THE LEGAL STATUS OF BERLIN

THE LEGAL STATUS
OF BERLIN

by

I. D. HENDRY

and

M. C. WOOD

A PUBLICATION OF
THE RESEARCH CENTRE FOR INTERNATIONAL LAW,
UNIVERSITY OF CAMBRIDGE

CAMBRIDGE
GROTIUS PUBLICATIONS LIMITED
1987

SALES & GROTIUS PUBLICATIONS LTD.
ADMINISTRATION PO BOX 115, CAMBRIDGE CB3 9BP, UK

British Library Cataloguing in Publication Data

Hendry, I. D.
    The legal status of Berlin.
    1. Berlin (Germany) — International status
    I. Title   II. Wood, M. C.
    341.2'9   JX4084. B38

ISBN 0-949009-05-9

Printed in Great Britain by
The Burlington Press (Cambridge) Limited
Station Road, Foxton, Cambridge, CB2 6SW

CONTENTS

PART FIVE. THE EXTERNAL REPRESENTATION OF
BERLIN'S INTERESTS

PREFACE

Over forty years have passed since the end of the Second World War, almost forty since the Berlin airlift and twenty-five since the building of the Wall. The majority of Germans do not have direct personal experience of the events which led to Berlin's unique legal status. Moreover, Berlin has not been at the centre of a major international crisis for many years, and even its "island position", some 110 miles behind the Iron Curtain, has less impact since the Quadripartite Agreement of 3 September 1971. Young people in West Berlin do not remember the delays and problems encountered when driving to the Federal Republic before 1972 or the very limited possibility of visiting East Berlin and the GDR.

The situation in and around Berlin has remained generally calm since the Quadripartite Agreement; but this does not mean that the legal position of Berlin is any less relevant than in the past. Together with the Western security guarantee, the preservation of Berlin's legal status remains essential to the freedom of the 1.9 million people living in the Western Sectors of the city. And looking beyond Berlin to Germany as a whole, the status of the city and that of Germany itself are inextricably linked. Berlin is more than a symbol of the open German question; it remains a key element in that question, and indeed in East-West relations generally.

The quadripartite status of Berlin is based upon the original rights which the four Powers acquired through the defeat and unconditional surrender of the German armed forces and the assumption of supreme authority with respect to Germany. The legal status of Berlin has remained essentially unchanged since 1945. Subsequent events have greatly altered the political context, and there have been important legal developments. But these have not affected the basic legal position. This is particularly true of the

Quadripartite Agreement of 3 September 1971, which cannot be considered in isolation but only in the context of the underlying status of the city.

The position of the Occupying Powers in Berlin may appear anachronistic. As the British Government said as long ago as 1958:

> It is certainly not normal that thirteen years after the end of the War there should still remain on a part of German territory a system of occupation instituted in 1945. Her Majesty's Government deplore this fact and the fact that Germany has not yet been re-unified so that Berlin might resume its rightful position as capital of a united Germany.[1]

It might be argued that the law should follow the facts, that the legal position cannot remain out of touch with reality indefinitely. Such an argument itself ignores two related political realities: that the German people, thus far denied their right of self-determination, retain a sense of nationhood and a desire for national unity; and that the Western Allies have consistently maintained, by word and by deed, the quadripartite status of Berlin and of Germany as a whole, thus preserving the legal basis for the security of the Western Sectors and for the eventual re-unification of Germany. The Allied legal position is part of the reality of Berlin. Thus 1986 has seen the Allied Kommandatura take exceptional measures to counter serious terrorist threats in Berlin, as well as the firm response of the three Powers, and indeed of the whole Western Alliance, to an attempt by the GDR to impose restrictions on their freedom of movement across the line between the Western Sectors and the Soviet Sector of Berlin. While there has been no major Berlin crisis in recent years, there is no reason to suppose that the underlying attitude of the Soviet Union and GDR has changed. The vital role of the Western Powers has been described in a recent publication as follows:

> Only the three Western Powers had and have the possibility of keeping Berlin as part of the Western world. And without remaining occupiers in the legal sense they could not be protectors.[2]

The legal position of Germany and Berlin may be thought complex and obscure, and at the level of detail this may sometimes be the case. But the obscurity comes, in part at least, from a

---

1. Note to the Soviet Government of 31 December 1958: *Selected Documents* I, p.350; Heidelmeyer, p.219.
2. *Berlin – Materialien zur Rechtslage und zur politischen Entwicklung seit 1945*, p.15. Wetzlaugk has recently written that "the Eastern interpretation of the Quadripartite Agreement points towards the longer term aim of dismantling the Western ties of the city and gradually replacing them by integration into the GDR": *Berlin und die Deutsche Frage*, p.193.

tendency to approach questions in an abstract way and to seek to describe the status of Germany and Berlin in terms of underlying theories of universal application. This no doubt has its place, and can be illuminating, but the present book is based on a different approach. It seeks to describe the legal position as it emerges from actual practice and the positions adopted by the various Governments and authorities concerned. It attempts to cover the whole field but, inevitably in a work of this length, not all matters can be considered in depth. It contains no extended analysis of certain more theoretical issues. A particular problem for anyone seeking to understand the quadripartite status of Berlin is the quantity, and variable quality, of the literature on the subject. Much of it is informative, even when one may disagree with the author's theoretical approach. We have therefore referred fairly widely to the existing literature without, however, attempting to be comprehensive.

The book is about the legal status of Berlin; policy questions are for others. It is, however, our firm view that policy decisions need to be taken in the light of a clear understanding of the legal position; this is especially true in relation to Berlin.

Our debt to others who have written on Berlin matters will be clear. We wish also to express our warmest thanks to those with whom we have worked on Berlin matters over the last few years, many of whom have been good enough to offer suggestions. Our special thanks go to Joan Brown, May McPhail and others for their untiring work and patience in typing the manuscript.

We are most grateful to Maureen MacGlashan of the Research Centre for International Law at Cambridge and to Robin Pirrie, Peter McCann and Diane Ilott of Grotius Publications for the great care with which they have prepared this book for publication.

Finally, we must point out that the views expressed are our own, and do not necessarily reflect those of the British authorities.

I D H
M C W

London
January 1987

ABBREVIATIONS

ACC	Allied Control Council
AFDI	*Annuaire français de droit international*
AJIL	*American Journal of International Law*
AK	Allied Kommandatura Berlin
AK Gazette	*Official Gazette of the Allied Kommandatura Berlin*
AöR	*Archiv des öffentlichen Rechts*
AVR	*Archiv des Völkerrechts*
BGBl	*Bundesgesetzblatt* (Federal Law Gazette of the Federal Republic of Germany)
BGH	*Bundesgerichtshof*
BKC/L	Berlin Kommandatura Commandants' Letter
BK/L	Berlin Kommandatura Letter
BK/O	Berlin Kommandatura Order
BVerfGE	*Entscheidungen des Bundesverfassungsgerichts* (Decisions of the Federal Constitutional Court of the Federal Republic of Germany)
BPIL	*British Practice in International Law* (1962–1968)
BYIL	*British Yearbook of International Law*
CC Gazette	*Official Gazette of the Control Council for Germany* (Nos. 1–19 and Supplement No. 1)
Cmd, Cmnd	(Command) Papers presented to Parliament by Command of Her Majesty

Cmd. 9368	Documents relating to the Termination of the Occupation Régime in the Federal Republic of Germany
Cmnd. 5135	Quadripartite Agreement signed at Berlin on 3 September 1971 (with related Agreement and Arrangements between the competent German Authorities and Final Quadripartite Protocol)
DA	Deutschland-Archiv
Das Vierseitige Abkommen	Das Vierseitige Abkommen über Westberlin und seine Realisierung: Dokumente 1971–1977 (1977)
DÖV	Die Öffentliche Verwaltung
DVBl	Deutsches Verwaltungsblatt
EA	Europa-Archiv
EuR	Europa-Recht
Fs	Festschrift
GBl. DDR	Gesetzblatt der Deutschen Demokratischen Republik (GDR Law Gazette)
GVBl*	Gesetz- und Verordnungsblatt für Berlin (Berlin Law Gazette)
Heidelmeyer	Heidelmeyer and Hindrichs, Documents on Berlin 1943–1963
Heidelmeyer Dokumente	Heidelmeyer and Hindrichs, Dokumente zur Berlin-Frage 1944–1966
ICLQ	International and Comparative Law Quarterly
JIR	Jahrbuch für Internationales Recht (before 1950: Jahrbuch für Internationales und Ausländisches Öffentliches Recht)
JR	Juristische Rundschau
JuS	Juristische Schulung
JZ	Juristenzeitung
Multilateral Treaties	Multilateral Treaties deposited with the Secretary-General: Status as at 31 December 1985 (United Nations Publication ST/LEG/SER.E/5)

NJW	*Neue Juristische Wochenschrift*
Pfennig/Neumann	Pfennig/Neumann, *Verfassung von Berlin*
PuK	*Politik und Kultur*
RGBl	*Reichsgesetzblatt* (Law Gazette of the German Reich)
RGDIP	*Revue générale de droit international public*
Riklin	Riklin, *Das Berlinproblem*
ROW	*Recht in Ost und West*
RuP	*Recht und Politik*
Schiedermair	Schiedermair, *Der völkerrechtliche Status Berlins nach dem Viermächte-Abkommen vom 3. September 1971*
Selected Documents I	Selected Documents on Germany and the Question of Berlin 1944–1961 (Cmnd. 1552)
Selected Documents II	Selected Documents on Germany and the Question of Berlin 1961–1973 (Cmnd. 6201)
UKTS	*United Kingdom Treaty Series*
UNTS	*United Nations Treaty Series*
US Documents	*Documents on Germany, 1944–1985* (United States Department of State Publication 9446)
VN	*Vereinte Nationen*
*VOBl**	*Verordnungsblatt der Stadt Berlin/für Gross-Berlin/ für Berlin* (Berlin Law Gazette)
ZaöRV	*Zeitschrift für ausländisches öffentliches Recht und Völkerrecht*

* Until October 1946 the Berlin Law Gazette was called the *Verordnungsblatt der Stadt Berlin*. Its name was then changed to *Verordnungsblatt für Gross-Berlin*. After the administrative division of the city in 1948, separate Gazettes with the name *Verordnungsblatt für Gross-Berlin* were issued in the Western Sectors by the lawful *Magistrat* and in the Soviet Sector by the "provisional *Magistrat*". The East Berlin publication changed its name in April 1974 to *Verordnungsblatt für die Hauptstadt der DDR Berlin*, but reverted to *Verordnungsblatt für Gross-Berlin* in May 1974. It ceased publication on 20 September 1976. The name of the Gazette published by the lawful *Magistrat* was changed in October 1950 to *Verordnungsblatt für Berlin*; and in April 1951 it was changed yet again to *Gesetz- und Verordnungsblatt für Berlin*, the title it still bears.

Zehn Jahre   *Zehn Jahre Deutschlandpolitik – Die Entwicklung*
Deutschlandpolitik   *der Beziehungen zwischen der Bundesrepublik*
                                Deutschland und der Deutschen Demokratischen
                                Republik 1969–1979

Zivier   Zivier, *The Legal Status of the Land Berlin* (3rd
                                ed.,1980)

Zündorf   Zündorf, *Die Ostverträge*

NOTE ON TERMINOLOGY

"Berlin", "Greater Berlin", "*Gross-Berlin*" and "the whole of Berlin" refer to the same area, i.e. the special Berlin area defined in the London Protocol of 12 September 1944 (and subsequently modified by quadripartite agreement).

"Western Sectors of Berlin", "West Berlin", "*Berlin (West)*" and "*West-Berlin*" refer to the British, French and American Sectors of Berlin. The Soviet Union and German Democratic Republic (GDR) often refer to the Western Sectors as "*Westberlin*".

"Soviet Sector", "Eastern Sector", "East Berlin" and "*Berlin (Ost)*" refer to the Soviet Sector of Berlin. The GDR and other Eastern European countries often refer to this Sector as "Berlin, capital of the GDR" ("*Berlin, Hauptstadt der DDR*").

In this book the term "Berlin" is used more often than "West Berlin" because in general –

> statements about Berlin's legal status are true of all four Sectors of the city. However it must be recognised that, since 1948, it has been impossible for any decisions of the Allied Kommandatura or the three Western Allies to be enforced in the Soviet Sector, and that consequently the position *de facto* differs from that *de jure*. (Lush, *ICLQ*, 14 (1965), p.742.)

The term "*Land* Berlin" is frequently used by the Federal authorities and by the municipal authorities in Berlin, and by West German authors. The Soviet Union objects to this expression, apparently because it is thought to imply that Berlin is a *Land* of the Federal Republic of Germany; it does not in fact carry this implication (see p.151 below). On the other hand, terms like *im übrigen Bundesgebiet* (in the rest of the Federal territory) do, and are best avoided.

The expression "the Allies" in the context of Berlin and Germany as a whole may refer to the four wartime Allies (also referred to as "the four Powers") – France, the Soviet Union, the United Kingdom and the United States – but nowadays it is often used when referring only to the three Western Allies. It is more precise to refer to France, the United Kingdom and the United States as "the Western Allies" or "the three Powers".

The official names of the organs established by the 1950 Constitution of Berlin are "*Senat* of Berlin", "Governing Mayor of Berlin", "House of Representatives of Berlin" etc. The Eastern side often refer to the "*Senat* of *Westberlin*" etc.

Differences in terminology between East and West often reflect fundamental legal differences. Joint documents normally use expressions that do not prejudice the positions of either side: for example, the Quadripartite Agreement of 3 September 1971 refers simply to "the *Senat*".

PART ONE

BERLIN AND GERMANY AS A WHOLE

The two chapters in Part One are of an introductory nature. The subject-matter of both Chapter 1 (principal developments since 1944) and Chapter 2 (legal status of Germany) could fill much longer books than the present one. Nevertheless, it is considered important to set the more detailed chapters in the broader context, since the status of Berlin is closely bound up with that of Germany as a whole and with wartime and post-war developments in Germany.

It is worth stating briefly at the outset the basic elements of the legal status of Berlin and of Germany as a whole. Details that may seem obscure or unduly complicated may be clearer if the following points are borne in mind:

(a) Germany continues to exist as a State in international law.

(b) The four Powers jointly assumed supreme authority in relation to Germany in 1945, and have retained their rights and responsibilities pending a peace settlement.

(c) The rights of the four Powers relating to Berlin and to Germany as a whole are original rights deriving from the defeat of the German armed forces and the assumption of supreme authority. These original rights underlie the structure of quadripartite agreements, decisions and practices.

(d) Quadripartite rights and responsibilities relating to Berlin apply to all four Sectors of the city. Neither Greater Berlin nor any part thereof forms part of the territory of the Federal Republic of Germany or of the German Democratic Republic.

(e)   The legal status of Berlin, and of Germany as a whole, cannot be changed unilaterally.

CHAPTER 1

PRINCIPAL DEVELOPMENTS SINCE 1944[1]

FROM THE OCCUPATION OF GERMANY TO THE BERLIN BLOCKADE

F ROM 18 September 1944, when Allied troops first occupied German territory, until the joint assumption of supreme authority on 5 June 1945, the territory of the German *Reich* came progressively under belligerent occupation.[2] The German High Command surrendered unconditionally to the Supreme Commander, Allied Expeditionary Force, and simultaneously to the Supreme High Command of the Red Army on 8 May 1945.[3] When the Allies jointly assumed supreme authority in respect of Germany on 5 June 1945,[4] the occupation ceased to be a belligerent occupation. The area to be occupied by each Power and the manner in which control was to be exercised were prescribed in agreements drawn up in 1944 and 1945 by the European Advisory Commission,[5] and duly approved by the Governments of the four Powers.[6] These agreements provided the basis for Statements on Zones of Occupation and on Control Machinery in Germany issued by the four Governments on 5 June 1945.[7] Following exchanges between the Governments concerned, which covered among other things access to Berlin, the areas actually occupied by their respective armed forces were adjusted to conform to the agreements. In July 1945 British and American forces withdrew from the Soviet zone — from a line running approximately through Wismar, Schwerin, Wittenberge, Magdeburg, Torgau and Chemnitz

---

[1] For more detailed treatment, see Davison, *The Berlin Blockade* (1958); Riklin, pp.19–225; Mahncke, *Berlin im geteilten Deutschland*, pp.11–94; Zieger, in: *Berlin Fibel* (1975), pp.11–66; Wetzlaugk, *Berlin und die Deutsche Frage*; *Selected Documents* I, pp.1–24; *Selected Documents* II, pp.1–27. For a Soviet account, see Vysotsky, *West Berlin*, pp.15–218.
[2] See Bathurst and Simpson, *Germany and the North Atlantic Community*, pp.3–17.
[3] *Selected Documents* I, p.37; *US Documents*, p.14.
[4] The Declaration of Berlin: see p.321 below and *Selected Documents* I, p.38; *US Documents*, p.33; Heidelmeyer, p.10.
[5] The European Advisory Commission was established by the Moscow Conference of Foreign Ministers of November 1943 (Heidelmeyer, p.1) and dissolved at the Potsdam Conference. It originally consisted of representatives of the Soviet Union, United Kingdom and United States; France joined on 27 November 1944. The documents of the Commission are published in *European Advisory Commission, Foreign Relations of the United States, Diplomatic Papers 1944*, Vol I (1968). See also Sharp, *The Wartime Alliance and the Zonal Division of Germany* (1975); Nelson, *Wartime Origins of the Berlin Dilemma* (1978); Mosely, *Foreign Affairs*, 28 (1949/50), pp.487–98, 580–604; Meissner, in Klein/Meissner, *Das Potsdamer Abkommen und die Deutschlandfrage* (1977), pp.43–57.
[6] At the Crimea Conference, the Soviet Union, United Kingdom and United States invited France to join the occupation, and the agreements were modified accordingly.
[7] *Selected Documents* I, p.43; *US Documents*, pp.38, 39; Heidelmeyer, p.12.

(Karl-Marx-Stadt) – and were replaced by Soviet forces, and British and American troops entered Berlin, where hitherto Soviet forces had been in sole occupation.

The Berlin (Potsdam) Conference, held from 17 July to 2 August 1945, reached important agreements on Germany, though it did not deal specifically with Berlin. First, the Conference provided for a Council of Foreign Ministers whose tasks included preparing "a peace settlement for Germany to be accepted by the Government of Germany when a Government adequate for the purpose is established". Second, the Conference laid down the political and economic principles to govern the treatment of Germany during the occupation. The political principles included the complete disarmament and demilitarisation of Germany, and denazification. But they also envisaged the reconstruction of German political life on a democratic basis. The economic principles were designed to eliminate Germany's war potential, to ensure adequate reparations, and to enable Germany to exist without outside assistance. It was fundamental to the economic principles that Germany should be treated as a unit. Third, the Conference made important territorial adjustments, while making it clear that final decisions on Germany's frontiers were left to the peace settlement. That part of Germany lying east of the Oder and Western Neisse rivers was placed provisionally under the administration of Poland, except for the northern part of East Prussia (the City of Königsberg and surrounding area), which was placed under Soviet administration.

In the period immediately following the assumption of supreme authority the Soviet Union participated fully in the quadripartite organs for the government of Germany, including the Allied Kommandatura Berlin, established pursuant to the agreements of 1944/45. Since these organs acted on the principle of unanimity Soviet representatives were able to block unwelcome decisions, though they could not of course impose their own will on the Western Powers. Difficulties arose, particularly in the application of somewhat imprecise language in the Potsdam Agreement. Nevertheless, many quadripartite agreements were concluded during this period which were of lasting importance for Berlin, for example as regards access to the city and demilitarisation.

The Russians had been in sole occupation of Berlin from April to July 1945. During this period they appointed their supporters to key positions, for example in the police force, and adopted a number of important measures. These early Soviet decisions were continued in force after the Western Powers had entered the city (Order No. 1 of the Allied Commandants) and – since unanimity was thereafter needed to change them – this step proved to be of major significance. In March 1946 the Berlin SPD voted decisively against merging with the Communist Party and was thus able to take part in the subsequent election independently of the Socialist Unity Party (SED). An election took place throughout Berlin on 20 October 1946 on the basis of the 1946 Temporary Constitution of Greater Berlin. The SED was overwhelmingly defeated.[8] Nevertheless, the 1946 Constitution, which was a compromise between Soviet and Western concepts, contained a number of features which enabled the Russians to maintain an important role in the detailed work of the local administration even after the defeat of the SED in the election of October 1946.

It was soon apparent that, largely because of Soviet obstruction, the Potsdam decisions could not be carried out. The United States then offered to agree to the economic fusion of its zone with any other zone. The United Kingdom agreed and the Bi-Zone was established on 1 January 1947; after some delay the French zone joined in March 1948 to form the Tri-Zone. The Council of Foreign Ministers, established by the Potsdam Conference, met on a number of occasions without reaching any agreement on a peace settlement for Germany. The three Western Powers therefore decided to permit the Western zones to develop in accordance with the Potsdam principles. They called a Six-Power Conference in London in March/June 1948 (the three plus Belgium, the Netherlands and Luxembourg), which recommended that representatives of the Western zones draw up a constitution.

Meanwhile events moved rapidly towards the first Berlin crisis (1948/9). The work of the Allied Kommandatura had become increasingly difficult following the 1946 elections, and its inability to take decisions in the face of the Soviet veto seriously impeded the administration of the city. A further disruptive element was the continued influence of the many Soviet nominees in the local administration and police. The immediate occasion for the crisis was the failure of the four Powers to reach agreement on a much-needed currency reform in Germany. Even after the Western Powers had introduced a new currency in their zones efforts to reach agreement on a single currency for Berlin continued. The Western Powers were prepared to accept that this could be the Soviet zone currency, provided it was issued in Berlin under quadripartite control. But these negotiations ended in failure, and

---

[8] 92.3% of the electorate cast their votes. The results were: SPD 48.7% (63 seats); CDU 22.2% (29 seats); SED 19.8% (26 seats); LDP 9.3% (12 seats). See Plischke, *Government and Politics of Contemporary Berlin*, pp.56–8; Fijalkowski, *Berlin – Hauptstadtanspruch und Westintegration*, pp.18–41.

in June 1948 separate currencies were introduced in Berlin by the Western Allies and the Soviet Union.[9]

In order to put pressure on the Western Allies the Russians had gradually introduced obstructive measures on the access routes (the so-called "creeping blockade"). Immediately following the introduction of the new currency in West Berlin, on 24 June 1948, the Russians imposed a total blockade on the land and water access routes to West Berlin, claiming that there were "technical difficulties". The Western Allies responded with a massive airlift.[10] Between July 1948 and May 1949 1.7 million tons of goods were carried on approximately 213,000 flights. The airlift, together with the determination of the Berliners, defeated Soviet efforts to force the West to abandon the city. The Western Allies and the Berliners were united in their determination to defend the freedom of the city.

Negotiations to resolve the crisis, both as regards the currency problem and the blockade, took place in Moscow and Berlin from July to September 1948, but were unsuccessful because of Soviet refusal to accept quadripartite control of the currency.[11] The Western Allies then brought the Berlin question before the Security Council and the General Assembly of the United Nations, though initially without concrete results.[12] Negotiations to end the blockade continued in the margins of the United Nations, and the blockade came to an end on 12 May 1949 following the Jessup–Malik agreement of 4 May 1949. This was confirmed at the Paris meeting of the Council of Foreign Ministers of June 1949. These agreements did not, however, prevent further Russian harassment of Berlin's links with the rest of Germany in the years which followed.

In the spring and early summer of 1948 the Soviet representatives withdrew from most of the quadripartite organs for the government of Germany. Marshal Sokolovsky left the Allied Control Council on 20 March 1948; and on 1 July 1948 the Soviet element ceased to participate in the Allied Kommandatura. The Control Council was thereafter in suspense. In December 1948, however, the three Western Allies announced that the Allied Kommandatura would resume its work forthwith, although it would only be possible for its

---

[9] Riklin, pp.76−8; Fijalkowski, *Berlin — Hauptstadtanspruch und Westintegration*, pp.200−25. The new *D-Mark* was introduced in West Berlin on 20 June 1948; on 23 June the new *E-Mark* was introduced throughout Berlin. On 20 March 1949 the *D-Mark* became the only legal tender in West Berlin: *US Documents*, p.207.

[10] Davison, *The Berlin Blockade;* Riklin, pp.76−137.

[11] *US Documents*, pp.163−74; Heidelmeyer, pp.83, 84; Riklin, pp.125−34.

[12] UN Security Council, Official Records, Third Year, No. 113−115/117−120; UN General Assembly, plenary, Official Records SR/372−374; *International Law Quarterly*, 1 (1948−9), pp.646−55; *US Documents*, pp.177−84, 191−2, 199−203; Heidelmeyer *Dokumente*, pp.85−97, 602−3; Jessup, *Foreign Affairs*, 50 (1971/72), pp.163−73.

decisions to be carried out in the Western Sectors for the present.

Also in 1948 the local city authorities in Berlin, which had hitherto functioned – albeit with difficulty – as a city-wide local government, split into two. Following the Communist defeat in the elections of October 1946 the Russians had used their powers under the 1946 Constitution to retain as much influence over the city government as possible. They had, for example, refused to approve the appointment of the democratically elected Mayor in 1947. The city authorities were for the most part based in the Soviet Sector (which included the historical and administrative heart of the city) and this enabled the Russians, through their control of the police, to instigate physical harassment of the authorities, for example by Communist-led riots. In July and August 1948 Communist demonstrators disrupted the City Assembly, and on 6 September they stormed the Assembly chamber. In order to continue the orderly conduct of its business the City Assembly therefore moved, as it was fully entitled to do, to the Western Sectors of the city, and has subsequently met at Schöneberg town-hall in the American Sector. On 30 November 1948, an "extraordinary City Assembly" was staged in the Admiralspalast (then the Opera House) in the Soviet Sector. This Assembly purported to relieve the existing city government (*Magistrat*) of its functions and to set up in its place a "provisional *Magistrat*", which was immediately recognised by the Soviet authorities. The lawful *Magistrat*, like the City Assembly, was forced to move to the Western Sectors. Thus by December 1948 the split in the city government was complete, and the election held on 5 December could only take place in the Western Sectors.[13]

FROM THE BLOCKADE TO THE WALL

On 21 September 1949 the Federal Republic of Germany came into being in accordance with a Basic Law promulgated by the Parliamentary Council on 23 May 1949. At the same time Military Government in the Western zones was terminated and its functions divided between High Commissioners (control functions) and Commanders-in-Chief (military functions). In their New York communiqué of 19 September 1950[14] the Foreign Ministers of the three Powers stated *inter alia* that:

Pending the reunification of Germany, the three Governments

---

[13] Krumholz, *Berlin ABC* (2nd ed.), pp.590–8; Mampel, *Der Sowjetsektor von Berlin*, pp.67–70; Riklin, pp.97–121; Heidelmeyer *Dokumente*, pp.97–105.
[14] *Selected Documents* I, p.136; *US Documents*, p.341; Heidelmeyer, p.124. This statement was frequently repeated: see Mann, *Studies in International Law*, p.683. See also the Interpretative Minute referred to in Bathurst and Simpson, *Germany and the North Atlantic Community*, p.188.

consider the Government of the Federal Republic of Germany as the only German Government freely and legitimately constituted and therefore entitled to speak for Germany as the representative of the German people in international affairs.

On 7 October 1949 the German Democratic Republic (GDR) was established in the Soviet zone; the Soviet Military Administration was replaced by a Soviet Control Commission.

In parallel with developments in the Western zones, the Allied Kommandatura redefined its relationship with the local German authorities in Berlin in 1949 and 1951 so as to give greater powers to the latter.[15] But the Western Allies declined to allow Berlin to become a *Land* of the Federal Republic of Germany; the Soviet Union, by contrast, permitted the GDR to refer to Berlin as its capital.

Further Western efforts to secure German re-unification have proved fruitless. The basic Western position was that a peace settlement with Germany could only be achieved once an all-German Government had been formed on the basis of free elections, and in 1950 they made proposals for such elections on an all-German basis.[16] The Soviet Union made counter-proposals for a constituent council from the two existing German Governments on a parity basis. Further proposals and counter-proposals followed throughout the 1950s.[17]

In 1951 each of the three Powers terminated the state of war with Germany.[18] Already in 1950 the Western Powers had decided that the Federal Republic of Germany could contribute to the defence of Western Europe through participation in the supra-national European Defence Community then under consideration. They proposed that at the same time the occupation régime should be terminated and a new relationship evolved between the three Powers and the Federal Republic. To this end the Bonn Conventions were signed by the three Powers and the Federal Republic on 26 May 1952[19] and the European Defence Community Treaty was signed on 27 May 1952.[20] The Bonn Conventions were to come into force simultaneously with the European Defence Community Treaty. When France failed to ratify the latter, a Conference was held in London on 3 October 1954 at which it was

---

[15] Statement of Principles and First Revision: *Selected Documents* I, pp.117, 140; *US Documents*, pp.262, 347; Heidelmeyer, pp.108, 126.
[16] Similarly, proposals were made in 1950 for free elections throughout Greater Berlin: Heidelmeyer *Dokumente*, pp.146–53.
[17] See, generally, Riklin, pp.138–83.
[18] von Münch, *Dokumente des geteilten Deutschland*, Vol. I, pp.57 (French decree), 57 (British Note), 59 (US Joint Resolution), 59 (US Proclamation). The British Proclamation is printed in *Re Grotian* [1955] Ch. 501, 502.
[19] Cmd. 8571.
[20] Cmd. 9127.

agreed that the Federal Republic (and Italy) should be invited to join an extended Brussels Treaty organisation, to be named Western European Union, and to join the North Atlantic Treaty Organization. As a result of these decisions, a number of agreements modifying the Bonn Conventions were signed at Paris on 23 October 1954. The Bonn/Paris Conventions[21] came into force on 5 May 1955. On that day the occupation régime in the Western zones was terminated and the Federal Republic became a member of Western European Union. On 6 May 1955 it became a member of NATO. Since 5 May 1955, and subject to retained Allied rights and responsibilities relating to Berlin and to Germany as a whole, the Federal Republic has had the full authority of a sovereign State over its external and internal affairs.

In connection with the Bonn/Paris Conventions, the Federal Republic of Germany issued a Declaration on Aid to Berlin. The Western Allies indicated that, while Berlin could not be part of the Federal Republic, they would facilitate the carrying out by the Federal Republic of this Declaration and permit the Federal Republic to ensure the representation of Berlin and the Berlin population outside Berlin; similarly, they would not object if Berlin adopted the same legislation as the Federal Republic.[22] On 5 May 1955 the Allied Kommandatura issued a Declaration on Berlin, further defining its relationship with the local German authorities; this remains the basis of the relationship to this day (p.332 below).

Parallel developments took place in the Soviet zone. On 25 March 1954 the Soviet Union declared that its relations with the GDR would be the same as with other sovereign States.[23] In January 1955 the Soviet Union terminated the state of war with Germany.[24] On 20 September 1955 it signed a treaty with the GDR; side-letters dealt with communications between the Federal Republic of Germany and West Berlin (p.116 below). Throughout these developments the Soviet Union took care to preserve its position as regards Germany as a whole.

The Heads of Government of France, the Soviet Union, the United Kingdom and the United States, meeting at Geneva from 18 to 23 July 1955, issued a directive to their Foreign Ministers,[25] which stated *inter alia* that:

The Heads of Government, recognising their common responsibility

---

[21] Cmd. 9368. See pp.43–4 below.
[22] Letter of the three High Commissioners to the Federal Chancellor in the version of letter X of 23 October 1954: see p.329 below.
[23] *Selected Documents* I, p.186; *US Documents*, p.418; Heidelmeyer *Dokumente*, p.208.
[24] *US Documents*, p.443; Heidelmeyer, p.170.
[25] *Selected Documents* I, p.220; *US Documents*, p.455. See also the Declaration of the four Foreign Ministers of 29 July 1957: *Selected Documents* I, p.276.

for the settlement of the German question and the reunification of Germany, have agreed that the settlement of the German question and the reunification of Germany by means of free elections shall be carried out in conformity with the national interests of the German people and the interests of European security.

The four Foreign Ministers met on various occasions over the next few years in order to give effect to this directive, but without success.

The situation in and around Berlin remained relatively calm until 1958. In that year various leading East Germans claimed "sovereignty" over Berlin.[26] Thus, in a speech in East Berlin on 27 October 1958, Ulbricht claimed that the whole of Berlin belonged to the territory of the GDR. On 10 November 1958, in a speech at the Sports Palace in Moscow, Krushchev declared that it was time to end the occupation of Berlin.[27] On 27 November 1958 the Soviet Union precipitated what became known as the second Berlin crisis (1958–62) by informing the three Western Allies that it regarded as null and void the London Protocol of 12 September 1944 and the related supplementary agreements, including the Agreement on Control Machinery in Germany, and declaring that the Western Allies had forfeited their occupation rights in Berlin. The principal reason given was alleged Western violations of the Potsdam Agreement. The Soviet Union proposed that Berlin should be re-unified under GDR control or, if this were not possible, that West Berlin should become a separate political entity (a demilitarised free city). Failing agreement within six months, complete land, water and air sovereignty would be transferred to the GDR.[28]

The Western Allies rejected this ultimatum and the Soviet assertions about the status of Berlin, and proposed in turn negotiations on the German question and on European security.[29] After further exchanges of notes,[30] the Conference of Foreign Ministers met at Geneva from 11 May to 20 June and 13 July to 5 August 1959. In addition to the four Powers, advisory delegations from the Federal Republic of Germany and GDR participated. By

[26] Heidelmeyer *Dokumente*, p.295.
[27] *Selected Documents* I, p.334; *US Documents*, p.542; Heidelmeyer *Dokumente*, p.296. On the second Berlin crisis, see Barker, *International Affairs*, 39(1963), pp.59−73; Schick, *The Berlin Crisis 1958−1962* (1971).
[28] *Selected Documents* I, p.318; *US Documents*, p.552; Heidelmeyer, p.180.
[29] Foreign Ministers' communiqué of 14 December 1958: *Selected Documents* I, p.303; *US Documents*, p.559; Heidelmeyer, p.210; Declaration of the North Atlantic Council on Berlin, 16 December 1958: *Selected Documents* I, p.334; *US Documents*, p.560; Heidelmeyer, p.211; Notes to the Soviet Government of 31 December 1958: *Selected Documents* I, p.346 (British Note); *US Documents*, p.573 (US Note); Heidelmeyer, pp.212 (French Note), 214 (British Note), 220 (US Note). See pp.106−7 below.
[30] Heidelmeyer, pp.242−7.

contrast with the position taken only a few months earlier, the Soviet representatives accepted the continuance of Allied rights in Berlin and of the occupation régime until the conclusion of a peace treaty.[31] The meeting ended with a brief final communiqué stating that the Conference had "considered questions relating to Germany, including a peace treaty with Germany and the question of Berlin" and that "the date and place for the resumption of the work of the Conference will be settled through diplomatic channels".[32] It has not met again.

Soviet and GDR harassment of West Berlin continued after the Geneva Conference: the access routes were obstructed in the summer of 1960, and access by residents of the Federal Republic to the Soviet Sector was made more difficult. At the Vienna summit in June 1961 the Soviet Union again demanded that West Berlin be declared a demilitarised free city. The Soviet Union continued to threaten to enter into a separate peace treaty with the GDR, while the GDR continued to claim that West Berlin was part of its territory. On 13 August 1961, the GDR began construction of the Wall sealing the Soviet Sector from the Western Sectors; and a few days later West Berliners were prevented from visiting the Eastern Sector of their city.[33]

AFTER THE WALL: *OSTPOLITIK*

The second Berlin crisis gradually became less intense. The Soviet Union apparently realised that its efforts to force the Western Allies to withdraw their troops from Berlin were not going to succeed. With the building of the Wall West Berlin ceased to be a point of intense annoyance to the East: its functions as a "shop window of the West" and as a place of easy escape for persons living in the East were drastically reduced. Since the end of the 1950s the Soviet Union had sought above all to attack the relationship between the Western Sectors and the Federal Republic of Germany, for example by provoking incidents on the occasion of major demonstrations of the ties between the Federal Republic and West Berlin and permitting the GDR to introduce new restrictive measures on the access routes. It sought to promote its view that the Western Sectors were a separate political entity, and to deny any quadripartite responsibility for East Berlin. In 1962 the Soviet Union dissolved the office of Soviet City Commandant, and in 1964 entered into a

---

[31] Statement of 15 May 1959 by the Soviet Foreign Minister: Heidelmeyer, p.250; see also Kruschev's statement of 19 March 1959: Heidelmeyer, p.248.
[32] *Selected Documents* I, p.425; *US Documents*, p.683; Heidelmeyer, p.265.
[33] Heidelmeyer, pp.271−91; Catudal, *Kennedy and the Berlin Wall Crisis* (1980).

further treaty with the GDR, in which both sides agreed to treat West Berlin as a "separate political entity".

The harsh effects of the Wall upon the Berlin population were to a limited degree mitigated by the wall pass arrangements of 1963 to 1966 worked out between the *Senat* of Berlin and the East German authorities. Towards the end of the 1960s both East and West showed interest in steps to reduce tensions in Europe. In this broader context the *Ostpolitik* of the Government of the Federal Republic of Germany, together with the Western Allies' efforts to secure practical improvements in the situation of Berlin, culminated in a series of important agreements between East and West.[34] Three of these agreements entered into force on 3 June 1972: the Treaty of 12 August 1970 between the Federal Republic of Germany and the Union of Soviet Socialist Republics;[35] the Treaty of 7 December 1970 between the Federal Republic of Germany and the People's Republic of Poland on the Bases of Normalising their Mutual Relations;[36] and the Quadripartite Agreement of 3 September 1971. The simultaneous entry into force of these three treaties indicates the close political linkage (*Junktim*) insisted upon by the various parties to them. These agreements gave rise to intense political controversy in the Federal Republic. Parliamentary approval for the Treaties with the Soviet Union and Poland was eventually achieved on 17 May 1972, together with the adoption by the *Bundestag* and *Bundesrat* of a joint resolution which described the Treaties as "important elements of a *modus vivendi*" between the Federal Republic and its Eastern neighbours and which contained other clarifications of the legal position.[37]

The way was then clear for further improvements in East-West relations, culminating in the thirty-five nation Conference on Security and Co-operation in Europe (CSCE) and the Helsinki Final

---

[34] See Zündorf; Frowein, *ICLQ*, 23 (1974), pp.105–26; Mahncke, *Berlin im geteilten Deutschland*, pp.11–32; Arndt, *Die Verträge von Moskau und Warschau* (1973); Arndt, *AJIL*, 74 (1980), pp.122–33.

[35] *BGBl.* 1972 II, p.353; *Selected Documents* II, p.221; *US Documents*, p.1103; *Zehn Jahre Deutschlandpolitik*, p.156. See *The Treaty of 12 August 1970 between the Federal Republic of Germany and the Union of Soviet Socialist Republics* (Press and Information Office of the Government of the Federal Republic of Germany, 1970); Zündorf, pp.50–61; Wengler, *JZ*, 25 (1970), pp.632–7; Steinburger, *ZaöRV*, 31 (1971), pp.63–161.

[36] *BGBl.* 1972 II, p.361; *Selected Documents* II, p.226; *US Documents*, p.1125. See *The Treaty between the Federal Republic of Germany and the People's Republic of Poland* (Press and Information Office of the Government of the Federal Republic of Germany, 1970); Frowein, *JIR*, 18 (1975), pp.11–61; Zündorf, pp.62–76. For the subsequent FRG–Poland agreement of October 1975/March 1976 see Zündorf, pp.77–91.

[37] *Zehn Jahre Deutschlandpolitik*, p.181; *Selected Documents* II, p.256; *US Documents*, p.1188; Zündorf, pp.92–5. The joint resolution, which was formally communicated to the Soviet Union and Poland, is of continuing importance: see, for example, the joint resolution of the *Bundestag* of 9 February 1984 (*BT–Drucksache 10/914*).

Act of 1 August 1975.[38] The Federal Republic entered into further important bilateral agreements with its Eastern neighbours: the Treaty of 26 May 1972 between the Federal Republic of Germany and the German Democratic Republic on Questions of Transport[39] (in force on 17 October 1972); the Treaty of 21 December 1972 on the Basis of Relations between the Federal Republic of Germany and the German Democratic Republic[40] (in force on 21 June 1973); and the Agreement of 11 December 1973 between the Federal Republic of Germany and the Czechoslovak Socialist Republic on their Mutual Relations[41] (in force on 19 July 1974). Following a long period of non-recognition,[42] the Western Allies recognised the GDR as having the full authority of a sovereign State and entered into diplomatic relations with it. The Federal Republic of Germany also entered into formal relations with the GDR, and a number of important inner-German agreements followed. The Federal Republic of Germany and the GDR joined the United Nations in September 1973 following a Quadripartite Declaration of 9 November 1972 in which the four Powers affirmed that this would not affect their rights and responsibilities.[43] In December 1973 the Federal Republic of Germany agreed to enter into diplomatic relations with Bulgaria and Hungary.[44] Throughout these developments the Western Allies and Federal Republic were careful to ensure that nothing was done which could harm the legal status of Berlin and Germany as a whole. They have not abandoned their view that Germany continues to exist as a State in international law, that the Potsdam territorial changes are provisional pending a peace settlement, and that the whole of Berlin remains under quadripartite occupation. The Soviet Union and other East bloc countries, on the other hand, appear to regard these agreements, together with the Helsinki Final Act of 1975, as a substitute for a peace settlement.

The agreements of the early 1970s have had a stabilising effect on the situation in Germany and in Europe. Berlin is no longer a source of major international tension; relations between the Federal

---

[38] Cmnd. 6198; *Documents relating to Problems of Security and Co-operation in Europe 1954–1977* (Cmnd. 6932); *US Documents*, p.1285.

[39] *BGBl.* 1972 II, p.1449; *Zehn Jahre Deutschlandpolitik*, p.183; *US Documents*, p.1191. See Zündorf, pp.202–10.

[40] See pp.21–2 below.

[41] *BGBl.* 1974 II, p.989; *Selected Documents* II, p.268; *US Documents*, pp.1256–62. See Zündorf, pp.96–111 (including a detailed discussion of the Munich Agreement of 29 September 1938).

[42] For the Hallstein doctrine, and other attempts to isolate the GDR, see Zündorf, pp.211–13; Zivier, p.21.

[43] Text at p.209 below.

[44] Zündorf, pp.115–6.

Republic of Germany and the GDR, while hardly normal and good-neighbourly, are in many respects little different from those between other States in East and West. But neither side has abandoned its fundamental positions and the East bloc countries in particular lose no opportunity to draw attention to their views in international fora. There have, moreover, been serious breaches of the status of Berlin since the Quadripartite Agreement of 3 September 1971; the Eastern side has sought to weaken the ties between the Federal Republic of Germany and West Berlin and to assimilate East Berlin even more completely into the GDR. In the 1970s there was considerable disappointment in the Federal Republic that the Quadripartite Agreement had not resolved all earlier problems. Nevertheless, the situation in and around Berlin remained calm even when détente came under great strain with the Soviet invasion of Afghanistan and events in Poland. And the *Ostpolitik* of the SPD/FDP coalition in Bonn was not significantly changed when, in 1982, the CDU-CSU/FDP coalition came to power. The Quadripartite Agreement has stood the test of time.

LIST OF PRINCIPAL WARTIME AND POST-WAR CONFERENCES CONCERNING GERMANY AND BERLIN

18–30 October 1943: Moscow Foreign Ministers Conference (UK, US, USSR)[45]

28 November – 1 December 1943: Tehran Heads of Government Conference (UK, US, USSR)[46]

14 January 1944 – 26 July 1945: European Advisory Commission, London (UK, US, USSR; France joined on 27 November 1944)[47]

4–11 February 1945: Crimea Heads of Government Conference, Yalta (UK, US, USSR)[48]

17 July – 2 August 1945: Potsdam Heads of Government Conference (UK, US, USSR)[49]

15 June – 12 July 1946: second meeting of the Council of Foreign Ministers, Paris (UK, US, USSR, France)[50]

---

[45] Heidelmeyer, p.1; Riklin, p.22.
[46] Riklin, pp.23–4.
[47] See footnote 5 above.
[48] *Selected Documents* I, p.34; *US Documents*, p.10; Heidelmeyer, p.8; Riklin, pp.27–9.
[49] See p.39 below.
[50] *US Documents*, p.88; Riklin, pp.47–9.

10 March – 24 April 1947: third meeting of the Council of Foreign Ministers, Moscow (UK, US, USSR, France)[51]

25 November – 15 December 1947: fifth meeting of the Council of Foreign Ministers, London (UK, US, USSR, France)[52]

23 February – 6 March and 20 April – 7 June 1948: London Six-Power Conference (UK, US, France, Belgium, Netherlands, Luxembourg)[53]

July – September 1948: talks in Moscow and Berlin concerning currency reform and the blockade (UK, US, USSR, France)[54]

23 May – 20 June 1949: sixth meeting of the Council of Foreign Ministers, Paris (UK, US, USSR, France)[55]

25 January – 18 February 1954: Berlin Conference of Foreign Ministers (UK, US, USSR, France)[56]

18–23 July 1955: Geneva Heads of Government Conference (UK, US, USSR, France)[57]

27 October – 16 November 1955: Geneva Conference of Foreign Ministers (UK, US, USSR, France)[58]

11 May – 20 June and 13 July – 5 August 1959: Geneva Conference of Foreign Ministers (UK, US, USSR, France; FRG and GDR advisory delegations)[59]

26 March 1970 – 3 September 1971: negotiations in Berlin between the four Ambassadors leading to the Quadripartite Agreement; and 3 June 1972: signature of the Final Quadripartite Protocol by the four Foreign Ministers (UK, US, USSR, France)[60]

---

[51] *Selected Documents* I, pp.73–91; *US Documents*, pp.117–23; Riklin, pp.54–5.
[52] *Selected Documents* I, p.92; *US Documents*, pp.135–9; Riklin, pp.60–2.
[53] *Selected Documents* I, pp.97–102; *US Documents*, pp.140–1, 143–9; Heidelmeyer *Dokumente*, p.599.
[54] *US Documents*, pp.156–74; Riklin, pp.127–33.
[55] Riklin, pp.138–41; Wetzlaugk, *Berlin und die Deutsche Frage*, pp.105–7.
[56] *US Documents*, pp.408–17; Riklin, pp.164–9.
[57] Cmnd. 868; *Selected Documents* I, pp.14, 215–24; *US Documents*, pp.448–55; Riklin, pp.177–9.
[58] *Selected Documents* I, pp.14–15, 232–48; *US Documents*, pp.465–72; Riklin, pp.181–2.
[59] *Selected Documents* I, pp.19–21, 387–425; *US Documents*, pp.624–70, 672–83; Heidelmeyer, pp.248–65; Riklin, pp.193–6; Wetzlaugk, *Berlin und die Deutsche Frage*, pp.110–13.
[60] See pp.335–50 below.

23 October – 5 November 1972: exchanges in Berlin between the four Ambassadors leading to the Quadripartite Declaration of 9 November 1972 (UK, US, USSR, France)[61]

---

[61] See p.209 below.

CHAPTER 2

THE LEGAL STATUS OF GERMANY[1]

THE DIVISION OF GERMANY FOR THE PURPOSES OF OCCUPATION

On 7/8 May 1945, when the German armed forces surrendered, most of the territory of the German *Reich* was occupied by Allied forces. As was provided in the London Protocol of 12 September 1944[2] between the Governments of the United Kingdom, the United States of America and the Union of Soviet Socialist Republics (as amended by the Agreement of 14 November 1944) Germany was occupied within its borders of 31 December 1937. The Allies acted on the basis that the absorption of territory into the *Reich* after 1937 was null and void. Under the London Protocol Germany within the 1937 borders was to be divided, for the purposes of the occupation, into three zones, one being allocated to each Ally, and a special Berlin area (Greater Berlin), which was to be occupied jointly. By July 1945 the areas actually occupied corresponded to those set out in the agreements. France joined the occupation in accordance with an Agreement of 26 July 1945 amending the London Protocol, and a fourth zone was established.

Under the London Protocol the Soviet zone comprised all of Germany east of a line running from Lübeck Bay to the 1937 Czechoslovak frontier (including East Prussia), with the exception of the special Berlin area. It was subsequently agreed at the Potsdam Conference in August 1945 that the northern part of East Prussia (the City of Königsberg and surrounding area) should be placed under Soviet administration and that the rest of Germany lying east of the Oder–Neisse line should be placed under Polish administration. It was further stated that the final determination of the frontiers of Germany must await a peace settlement. In the

---

[1] See Mann, *Studies in International Law* (1973), pp.634–59 (based on a paper read to the Grotius Society on 5 March 1947) and pp.660–705; Jennings, *BYIL*, 23 (1946), pp.112–41; Bathurst and Simpson, *Germany and the North Atlantic Community*. See also Kelsen, *AJIL*, 38 (1944), pp.689–94 and *AJIL*, 39 (1945), pp.518–26; Kaufmann, *Deutschlands Rechtslage unter der Besatzung* (1948); Grewe, *Ein Besatzungsstatut für Deutschland* (1948); Stödter, *Deutschlands Rechtslage* (1948); Ress, *Die Rechtslage Deutschlands nach dem Grundlagenvertrag vom 21. Dezember 1972*; Zündorf, *Die Ostverträge*; Schmid, *Die deutsche Frage im Staats- und Völkerrecht* (1980); Frowein, in: *Handbuch des Verfassungsrechts der Bundesrepublik Deutschlands* (1983), pp.29–58 (cited in this chapter as Frowein); Seiffert, in: *Deutschland als Ganzes* (1985), pp.279–84; Schröder, *ROW*, 30 (1986), pp.154–60.

[2] For text see p.313 below.

immediate post-war period certain minor adjustments were made to the zonal boundaries.[3]

Thus by August 1945 Germany within its frontiers of 31 December 1937 was divided into the following areas (see Map 1):

(i)   the British zone of occupation;[4]
(ii)   the American zone of occupation;
(iii)   the Soviet zone of occupation, less the areas listed at (vi) and (vii) below;
(iv)   the French zone of occupation;
(v)   the special Berlin area, which did not form part of any zone;
(vi)   that part of the Soviet zone of occupation which was placed under Soviet administration, that is to say, the northern part of East Prussia (the City of Königsberg and surrounding area);
(vii)   that part of the Soviet zone of occupation which was placed under Polish administration, that is to say, the territory of Germany east of the Oder-Neisse line, except for the northern part of East Prussia.

THE ASSUMPTION OF SUPREME AUTHORITY

On 5 June 1945 the four Powers assumed supreme authority with respect to Germany. The Declaration issued at Berlin that day regarding the defeat of Germany and the assumption of supreme authority with respect to Germany reads in part as follows:

> The Governments of the United Kingdom, the United States of America and the Union of Soviet Socialist Republics, and the Provisional Government of the French Republic, hereby assume supreme authority with respect to Germany, including all the powers possessed by the German Government, the High Command and any state, municipal, or local government or authority. The assumption, for the purposes stated above, of the said authority and powers does not effect the annexation of Germany.
>
> The Governments of the United Kingdom, the United States of America and the Union of Soviet Socialist Republics, and the Provisional Government of the French Republic, will hereafter determine the boundaries of Germany or any part thereof and the status of Germany or of any area at present being part of German territory.

The four Governments reserved to themselves the exercise of

---

[3] Frowein, p.32.
[4] In accordance with paragraph 2 of the London Protocol of 12 September 1944 (as amended on 14 November 1944) and an arrangement between the British and United States authorities, the area around Bremen was administered by the United States authorities.

supreme authority over Germany's external affairs, but delegated the exercise of "supreme authority in Germany" to the four Commanders-in-Chief.[5]

GERMANY'S CONTINUED EXISTENCE

Germany continues to exist as a State in international law though since 1945 it has not had a central government (apart from the organs established by the four Powers to govern Germany). The State of Germany was not extinguished in 1945 at the time of the unconditional surrender of the German armed forces and the assumption of supreme authority and occupation by the four Powers.[6] In the Declaration of Berlin of 5 June 1945 the four Powers expressly disclaimed any intention to annex Germany. The continued existence of Germany was recognised by the four Powers,[7] as well as by the authorities and courts of a number of States,[8] including those of the Federal Republic.[9] This position was not affected by the termination of the state of war with Germany, or by the establishment in 1949 of the Federal Republic of Germany and the GDR, or by their recognition as States having the full authority of sovereign States over their internal and external affairs. These developments were accompanied by clear reservations of the legal position of the four Powers. By the Protocol on the Termination of the Occupation Régime in the Federal Republic of

---

[5] Mann, *Studies in International Law*, pp.658, 663–4.

[6] The contrary view was held by Kelsen, *AJIL*, 39 (1945), pp.518–26; Virally, *L'administration internationale de l'Allemagne* (1948), p.87.

[7] This follows from their agreements and actions, e.g. the Accord of 10 May 1948 between the three Powers and Spain concerning German Enemy Property: *UKTS* 71 (1948). The New York communiqué of the three Foreign Ministers of 19 September 1950 (pp. 7–8 above) was clearly predicated upon the fact that Germany existed. See also the Secretary of State's certificates in *R v Bottrill, ex p. Kuechenmeister* [1947] 1 K.B.41 and *Trawnik v Lennox* [1985] 1 W.L.R. 532: *BYIL*, 55 (1984), p.525. In *Carl Zeiss Stiftung v Rayner and Keeler and Others* [1967] 1 A.C. 853, Lord Wilberforce stated at p.955 that "The State of Germany remained (and remains) in existence": for a discussion of other aspects of this case, see Mann, *Studies in International Law*, pp.674–9; Mann, *Foreign Affairs in English Courts* (1986), pp.56–7. See also the decision of the US Supreme Court in *Clark v Allen*, 331 U.S.503 and the decisions of the French Conseil d'État referred to at p.55 below. For a Soviet reference to continued quadripartite rights and responsibilities, see the aide–mémoire of 5 July 1968: *EA*, 23 (1968), p.D378.

[8] See the decisions of the Court of Appeal in Zurich in the *Occupation of Germany* case (*Annual Digest*, 13 (1946), p.187); the Swiss Federal Tribunal in the case of *Landis v Goens* (*International Law Reports*, 19 (1952), p.31); the Rotterdam District Court in *Gevato v Deutsche Bank* (*International Law Reports*, 19 (1952), p.29); the Dutch Supreme Court in *In re Swane* (*International Law Reports*, 26 (1958), p.577); and the High Court of Singapore in *Simon v Taylor* (*International Law Reports*, 56, p.40; *ZaöRV*, 35 (1975), pp.364–74).

[9] See the materials summarised in *ZaöRV*, beginning with *ZaöRV*, 23 (1963), p.301 ; see also Mann, *Studies in International Law*, pp.680–1; the decision of the Federal Supreme Court in *Re Lachinger* (*International Law Reports*, 21 (1954), p.43); and the constant jurisprudence of the Federal Constitutional Court (*BVerfGE* 2, 266; 3, 319; 5, 126; 6, 338; 36, 16).

Germany and the Convention on Relations between the Three Powers and the Federal Republic of Germany (text at p.323 below), the three Powers terminated the Occupation régime (but not, strictly speaking, the occupation as such); and in Article 1.2 of the Relations Convention the three Powers agreed that:

> The Federal Republic shall have accordingly the full authority of a sovereign State over its internal and external affairs.

At the same time, Article 2 provided that:

> In view of the international situation, which has so far prevented the re-unification of Germany and the conclusion of a peace settlement, the Three Powers retain the rights and the responsibilities, heretofore exercised or held by them, relating to Berlin and to Germany as a whole, including the re-unification of Germany and a peace settlement.

The same language was used upon recognition of the GDR. Thus on 6 February 1973 the Minister of State at the Foreign and Commonwealth Office informed Parliament that:

> Subject to the rights and responsibilities of the Four Powers in respect of Berlin and Germany as a whole, Her Majesty's Government recognise that the GDR has the full authority of a sovereign State over its internal and external affairs. This does not in any way indicate a change in our position on the special situation in Germany as set out in the NATO communiqué of 8th December, 1972.[10]

The Federal Republic of Germany essentially shares the view of the three Western Allies. It likewise considers that Germany continues to exist as a State in international law. Authors in the Federal Republic have devised many theories to explain the Federal Republic's relationship to Germany.[11] It will be recalled that in their communiqué of 19 September 1950 (pp.7–8 above), the three Powers stated that they considered the Federal Government as the only German Government entitled to speak for Germany as the representative of the German people in international affairs. The Federal Government's position has been given on various occasions. For example, in reply to a parliamentary question in November 1971 the Federal Government stated:

> At the time of its establishment and since, the Federal Republic of Germany has acted on the assumption that the state authority,

---

[10] *Selected Documents* II, p.266. The Minister stated that the Foreign Secretary's telegram of 22 December 1972 proposing talks constituted recognition. For the NATO communiqué see *Selected Documents* II, p.265; *US Documents*, p.1213.
[11] See, in addition to the works listed at footnote 1 above, Guérin, *L'Evolution du Statut Juridique de l'Allemagne de 1945 au Traité Fondemental* (1978).

embodied until 1945 in the German *Reich*, was reorganised in it [the Federal Republic]. In accordance with the will of the German people, it has accepted the moral responsibilities that the German past lays upon it; accordingly it largely took over the positions – rights and responsibilities – of the German *Reich*. The Federal Republic of Germany was thus, after its establishment and since, considered and treated, also abroad, as above all the State which defended and defends the continuity of Germany . . .

The Federal Government agrees with the Federal Constitutional Court's position of principle concerning the role of the Federal Republic of Germany in relation to the German *Reich*; it therefore remains called upon to assume the latter's legal positions where and insofar as that is possible.[12]

The Soviet Union and other East bloc countries also originally maintained that Germany continued to exist, but no longer hold this position. Their current view seems to be that Germany ceased to exist in 1945 (or 1949) and that two sovereign States came into being on its territory. Nevertheless, they accept the continuance of quadripartite rights and responsibilities. For example, the Quadripartite Declaration of 9 November 1972 (p.209 below) affirmed that the membership of the Federal Republic of Germany and the GDR in the United Nations "shall in no way affect the rights and responsibilities of the Four Powers and the corresponding, related quadripartite agreements, decisions and practices".

QUADRIPARTITE RIGHTS AND RESPONSIBILITIES[13]

The continued existence of quadripartite rights and responsibilities is not in doubt. It was confirmed *inter alia* by the Quadripartite Declaration of 9 November 1972, referred to above. For their part, the Federal Republic of Germany and GDR agreed in Article 9 of the Treaty on the Basis of Relations of 21 December 1972[14] that the Treaty did not affect treaties and agreements

---

[12] *Bundestag Drucksache* VI/2828, p.4.

[13] Bathurst and Simpson, *Germany and the North Atlantic Community*, pp.135–46; von Richthofen, in: *Fs. Herwath* (1974), pp.240–7; Schenk, *Die Viermächteverantwortung für Deutschland als Ganzes* (1976); Frowein, pp.40–6.

[14] *BGBl.* 1973 II, p.421; *Zehn Jahre Deutschlandpolitik*, p.210. The most complete set of documents connected with this Treaty is to be found in *Verträge, Abkommen und Vereinbarungen zwischen der Bundesrepublik Deutschland und der Deutschen Demokratischen Republik* (Press and Information Office of the Federal Government, 1973); for English translations, see *Selected Documents* II, p.261; *US Documents*, p.1215. The preamble states that the Treaty is "without prejudice to the differing views of the Federal Republic of Germany and the German Democratic Republic on questions of principle, including the national question": see Zündorf, pp.222–5. The expression "the two German States", which occurs in the Treaty, is a further hint of the special nature of inner-German relations. On the Treaty in general see Zündorf, pp.211–319; Ress, *Die Rechtslage Deutschlands nach dem Grundlagenvertrag vom 21. Dezember 1972.*

previously concluded by them "or concerning them"; and in a related exchange of letters they set out the following text of Notes they would transmit to the four Powers:

> The Federal Republic of Germany and the German Democratic Republic, with reference to Article 9 of the Treaty on the Basis of Relations of 21 December 1972, affirm that the rights and responsibilities of the Four Powers and the corresponding, related quadripartite agreements, decisions and practices cannot be affected by this Treaty.

The Federal Republic of Germany and GDR thus clearly acknowledged the continuation of the reserved rights and responsibilities of the four Powers relating to Berlin and to Germany as a whole; they also acknowledged their legal incapacity to affect those rights and responsibilities.

The Allies have been most careful to safeguard their rights and responsibilities wherever there was a need to do so. For example, the third paragraph of the final clauses of the Declaration on Principles in the Helsinki Final Act[15] reads:

> The participating States, paying due regard to the principles above and, in particular, to the first sentence of the tenth principle, "Fulfilment in good faith of obligations under international law", note that the present Declaration does not affect their rights and obligations, nor the corresponding treaties and other agreements and arrangements.

This paragraph was included to reaffirm quadripartite rights and responsibilities. As the British Prime Minister said immediately prior to signature of the Final Act:

> Subject to quadripartite rights and responsibilities the Government of the United Kingdom considers that the documents emerging from the Conference relate also to Berlin.
>
> The Final Act of this Conference is not a treaty; nor is it a peace settlement. It does not, and it cannot, affect the status of present frontiers. It does not, and it cannot, in any way affect Four-Power rights and responsibilities relating to Berlin and to Germany as a whole.[16]

---

[15] Cmnd. 6198, pp.2, 6; Cmnd. 6932, pp.225, 232. See Blech, *EA*, 31 (1976), pp.257–70; Mahnke, *ROW*, 21 (1977), pp.45–56. Other important occasions on which quadripartite rights and responsibilities were expressly safeguarded were in connection with the FRG-USSR Treaty of 12 August 1970 (*Selected Documents* II, p.220; *US Documents*, pp.1100, 1101); the FRG-USSR Air Services Agreement of 11 November 1971 (*BGBl.* II 1972, pp.1525, 1533); the FRG-Poland Treaty of 7 December 1970 (*Selected Documents* II, p.229; *US Documents*, pp.1112–3); the USSR-GDR Treaty of 1975 (*US Documents*, p.1301).
[16] Cmnd. 6932, p.218. Statements were also made by the three Powers and the Soviet Union at the Stockholm CDE Conference in September 1986: to be published in *BYIL* 1986.

Quadripartite rights and responsibilities exist independently of any treaties, agreements and other arrangements. They result from the joint assumption of supreme authority by the Allies; they are original rights, and are in no way inconsistent with any rule of international law.[17] Their precise scope has nowhere been defined: thus Article 2 of the Convention on Relations between the Three Powers and the Federal Republic of Germany ("the Relations Convention") refers in general terms to "the rights and responsibilities relating to Berlin and to Germany as a whole, including the re-unification of Germany and a peace settlement". Quadripartite rights and responsibilities relating to Germany as a whole include those mentioned in the following paragraphs.

(i) re-unification and a peace settlement[18]

The wartime and post-war agreements of the four Powers envisaged that a peace settlement would be concluded with Germany when a German government suitable for that purpose was in place.[19] So far this has not come about. In Article 7 of the Relations Convention the three Western Allies and the Federal Republic of Germany set out their policy towards the German question as follows:

> 1. The Signatory States are agreed that an essential aim of their common policy is a peace settlement for the whole of Germany, freely negotiated between Germany and her former enemies, which should lay the foundation for a lasting peace. They further agree that the final determination of the boundaries of Germany must await such a settlement.

---

[17] Contrary to the view held by some the "enemy states clauses" of the United Nations Charter (Articles 107 and 53) are of continuing significance since they make it clear that nothing in the Charter invalidates or precludes the continued exercise of quadripartite rights and responsibilities, for example, as regards access. At the same time they afford no right to the Soviet Union to intervene unilaterally in the affairs of the Federal Republic: see UK aide-mémoire of 20 September 1968 (*Selected Documents* II, p.200); US aide-mémoire of 17 September 1968 (*AJIL*, 63 (1969), p. 121); French aide-mémoire (*Le Monde* of 19 September 1968). See generally Schiedermair, pp.26–39, and authors cited at footnote 68 therein; Krakau, *Feindstaatenklauseln und Rechtslage Deutschlands nach den Ostverträgen* (1975); Frowein, pp.41–2; Forbes, *Feindstaatenklauseln, Viermächteverantwortung und Deutsche Frage* (1983).

[18] Frowein, p.44; Meissner, in: *Deutschland als Ganzes* (1985), pp.191–219; Fiedler, *NJW*, 38 (1985), pp.1049-55.

[19] The Western position remains essentially as stated by the US Secretary of State, Mr Herter, at the Geneva conference on 18 May 1959: *ICLQ*, 10 (1961), pp.583-6; Cmnd. 868, p.30. East bloc countries appear to regard the Eastern treaties of the early 1970s, and the Helsinki Final Act, as a kind of substitute peace settlement. However, the Eastern treaties are essentially a *modus vivendi* (but not in the sense that they can be unilaterally terminated at any moment) and do not affect the status of Germany. See, for example, the NATO communiqué of 4 December 1970: *US Documents*, p.1121. The Western Allied position on the Helsinki Final Act has been described at p.22 above.

2. Pending the peace settlement, the Signatory States will co-operate to achieve, by peaceful means, their common aim of a re-unified Germany enjoying a liberal-democratic constitution, like that of the Federal Republic, and integrated within the European community.
3. Deleted
4. The Three Powers will consult with the Federal Republic on all matters involving the exercise of their rights relating to Germany as a whole.

It will be seen that this is not a commitment to re-unification on any terms, but specifically to "a re-unified Germany enjoying a liberal-democratic constitution, like that of the Federal Republic, and integrated within the European community".

(ii) questions relating to borders

Germany was occupied within its frontiers of 31 December 1937, and divided for the purposes of the occupation into four zones and a special Berlin area. Any change in these frontiers, or in the borders within Germany, falls within the field of quadripartite rights and responsibilities. All changes in the frontiers of 31 December 1937 are of a provisional nature, pending a peace settlement.[20] The border between the Federal Republic of Germany and the GDR is the zonal border laid down by the London Protocol of 12 September 1944, subject to some adjustments made by the occupation authorities in the early post-war period. The Treaty on the Basis of Relations between the Federal Republic of Germany and the GDR of 21 December 1972 provides for a Border Commission to ascertain and mark the border. This it has done, except in the controversial Elbe section.[21]

(iii) the stationing of armed forces[22]

The stationing of British, American and French armed forces in the Federal Republic of Germany is now largely governed by

---

[20] In this sense, "according to international law, Germany continues to exist within its frontiers of 31 December 1937": Note of the Federal Government of 25 March 1966: *US Documents*, p. 914. On the much discussed question of the Oder-Neisse line and the areas of Germany to the east thereof, see Whiteman, *Digest of International Law*, Vol. 3, pp.283–392; *Selected Documents* II, p.229; Krülle, *Die völkerrechtlichen Aspekte des Oder-Neisse-Problems* (1970); Skubiszewski, *AJIL*, 67 (1973), pp.23–43; Frowein, *ICLQ*, 23 (1974), pp.105–26; Lehmann, *Der Oder-Neisse-Konflikt im Spannungsfeld zwischen Ost und West* (1979); Blumenwitz, *Die Darstellung der Grenzen Deutschlands in Kartographischen Werken* (1980); Gelberg, *AJIL*, 76 (1982), pp.119–29; Frowein, pp.44–6. On the provisional nature of changes to the western frontier of Germany, see Whiteman, *Digest of International Law*, Vol. 3, pp.392–425; *BYIL* 1984, p.534 (Mundatwald).
[21] Schröder, *Die Elbe-Grenze* (1986), and works cited therein.
[22] Frowein, pp.42–4.

treaties with the Federal Republic.[23] Nevertheless, it continues to rest in part on original occupation rights. Article 4.2 of the Relations Convention expressly confirms that the rights of the three Powers, heretofore exercised or held by them, which relate to the stationing of armed forces in Germany and which are retained, are not affected insofar as they are required for the exercise of their rights and responsibilities relating to Berlin and to Germany as a whole. The Treaty of 20 September 1955 between the Soviet Union and GDR provides for Soviet troops to remain in the GDR in accordance with the existing international agreements.[24] The presence of the military liaison missions of the four Powers at Potsdam, Bünde (until 1957, Bad Salzuflen), Baden-Baden and Frankfurt-on-Main also demonstrates the continuance of original occupation rights in this field.[25]

(iv) aviation

The Allies retain original rights relating to aviation in Germany. Article 6 of Chapter Twelve (Civil Aviation) of the Convention on the Settlement of Matters arising out of the War and the Occupation provides:

> In the exercise of their responsibilities relating to Germany as a whole, the Three Powers will continue to exercise control with respect to aircraft of the Union of Soviet Socialist Republics utilizing the air space of the Federal Republic.[26]

Air access to Berlin is dealt with in Chapter 8 below.

INNER-GERMAN RELATIONS[27]

The Federal Republic of Germany and the GDR currently have very different views on the German question, as they recognised in the Basis of Relations Treaty. The Federal Republic is committed to

---

[23] The Bonn/Paris Conventions; the NATO Status of Forces Agreement and the Supplementary Agreement thereto. There are also Belgian, Canadian and Dutch forces stationed in the Federal Republic.

[24] The Soviet troops stationed in the GDR are known as the "Group of Soviet Forces Germany". The British forces in the Federal Republic are referred to as "British Forces Germany".

[25] See Article 2 of the Agreement on Control Machinery in Germany of 14 November 1944 (p.317 below). For the US-USSR Huebner-Malinin Agreement of 5 April 1947, see *US Documents*, p.114; see also Whiteman, *Digest of International Law*, Vol. 2, p.592.

[26] Cmd. 9368, p.104; see also *US Documents*, p.525. For the corresponding Soviet responsibilities for GDR airspace, see Heidelmeyer *Dokumente*, pp.247–8; *US Documents*, pp.862, 864. See also Bentzien, *Zeitschrift für Luft- und Weltraumrecht*, 28 (1979), p.335.

[27] Kewenig, *EA*, 28(1973), pp.37–46; Wilke, *Bundesrepublik Deutschland und Deutsche Demokratische Republik* (1976); Zündorf, pp.214–5; Mahnke, in: *Fünf Jahre Grundvertragsurteil des Bundesverfassungsgerichts* (1979), pp.145–86; Zieger, in: *Deutschland als Ganzes* (1985), pp.285–98.

eventual German re-unification, to the continued existence of Germany as a State in international law, and to the view that the GDR is not a foreign State. Its policy is to work towards a state of peace in Europe, in which the German people will recover its unity in free self-determination.[28] It insists on the special nature of its relations with the GDR. In his address to the *Bundestag* on the State of the Nation in a Divided Germany on 27 February 1985,[29] the Federal Chancellor said that the Federal Government's *Deutschlandpolitik* remained determined by –

- the Basic Law for the Federal Republic of Germany;
- the Convention on Relations between the Three Powers and the Federal Republic of Germany;
- the Moscow and Warsaw Treaties of 1970;
- the Letters on German Unity as well as the Joint Resolution of the German *Bundestag* adopted on 17 May 1972;
- the Basic Treaty with the GDR and the judgments handed down by the Federal Constitutional Court in July 1973 and July 1975.

The GDR, on the other hand, would like to see its relations with the Federal Republic placed on the same footing as those with any other State. Thus in a speech at Gera on 13 October 1980, Honecker put forward four demands (the so-called Gera demands):

(i) the closing of the Salzgitter central collection centre (*Zentrale Erfassungsstelle*) for information on crimes committed on the inner-German border, and within the GDR;

(ii) agreement on the border along the Elbe;

(iii) recognition of GDR citizenship;

(iv) the exchange of Ambassadors.[30]

The special nature of inner-German relations is shown in many ways. As the Federal Republic of Germany does not recognise the GDR as a foreign State, it has not entered into diplomatic relations with the GDR. Instead, the two German States exchange Permanent Representations established at each other's seat of government (pp.78–9, 301–2 below).

As was confirmed by the Additional Protocol to Article 7 of the Basis of Relations Treaty, inner-German trade continues to be based on special agreements, in particular the Berlin Agreement of 20

---

[28] See, for example, the Federal Republic's letter on German unity which was sent to the GDR in connection with the Basis of Relations Treaty: *US Documents*, p.1217.

[29] *US Documents*, p.1388.

[30] *Neues Deutschland* of 14 October 1980; *DA*, 13 (1980), pp.1220–6; *ZaöRV*, 46 (1986), pp.376–7.

September 1951, as amended on 16 August 1960.[31] For the Federal Republic of Germany inner-German trade is not foreign trade;[32] and the position has been made clear in connection with both GATT[33] and the EEC.[34]

The question of German nationality is a further special aspect of inner-German relations.[35] In the view of the Federal Republic of Germany there is a single German nationality, based on the *Reich* Nationality Law of 1913.[36] However, since 1967 the GDR has had its own separate Citizenship Law.[37] In connection with the Basis of Relations Treaty the Federal Republic declared that nationality questions were not resolved, to which the GDR responded that it proceeded from the assumption that the Treaty would make a solution easier. One particular area where the question of German nationality may cause problems for other States is in connection with bilateral consular matters.[38]

---

[31] Agreement on Trade between the currency areas of the German Mark (DM-West) and the currency areas of the German Mark of the *Deutsche Notenbank* (DM–Ost): *Bundesanzeiger* No.32 of 15 February 1961. On legal aspects of inner-German trade see Ress, *Die Rechtslage Deutschlands nach dem Grundlagenvertrag vom 21. Dezember 1972*, pp.363–71; Bopp, *Wirtschaftsverkehr mit der DDR* (1983).

[32] *BVerfGE* 36, 33.

[33] *GATT Basic Instruments and Selected Documents*, Vol.2 (1972), p.34.

[34] Protocol to the EEC Treaty on German internal trade and connected problems, and OJ 1973 C 57/3 and 73/21: see Rösch, in Groeben/Boekh/Thiesing/Ehlermann, *Kommentar zur EWG-Vertrag* (3rd ed.,1983), pp.1355–62, and articles cited therein.

[35] Schröder, *ROW*, 30 (1986), pp.154–60. See Chapter 19 below.

[36] *Reichs- und Staatsangehörigkeitsgesetz* of 22 July 1913: *RGBl.* p. 583; *BGBl.* III No. 102–1.

[37] *Staatsbürgerschaftsgesetz* of 20 February 1967: *GBl. DDR* I, p. 3; *von Münch I*, p.369. See Rieger, *Die Staatsbürgerschaft der DDR* (1982).

[38] See Frowein, in: *Fs Mann* (1977), pp.367–80; Blumenwitz, *Die deutsche Staatsangehörigkeit und die Konsularverträge der DDR mit dritten Staaten* (1975); Majoros, *Die Konsularabkommen der DDR* (1984); von Mangoldt, *AVR*, 22 (1984), pp.138–71.

PART TWO

BERLIN: GENERAL

This Part covers some general legal matters that are fundamental to the status of Berlin. Certain basic elements of the quadripartite status of Berlin are considered in Chapter 3, which also introduces the principal instruments concerned. The institutional framework for the governance of Berlin is dealt with in Chapter 4, which describes both the Allied and local German authorities, as well as the status of certain governmental representatives and international organisations in Berlin. Chapter 5 examines the different bodies of law applicable in Berlin and their relationship with one another. The territorial extent of the special Berlin area, and its division into Sectors, is described in Chapter 6.

CHAPTER 3

THE LEGAL FRAMEWORK

THE freedom of the 1.9 million inhabitants of West Berlin depends upon the maintenance of Berlin's special legal status and upon the Allied security guarantee.[1] The close economic, legal, social and cultural, and indeed political, ties between West Berlin and the Federal Republic of Germany, together with West Berlin's democratic system and adherence to the rule of law, are the work of Germans, in Berlin and in the Federal Republic, but they ultimately depend upon the maintenance of the quadripartite status of Berlin. The main elements of Berlin's status, which has remained essentially unchanged since 1945, will be described in this introductory chapter, which will also list the principal quadripartite and tripartite agreements and decisions.

An understanding of Berlin's status requires an appreciation of the different levels of applicable legal rules. The most fundamental are the original rights of the four wartime Allies. Based on these original rights, but in no way detracting from them, are a series of quadripartite agreements, decisions and practices, most of which date from the period 1944 to 1949. The Quadripartite Agreement of 3 September 1971, while of considerable political importance, deals primarily with certain practical matters that had caused particular difficulty in the past. It is expressly stated not to affect quadripartite rights and responsibilities, and the corresponding wartime and post-war agreements and decisions of the four Powers, and to be without prejudice to the legal positions of the four Powers.

The breakdown of day-to-day quadripartite administration of Berlin left the three Western Allies no option but to continue the administration of the Western Sectors on a tripartite basis, and from 1948 onwards agreements and decisions were reached to this end. With the establishment of the Federal Republic of Germany in 1949

---

[1] "It is important for the West to underline that the status of the whole of Berlin has remained *de jure* unchanged, since only thus, decades after the end of the Second World War, can one provide the basis for Berlin's protection by the three Western Allies and with it the Western parts of the city's attachment to the Western world ... Maintaining the original status is a response to the Soviet Union's efforts to detach the Western Sectors from their attachment to the West and to incorporate them into its own sphere. There remains no acceptable alternative to this position even against the background of the Berlin arrangement [i.e. the arrangements of 1971/72] ... The Western Powers no longer preserve the occupation in order to control the Germans but to safeguard the Western Sectors in their extremely difficult position vis-à-vis the Eastern side": *Berlin – Materialien zur Rechtslage und zur politischen Entwicklung seit 1945*, p.11.

it became necessary to define the relationship between Berlin and the Federal Republic; and the Allies likewise redefined their relationship to the local Berlin authorities established under the new Constitution of 1950. This was done in a series of tripartite decisions; shortly thereafter the Bonn/Paris Conventions of 1952/54 placed on a new footing the relations between the three Powers and the Federal Republic of Germany. The Western Allies were careful, throughout these developments, to ensure that no steps were taken that would detract from the quadripartite status of Berlin and Germany as a whole.

In addition to the principal quadripartite and tripartite agreements and decisions, the Allies have enacted a large body of law applicable in Berlin, either on a quadripartite, tripartite or individual basis. And there are the local German legal rules, both constitutional and other, applicable to and in Berlin. These rules are in large measure compatible with Allied law, but in so far as they are not, Allied law prevails (Chapter 5 below).

ORIGINAL OCCUPATION RIGHTS

Allied rights in relation to Berlin (as in relation to Germany as a whole) are original rights deriving from the defeat of the German armed forces, the unconditional surrender of Germany and the assumption by the four Powers jointly of supreme authority with respect to Germany. These rights exist independently of and underlie the series of agreements specifying the areas in which and the methods by which they are to be exercised.[2] The occupation of Germany was agreed upon by the Allies during the war, and took place in accordance with the wartime agreements. The rights that flow from the defeat of Germany do not themselves depend upon the wartime and post-war agreements and decisions of the four Powers, still less upon any agreement on the part of Germany itself.

The Soviet position on the status of Berlin has been less consistent than that of the Western Powers, and has changed over time to suit changing Soviet policy. The Soviet Union has from time to time sought to deny that the three Powers have original rights in Berlin,

---

[2] As was stated in the British note to the Soviet Union of 31 December 1958: "the right of the Western Powers to be in Berlin rests not on the agreements . . ., but on the unconditional surrender of Germany and the assumption by the victorious Powers of supreme authority in Germany": *Selected Documents* I, pp.346, 349; Heidelmeyer, pp.214, 218. See also the US note of 31 December 1958 (*US Documents*, p.573) and the State Department's legal analysis of 20 December 1958: *Selected Documents* I, p.335; *US Documents*, p.560. For the French position see Heidelmeyer, p.212. The position of the Federal Republic of Germany is the same: see, for example, Heidelmeyer, p.346.

and has argued that they merely have rights under four-Power agreements, which can be lost if these agreements terminate for any reason.[3] For example, in statements to the Embassies of the three Powers of 10 March 1977[4] the Soviet Foreign Ministry said that:

> With regard to the assertions of the American side about "Greater Berlin" which allegedly still has a quadripartite status, the Soviet point of view on this question is well-known and has repeatedly been brought to the attention of the Western Powers. The Soviet side considers it necessary to emphasise again that the USA, Great Britain and France never had any "original" extra-contractual rights with regard to Berlin. Berlin in the territorial sense has never been separated from the area of the former Soviet occupation zone of Germany, and this has been reflected in the relevant quadripartite documents. The joint administration of Berlin which existed in the immediate post-war years was brought to an end in its day by the Western Powers themselves, who violated the implementation of quadripartite agreements and decisions and separated the Western Sectors of Berlin from their natural environment.
>
> Thus, there has for a long time been no "Greater Berlin" nor a "quadripartite status for Greater Berlin". There is Berlin the capital of the GDR, which is an indissoluble and integral part of the Republic and has the same status as any other area of the GDR. And there is West Berlin – a city with special status where an occupation regime is still maintained. It is precisely from these legal and factual realities, which are recognised and respected by the great majority of States of the world, that the Quadripartite Agreement flows.

The Eastern position on the Western Sectors of Berlin (which they often refer to as *"Westberlin"*) is that they form a "separate [independent] political entity" located "on the territory of the GDR". Sometimes West Berlin is referred to as a subject of international law with limited powers, and it has been suggested that it is, or should be, an "internationalised" or "free" city. Article 6 of

---

[3] For important statements of the Soviet position see the Soviet Note of 14 July 1948 (*US Documents*, p.158); the Soviet Note of 27 November 1958 (*Selected Documents* I, p.318; *US Documents*, p.552; Heidelmeyer, p.180). See *Das Vierseitige Abkommen über Westberlin und seine Realisierung* (1977), prepared by the Soviet and GDR Ministries for Foreign Affairs; *Documentation on the question of West Berlin* (1964) issued by the GDR Ministry for Foreign Affairs. Soviet and GDR statements are also set out in the various collections of documents published in the West. Among Eastern writings on Berlin's status are: Kröger, *Deutsche Aussenpolitik*, 3 (1958), pp.10–26; Steiniger, *West-Berlin. Ein Handbuch zur Westberlin-Frage* (1959); Arzinger and Poeggel, *Westberlin – selbständige politische Einheit* (1965); Rshewski, *Westberlin – ein politisches Gebilde sui generis* (1966/67); Görner, *DDR gewährleistet friedlichen Westberlin – Transit*, pp.7–33; Boldyrew, *Westberlin und die Europäische Sicherheit* (1973); Vysotsky, *West Berlin* (1974); Abrasimov, *West Berlin – Yesterday and Today*; Oeser, Poeggel (ed.), *Völkerrecht: Grundriss* (1983), pp.265–75; Kröger, *Deutsche Aussenpolitik* (1977), pp.57–65. See Hacker, in: *Zehn Jahre Berlin-Abkommen*, pp.218–22.

[4] *Das Vierseitige Abkommen*, p.308.

the USSR-GDR Treaty of Friendship of 12 June 1964[5] referred to West Berlin in the following terms:

> The High Contracting Parties will regard West Berlin as an independent political entity.

Article 7 of the USSR/GDR Treaty of Friendship, Co-operation and Mutual Assistance of 7 October 1975[6] provides as follows:

> The parties to the Treaty in agreement with the Quadripartite Agreement of 3 September 1971 will maintain and develop their connections (*Verbindungen*) to West Berlin, proceeding from the fact that it is not a part of the Federal Republic and that it also continues not to be governed by it.[7]

This language reflects in part, and somewhat inaccurately, that used in Part IIB of the Quadripartite Agreement of 3 September 1971 to describe the ties between the Federal Republic of Germany and the Western Sectors of Berlin. With this Treaty the Eastern side may be asserting that their own relations with West Berlin are those between subjects of international law, and that the Federal Republic's relations with West Berlin, as set out in the Quadripartite Agreement, are of the same nature.

The Eastern emphasis on the separateness of West Berlin serves two closely related purposes. First, it is intended to suggest that West Berlin, and not Greater Berlin, is a territory with special status, thus denying the continued quadripartite status of the whole of the city (and perhaps also, indirectly, Allied rights and responsibilities for Germany as a whole) and supporting the claim that the Soviet Sector is part of the GDR's territory and indeed its capital. Second, it seeks to deny the close ties between the Federal Republic of Germany and the Western Sectors of Berlin, and in particular the Federal Republic's power to represent the interests of the Western Sectors externally.

The Soviet Union has pointed to the fact that the occupation of Berlin was carried out from April to July 1945 solely by Soviet troops, and that the armed forces of the Western Allies entered the city in July and August 1945 with Soviet agreement. Despite the

---

[5] *Selected Documents* II, p.106; *US Documents*, p.869; *GBl. DDR*, 1964 I, p.132. The Western Allies rejected this assertion, stating that West Berlin was not an "independent political entity" and that, "within the framework of their responsibilities regarding Germany as a whole, the Four Powers have put the German capital, the city of Greater Berlin, under their joint administration": *Selected Documents* II, p.109; *US Documents*, p.877; Heidelmeyer *Dokumente*, p.556.

[6] Cmnd. 6932, p.285; *US Documents*, p.1297; *GBl. DDR*, 1975 II, p. 237. The Western Allies stated on this occasion that "no treaty concluded by any of the Four Powers with a third state can in any way affect the rights and responsibilities of the Four Powers": *US Documents*, p.1301.

[7] The same provision appears in the GDR's treaties with other Warsaw Pact countries and with the Mongolian People's Republic.

clear language of the London Protocol, the Soviet Union has claimed that Greater Berlin was part of the Soviet zone of occupation.[8] It is, however, clear from the text of the London Protocol, and confirmed by the practice of the four Powers, that the whole of the special Berlin area (that is, Greater Berlin) was to be under the joint occupation of the four Powers, and that neither Berlin nor any Sector thereof formed part of the Eastern (Soviet) zone of occupation.[9] Paragraph 1 of the London Protocol provides that "Germany ... will ... be divided into four zones, one of which will be allotted to each of the four Powers, and a special Berlin area, which will be under joint occupation by the four Powers". Paragraph 2, which sets out in detail the "boundaries of the four zones and of the Berlin area", defines the Eastern zone in the following terms: "the territory of Germany (including the province of East Prussia) situated to the East of" a precisely-defined line "will be occupied by armed forces of the U.S.S.R., with the exception of the Berlin area, for which a special system of occupation is provided below". After defining each of the four zones, paragraph 2 goes on to state, under a separate heading, that "the Berlin area ... will be jointly occupied by armed forces of the U.K., U.S.A. and U.S.S.R., and the French Republic".

While Allied rights are often described as occupation rights, they are not, following the assumption of supreme authority on 5 June 1945, those of a belligerent occupant. Allied rights are more extensive than those of a belligerent occupant, and in particular are not subject to the limitations set out in the Hague Regulations of 1907.[10] A belligerent occupant has no right to make changes in the laws or in the administration of occupied territory other than those which are temporarily necessitated by his interest in the maintenance and safety of his army and the realisation of the purpose of the war. On the contrary, he has a duty to administer the

---

[8] A claim first advanced in 1947/1948, revived in 1958/1961 and repeated as recently as 1977: see the Soviet statement of 10 May 1977 cited at p.33 above. See also the Western replies of 17 July 1961 to the Soviet Memorandum of 4 June 1961: *US Documents*, pp.729, 753; *Selected Documents* I, pp.443, 448; Heidelmeyer *Dokumente*, pp.413, 424.

[9] See the Notes referred to at footnote 2 above. For more detailed analysis see Bathurst, *BYIL*, 38 (1962), pp.263–5; Riklin, pp.187–8, 244–61; Mahnke, *DA*, 2 (1969), pp.473–82. For the Eastern argument see Kröger, *Deutsche Aussenpolitik*, 3 (1958), pp.10–26.

[10] *Grahame v The Director of Prosecutions*, Control Commission Courts: Court of Appeal Reports (1947) No. 348, p.168; Whiteman, *Digest of International Law*, Vol. 10, pp.595–8; Mann, *Studies in International Law*, pp.641–5, 668–9 (including references to the jurisprudence of Allied and German Courts); Jennings, *BYIL*, 23 (1946), pp.135–6; Friedmann, *The Allied Military Government of Germany* (1947), pp.65–8; Kaufmann, *Deutschlands Rechtslage unter der Besatzung* (1948), p.18; Guggenheim, *Traité de Droit international public*, Vol II (1954), pp.464, 469–73; Lauterpacht, *ICLQ*, 8 (1959), p.207; Schröder, *RuP*, 5 (1969), p.15; Donnison, *Civil Affairs and Military Government: Central Organization and Planning* (1966), pp.119–36; Zivier, p.38; Roberts, *BYIL*, 55 (1984), pp.268–70; see also the Decision of the European Commission of Human Rights on Applications Nos. 7655/76, 7656/76, and 7657/76, *Decisions and Reports* 12, pp.111, 128.

occupied area according to existing laws and existing rules of administration. The Allies only exercised rights as belligerent occupants until 5 June 1945 when they assumed "supreme authority with respect to Germany, including all the powers possessed by the German Government, the High Command and any state, municipal, or local government or authority".[11] The four Allies thereby deliberately assumed more sweeping powers than are enjoyed by a belligerent occupant. Their supreme authority was not subject to limitations deriving from German law.

In short, the Allies retain original rights in respect of Germany as a whole, including those connected with Berlin and with a peace settlement. As regards Berlin, they retain the plenitude of supreme authority assumed in 1945. They have not subsequently relinquished any part of their supreme authority, though under normal conditions they only exercise their rights in certain specified fields.

WARTIME AND POST-WAR AGREEMENTS AND DECISIONS OF THE FOUR POWERS

The practical application of quadripartite rights and responsibilities in relation to Berlin is to a large extent covered by quadripartite agreements, decisions and practices concluded in various forms and at various levels. This complex superstructure, which does not detract from the underlying original rights, is an essential element in any consideration of the legal status of Berlin. Some areas are covered by detailed texts; others by more general texts or by practices. Some of the principal agreements have been registered in accordance with Article 102 of the Charter of the United Nations; others have not, but this does not detract from their binding quality. The whole complex has as much in common with an internal constitutional arrangement (that is, internal to Germany) as with a series of international agreements in the usual sense. The following are among the more important written quadripartite agreements and decisions affecting Berlin from the wartime and immediate post-war period:

The London Protocol of 12 September 1944[12]
(Protocol of 12 September 1944 between the Governments of the

---

[11] Declaration of Berlin of 5 June 1945: see p.38 below. See further Bathurst and Simpson, *Germany and the North Atlantic Community*, pp.47–9.
[12] 227 *UNTS* 280. The English text of the Protocol as amended is at p.313 below. The Protocol as amended in November 1944 entered into force on 6 February 1945; the July 1945 amendment entered into force on 13 August 1945. The English texts of the original Protocol and the two amendments are in *Selected Documents* I, pp.27, 29, 45; *US Documents*, pp.1, 4, 44; Heidelmeyer, pp.2, 5, 14. For more detailed treatment of the London Protocol, see pp.17–18, 35, 91–2.

United Kingdom, the United States of America and the USSR on the Zones of Occupation in Germany and the Administration of Greater Berlin, as amended by the three-Power Agreement of 14 November 1944 regarding Amendments to the Protocol of 12 September 1944 and the four-Power Agreement of 26 July 1945 regarding Amendments to the Protocol of 12 September 1944)

The London Protocol, which was elaborated by the European Advisory Commission, defined the four zones and the special Berlin area into which Germany within its frontiers of 31 December 1937 was to be divided for the purposes of occupation.[13] The Protocol further provided for an Allied Kommandatura to direct jointly the administration of the Greater Berlin area. The basic provisions of the Protocol were made known to the German people in a Statement of 5 June 1945 on the zones of occupation in Germany.[14] The Soviet Union announced in its Note of 27 November 1958[15] that the London Protocol, as well as the Agreement on Control Machinery, had ceased to be in force. This was rejected by the Western Allies,[16] and has not been pressed by the Soviet Union.

The Agreement of 14 November 1944 on Control Machinery[17]

(Tripartite Agreement of 14 November 1944 on Control Machinery in Germany, as amended by the Quadripartite Agreement of 1 May 1945 regarding Amendments to the Agreement of 14 November 1944 on Control Machinery in Germany)

This Agreement, which was also elaborated by the European Advisory Commission, set out the basic elements of the control machinery in Germany. Unlike the London Protocol, it was expressed to govern the position "during the initial period of the occupation of Germany", and looked forward to a separate

---

[13] The Eastern side has wrongly sought to argue that "the purposes of occupation" here means "the objectives of the occupation"; compare the Potsdam Agreement where the different expression "for the purposes of *the* occupation" does have this meaning: Riklin, p.243.

[14] *CC Gazette, Supplement No. 1*, p.11; *Selected Documents* I, p.45; *US Documents*, p.38; Heidelmeyer, p.12.

[15] *Selected Documents* I, p.318; *US Documents*, p.552; Heidelmeyer, p.180.

[16] *Selected Documents* I, p.346 (British Note); *US Documents*, p.573 (US Note); Heidelmeyer, pp.212 (French Note), 214 (British Note), 220 (US Note). See also the Department of State Analysis: *Selected Documents* I, p.335; *US Documents*, p.560; Lauterpacht, *ICLQ*, 8 (1959), pp.202–12; Bathurst, *BYIL*, 38 (1962), p.255; Mampel, *Der Sowjetsektor von Berlin*, pp.22–36; Rottman, *Der Viermächte-Status Berlins*, pp.63–82.

[17] 236 *UNTS* 360, 400. The English text, as amended, is at p.317 below. The English texts of the Agreement and its amendment are in *Selected Documents* I, pp.31, 35; *US Documents*, pp.6, 12. The Agreement entered into force on 6 February 1945; the amendment on 25 May 1945. For more detailed treatment of the Agreement, see pp.56–8 below.

agreement on the Allied control machinery thereafter.[18] The Agreement provided that supreme authority in Germany would be exercised, on instructions from their respective Governments, by the four Commanders-in-Chief, each in his own zone of occupation, and also jointly, in matters affecting Germany as a whole, in their capacity as members of the Allied Control Council. It outlined the functions of the Control Council and of the Allied Kommandatura Berlin. It further provided for the exchange between the Commanders-in-Chief of military liaison missions (p.25 above), and for liaison with the Governments of other United Nations, who might appoint military missions to the Control Council (pp.73–4 below). The basic provisions of the Agreement were made known to the German people in a Statement of 5 June 1945 on control machinery in Germany.[19] In a third Statement of 5 June 1945 the four Governments announced their intention to consult with the Governments of other United Nations in connection with the exercise of supreme authority in Germany.[20]

The Declaration of Berlin of 5 June 1945[21]

(Declaration of 5 June 1945 regarding the defeat of Germany and the assumption of Supreme Authority with respect to Germany by the Governments of the United Kingdom, the United States of America and the USSR, and the Provisional Government of the French Republic)

In this Declaration the four Powers jointly assumed supreme authority with respect to Germany, while expressly disclaiming any intention to annex Germany. They also announced certain requirements with which Germany must comply, and looked forward to additional requirements to be carried out uncon-ditionally by all German authorities and the German people. Other requirements were imposed by acts of the Allied Control Council, such as Control Council Proclamation No. 2 of 20 September 1945.[22]

---

[18] See Bathurst, *BYIL*, 38(1962), pp.289–90.
[19] *CC Gazette, Supplement No. 1*, p.10; *Selected Documents* I, p.43; *US Documents*, p.39; Heidelmeyer, p.12.
[20] *CC Gazette, Supplement No. 1*, p.12; *Selected Documents* I, p.44.
[21] *CC Gazette, Supplement No. 1*, p.7; 68 *UNTS* 190; *Selected Documents* I, p.38; *US Documents*, p.33. The text of the preamble is at p.321 below. See Jennings, *BYIL*, 23 (1946), pp.112–41; Gross, *RGDIP*, 50 (1946), pp.67–78; Arndt, *Völkerrechtliche und staatsrechtliche Bedeutung der Berliner Erklärung vom 5. Juni 1945* (Dissertation, Göttingen 1970).
[22] *CC Gazette*, p.8. Proclamation No. 2 gave effect to a European Advisory Commission agreement of 25 July 1945.

The Potsdam Agreement of 2 August 1945[23]

The Berlin (Potsdam) Conference of 17 July – 2 August 1945 was attended by the Heads of State or Government of the United Kingdom, United States and Soviet Union. In six Notes dated 7 August 1945 France agreed to a number of points in the Potsdam Agreement, with certain reservations.[24] The Agreement deals extensively with the German question, including the German territories east of the Oder-Neisse line. While it does not deal specifically with Berlin, certain of its provisions, especially those concerning demilitarisation, are of continuing relevance to Berlin. Effect was given to many of the Agreement's provisions by Control Council legislation. The Soviet Union has sought to argue that the Western Allies' rights in Berlin have been forfeited because of their alleged failure to implement the Potsdam Agreement. This assertion has been consistently rejected by the Western Allies.

The Control Council decision of 30 November 1945 on air corridors[25]

After prolonged negotiation the Allied Control Council approved the establishment of three air corridors from Berlin to the Western zones, that is, Berlin-Hamburg, Berlin-Bückeburg and Berlin-Frankfurt-on-Main. The air corridors have not subsequently been altered.

The 1946 Flight Rules[26]

The 1946 Flight Rules, which were finally adopted by the Allied Control Authority Air Directorate on 22 October 1946, and which have not subsequently been amended, provide the only quadri-partitely agreed rules concerning flight in the three corridors

---

[23] The term "Potsdam Agreement" is inexact. Two principal texts have been published: (i) The Protocol of the Proceedings of the Berlin (Potsdam) Conference: *Selected Documents* I, p.49; *US Documents*, p.54; Heidelmeyer, p.15; (ii) The Report on the Tripartite Conference of Berlin: *CC Gazette, Supplement No. 1*, p.13. While they cover much the same ground as regards the German question, the former may be regarded as the basic agreement of the Potsdam Conference; the latter was the version published at the conclusion of this Conference. The literature on the Potsdam Agreement is extensive, both in East and West. For an introduction, see Hacker, in: Klein, Meissner, *Das Potsdamer Abkommen und die Deutschlandfrage* (1977), pp.5–41; see also Faust, *Das Potsdamer Abkommen und seine völkerrechtliche Bedeutung* (4th ed., 1969). For a detailed account of the Conference itself, see Deuerlein, *Deklamation oder Ersatzfrieden?: Die Konferenz von Potsdam 1945* (1970).

[24] *JIR*, 4 (1952/53), pp.179–83.

[25] CONL/M(45)13: *Selected Documents* I, p.63; *US Documents*, p.72; Heidelmeyer, p.36. See pp.110–12 below.

[26] DAIR/P(45)71 Second Revise: *US Documents*, p.99; Heidelmeyer, p.39. See pp.112–14 below.

and in the Berlin Control Zone. The Rules are quite detailed, covering among other things the definition of the corridors and Berlin Control Zone, the functions of the Berlin Air Safety Center, and technical Visual and Instrument Flight Rules.

The New York agreement of 4 May 1949[27]

This agreement (the "Jessup-Malik agreement") ended the Berlin blockade. The four Powers agreed that all the restrictions imposed since 1 March 1948 by the Soviet Union on communications, transportation, and trade between Berlin and the Western Zones would be removed. At the same time restrictions imposed by the Western Allies (the counter-blockade) were also removed.

The communiqué on the Sixth Session of the Council of Foreign Ministers of 20 June 1949[28]

The New York agreement had provided for a meeting of the Council of Foreign Ministers to consider Germany and Berlin. The meeting duly took place in Paris from 23 May to 20 June 1949. While it made no progress on more fundamental issues, an agreement was reached confirming the New York agreement and containing an additional specific obligation to take the measures necessary to ensure the normal functioning and utilisation of transit traffic. The communiqué also dealt with the resumption of interzonal trade.

The above list of quadripartite agreements and decisions from the wartime and immediate post-war period is not exhaustive. Other decisions of the four Powers, for example the enactment of certain laws such as Control Council Law No.43 (p.275 below), are also of great importance, as are their practices, for example in connection with access.

TRIPARTITE AGREEMENTS AND DECISIONS

Since 1948 and the breakdown of quadripartite administration, the three Western Allies have themselves concluded a number of agreements relating to Berlin. Among the most significant are the Allied security guarantee for the city, and a series of agreements

---

[27] 138 *UNTS* 123; *Selected Documents* I, p.115; *US Documents*, p.221; Heidelmeyer, p.100. On the negotiation of the New York agreement see *US Documents*, p.218; Heidelmeyer, p.98. See Chapter 7 below.
[28] *Selected Documents* I, p.122; *US Documents*, p.269; Heidelmeyer, p.104. See Chapter 7 below.

and decisions dealing with the manner of exercising supreme authority.

The Allied security guarantee[29]

The Allied security guarantee for Berlin is clear and unequivocal. While the North Atlantic Treaty[30] has not itself been extended to Berlin, under Article 5 thereof an armed attack against one or more of the Parties in Europe or North America is to be considered an attack against them all. And under Article 6, as amended, the reference to an armed attack on one or more of the Parties is deemed to include an armed attack "on the forces, vessels or aircraft of any of the Parties, when in or over ... any ... area in Europe in which occupation forces were stationed" on 24 August 1949.[31] The Western Sectors of Berlin are thus under the protection of the North Atlantic Treaty Organization, since any armed attack on these Sectors would involve an armed attack on the American, French and British forces there.[32] This was reaffirmed in the communiqué of 19 September 1950,[33] in which the three Foreign Ministers stated that the Western Allies would "treat an attack against the Federal Republic or Berlin from any quarter as an attack upon themselves". The London three-Power Declaration of 3 October 1954 includes the following:

5. The security and welfare of Berlin and the maintenance of the position of the Three Powers there are regarded by the Three Powers as essential elements of the peace of the free world in the present international situation. Accordingly, they will maintain armed forces within the territory of Berlin as long as their responsibilities require it. They therefore reaffirm that they will treat any attack against Berlin from any quarter as an attack upon their forces and themselves.[34]

---

[29] Riklin, pp.156–7, 169, 218; Mahncke, *Berlin im geteilten 'Deutschland*, pp.133–47; Wetzlaugk, *Berlin und die Deutsche Frage*, p.80.

[30] 34 *UNTS* 243. See also the Protocols of Accession of 17 October 1951 (126 *UNTS* 350), 23 October 1954 (243 *UNTS* 308) and 10 December 1981: *UKTS* 45 (1982).

[31] As amended by the 1951 Protocol of Accession. Article 6 previously referred to "an armed attack ... on the occupation forces of any Party in Europe". See Bathurst and Simpson, *Germany and the North Atlantic Community*, pp.80–1; Wetzlaugk, *Berlin und die Deutsche Frage*, pp.79–83, 88–9; Wetzlaugk, *Die alliierten Schutzmächte in Berlin*, pp.16–27.

[32] See also *Selected Documents* I, pp.129, 161. It is beyond the scope of this book to consider the military and psychological function of the presence of some 12,000 troops; any suggestion that their purpose could be achieved if the numbers were significantly reduced would need to take account of such matters.

[33] *Selected Documents* I, p.136; *US Documents*, p.341; Heidelmeyer, p.124.

[34] Declaration by the Governments of the United States of America, the United Kingdom and France, contained in the London communiqué of 3 October 1954: *Selected Documents* I, p.188; *US Documents*, p.424; Heidelmeyer, p.137.

The other Parties to the North Atlantic Treaty associated themselves with this Declaration.[35] The Allied security guarantee has been reaffirmed on many occasions.[36] In addition, Article 4 of the Convention on Relations between the Three Powers and the Federal Republic of Germany records that the mission of the Allied forces stationed in the Federal Republic is "the defence of the free world, of which Berlin and the Federal Republic form part".

Apart from the security guarantee, the principal tripartite agreements and decisions on Berlin are as follows:

The Declaration by the Western Commandants of 21 December 1948[37]

Following the Soviet Commandant's withdrawal from the Allied Kommandatura on 1 July 1948, the three Western Commandants declared that the Allied Kommandatura would resume its work. It was recognised that for the time being the Allied Kommandatura would only be able to carry out its decisions in the Western Sectors.

The Allied Kommandatura Statement of Principles of 1949/1951

The Statement of Principles of 14 May 1949 governing the Relationship between the Allied Kommandatura and Greater Berlin[38] and the First Instrument of Revision of 7 March 1951[39] defined the relationship between the Allied Kommandatura and the local German authorities in Berlin. They were replaced by the Declaration on Berlin of 5 May 1955.

The Agreement of 23 October 1954 on the exercise of reserved rights in Germany[40]

In this Agreement the three Western Allies agreed that, upon the termination of the occupation régime in the Federal Republic of Germany, their retained rights would be exercised by their Chiefs of Mission in the Federal Republic of Germany, and that those rights which relate to Berlin would continue to be exercised in Berlin pursuant to existing procedures.

---

[35] Resolution of the North Atlantic Council of 22 October 1954 associating the other NATO Partners with the three–Power security guarantee: Heidelmeyer, p.137.

[36] See, for example, the declaration of the North Atlantic Council of 16 December 1958, to which reference was frequently made thereafter: *US Documents*, p.560; Heidelmeyer *Dokumente*, p.338.

[37] *Selected Documents* I, p.114; *US Documents*, p.194; Heidelmeyer, p.77. See pp.58–9 below.

[38] *Selected Documents* I, p.117; *US Documents*, p.262; Heidelmeyer, p.108. For an account of the Statement of Principles and the 1951 Revision, see Plischke, *Berlin: Development of its Government and Administration*, pp.11–29.

[39] The Instrument of Revision came into effect on 8 March 1951: *Selected Documents* I, p.140; *US Documents*, p.347; Heidelmeyer, p.126.

[40] *Selected Documents* I, p.209; *US Documents*, p.431; Heidelmeyer, p.145. See p.57 below.

The Declaration on Berlin of 5 May 1955[41]

The Declaration on Berlin, which replaced the Statement of Principles of 14 May 1949, as revised on 7 March 1951, sets out the current relationship between the Allied Kommandatura and the local German authorities in Berlin. Under Article II the Allied authorities retain –

> the right to take, if they deem it necessary, such measures as may be required to fulfil their international obligations, to ensure public order and to maintain the status and security of Berlin and its economy, trade and communications.

In Article III they indicate that they will normally exercise powers only in certain fields.

Many tripartite decisions have taken the form of Allied Kommandatura Laws, Directives, BK/Os, BKC/Ls and BK/Ls.[42] Among the more important are BK/O(50)75 of 29 August 1950 conveying reservations to the Constitution of Berlin (p.146 below); BK/O(51)63 of 13 November 1951 concerning the delegation of authority to officials or agencies outside Berlin (p.168 below); and BK/O(51)56 of 8 October 1951, BKC/L(52)6 of 21 May 1952 and BK/O(74)11 of 30 September 1974 concerning the extension of laws and treaties to Berlin (pp.157–8, 196–7, 199 below).

THE BONN/PARIS CONVENTIONS OF 1952/54[43]

The Convention on Relations between the Three Powers and the Federal Republic of Germany (the Relations Convention[44] – often, somewhat misleadingly, referred to in West Germany as the *Deutschland-Vertrag*), and the related Conventions, all of which

---

[41] BKC/L(55)3: the English text is at p.332 below. An earlier version of the Declaration, which did not come into force, was attached to BKC/L(52)7 of 26 May 1952: Heidelmeyer *Dokumente*, p.164.

[42] For the form of Allied legislation, see Chapter 5 below.

[43] Four Conventions and a Tax Agreement were signed at Bonn on 26 May 1952, and amended by the five Schedules to the Protocol on the Termination of the Occupation Régime in the Federal Republic of Germany, signed at Paris on 23 October 1954. They entered into force on 5 May 1955. The "Bonn/Paris Conventions" were the Convention on Relations between the Three Powers and the Federal Republic of Germany (the Relations Convention); the Convention on the Settlement of Matters arising out of the War and the Occupation (the Settlement Convention); the Convention on the Rights and Obligations of Foreign Forces and their Members in the Federal Republic of Germany (now superseded by the NATO Status of Forces Agreement and its Supplementary Agreement); the Finance Convention; and the Agreement on the Tax Treatment of the Forces and their Members. The Bonn/Paris Conventions, as they came into force, and associated documents, are set out in *Germany No. 1* (1955) Cmd. 9368. See Heidelmeyer *Dokumente*, p.218; Bathurst and Simpson, *Germany and the North Atlantic Community*, pp.132–83; Bishop, *AJIL*, 49 (1955), pp.125–47; Grewe, *AöR*, 80 (1955/56), pp.231–40; Grewe, in: Kutscher, *Bonner Vertrag* (1952); Blumenwitz, *ROW*, 29 (1985), pp.317–23.

[44] Text at p.323 below.

entered into force on 5 May 1955, placed the relations between the three Powers and the Federal Republic on a new footing. But they did not alter the position of the Allies in relation to Berlin. Article 2 of the Relations Convention records that "the Three Powers retain the rights and the responsibilities, heretofore exercised or held by them, relating to Berlin and to Germany as a whole, including the re-unification of Germany and a peace settlement". Article 4.2 of the Convention provides that the rights of the three Powers which relate to the stationing of armed forces in Germany are not affected insofar as they are required for the exercise of retained rights relating to Berlin and Germany. Article 9 excludes from the jurisdiction of the Arbitration Tribunal or any other tribunal or court any dispute concerning retained rights. Article 6 provides that the three Powers will consult with the Federal Republic in regard to the exercise of their rights relating to Berlin, and that the Federal Republic, for its part, will co-operate with the three Powers in order to facilitate the discharge of their responsibilities with regard to Berlin (p.72 below). An associated letter from the three High Commissioners to the Federal Chancellor reaffirmed the Allied position on the relationship between the Federal Republic and Berlin and noted the Federal Republic's Declaration on Aid to Berlin.[45] In addition, Article 5 of Chapter 12 of the Convention on the Settlement of Matters arising out of the War and the Occupation[46] contains provisions concerning air traffic to and from the Berlin air corridors (pp.114–15 below).

THE QUADRIPARTITE AGREEMENT OF 3 SEPTEMBER 1971[47]

The Quadripartite Agreement was signed on behalf of the Governments of the United Kingdom, France, the Soviet Union and

---

[45] Text at p.329 below.

[46] 332 UNTS 219; Cmd. 9368, p.103; US Documents, p.430; Heidelmeyer, p.140.

[47] 880 UNTS 116. The English text is at p.335 below. For an analysis of the Western proposals of 5 February 1971 and the Soviet drafts of 26 March 1971 see Wagner, EA, 26 (1971), pp.375–82. For extensive extracts from these drafts see Quick of 4 August 1971, pp.8–11; certain extracts may also be found in Catudal, A Balance Sheet of the Quadripartite Agreement on Berlin, pp.191–4. The literature on the Quadripartite Agreement is extensive: see, for example, The Berlin Settlement. The Quadripartite Agreement on Berlin and the Supplementary Agreements (Press and Information Office of the Government of the Federal Republic of Germany, 1972); Doering/Ress, Staats- und Völkerrechtliche Aspekte der Berlin-Regelung; Doeker/Melsheimer/Schröder, AJIL, 67 (1973), pp.44–62; Mahncke, Berlin im geteilten Deutschland; Schiedermair; Zivier; Hacker, in: Berlin Fibel (1975), pp.321–48; Frowein, AöR, 101 (1976), pp.638–45; Wilke, German Yearbook of International Law, 21 (1978) pp.252–71; Zündorf, pp.117–75; Wettig, Das Viermächte Abkommen in der Bewährungsprobe; Catudal, ICLQ, 25 (1976), pp.766–800; Catudal, The Diplomacy of the Quadripartite Agreement on Berlin; Catudal, A Balance Sheet of the Quadripartite Agreement on Berlin; Bark, Agreement on Berlin – a Study of the 1970–1972 Quadripartite Negotiations (1974); Zieger (ed.), Zehn Jahre Berlin-Abkommen 1971–1981. For the Eastern position see Vysotsky, West Berlin; Kröger, Deutsche Aussenpolitik (1977), pp.57–65; Abrasimov, West Berlin – Yesterday and Today.

the United States of America on 3 September 1971 and entered into force on 3 June 1972 in accordance with a Final Quadripartite Protocol signed that day by the Foreign Ministers of the four Powers.

The Quadripartite Agreement itself consists of a preamble, three Parts, a testimonium and four Annexes. There are also two Agreed Minutes dated 3 September 1971, which are to be read together with the Agreement: Agreed Minute I (personal documentation of Berliners) and Agreed Minute II (certain Soviet activities in the Western Sectors of Berlin). The Final Quadripartite Protocol is an essential part of the treaty complex, as are the inner-German arrangements listed in the Protocol. In addition, Notes were exchanged on 3 September 1971, before signature of the Quadripartite Agreement, between the three Western Ambassadors and the Soviet Ambassador; these concerned the letter which the three Ambassadors sent after signature to the Federal Chancellor containing clarifications and interpretations which represented the understanding of the three Governments on the statements contained in Annex II. This letter is an instrument of the kind described in Article 31.2(b) of the Vienna Convention on the Law of Treaties (that is to say, an instrument made by one or more parties in connection with the conclusion of a treaty and accepted by the other parties as an instrument related to the treaty), and thus forms part of the context for the purpose of interpreting the Quadripartite Agreement. A second letter sent by the three Ambassadors to the Federal Chancellor on 3 September 1971 conveyed the text of the Quadripartite Agreement and dealt with matters arising thereunder of concern to the three Western Allies and the Federal Republic of Germany. This letter, which was not formally transmitted to the Soviet Union (but which the Soviet Ambassador knew about in advance), is concerned solely with the relationship between the three Western Allies and the Federal Republic of Germany.

As is stated in the testimonium, the Quadripartite Agreement is done in the English, French and Russian languages, all texts being equally authentic. Throughout the negotiations the detailed drafting work was done on the basis of the English language text. A full Russian language text was only introduced a few days before signature. This text was accepted by the Western negotiators on the clear understanding that, as the Soviet Ambassador said prior to signature, it was the exact equivalent in substance of the English and French texts.[48] Federal German and GDR

[48] Wettig, *DA*, 12 (1979), p.284; Catudal, *A Balance Sheet of the Quadripartite Agreement on Berlin*, p.12; Zivier, p.32. Thus, for example, the Soviet Union would have difficulty in basing a divergent interpretation of the Agreement on the Russian text of certain terms in Part IIB ("taking into account", "continue not to be"); Schiedermair, footnote 238.

representatives agreed on a German translation of the Agreement.[49]

The provisions of Part II of the Quadripartite Agreement, and the Annexes, which relate to certain practical matters concerning the Western Sectors of Berlin, are considered in detail elsewhere. The present chapter deals with the Agreement in general and with its provisions of general application, that is, the preamble, Parts I and III, and the Final Quadripartite Protocol.

The nature of the Agreement

The nature of the Quadripartite Agreement has been described by the three Western Allies in the following terms:

> The Quadripartite Agreement is an international treaty concluded between the four contracting parties and not open to participation by any other State. In concluding this Agreement, the Four Powers acted on the basis of their quadripartite rights and responsibilities, and of the corresponding wartime and post-war agreements and decisions of the Four Powers, which are not affected. The Quadripartite Agreement is a part of conventional, not customary international law.[50]

Eastern European countries often act as though they were parties to the Quadripartite Agreement, for example by protesting at alleged breaches.[51] The Western Allies do not normally respond in substance to such allegations, but merely reaffirm that States which are not parties to the Quadripartite Agreement are not competent to comment authoritatively on its provisions.[52]

The Quadripartite Agreement does not and was not intended to alter the legal status of Berlin; still less does it represent an overall solution to, or settlement of, the Berlin question.[53] This is clear from the preamble, paragraph 3 of Part I and the Final Quadripartite Protocol. The Agreement deals in large part with certain practical

---

[49] See Wettig, *DA*, 12 (1979), p.286; Zündorf, p.126; Mahncke, *Berlin im geteilten Deutschland*, p.26. The agreed German text was published in West Germany. A somewhat different East German text was published in *Neues Deutschland* on 4 September 1971: see *Das Vierseitige Abkommen*, pp.44, 108. As is the nature of translations, neither is perfect – but then neither is authentic. Among the differences are the title ("*Das Vierseitige Abkommen*"), where the East German text is closer to the authentic language texts; and Part IIB (e.g. "*Verbindungen*" instead of "*Bindungen*"), where the East German text is substantively less accurate.

[50] *Multilateral Treaties*, Chapter III. 1, note 2 and Chapter III. 11, note 2. The Federal Republic of Germany supported this position. See also the third preambular paragraph of the Agreement ("Acting on the basis of ..."); and the letter to the Federal Chancellor conveying the text of the Quadripartite Agreement: Cmnd. 5135, p.52.

[51] For the Soviet position, see *Multilateral Treaties*, Chapter XXVII.1,note 2.

[52] E.g. *BYIL*, 55 (1984), p.530.

[53] *The Berlin Settlement* (footnote 47 above), p.179; Zivier, p.149; Zündorf, p.217. For a brief account of the constitutional controversy that the Quadripartite Agreement provoked in the Federal Republic, see Zivier, pp.165–7.

matters which had given rise to difficulties in the past. The Final Quadripartite Protocol records that the Quadripartite Agreement and the consequent inner-German arrangements "settle important issues examined in the course of the negotiations". Other such important issues were not settled, including those concerning the Soviet Sector.

The subject-matter of the Agreement

There is an important difference between the Western Allies and the Soviet Union concerning the subject-matter of the Quadripartite Agreement. In the view of the Western Allies the Agreement relates to the whole of the special Berlin area, that is to say, to all four Sectors of the city. The Soviet Union, on the other hand, insists that only the three Western Sectors are the subject-matter of the Agreement and that the negotiators were not concerned with East Berlin. It often refers to the Agreement as "the Quadripartite Agreement on West Berlin".[54]

Nowhere does the Agreement refer to "Berlin", as opposed to the "Western Sectors of Berlin" (Part II) or the "American Sector of Berlin" (preamble). Instead there is a deliberate ambiguity in the term "the relevant area", which is not defined and which has to be interpreted in context. The term can be regarded by the West as covering West and East Berlin and by the East as relating to West Berlin in its geographical context (that is, including the access routes and the areas immediately surrounding West Berlin in their relation thereto). The text of the Agreement tends to support the Western view. The term "relevant area" first appears in the preamble, where it follows references to the Allied Control Council, the American Sector of Berlin, quadripartite rights and responsibilities, and the wartime and post-war agreements and decisions of the four Powers, all of which recall arrangements concerning the whole of Berlin and the access routes. Part I, entitled "General provisions", likewise refers to "the relevant area", whereas Part II is headed "Provisions

---

[54] See the interview with Honecker in *Neues Deutschland* of 5 September 1971; and the remarks of Abrasimov, the Soviet Ambassador in East Berlin, upon being made an "honorary citizen of the capital of the GDR" on 12 September 1971: *Neues Deutschland* of 13 September 1971. See also the address by Ambassador Rush to the Berlin Chamber of Industry and Commerce on 27 September 1971: *US Documents*, pp.1155–67. See also Jung, *ROW*, 19 (1975), pp.217–23; Zivier, *ROW*, 19 (1975), pp.223–5; Schiedermair, pp.14–18, 42–9, 53–4; Frowein, *AöR*, 101 (1976), pp.638–40; Zivier, pp.171–4; Silagi, in: *Zehn Jahre Berlin-Abkommen 1971–1981*, p.103; Vysotsky, *West Berlin*, p.212. The legal position was not affected by the reference to "the September 3, 1971 Quadripartite Agreement relating to the Western Sectors of Berlin" in the joint communiqué of 29 May 1972 on the occasion of President Nixon's visit to Moscow (*US Documents*, p.1202), on which see the US Secretary of State's comments (*Frankfurter Allgemeine Zeitung* of 10 June 1972).

relating to the Western Sectors of Berlin". This heading is difficult to reconcile with the Soviet view that the Agreement as a whole relates only to the Western Sectors. Even though the more detailed provisions of the Quadripartite Agreement (Part II and Annexes I to IV) are primarily concerned with the Western Sectors, including the access routes and communications with East Berlin and the GDR, the Western Allies could not have accepted an Agreement limited to the Western Sectors. Such an Agreement would have tended to confirm the Soviet view that the quadripartite status of Berlin was now confined to the Western Sectors and that the Eastern Sector was now part of the territory of the GDR.

The preamble

The preamble to the Quadripartite Agreement first recalls the basis on which the Agreement was concluded:

Acting on the basis of their quadripartite rights and responsibilities, and of the corresponding wartime and post-war agreements and decisions of the Four Powers, which are not affected.

It will be noted that this refers both to quadripartite rights and responsibilities and to the wartime and post-war agreements and decisions. The wartime and post-war agreements and decisions are essentially those from the period 1944–49, from the London Protocol of 12 September 1944 and the Agreements of 14 November 1944 and 5 June 1945 to the New York and Paris agreements of 1949, and the decisions reached through the quadripartite machinery, including the arrangements on access. The paragraph expressly states that neither quadripartite rights and responsibilities nor the corresponding quadripartite agreements and decisions are affected by the Quadripartite Agreement. Similar language is to be found in Part I, paragraph 3, and in paragraph 1 of the Final Quadripartite Protocol. The fact that the 1971 Agreement primarily regulates practical matters, and does not affect more fundamental aspects of Berlin's legal status, is further emphasised by the concluding preambular paragraphs:

Guided by the desire to contribute to practical improvements of the situation,
Without prejudice to their legal positions.

Part I

The four paragraphs of Part I (General provisions) are of considerable importance for the relations of the four Powers in connection with Berlin. The difference of view over the subject-matter of the Agreement is of particular relevance in this regard. In the Western view the four general provisions are equally applicable to all four Sectors of Berlin.

Part I, paragraph 1, reads:

The four Governments will strive to promote the elimination of tension and the prevention of complications in the relevant area.[55]

This provision has to be read in context and against the background of the tension and complications in and around Berlin in the past. The paragraph is likely to be of more political than legal interest. The four Powers "will strive to promote" the elimination of tension and the prevention of complications "in the relevant area". They must avoid taking steps themselves which cause tension or complications, and within their powers they must ensure that others do not do so. The paragraph is in very general terms, and differing views may well be held on its application in particular circumstances.

Part I, paragraph 2, reads:

The four Governments, taking into account their obligations under the Charter of the United Nations, agree that there shall be no use or threat of force in the area and that disputes shall be settled solely by peaceful means.[56]

This provision is closely connected with the existing obligations of the four Powers under the Charter of the United Nations and general international law. Its inclusion in the Quadripartite Agreement precludes any possible argument that these central principles of international law are in some way inapplicable to the situation in and around Berlin. Moreover, as with paragraph 1 the undertaking of the four Powers relates not only to their own acts but to those of others.

The term "threat or use of force" in this context refers to the threat or use of force in international relations referred to in Article 2.4 of the Charter of the United Nations. The paragraph does not deal with the internal use of force, for example in exercise of police power. Similarly, the reference to the peaceful settlement of disputes covers disputes between States referred to in Article 2.3 of the Charter. As will be noted later, the Final Quadripartite Protocol provides a mechanism for resolving certain disputes.

Part I, paragraph 3, reads:

The four Governments will mutually respect their individual and joint rights and responsibilities, which remain unchanged.[57]

[55] Zündorf, p.129; Schiedermair, pp.19–24.
[56] Zündorf, footnote 426; Schiedermair, pp.24–42. The obligations on the non-use of force remain subject to the Charter exceptions; for the "enemy states clauses" (Articles 53 and 107 of the Charter) see p.23 above.
[57] Schiedermair, pp.49–52.

This paragraph too adds little to the existing obligations of the parties. It does, however, further describe the "quadripartite rights and responsibilities" referred to in the preamble. They are both individual and joint, as is reflected in the respective powers of the Allied Kommandatura and the Commandants. The affirmation that the rights and responsibilities "remain unchanged" indicates both that they have not changed in the past and that they are not changed by the Quadripartite Agreement. The reference is comprehensive, covering all individual and joint rights in and in respect of Berlin. It embraces both original rights, including the right to occupy Berlin and the right of access, and the rights and responsibilities deriving from quadripartite agreements, decisions and practices.

Part I, paragraph 4, reads:

> The four Governments agree that, irrespective of the differences in legal views, the situation which has developed in the area, and as it is defined in this Agreement as well as in the other agreements referred to in this Agreement, shall not be changed unilaterally.[58]

This is the most concrete of the general provisions in Part I of the Quadripartite Agreement, and the one most often cited, for example, in connection with the establishment in Berlin of the Federal Environment Agency (pp.184–5 below) and East Berlin's participation in the 1981 *Volkskammer* elections (pp.303–4 below).

The exclusion of unilateral change in the situation raises two main questions: what is the situation referred to, and what amounts to a change? The situation is described as "the situation which has developed in the area, and as it is defined in this Agreement as well as in the other agreements referred to in this Agreement". The area means "the relevant area" and thus, for the Western Allies, embraces the whole of Berlin and the access routes. The situation was not frozen at any arbitrary point in the past or upon the coming into force of the Quadripartite Agreement, as is made clear by the reference to the Quadripartite Agreement and to the other agreements. The Quadripartite Agreement itself includes dynamic elements, such as the provision for the "development" of the ties between the Western Sectors of Berlin and the Federal Republic of Germany and the recognition that, as in the past, legislation and international agreements will be extended to Berlin. The "other agreements referred to in this Agreement" are both the wartime and post-war agreements of the four Powers and the inner-German arrangements referred to in Parts IIA and IIC, which in turn contain dynamic elements.

---

[58] Zivier, pp.176–8; Zündorf, pp.130–2; Schiedermair, pp.52–61.

The changes concerned could be brought about either by one or more of the four Powers or by German authorities. In any case, only changes affecting fundamental aspects of the situation are excluded. Minor changes of a day-to-day kind, which become necessary with the passage of time (for example, in certain Allied legislation), are not excluded. Moreover, non-fundamental changes falling within the "dynamic" provisions of the Quadripartite Agreement, referred to above, are permissible, though there is room for debate about how far these dynamic elements can be developed without introducing the kind of changes excluded by Part I, paragraph 4.

Part I, paragraph 4, does not mean that any party to the Agreement has to regard the situation which has developed in the area as lawful. This is underlined by the phrase "irrespective of the differences in legal views". No party is precluded from challenging the lawfulness of the existing situation, for example by diplomatic protest; what is excluded are unilateral attempts to change the situation.

Part III and the Final Quadripartite Protocol

The Quadripartite Agreement entered into force on 3 June 1972 in accordance with Part III, which reads:

> This Quadripartite Agreement will enter into force on the date specified in a Final Quadripartite Protocol to be concluded when the measures envisaged in Part II of this Quadripartite Agreement and its Annexes have been agreed.

The measures referred to are the "detailed arrangements between the competent German authorities" referred to in Part IIA and C. These arrangements fall within the area of quadripartite rights and responsibilities, and were negotiated pursuant to and in implementation of the Quadripartite Agreement. The following arrangements are listed in the Final Quadripartite Protocol:

> Agreement between the Government of the Federal Republic of Germany and the Government of the German Democratic Republic on the Transit Traffic of Civilian Persons and Goods between the Federal Republic of Germany and Berlin (West) dated 17 December 1971;[59]
>
> Arrangement between the Senat and the Government of the German Democratic Republic on Facilitations and Improvements in Travel and Visitor Traffic dated 20 December 1971;[60]
>
> Arrangement between the Senat and the Government of the

---

[59] Cmnd. 5135, p.62; US Documents, p.1169. See pp.129–39 below.
[60] Cmnd. 5135, p.104; US Documents, p.1179. See pp.248–52 below.

German Democratic Republic on the Resolution of the Problem of Enclaves by Exchange of Territory dated 20 December 1971;[61]

Points 6 and 7 of the Protocol on Negotiations between a Delegation of the Federal Ministry for Post and Telecommunications of the Federal Republic of Germany and a Delegation of the Ministry for Post and Telecommunications of the German Democratic Republic dated 30 September 1971.[62]

Part III, together with the Final Quadripartite Protocol, confirms that, as is clear from Part IIA and C and Annexes I and III, the Quadripartite Agreement, the consequent inner-German arrangements and the Final Quadripartite Protocol together form a single whole. This means in particular that the inner-German arrangements have to be read as one with the Quadripartite Agreement, to which they are subordinate and which is an essential basis for their interpretation and application; and, as is clear from the consultation provision in the Final Quadripartite Protocol, their interpretation and application are matters of direct concern to the four Powers. The German parties negotiated the inner-German arrangements pursuant to the Quadripartite Agreement and under a four-Power roof, that is to say, under a mandate from the four Powers. The Final Quadripartite Protocol was only signed once the inner-German arrangements were agreed, and the "consequent" inner-German arrangements entered into force simultaneously with the Quadripartite Agreement and are to remain in force together with it. In other words, the German parties to the inner-German arrangements are not free to derogate from them; if they sought to do so this could bring into question the whole of the Quadripartite Agreement.

Paragraph 4 of the Final Quadripartite Protocol provides for quadripartite consultations at the request of any one of the four Governments.[64] It has so far not been invoked, but is nevertheless of great importance. No party to the Quadripartite Agreement would be justified in engaging in reprisals, or seeking to denounce the Agreement, before the consultation procedure specifically provided therein had been exhausted. Paragraph 4 reads:

In the event of a difficulty in the application of the Quadripartite

---

[61] Cmnd. 5135, p.122; *US Documents*, p.1182. See Chapter 6 below.

[62] Cmnd. 5135, p.59; *US Documents*, p.1167. See Zivier, p.220; Catudal, *A Balance Sheet of the Quadripartite Agreement on Berlin*, pp.95–9.

[63] See the remarks of Ambassador Rush, *US Documents*, pp.1163–4; Zivier, pp.162–5; Schiedermair, pp.185–90; Zündorf, pp.167–70. East bloc authors accept that the Quadripartite Agreement and the arrangements between the Federal Republic of Germany and the GDR "operate together as a whole", but say that they are "independent juridical acts", concluded on the basis of the German authorities' own competences: e.g. Vysotsky, *West Berlin*, p.282.

[64] Zivier, pp.180–1; Schiedermair, pp.46, 190–3; Zündorf, pp.170–1.

Agreement or any of the above-mentioned agreements or arrangements which any of the four Governments considers serious, or in the event of non-implementation of any part thereof, that Government will have the right to draw the attention of the other three Governments to the provisions of the Quadripartite Agreement and this Protocol and to conduct the requisite quadripartite consultations in order to ensure the observance of the commitments undertaken and to bring the situation into conformity with the Quadripartite Agreement and this Protocol.

It will be seen that the scope of the consultation procedure is wide. It may be invoked (i) in the event of a difficulty in the application of the Quadripartite Agreement (including the broad "general provisions" in Part I) or any of the inner-German arrangements which any one of the four Governments considers serious; or (ii) in the event of non-implementation of any part of the Quadripartite Agreement or the inner-German arrangements. In each case, the Government or Governments concerned may draw the attention of the other Powers to "the provisions of the Quadripartite Agreement and this Protocol" and, invoking the Protocol, conduct quadripartite consultations. The purpose of the consultations may be twofold: to ensure the observance of "the commitments undertaken", and "to bring the situation into conformity with the Quadripartite Agreement and this Protocol". The "commitments undertaken" include the commitments of the German parties under the inner-German arrangements. They are indissolubly linked to provisions of the Quadripartite Agreement and the Protocol, and consequently difficulties with them or non-implementation of any part thereof would be grounds for quadripartite consultations under the Protocol. The quadripartite consultation procedure is independent of the dispute settlement procedures in the inner-German arrangements, though it is unlikely in practice to be invoked in connection therewith until these have been tried.

THE QUADRIPARTITE DECLARATION OF 9 NOVEMBER 1972

This four-Power Declaration, like the Quadripartite Agreement, was negotiated by the four Ambassadors in the Control Council building in Berlin. The particular occasion was the application of the Federal Republic of Germany and the German Democratic Republic to join the United Nations, and it is considered in Chapter 16 below in that context.[65] It is an important reaffirmation of "the rights and responsibilities of the Four Powers and the

[65] See pp.208–10 below.

corresponding, related quadripartite agreements, decisions and practices". Although it does not expressly indicate the subject-matter of these rights, responsibilities, agreements, decisions and practices, it is clear from the context that these relate to Berlin and to Germany as a whole. The express mention of "practices" is a recognition of their importance in connection with quadripartite rights and responsibilities.

CHAPTER 4

THE INSTITUTIONAL FRAMEWORK

THIS chapter deals first with the occupation authorities and the local German authorities, which together conduct the government of the city. It then looks at the institutions and offices in Berlin established by foreign States, in particular the Military Missions and consular posts, as well as the position of certain other governmental representatives and international organisations.[1]

OCCUPATION AUTHORITIES

The nature of the Allied occupation authorities in Germany has been much discussed. By the Declaration of Berlin of 5 June 1945 the four Allies assumed–

> supreme authority with respect to Germany, including all the powers possessed by the German Government, the High Command and any state, municipal, or local government or authority.

They further specified that the assumption of the said authority and powers did not effect the annexation of Germany. From the outset the Western Allies have been clear that the acts of the occupation authorities in Germany "are in law attributable not to the Allied States but to the State of Germany, which is accordingly deliberately maintained in being as a legal person".[2] The occupation authorities, whether acting jointly or individually, constituted the government of Germany. Thus in a series of decisions the French *Conseil d'État* held that the French occupation authorities in Germany exercised powers attributable to the government of Germany and not the authority of the French State.[3] Similarly the British Government has stated that the persons to be regarded for the purposes of the United Kingdom State Immunity Act 1978 as the government of Germany include the members of the Allied Kommandatura of Berlin, including the British Military Commandant.[4] Even when

---

[1] For the local German authorities in the Soviet Sector and missions situated there, see Chapter 24 below.
[2] Jennings, *BYIL*, 23 (1946) p.122.
[3] See the constant jurisprudence of the *Conseil d'État*: judgments of 29 June 1951 (*Société Bonduelle* case); 21 November 1952 (*Association pour la réconstruction à Paris et à Metz du monument du général Mangin* case); 10 July 1954 (*Kelm* case); 15 December 1954 (*Roucante* case); and 17 June 1955 (*Groupement des scieurs alsaciens et mosellans* case): Kiss, *Répertoire de la pratique française en matière de droit international public*, Vol II, pp.496–501.
[4] Certificate of the Secretary of State for Foreign and Commonwealth Affairs dated 17 September 1984 issued in connection with the case of *Trawnik v Lennox*: *BYIL*, 55 (1984), p.525.

exercising occupation powers individually the respective occupation
authorities are exercising joint authority and are in law the agents or
delegates of the Allies jointly.[5]

The Allied Control Council[6]

The Allied Control Council was established in accordance with
the Agreement of 14 November 1944 on Control Machinery in
Germany, as amended by the Agreement of 1 May 1945.[7] Article 1
provided that supreme authority in Germany would be exercised,
on instructions from their respective Governments, by the four
Commanders-in-Chief, each in his own zone of occupation, and also
jointly, in matters affecting Germany as a whole, in their capacity as
members of the supreme organ of control constituted under the
Agreement. Article 3 provided that the four Commanders-in-Chief,
acting together as a body, would constitute a supreme organ of
control called the Control Council. The Control Council's seat was
Berlin. One of the functions of the Control Council listed in Article
4 was to direct the administration of Greater Berlin through
appropriate organs. Decisions of the Control Council were to be
unanimous. Its principal subordinate organ was the Co-ordinating
Committee.[8] The Control Council, which first met on 30 July 1945,
issued many laws for Germany, some of which remain in force in
Berlin and elsewhere. The Soviet Commander-in-Chief withdrew
from the Control Council on 20 March 1948, and it was thereafter
in suspense.[9] However, as will be seen later in this chapter, the
Military Missions continue to be accredited to the Control Council;

---

[5] Referring to the position of the Commanders-in-Chief (Military Governors) in
Germany, Bathurst and Simpson write that "it seems clear the authority in the zones,
though exercised severally, was nonetheless in law joint authority, exercised by each
Power not in its own right but on behalf of the four Powers ... the Military Governor was,
even in his own zone, in law the agent of the four Powers jointly ... The Governments of
the Occupying Powers ... had no direct power over the inhabitants of Germany. Their
decisions required transformation into the law of Germany by the Control Council or the
Military Governors": *Germany and the North Atlantic Community*, pp.43–4; Friedman, *The
Allied Military Government of Germany*, p.67; Jennings, BYIL, 23 (1946), p.138; Mann,
Studies in International Law, pp.645–7, 653–6, 665.
[6] See Schröder, *AVR*, 23 (1985), pp.42–73; Friedmann, *The Allied Military Government of
Germany*, pp.49–53. The Control Council building at Kleistpark in the American Sector is
still occupied by the Berlin Air Safety Center. The flags of the four Powers still fly outside
the building. Before 1945 it was the seat of the *Kammergericht*, and used by the Nazi
Volksgerichtshof.
[7] The English text of the Agreement, as amended, is at p.317 below.
[8] The Control Council had various other subordinate organs and staff. The collective
term was "Allied Control Authority", defined in Control Council Directive No.1 as "the
entire control machinery in Germany, including the Control Council, the Co-ordinating
Committee and the Control Staff": CONL/P(45)7: *US Documents*, p.48.
[9] For a Soviet account of the events of 20 March 1948, see Vysotsky, *West Berlin*, p.73.
For subsequent Allied attitudes to the Control Council, see Schröder, *AVR*, 23 (1985),
p.42.

and the Control Council established the Berlin Air Safety Center and directed the Allied Kommandatura to establish Spandau Allied Prison, both of which continue to function on a four-Power basis.

The Western Ambassadors in Bonn

Upon the establishment of the Federal Republic of Germany in 1949, the Charter of the Allied High Commission for Germany[10] transferred to the High Commissioners –

> all authority with regard to the control of Germany or over any governmental authority thereof vested in or exercised by the respective Commanders-in-Chief of the forces of the occupation of the three Powers in Germany, from whatever source derived and however exercised.

The retention by the Allies of their rights and responsibilities relating to Berlin and to Germany as a whole was expressly referred to in the Convention on Relations between the Three Powers and the Federal Republic of Germany, which entered into force on 5 May 1955.[11] The Allied High Commission was abolished on that day, but the three Allied Ambassadors in Bonn retained the powers previously vested in them as High Commissioners. These powers, originally vested in the Commanders-in-Chief, include the power to appoint the respective Commandants, to give general direction to the Allied Kommandatura, and to treat with the Soviet Ambassador in East Berlin on matters of quadripartite concern. Paragraph 3 of the Tripartite Agreement on the Exercise of Retained Rights in Germany, signed by the Foreign Ministers of the three Powers on 23 October 1954 (p.42 above), provided that "those rights which relate to Berlin will continue to be exercised in Berlin pursuant to existing procedures, subject to any future modification which may be agreed". The three Allied Ambassadors in Bonn are thus the repositories of the reserved rights and powers of the High Commissioners for Germany.

The Allied Kommandatura Berlin[12]

The supreme legislative and executive authority in Berlin is the Allied Kommandatura Berlin. This body was established in accordance with Article 7 of the Agreement of 14 November 1944

---

[10] Charter of the Allied High Commission for Germany, signed on 20 June 1949: *Selected Documents* I, p.123; *US Documents*, p.270. For the work of the Allied High Commission, see Bathurst and Simpson, *Germany and the North Atlantic Community*, pp.93–105.

[11] Text at p.323 below.

[12] See Plischke, *Berlin: Development of its Government and Administration*, pp.30–62, 79–181; Plischke, *Government and Politics of Contemporary Berlin*, pp.14–20, 65–7; Krumholz, *Berlin ABC* (2nd ed.), pp.28–31. For the legislative authority of the Allied Kommandatura, see pp.85–6 below.

on Control Machinery in Germany, as amended, which provided that an Inter-Allied Governing Authority (Komendatura)[13] consisting of four Commandants, one from each Power, appointed by their respective Commanders-in-Chief, would be established to direct jointly the administration of the Greater Berlin area. The Allied Kommandatura was responsible in Berlin for matters which, in each zone, were within the competence of the individual Commander-in-Chief. Article 7 also provided that the Kommandatura would operate under the general direction of the Control Council, but its existence was in no way dependent on the Control Council.[14]

The Allied Kommandatura began its work on 11 July 1945, and at first functioned reasonably smoothly. But a Soviet campaign of obstruction, including constant use of the veto, ensued after the Communist-controlled Socialist Unity Party (SED) lost its predominant position in the local city administration in the first post-war election in October 1946. Following the Soviet withdrawal from the Control Council on 20 March 1948 and the breakdown of quadripartite control machinery for Germany, the Soviet Commandant withdrew from the Allied Kommandatura on 16 June 1948, and the Russians announced on 1 July 1948 that they would no longer participate in Allied Kommandatura staff meetings.[15] In the following months the Allied Kommandatura did not meet owing to the refusal of the Soviet Commandant to attend and this had an increasingly serious effect on the government of Berlin. Many proposed legislative and executive acts of the local Berlin authorities could not be carried out in the absence of Allied Kommandatura approval, which was required by Article 36 of the Temporary Constitution of Berlin. Moreover the supreme legislative and executive authority in the city was itself paralysed.

Accordingly, on 21 December 1948 the three Western Commandants formally declared that the Allied Kommandatura, having been established by agreements which could only be altered or abrogated by agreement of all the Governments party to them, had not ceased to exist, though its work had been in suspense since 1 July owing to Soviet refusal to attend its meetings. It would resume its work forthwith. If the Soviet authorities decided to abide by the agreements to which the four Powers were committed, the quadripartite administration of Berlin could be resumed; but as

---

[13] Komendatura very soon became Kommandatura in English and French; it is often rendered as *Kommandantur* in German.
[14] Mampel, *Der Sowjetsektor von Berlin*, p.31. For the relationship between the Allied Kommandatura and the Allied Control Council, see Riklin, pp.250–5.
[15] *Selected Documents* I, p.113; *US Documents*, p.151; Heidelmeyer, p.67. For a Soviet account of these events, see Vysotsky, *West Berlin*, p.87.

long as the Soviet authorities abstained from attendance, the three Western Allies would "exercise the powers of the Allied Kommandatura although it is realised that owing to Soviet obstruction it will only be possible for them to carry out their decisions in the Western Sectors for the present".[16] They have done so ever since. The Western Sectors of Berlin are thus under effective three-Power administration, while the whole of Berlin remains under four-Power occupation.

The Allied Kommandatura remains in law a quadripartite organ, though in practice only the British, American and French Commandants now participate. The three Commandants meet at least once a month, accompanied by the Deputy Commandants, who are the Western Allied Ministers in Berlin, that is to say, the senior Allied civilian officials resident in the city. The Allied Kommandatura generally conducts its detailed work in four Committees: the Civil Affairs Committee, Legal Committee, Economic Committee and Public Safety Committee. Broadly speaking, these deal respectively with political affairs, legal questions, economic matters (including communications), and aspects of public safety and security (including supervision of the Berlin police). The Committees are composed of the appropriate officials of the three Western military governments in Berlin. They meet regularly to conduct business falling within their spheres of responsibility, and make recommendations to the Commandants and Deputy Commandants; they also deal directly with the local Berlin authorities in the name of the Allied Kommandatura in their respective fields of competence. In addition, the Kommandatura has a tripartite Secretariat of Allied officials.[17] The chairmanship of the Kommandatura, including its Committees, rotates between the three Western Allies on a monthly basis.[18]

The Western Commandants, their officials and forces

Subject to the Allied Kommandatura, the Western Commandants

---

[16] *Selected Documents* I, p.114; *US Documents*, p.194; Heidelmeyer, p.77.

[17] Allied Kommandatura meetings are held, and the Secretariat maintains offices, at the Allied Kommandatura building in Dahlem in the American Sector. Four flagpoles stand outside the building although only the flags of the three Western Powers are now flown. Housed in the same building are the Allied Travel Office and Inter-Zonal Facilities Bureau, Allied authorities which issue certain residence permits and travel documents (see p.293 below).

[18] The chairmanship in January, April, July and October is British; in February, May, August and November it is American; and in March, June, September and December it is French. The Allied Kommandatura's Internal Procedure originally provided for decisions to be taken unanimously; as revised on 7 June 1949 (*Selected Documents* I, p.120; *US Documents*, p.265; Heidelmeyer *Dokumente*, pp.118, 605) it provided for majority voting. In practice, decisions of the Allied Kommandatura and its Committees are taken by consensus.

have legislative and executive authority within their respective Sectors of Berlin; they may also establish civil courts.[19] The Commandants act under the general political direction of the three Ambassadors in Bonn and, ultimately, of the Foreign Ministers and Governments in London, Washington and Paris. But this does not alter the fact that, in Berlin, the powers deriving from the supreme authority jointly assumed by the Allies in 1945 vest in, and are exercised by, the Allied Kommandatura and, subordinate to it, the Commandants or persons acting on their behalf.[20]

The Commandants are supported and advised by civilian and military staffs. Their administrations in Berlin are known respectively as the British Military Government, Berlin; the United States Mission Berlin; and the *Gouvernement Militaire Français de Berlin*. The civilian staffs consist of persons from the respective diplomatic and civil services, as well as locally-engaged personnel, most of whom are German nationals. The civilian staffs assist the Commandants in carrying out their civil or political functions in the government of Berlin. They each include Ministers (Deputy Commandants), Political Advisers, Deputy Political Advisers, Legal Advisers, Economic Advisers, Public Safety Advisers, Protocol Officers and *Senat* Liaison Officers. The *Senat* Liaison Officers act as the channel of Allied-*Senat* communication at the working level, and maintain offices at Schöneberg town hall, the seat of the House of Representatives and the *Senat*. The Consulates-General of the three Powers are also part of the respective Allied administrations in Berlin, and their staff have the same status as the other staff of those administrations.

[19] Such courts are distinct from courts-martial. Provision is made for Allied courts as follows: American Sector: High Commissioner Law No. 46 of 28 April 1955 (*AK Gazette*, p.1056), as amended by Sector Ordinances (*AK Gazette*, pp.1083, 1132, 1220); British Sector: Ordinances No. 68 of 2 July 1951 (*AK Gazette*, p.286), No. 206 of 28 June 1952 (*AK Gazette*, p.525) and No. 208 of 30 July 1955 (*AK Gazette*, p.1068); French Sector: *Ordonnance* No. 242 of 1 June 1950 (*AK Gazette*, p.421), and *Ordonnances* of 5 July 1955 (*AK Gazette*, p.1070) and 5 April 1956 (*AK Gazette*, p.1094). Such courts have only exercised criminal jurisdiction, and the French court still does so on a regular basis. Notable cases include the *French hijacking* case in 1969 (*La Semaine Juridique* 1970, No.16540; Ruzié, *AFDI* (1969), pp.784–92; von Mangoldt, *ZaöRV* (1970), pp.528–41); the *Weil* case (shooting of Soviet guard at the Tiergarten war-memorial, tried in a British Military Government Court); and *United States v Tiede* (diversion of a Polish aircraft to Tempelhof airport, tried in the US Court for Berlin: *International Legal Materials*, 19 (1980), pp.179–207; Forch, *ZaöRV*, 40 (1980), pp.760–81; Stern, *Judgment in Berlin* (1984)).
[20] When a Commandant exercises powers "he does so in law as Sector Commandant, not as a subordinate to his Commander-in-Chief. This applied also in the Soviet Sector. The Commandant of this Sector was not empowered to issue Orders independently because the Soviet Occupying Power exercised territorial sovereignty in the Eastern Sector but rather because the Allied Kommandatura had permitted the Sector Commandants to exercise such powers to a limited degree within their Sectors": Mampel, *Der Sowjetsektor von Berlin*, p.37. The position of all the occupation authorities in Germany was similar: see pp.55–6 above.

In exercising their military functions as officers commanding the occupying forces, the Commandants are assisted by military staffs. They have under their command substantial forces (over 12,000 men in all). To promote coordination the Commandants maintain a tripartite military staff, known as Allied Staff Berlin.

The additional costs of the occupation[21] are borne by the German authorities. In Article III of the Declaration on Berlin of 5 May 1955 the Allied Kommandatura declared that the Allied authorities would normally exercise powers only in certain fields, including:

> (d) Satisfaction of occupation costs. These costs will be fixed after consultation with the appropriate German authorities and at the lowest level consistent with maintaining the security of Berlin and of the Allied Forces located there.

The Allied Kommandatura fixes the occupation costs each year in an unpublished BK/O.[22] The costs are in fact satisfied from monies paid to the *Senat* by the Federal Government, and in recognition of this the three Powers have stated that they would "be prepared to consult with the Federal Government prior to the establishment of their Berlin occupation cost budgets".[23] In practice, consultations are held each year between the Embassies of the three Powers in Bonn and the Federal Ministry of Finance with a view to agreeing the level of the occupation cost budgets.

The Soviet Ambassador in East Berlin

Following the breakdown of the quadripartite machinery for the government of Germany, the Soviet Military Governor announced in October 1949 that the functions of administration which hitherto belonged to the Soviet Military Administration in Germany would be transferred to the Provisional Government of the German Democratic Republic, and that:

> In place of the Soviet Military Administration in Germany, a Soviet Control Commission will be established charged with exercising control over the fulfilment of the Potsdam and other joint decisions of the four Powers in Germany.

The representative of the Soviet Control Commission in Berlin

---

[21] By "additional costs" are meant those costs incurred by the Allied forces additional to those that they would have incurred had they not been in Berlin. This includes, for example, accommodation and certain items of equipment, but not basic salaries.

[22] The rules relating to contributions set forth in Articles 49, 51 and 52 of the Hague Regulations are not applicable to the occupation of Berlin: see pp.35–6 above. Nor is it useful to seek to apply these rules by analogy; the rules for fixing Berlin occupation costs, and in particular the level of such costs, are set forth in Allied instruments.

[23] Letter from the three High Commissioners to the Federal Chancellor concerning the exercise of the reserved Allied rights relating to Berlin: see p.329 below.

was to conduct the necessary relations with the corresponding representatives of the Western occupation authorities.[24] In 1953 the command of the Soviet Forces in Germany was separated from the other functions of occupation (as had happened in the Western zones in 1949) and the Control Commission was renamed High Commission. The offices of Ambassador and High Commissioner were held by the same person.[25] Upon the conclusion of the Treaty of 20 September 1955 between the Soviet Union and GDR the office of the High Commissioner was dissolved and, parallel to developments in the Western zones, the functions of the Soviet High Commissioner were transferred to the Soviet Ambassador in East Berlin.[26] Thus the Quadripartite Agreement of 3 September 1971 was negotiated and signed by the three Western Ambassadors in Bonn and the Soviet Ambassador in East Berlin, and the Quadripartite Declaration of 9 November 1972 was likewise negotiated by the four Ambassadors. Regular meetings take place between each of the Western Allied Ambassadors and the Soviet Ambassador, and communications are exchanged between them.

After the withdrawal of the Soviet authorities from the Allied Kommandatura, there continued to be a Soviet Commandant to whom the three Western Commandants still addressed themselves on matters of quadripartite responsibility.[27] Since the abolition of the post of Soviet Commandant on 23 August 1962,[28] contacts in Berlin about four-Power matters have taken place between the Allied authorities of the Western Sectors and officials of the Soviet Embassy in East Berlin.

The Soviet Ambassador in East Berlin has thus become the repository of Soviet rights and responsibilities relating to Berlin and to Germany as a whole. The Soviet Embassy is the only governmental authority in Germany with which the Western Allied authorities in Germany conduct four-Power business, and it is in practice the regular channel for this purpose.

[24] Statement by General Chuikov: *Selected Documents* I, p.124; *US Documents*, p.306. See also Chuikov's statement of 11 November 1949: *Selected Documents* I, p.127; Heidelmeyer *Dokumente*, p.141.

[25] See announcement of 28 May 1953: *Selected Documents* I, pp.11, 174; *US Documents*, p.400.

[26] Decision of USSR Council of Ministers of 20 September 1955: Heidelmeyer *Dokumente*, p.241. For these events, see Vysotsky, *West Berlin*, pp.250–1, where it is stated that the Soviet Ambassador "assumed responsibility for maintaining contacts on West Berlin and German affairs as a whole with the ambassadors of the three Western Powers in the FRG".

[27] Shortly after the Soviet-GDR Treaty of 1955 the Soviet "Kommandatura of Berlin" was replaced by a "Kommandatura of the Garrison of Soviet Troops in Berlin": Vysotsky, *West Berlin*, p.251.

[28] Mampel, *Der Sowjetsektor von Berlin*, pp.384–5; *Selected Documents* II, p.59; *US Documents*, p.823; Heidelmeyer, p.330. For the Western Allied statement, see *Selected Documents* II, p.60; *US Documents*, p.824; Heidelmeyer, p.332. See p.298 below.

Particular four-Power institutions

While most four-Power business concerning Berlin is conducted between the Western Allied authorities in Berlin and the Soviet Embassy, or by the four Ambassadors, there remain two institutions in which representatives of the four Powers continue to work together on a day-to-day basis: the Berlin Air Safety Center, located in the building formerly occupied by the Allied Control Council in the American Sector of Berlin; and Spandau Allied Prison in the British Sector.

The Berlin Air Safety Center (BASC) was established by the Allied Control Authority Co-ordinating Committee in December 1945,[29] and began to operate in February 1946 in accordance with quadripartite Flight Rules. Its functions are now set out in the "Flight Rules by Allied Control Authority Air Directorate for Aircraft Flying in Air Corridors in Germany and Berlin Control Zone" of 22 October 1946.[30] Paragraph 4 of the Rules begins:

> The Berlin Air Safety Center has been established in the Allied Control Authority Building with the object of ensuring safety of flight for all aircraft in the Berlin area. The Safety Center regulates all flying in the Berlin Control Zone and also in the corridors extending from Berlin to the boundaries of adjacent control zones.

Paragraph 4 then lists the detailed functions of the Center, and further specific functions are assigned to it in other paragraphs of the Flight Rules. The Center continues to this day to fulfil its task of "ensuring safety of flight for all aircraft in the Berlin area". Each of the four Powers is represented by a Chief Controller, with a Deputy Controller and several Duty Controllers, all of whom are air force officers. They work together at close quarters twenty-four hours a day. The Center is thus a unique and living institution, which was established and still operates to perform functions made necessary by the joint occupation of Berlin.

Spandau Allied Prison was established by the Allied Kommandatura for the confinement of persons sentenced to imprisonment by the International Military Tribunal, Nuremberg. The Tribunal was established by the London Agreement of 8 August 1945, and its Charter was annexed to the Agreement and formed an integral part of it.[31] Article 27 of the Charter empowered

---

[29] *US Documents*, p.74.

[30] DAIR/P(45)71 Second Revise: *US Documents*, p.72; Heidelmeyer, p.39. See Chapter 8 below.

[31] 82 *UNTS* 279. The Agreement and Charter are also reproduced in Volume 1 of the forty-two volume report of the trial: *Trial of the Major War Criminals before the International Military Tribunal* (1947–49).

the Tribunal to impose on defendants a sentence of death or such other punishment as was determined by it to be just. Article 29 of the Charter required sentences to be carried out in accordance with the orders of the Control Council for Germany. In accordance with this provision the Control Council directed the Allied Kommandatura Berlin to select and provide prison facilities with full quadripartite administration and supervision within the area of the Kommandatura's authority for effectuating prison sentences in accordance with the judgments of the Tribunal; and the Allied Kommandatura established an Allied Prison at Spandau in the British Sector. Supreme executive authority over Spandau Allied Prison was vested in the Allied Kommandatura itself; and under the supervision of a Higher Executive Authority consisting of the four Legal Advisers, an executive authority was established consisting of four governors acting by unanimous decision. The Western Legal Advisers continue to have a supervisory role in relation to the administration of the Prison. Day-to-day administration is in the hands of the four governors, each of whom is the delegate and representative of one of the four Powers. The quadripartite administration and supervision of Spandau Allied Prison continue notwithstanding the Soviet withdrawal from the Allied Kommandatura. The Soviet authorities continue to provide a governor and warders and to take their turn in the monthly rota for the military guard. Matters concerning the Prison are dealt with as appropriate by the four governors, by the authorities of the four Sectors, which since 1962 have been the Allied military governments in Berlin and the Soviet Embassy in East Berlin, and by the four Ambassadors, as successors to the Commanders-in-Chief/High Commissioners. Of the seven Nazi leaders imprisoned at Spandau in accordance with sentences imposed by the Tribunal, Doenitz, von Schirach and Speer were released after serving their sentences, and von Neurath, Raeder and Funk were released early on account of illness; only Hess remains, the Soviet Union having repeatedly refused high level appeals by the Western Allies for his release.[32]

---

[32] To release Hess without Soviet agreement "would constitute a violation of a binding international agreement", which "would put at risk other more fundamental agreements on which the security of West Berlin is based": *BYIL*, 55 (1984), p.524; see also *BYIL*, 51 (1980), p.440; *BYIL*, 53 (1982), p.441. The European Commission of Human Rights has declared inadmissible three applications concerning Hess's imprisonment: No. 6231/73, *Ilse Hess v. UK*, *Decisions and Reports* 2, p.72; 6953/75, *R. Hess v. UK*, unpublished, but cited in part (and somewhat inaccurately) in *Digest of Strasbourg Case-Law relating to the European Convention on Human Rights*, Vol.1, p.17; 8766/79, *R. Hess v. UK and France*, *Europäische Grundrechte-Zeitung*, (1982), p.15. The Federal Constitutional Court has also rejected constitutional complaints against Hess's continued imprisonment. For a collection of documents, see Seidl, *Der Fall Rudolf Hess 1941–1984* (1984). See also Bird, *Prisoner No. 7: Rudolf Hess* (1974).

Status of the occupation authorities and forces in Berlin

The occupation authorities and forces in Berlin are not subject to the jurisdiction of the local German authorities or to local German law, except insofar as they have expressly consented thereto. The immunities of the Allied forces and persons connected therewith are one of the reserved fields under the Declaration on Berlin of 5 May 1955.[33] Such exemption from local jurisdiction is a normal feature of any occupation, but in the special case of Berlin it is also of central importance to the status of the city, since it enables the Allies to continue to exercise to the full their quadripartite rights and responsibilities. Otherwise the exercise of their supreme authority could be limited, or even prevented altogether, by the very authorities, whether legislative, executive or judicial, over which the Allies have assumed that authority.

In the Western Sectors of Berlin, the status of the occupation authorities and forces is dealt with in various pieces of Allied legislation. Of these the most important is Allied Kommandatura Law No. 7 of 17 March 1950.[34] Under Articles 1 and 2, the German courts are prohibited from exercising criminal or civil jurisdiction over the Allied forces,[35] or in respect of acts arising out of or in the course of performance of duties or services with the Allied forces, except when expressly authorised, either generally or in specific cases, by the Allied Kommandatura or the appropriate Sector Commandant. The German courts also require such authorisation before they may exercise jurisdiction in cases of alleged criminal offences committed against the person or property of the Allied

---

[33] Article III of the Declaration (p.332 below) provides that the Allied authorities will normally exercise powers only in certain fields, which include –

    (a) Security, interests and immunities of the Allied Forces, including their representatives, dependents and non-German employees. German employees of the Allied Forces enjoy immunity from German jurisdiction only in matters arising out of or in the course of performance of duties or services with the Allied Forces.

[34] *AK Gazette*, p.11, as amended by Allied Kommandatura Law No. 17 of 27 August 1951 (*AK Gazette*, p.382) and interpreted by Allied Kommandatura Law No. 21 of 20 February 1952 (*AK Gazette*, p.458).

[35] Allied Kommandatura Law No. 2 of 9 February 1950 (*AK Gazette*, p.4) defines the expression "Allied Forces", for the purposes of Allied Kommandatura legislation (and thus Law No. 7), as including the Occupation Authorities; the Occupation Forces and their members; members of the families and non-German persons in the service of persons in the foregoing categories; and non-German persons whose presence in Berlin is certified to be necessary for the purposes of the occupation. Law No. 2 also defines the term "Occupation Authorities" as including the Allied Kommandatura and the Commandants of the Sectors of Berlin concerned and persons exercising power on behalf of such Commandants. It further defines the expression "Occupation Forces" as including the Armed Forces of the Occupying Powers and auxiliary contingents of other Powers serving with them.

forces and in cases of alleged offences against Allied laws.[36] In non-criminal cases, such authorisation is also required where the issues to be decided may affect the right of control of any Power in occupation. It is appropriate that the decision whether or not to grant authorisation should be taken by the Allied Kommandatura rather than by an individual Sector Commandant whenever such authorisation could affect generally the exercise of Allied rights and responsibilities or otherwise cut across Sector lines.

Article 3 of Allied Kommandatura Law No. 7 provides that no German court shall render a decision which impeaches the validity or legality of any legislation, regulation, directive, decision or order published by the occupation authorities. Provision is also made in Article 3 for the appropriate Sector Commandant to give a certificate, binding on the court, as to the existence, terms, validity and intent of any order of the occupation authorities in cases where this is in question.[37] Article 4 provides that all proceedings and every decision taken by a German court on any matter excluded from its jurisdiction shall be null and void. Under Article 7, the Commandants also have the power, in certain circumstances, to withdraw cases from the German courts and to suspend German court decisions; this is rarely done.[38] Article 8 provides that in cases outside the jurisdiction of the German courts under the Law, no German authority may, except when expressly authorised either generally or in specific cases by the appropriate Sector Commandant, impose any penalty or coercive measure of any description. And under Article 10 the Sector Commandants may take such measures as they deem necessary to provide for the determination of cases which under the Law are not within the jurisdiction of the German Courts.

The occupation authorities and forces are thus immune from the jurisdiction of the German courts in the Western Sectors of Berlin except in so far as, by prior Western Allied consent, those courts are authorised to exercise jurisdiction. They are similarly immune from the jurisdiction of other local Berlin authorities. Allied Kommandatura Law No. 7 covers not only the Western Allied occupation authorities and forces, but also those of the Soviet Union. Thus, the immunity from local German jurisdiction enjoyed

---

[36] General authorisations for German courts to exercise jurisdiction in certain matters have, for example, been granted by Allied Kommandatura Regulations Nos. 1, 2, 3 and 4 pursuant to Allied Kommandatura Law No. 7 (*AK Gazette*, pp.30, 1154, 1158, 1178), as well as by Regulations pursuant to Ordinance No. 508 of the British, French and US Sectors (*AK Gazette*, p.257) and by BK/O(80)13 of 30 December 1980 (p.284 below) and by BK/O(70)8 of 26 October 1970 (pp.75–6 below).

[37] See pp.89–90 below.

[38] This power was used, for example, in the *Tiede* case (p.60 above).

in the Western Sectors by the Western Allied occupation authorities and forces is also enjoyed by members of the Soviet Embassy in East Berlin and by members of the Soviet armed forces.

In practice, the Western Allied authorities frequently authorise the German courts to exercise civil jurisdiction in private disputes involving individual members of the Allied forces. However, the Allied authorities deal with criminal cases against members of their forces in their own courts-martial. With some exceptions involving civilians, the German courts are not authorised to exercise criminal jurisdiction over members of the Allied authorities and forces. Likewise, Berlin police initially involved in a suspected offence by a member of the Western Allied forces do not exercise jurisdiction (beyond, where necessary, immediate apprehension) but hand the matter over as soon as possible to the appropriate Allied authorities. Cases involving members of the Soviet Embassy or of the Soviet armed forces in the Western Sectors are treated similarly and, in accordance with long-standing four-Power arrangements, are dealt with by the appropriate Allied Sector authorities who return the person concerned to the Soviet authorities and transmit a report of the incident if necessary.

In addition to being immune from local German jurisdiction, the occupation authorities and forces are not subject to the German law in force in Berlin except where they have expressly subjected themselves thereto. The Allied Kommandatura has frequently made clear that local German legislation cannot affect Allied rights and responsibilities. As BK/O(74)11 of 30 September 1974[39] recalled, in relation to laws and treaties being extended to Berlin –

> Even in those cases where no reservations are laid down expressly by the Allied Kommandatura, such laws and treaties do not affect the rights and responsibilities of the Allies or Allied legislation.

The Allied authorities have, however, on occasion consented to conduct their activities in accordance with, or at least taking account of, provisions of German law, inasmuch as to do so would not prejudice their rights and responsibilities. In addition, when authorising the German courts to exercise civil jurisdiction in private disputes or transactions involving individual members of the Allied forces, which is often done, the Allied authorities implicitly accept that those courts will apply rules of German law. The Allied authorities have also occasionally legislated to provide expressly for the application of German law to the activities of their forces. For example, Allied legislation subjects members of the Allied forces to the provisions of German road traffic legislation, with certain

---

[39] *GVBl.* p.2576.

exceptions.[40] In other cases, Allied legislation makes provision for the relevance of German law, while not accepting its direct application to Allied activities or that those activities give rise to any Allied liability under German law. For example, the parallel Sector Ordinances No.508 of 21 May 1951[41] deal with compensation for loss or damage caused by the occupation authorities and forces, and provide in Article 3 that "the act or omission must be such as would have given the person who suffered the loss or damage a right according to the provisions of German law to recover compensation from the person who committed the act or omission or who was responsible for it". This provision reflects the fact that the occupation authorities and forces are not subject to German law; Ordinance No.508 mitigates this fact, in certain circumstances, by providing a statutory scheme for compensation by the local German authorities. In adjudicating on claims, one of the tests those authorities must apply is whether the act or omission would have given rise to liability under German law if German law had been applicable.

Members of the Western Allied occupation authorities and forces are likewise not subject to the jurisdiction of the local German authorities or to the local German law in force in the Soviet Sector; but there is no clear legislation to this effect comparable to Allied Kommandatura Law No.7. If in difficulties, they insist on the matter being handled by the Soviet authorities. In accordance with long-standing four-Power arrangements, the Soviet authorities hand the person concerned over to be dealt with by the appropriate Western Allied Sector authorities and transmit a report of the incident where necessary, just as happens when a Soviet soldier is in difficulties in the Western Sectors. In general, these arrangements operate satisfactorily and are respected by the local German authorities in the Soviet Sector.

GERMAN AUTHORITIES

In the Allied view, Berlin is not a *Land* of the Federal Republic of Germany and may not be governed by it. This does not, however, preclude the presence in Berlin of certain Federal officials, courts and agencies (Chapter 13 below). Their authority over Berlin, and indeed that of Federal officials, courts and institutions located elsewhere, is derived from the Berlin legislature or government; and they are subject to the same powers and jurisdiction of the

---

[40] Ordinance No. 535 of 1 March 1971 of the British, French and US Sectors (*AK Gazette*, p.1196) as amended by Ordinance No. 536 of 1 June 1976 (*AK Gazette*, p.1216).
[41] *AK Gazette*, p.257. See p.283 below.

occupation authorities as local Berlin authorities (Chapter 12 below).

The local German authorities in Berlin exercise authority under the Constitution of Berlin of 1 September 1950,[42] which was adopted by the City Assembly to replace the Temporary Constitution of Greater Berlin of 13 August 1946.[43] It sets out a number of basic individual rights and freedoms, and provides for the municipal authorities of Berlin: the House of Representatives (*Abgeordnetenhaus*) as legislature, and the *Senat* as executive. It further provides for the administration of justice and the regulation of public finance. According to Article 4 it applies to the whole of Berlin, though in practice effect can only be given to its provisions in the twelve districts (*Bezirke*) in the Western Sectors.

The House of Representatives

The legislature established by the 1950 Constitution is the House of Representatives. Article 25 provides that it shall consist of at least 200 members, but because of the absence of elected members from the Soviet Sector, it actually has about 145 members. The precise number varies with each election because of a complex voting system involving both proportional representation and the direct election of constituency members. Under Article 26 representatives are elected in general, equal, secret and direct elections. All Germans who have attained the age of eighteen and have been domiciled in Berlin for at least three months are entitled to vote. Every person entitled to vote who has attained the age of twenty-one is eligible to stand for election. Under Article 39 the House of Representatives is elected for four years, though it may dissolve itself prematurely by a majority of two-thirds of its members and thus precipitate an election. Article 39(3) provides for premature dissolution by referendum.

The House of Representatives elects several committees of its members, in which the political parties must be represented according to the principles of proportional representation. Under Article 34 the House and its committees may insist on the presence of the members of the *Senat*, and the *Senat* is to be invited to the meetings of the House and its committees.

[42] *Verfassung von Berlin (VOBl.* I, p.433), last amended by a Law of 20 June 1977 *(GVBl.* p.1126). For an English translation see *US Documents*, p.324. For a commentary, see Pfennig/Neumann, *Verfassung von Berlin.* See also Plischke, *Berlin: Development of its Government and Administration*, pp.67–110; Plischke, *Government and Politics of Contemporary Berlin*, pp.21–48; Sendler, *JR* (1985), pp.441–52.
[43] *Vorläufige Verfassung von Gross-Berlin* promulgated by BK/O(46)326 of 13 August 1946 *(VOBl.* p.294). For an English translation see Plischke, *Berlin: Development of its Government and Administration*, p.214. For a commentary see Haas, *Verfassung von Gross-Berlin*, 4th ed. (1947).

Article 3 provides that legislative power rests exclusively with the parliament, that is to say, the House of Representatives. Articles 45 and 46 make provision for the general procedure for enacting Laws (*Gesetze*), and Articles 73 to 83 deal with budget and other financial legislation. Other Articles confer particular powers and functions on the House, as well as providing that the details of certain constitutional provisions shall be regulated by Law (*Gesetz*), that is to say, by legislation enacted by the House of Representatives.

The Senat

The executive body established by the Constitution is the *Senat*, which according to Article 40 consists of the Governing Mayor (*Regierende Bürgermeister*), the Mayor (*Bürgermeister*), who is his deputy, and up to sixteen Senators. Article 41 provides that the Governing Mayor shall be elected by the House of Representatives by a majority of the votes cast, and that the Mayor and Senators shall be elected by the House upon the proposal of the Governing Mayor. Under Article 42 the House of Representatives may remove the *Senat* or any of its members from office by a vote of no confidence carried by a majority of the members of the House.

Under Article 43 the Governing Mayor presides over the *Senat*, formulates in agreement with the *Senat* the guidelines of government policy and controls their observance. Article 44 places the main administration of the city, including the administration of justice and the police, directly within the competence of the *Senat*. Article 47 empowers the *Senat* to issue legally-binding ordinances (*Rechtsverordnungen*) required for the execution of a Law (*Gesetz*) unless the Law otherwise provides, but subject to amendment or revocation by the House of Representatives. It also empowers the *Senat* to issue administrative provisions (*Verwaltungsvorschriften*) required for the execution of a Law, which must be submitted to the House for information on request.

District authorities

Section VI of the Constitution regulates the central administration of Berlin and the administration of the districts (*Bezirke*), as well as the relationship between the two. The *Senat* is required to exercise supervision over the district administrations. Provision is made for each district to have an Assembly of elected district representatives (*Bezirksverordnetenversammlung*) consisting of 45 members, the term of which coincides with that of the House of Representatives. Each District Assembly elects the members of the District Office (*Bezirksamt*), which is composed of the District Mayor

(*Bezirksbürgermeister*) and the District Counsellors (*Bezirksstadträte*). The District Office is the administrative authority of the district.

Courts

Article 63 of the Constitution provides that judicial power shall be exercised in the name of the people by independent courts subject only to the law. The Constitution does not expressly provide for their structure and jurisdiction. As in *Länder* of the Federal Republic of Germany, ordinary civil and criminal jurisdiction is exercised at three ascending levels: *Amtsgericht, Landgericht* and *Kammergericht.* Similarly, there are courts with specialist jurisdiction: administrative courts (*Verwaltungsgerichte*), labour courts (*Arbeitsgerichte*), social courts (*Sozialgerichte*) and a fiscal court (*Finanzgericht*).[44]

Article 72 of the Constitution provides for the establishment of a Berlin Constitutional Court.[45] But no such court has been established, and Article 72 was suspended in 1974 by a new Article 87a. Although the establishment of a Berlin Constitutional Court had often been discussed, no agreement could be reached between *Senat* and Allies as to its jurisdiction to review the constitutionality of legislation. The *Senat* wished such jurisdiction to be limited to the review of the constitutionality of Berlin legislation other than Federal legislation taken over in Berlin (Chapter 11 below). As it viewed such adopted legislation as retaining the quality of Federal law, the *Senat* considered that review of such legislation should be a matter for the Federal Constitutional Court. But the Allies had, by BK/O(50)75 of 29 August 1950,[46] determined that the provisions of any Federal Law should apply to Berlin only after they had been passed by the Berlin legislature as a Berlin Law. The Allies had also, by BK/O(52)35 of 20 December 1952,[47] declined to permit the Federal Constitutional Court to exercise jurisdiction in relation to Berlin, and had subsequently reaffirmed on several occasions that this precluded review by that Court of Berlin Laws adopting the provisions of Federal Laws (pp.173–7 below).

THE ROLE OF THE FEDERAL GOVERNMENT

While Berlin may not be governed by the Federation, the ties

---

[44] For accounts in English of the German legal system, see Cohn, *Manual of German Law*, Vols. I and II (2nd ed. 1968), Vol. II (1st ed. 1952); Horn and Kötz, *German Private and Commercial Law – An Introduction* (1981).

[45] Finkelnburg, *JR*, 6, (1965), p.361; Wassermann, *JR*, 9, (1963), p.338; Stern, *DVBl*, 78 (1963), pp.696–704; Pestalozza, in: *Landesverfassungsgerichtsbarkeit* (1983), pp.183–230; Dehnhard, *DVBl*, 101 (1986), pp.176–81.

[46] *VOBl.* p.440; *Selected Documents* I, p.135; *US Documents*, p.340; Heidelmeyer, p.121. See p.146 below.

[47] Heidelmeyer *Dokumente*, p.127. See p.173 below.

between Berlin and the Federal Republic are very close and the Federal Government has important functions in relation to Berlin. Arrangements exist for the Federal Republic to represent the interests of Berlin abroad, subject always to Allied rights and responsibilities in this regard (Part V below). And the Federal Republic plays a vital role in assisting and promoting Berlin in the economic and other fields. In connection with the Convention on Relations between the Three Powers and the Federal Republic of Germany of 1952/1954, the Western Allies undertook to exercise their rights and responsibilities relating to Berlin in such a way as to facilitate the carrying out of these tasks by the Federal Republic.[48]

Article 6 of the Relations Convention provides as follows:

1. The Three Powers will consult with the Federal Republic in regard to the exercise of their rights relating to Berlin.
2. The Federal Republic, on its part, will co-operate with the Three Powers in order to facilitate the discharge of their responsibilities with regard to Berlin.

There are, in fact, regular consultations between the Western Allies and the Federal Republic, in particular in the Bonn Group (*Vierergruppe*), in which representatives of the three Western Allied Embassies in Bonn and the Federal Foreign Office take part.[49] And consultations on Berlin civil aviation matters take place within the Berlin Civil Air Transport Advisory Group (BCATAG).

The Government of the Federal Republic of Germany is represented in Berlin to the three Allied Commandants and to the *Senat* by a permanent liaison agency,[50] headed by an official called the Plenipotentiary of the Federal Government in Berlin (*Bevollmächtigter der Bundesregierung in Berlin*). The *Senat* is represented in Bonn by a Plenipotentiary of *Land* Berlin to the Federation (*Bevollmächtigter des Landes Berlin beim Bund*), who is also in practice the Senator for Federal Affairs (*Senator für Bundes-angelegenheiten*).

---

[48] See the Declaration of the Federal Republic on Aid to Berlin of 26 May 1952 and the letter from the Three High Commissioners to the Federal Chancellor concerning the exercise of the reserved Allied rights relating to Berlin of 26 May 1952 in the version of letter X of 23 October 1954 (p.329 below).

[49] See Mahncke, *Berlin im geteilten Deutschland*, pp.130–1. A representative of the *Senat* is also present. The Bonn Group likewise deals with matters relating to Germany as a whole. Consultations also take place at other levels, for example at regular meetings between the three Western Ambassadors in Bonn and the State Secretary in the Federal Ministry of Foreign Affairs, and between the Foreign Ministers of the three Powers and of the Federal Republic of Germany (for example, on the occasion of the twice-yearly NATO Ministerial meetings).

[50] See p.183 below.

MILITARY MISSIONS

Among the various types of mission representing the interests of a State abroad, the Military Missions in Berlin are unique.[51] At present, such Missions with premises in Berlin are maintained by Australia, Belgium, Canada, Czechoslovakia, Denmark, Greece, the Netherlands, Norway, Poland and Yugoslavia; in addition, Luxembourg and South Africa have Military Missions, but their accredited staff are all resident in Bonn and operate from the respective Embassies there. The existence of Military Missions in Berlin derives from Article 8 of the Agreement of 14 November 1944 on Control Machinery in Germany, which reads:

> The necessary liaison with the Governments of other United Nations chiefly interested will be ensured by the appointment by such Governments of military missions (which may include civilian members) to the Control Council, having access, through the appropriate channels, to the organs of control.

The actual conditions for the establishment of the Military Missions were determined by quadripartite decision recorded in document CORC/P(45)86, approved by the Control Council on 3 October 1945.[52] It was provided that each Government whose application to accredit a Military Mission was accepted should be free to decide the composition of its Mission, but that the number of all ranks belonging to each Mission should be limited to ten. Accordingly each Military Mission has a maximum of ten accredited members (in fact, many have less than ten); in addition they have employees who are not accredited members of the Mission.

Members of Military Missions are accredited to the Allied Control Council. They are issued with an Allied Control Authority identity card, and require no further permission to reside in Berlin. The heads of the Military Missions present their credentials to the Allied authorities (in practice, the Chairman Commandant attended by the three Allied Ministers) at a formal ceremony in the Allied Control Council building. However, since 1958 and 1965 respectively, the heads of the Czechoslovak and Polish Military Missions have not done so, and are therefore called "acting head of mission". In practice the process of accreditation and the ceremony of presentation of credentials is undertaken by the Western Allies without the active participation of the Soviet authorities, although the latter are kept fully informed.

---

[51] The Military Missions are listed in the *Official List of Military Missions and Consular Offices in Berlin*, published annually by the Allied Liaison and Protocol Offices. For a more detailed treatment see Schröder, *Die ausländischen Vertretungen in Berlin*, especially pp.33–6, 70–6, 99–102.

[52] Text in Schröder, *Die ausländischen Vertretungen in Berlin*, pp.125–8.

The status of members of the Military Missions is comparable to that of members of the Allied Forces under Allied Kommandatura Law No.7 of 17 March 1950 (pp.65–7 above). Under Articles 1 and 2, the German courts may not exercise criminal or civil jurisdiction over "persons accredited to the Allied Control Council" and "the members of their families", except when expressly authorised, either generally or in specific cases, by the Allied Kommandatura or the appropriate Sector Commandant. Nor are members of Military Missions subject to the jurisdiction of other local Berlin authorities, such as the police. Traffic accidents and similar incidents are in practice dealt with by the Allied authorities of the Sector concerned. Similarly, protocol questions and administrative matters, such as vehicle licensing, are handled for each Mission by the Allied authorities of the Sector in which its office is located.[53]

The origin of the Military Missions in Berlin lies in the four-Power occupation of Germany and the readiness of the Occupying Powers to accept liaison missions from their principal wartime allies. Their presence in Berlin is explained by the location there of the Control Council, the supreme organ of control for Germany. They are an element of the control machinery established for the occupation of Germany. Just as the existence and the status of the Military Missions are unique, so are the rules governing them, which are based upon agreements and decisions of the four Powers and Allied legislation in force in Berlin. While the Missions now generally perform functions similar to those of consular posts, their status and legal basis are different, as are the privileges and immunities associated with them.

As was agreed quadripartitely in document CORC/P(45)86 and as their Allied Control Authority identity cards indicate, members of the Military Missions have the right of free movement throughout all four Sectors of Berlin. The status of members of the Military Missions whilst in the Soviet Sector is in practice respected by the GDR authorities. They are not bound by the GDR minimum currency exchange requirement upon entry into the Soviet Sector. An attempt by the GDR to put an end to this in 1980 was dropped after the Western Allies protested to the Soviet Union.

CONSULAR POSTS[54]

Each of the three Powers maintains a Consulate-General in the Western Sectors of Berlin. Consular posts headed by career consular

---

[53] Following Yugoslavia's break with the Soviet Union, the Yugoslav Military Mission moved from the Soviet Sector to the British Sector.
[54] For a more detailed treatment, see Schröder, *Die ausländischen Vertretungen in Berlin*, especially pp.77–83, 102–4.

officers are also maintained by Brazil, Bulgaria, Chile, Hungary, India, Indonesia, Iran, Italy, Japan, the Republic of Korea, Romania, Spain, Sweden, Switzerland, Thailand and Turkey; and the Soviet Union has established a Consulate-General pursuant to the Quadripartite Agreement of 3 September 1971. The Austrian Delegation in the Western Sectors is also treated as such a post, the Head of Delegation having the rank of Consul-General. A further twenty-eight States are represented by honorary consuls.[55]

The British, French and United States Consulates-General are part of the respective Allied administrations (p.60 above). The legal position of consular posts of countries other than the three Powers is regulated by the Vienna Convention on Consular Relations of 1963, the application of which in Berlin is however subject to Allied legislation. The Federal Law of 26 August 1969 ratifying the Vienna Convention[56] was taken over in Berlin by a Berlin Law of 21 December 1970.[57] In anticipation of this, the Allied Kommandatura issued BK/O(70)8 of 26 October 1970.[58] The provisions of this BK/O make clear the reserved Allied rights and powers as regards consular representation in Berlin. Paragraph 1 provides that the application in Berlin of both the Federal Law and the Vienna Convention is subject to the rights and responsibilities of the Allies with respect to consular matters. Paragraph 2 provides:

> In particular, the right of the Sector Commandants in their respective Sectors to decide on the establishment of consular posts, on the appointment and admission of the heads of consular posts including their admission on a provisional basis and of members of consular posts, and to determine the formalities for such admission and the extent of consular privileges and immunities shall remain unaffected.

Paragraph 3 provides that the establishment of consular relations, referred to in Article 2 of the Convention, which involves the consular representation of any State in respect of Berlin shall require the consent of the Sector Commandants; and that such consent is not implied by the establishment of diplomatic relations between the Federal Republic of Germany and any other State. By virtue of paragraph 4 the BK/O applies to any consular post, defined by Article 1 of the Convention to mean any consulate-general, consulate, vice-consulate or consular agency; it applies also to any Delegation which performs consular functions (now only the Austrian Delegation), except as otherwise directed by the Sector

---

[55] The consular posts are listed in the *Official List of Military Missions and Consular Offices in Berlin*, published annually by the Allied Liaison and Protocol Offices.
[56] *BGBl.* II, p.1585.
[57] *GVBl.* p.2075.
[58] *GVBl.* p.2094.

Commandants, each for his Sector. Paragraph 5 applies the BK/O to the régime relating to honorary consular officers and consular posts headed by such officers. Pursuant to Allied Kommandatura Law No.7, paragraph 6 authorises the competent German courts to exercise jurisdiction in accordance with the provisions of the Federal Law in relation to persons and property to whom or to which that Law applies; the authorisation does not however apply to members of the Allied forces (as defined in Allied Kommandatura Law No.2) and property of such persons or forces, or to any offence alleged to have been committed against enactments of the occupation authorities.

The important governmental rights of the Sector Commandants, exercised each in their respective Sectors, to decide on the establishment of consular relations and consular posts, the appointment and admission of their members and the formalities for such admission, and the extent of consular privileges and immunities, are expressly reserved by BK/O(70)8. Members of consular posts are issued with identity cards signed by the three Western Commandants, and require no further permission to reside in Berlin. In all fundamental respects the Commandants in their respective Sectors have the rights and powers of the "receiving State" under the Vienna Convention; although as paragraph 2 of the BK/O makes clear, the rights reserved to the Commandants derive not from the Convention but from the·supreme authority exercised by them.

The Soviet Consulate-General was established in the Western Sectors of Berlin following the Quadripartite Agreement of 3 September 1971.[59] Part IID of the Agreement provides that "consular activities of the Union of Soviet Socialist Republics in the Western Sectors of Berlin can be exercised as set forth in Annex IV". In paragraph 3 of their communication to the Soviet Government at Annex IVA, the three Powers authorised –

> the establishment of a Consulate-General of the USSR in the Western Sectors of Berlin accredited to the appropriate authorities of the three Governments in accordance with the usual procedures applied in those Sectors, for the purpose of performing consular services, subject to provisions set forth in a separate document of this date.

The Soviet Government took note of this in paragraph 3 of their communication to the three Western Governments at Annex IVB. The "separate document" referred to is Agreed Minute II of 3 September 1971, which begins as follows:

> Provision is hereby made for the establishment of a Consulate-

---

[59] See Schiedermair, pp.125–32. Soviet commercial organisations are considered at pp.292–3 below.

General of the USSR in the Western Sectors of Berlin. It is understood that the details concerning this Consulate-General will include the following. The Consulate-General will be accredited to the appropriate authorities of the three Governments in accordance with the usual procedures applying in those Sectors. Applicable Allied and German legislation and regulations will apply to the Consulate-General. The activities of the Consulate-General will be of a consular character and will not include political functions or any matters related to quadripartite rights or responsibilities.

Agreed Minute II also provides that the assignment of personnel to the Consulate-General will be subject to agreement with the appropriate authorities of the three Governments; that the number of such personnel will not exceed twenty Soviet nationals; and that such personnel and their dependents may reside in the Western Sectors of Berlin upon individual authorisation.

The Soviet Consulate-General is in no sense part of the Soviet occupation authorities in Berlin. Its establishment was authorised by the three Powers "for the purpose of performing consular services". Its activities are expressly limited to those of a consular character and exclude "political functions or any matters related to quadripartite rights or responsibilities".[60] So far as concerns the Russians in Berlin, quadripartite rights and responsibilities remain exclusively a matter for the Soviet Embassy in East Berlin. Agreed Minute II also makes it clear that the usual accreditation procedures[61] and applicable legislation and regulations in the Western Sectors apply to the Soviet Consulate-General, which is thus in the same position as the consular posts established by other countries in the Western Sectors (except those of the three Powers).

OTHER REPRESENTATIVES OF STATES

The Vienna Convention on Diplomatic Relations of 1961 applies in the Western Sectors of Berlin, subject to Allied legislation. In connection with the adoption in Berlin of the Federal Law ratifying the Vienna Convention,[62] the Allied Kommandatura issued BK/O(64)3 of 11 September 1964.[63] This provided that the

---

[60] See the remarks by Ambassador Rush: *US Documents*, p.1164. Attempts by the Soviet Consulate-General to exceed these limitations are resisted by the Western Allies and *Senat*.

[61] In practice, the Soviet Embassy in East Berlin approaches the Western Allied authorities regarding accreditation, while in the case of other sending States the initial approach is made by the respective Embassies in Bonn to the Western Allied Embassies in Bonn. For a comparison of the procedures, see Schröder, *Die ausländischen Vertretungen in Berlin*, pp.79–81. See also *Das Vierseitige Abkommen*, p.266.

[62] *BGBl.* II, p.957; *GVBl.* p.1151.

[63] *GVBl.* p.1162.

promulgation in Berlin of the Law taking over the Federal Law —

(i) . . . shall in no way affect the legal provisions in force in Berlin with regard to the definition of privileges and immunities or the designation or status of the persons entitled thereto.

(ii) In particular it shall in no way affect the competence of the Allied Commandants to determine at any time, if and so far as may appear to them to be necessary, the extent of entitlement to privileges and immunities in Berlin.

Thus, as with the application in Berlin of the Vienna Convention on Consular Relations, the Allied Kommandatura expressly reserved the rights of the Commandants in the field of privileges and immunities.

The extension of the Vienna Convention on Diplomatic Relations to Berlin was designed to enable its provisions concerning privileges and immunities to be given effect with respect to the staff of diplomatic missions accredited to the Federal Republic while in the Western Sectors of Berlin. Accordingly, subject to Allied control and the reservations in BK/O(64)3, the members of diplomatic missions accredited to the Federal Republic enjoy the same privileges and immunities in the Western Sectors of Berlin as in the Federal Republic. In the case of members of the Western Allied Embassies in Bonn, and of those members of Embassies in Bonn who are also accredited to the Allied Control Council as members of Military Missions, Allied legislation, in particular Allied Kommandatura Law No.7, would also be relevant.

The position in the Western Sectors of members of the Permanent Representation (*Ständige Vertretung*) of the GDR in Bonn is governed by special provisions. The Vienna Convention on Diplomatic Relations does not apply directly since the Permanent Representation is not a diplomatic mission. By a Protocol of 14 March 1974,[64] however, the Vienna Convention was applied *mutatis mutandis* to the Permanent Representations in East Berlin and Bonn. In implementation thereof, the Federal Law to provide Privileges and Immunities to the Permanent Representation of the German Democratic Republic of 16 November 1973[65] authorised the Federal Government, subject to the principle of reciprocity, to grant by Ordinance to the GDR Permanent Representation, and to its members, their families and servants, privileges and immunities comparable to those granted to diplomatic missions under the Vienna Convention. This Law has been taken over in Berlin[66]

---

[64] *BGBl.* II, p.933; *US Documents*, p.1265.
[65] *Gesetz über die Gewährung von Erleichterungen, Vorrechten und Befreiungen an die Ständige Vertretung der Deutschen Demokratischen Republik: BGBl.* I, p.1673. See Mahnke, *ROW*, 19 (1976), pp.49–53.
[66] *GVBl.* p.2086.

subject to BK/O(73)7 of 28 September 1973.[67] Paragraphs 1 and 2 of the BK/O read:

1. The taking over in Berlin of the Federal Law cited above shall in no way affect the legal provisions in force in Berlin with regard to the definition of privileges and immunities or the designation or status of persons entitled thereto.

2. In particular, it shall in no way affect the competence of the Allied authorities to determine at any time, if and in so far as may appear to them to be necessary, the extent of entitlement to privileges and immunities in Berlin, as well as the persons entitled thereto, and to take any measures which the Allied Kommandatura might deem necessary with regard to these privileges and immunities.

Paragraph 3 requires the express approval of the Allied Kommandatura before any Ordinance issued under the Law may enter into force in Berlin. In pursuance of the Law, the Federal Government duly issued an Ordinance on 30 April 1974.[68] By BK/O(74)6 of 19 June 1974[69] the Allied Kommandatura ordered that:

1. The *Senat* is authorised to apply the provisions laid down in the Ordinance cited above to the extent necessary to avoid any impediment to the due performance by the Permanent Representation of the German Democratic Republic of its functions.

2. The provisions of the present Order do not deprive the provisions of BK/O(73)7 of effect.

Accordingly, subject to the reservations in BK/O(73)7 and BK/O(74)6, and thus subject to Allied control, members of the GDR Permanent Representation would enjoy in the Western Sectors the same privileges and immunities as in the territory of the Federal Republic; these are comparable to the privileges and immunities enjoyed by members of diplomatic missions under the Vienna Convention.

The position of members of diplomatic missions in East Berlin whilst in the Western Sectors of Berlin is quite different. As noted above, members of the Soviet Embassy are treated as members of the occupation authorities and their position is comparable to that of members of the Western Allied forces in the Western Sectors of Berlin. The same applies to officials of the three Powers when visiting the Western Sectors, at least in connection with official business. Members of other Embassies enjoy in the Western Sectors

---

[67] *GVBl.* p.2108.
[68] *Verordnung über die Gewährung von Erleichterungen, Vorrechten und Befreiungen an die Ständige Vertretung der Deutschen Demokratischen Republik: BGBl.* I, p.1022; *GVBl.* p.1551.
[69] *GVBl.* p.1560.

only the limited immunity concerning transit accorded by Article 40 of the Vienna Convention on Diplomatic Relations, subject to Allied reserved rights. Members of consular posts in East Berlin and the GDR likewise enjoy only a limited immunity concerning transit, accorded by Article 54 of the Vienna Convention on Consular Relations. Members of the Permanent Representation (*Ständige Vertretung*) of the Federal Republic in East Berlin have no privileges and immunities in the Western Sectors.

A further category of government representatives with immunity in Berlin are state visitors officially invited to the city. Article 4 of the Second Law to amend the Federal Central Register Law of 17 July 1984[70] confers immunity from German jurisdiction upon representatives of other States who visit the Federal Republic of Germany or Berlin at the official invitation of the Federal Republic. This provision has been taken over in Berlin,[71] but is qualified in two ways by BK/O(84)7 of 26 July 1984.[72] First, paragraph 2 of the BK/O provides:

> Article 4 of the Law cannot affect Allied rights and responsibilities nor Allied legislation, in particular Article III (C) of the Berlin Declaration of 5 May 1955 and BK/O(64)3 of 11 September 1964.

Thus the Allied Kommandatura specifically recalled the rights reserved in the Declaration on Berlin concerning "relations of Berlin with authorities abroad", and the reservation in BK/O(64)3 of "the competence of the Allied Commandants to determine at any time, if and so far as may appear to them to be necessary, the extent of entitlement to privileges and immunities in Berlin". Second, paragraph 3 of BK/O(84)7 provides:

> In the application of Article 4 of the Law in Berlin, the reference to an official invitation of the Federal Republic of Germany shall be construed to include an official invitation issued on behalf of the *Senat* of Berlin by the Federal Republic of Germany in exercise of its function of representing the interests of Berlin outside Berlin.

This reflects the role of the Federal Republic of Germany in issuing invitations for foreign representatives to visit Berlin.

INTERNATIONAL ORGANISATIONS

The status, privileges and immunities of international organisations (and representatives and staff members) in the Western Sectors of Berlin are likewise governed by Allied legislation

---

[70] *Zweites Gesetz zur Änderung des Bundeszentralregistergesetzes*: BGBl. I, p.990.
[71] *GVBl.* p.1093.
[72] *GVBl.* p.1122.

and reserved rights. Subject thereto, their position is regulated by the provisions of the relevant treaties entered into by the Federal Republic of Germany and extended to Berlin, and by the provisions of Federal legislation taken over in Berlin.[73] In BK/O(75)10 of 7 August 1975,[74] the Allied Kommandatura laid down general reservations covering these provisions:

> The Allied Kommandatura has noted that an increasing number of international agreements or ordinances provide for privileges and immunities in favour of international organisations the activities of which may possibly be extended to Berlin. The Allied Kommandatura wishes to take this opportunity to recall that although it may approve in accordance with established procedure the adoption in Berlin of such international agreements or of such ordinances, they cannot affect Allied rights and responsibilities nor Allied legislation, in particular, Article III (C) of the Berlin Declaration of 5 May 1955 and BK/O(64)3 of 11 September 1964.

Thus, as was the case with BK/O(84)7 referred to above, Allied rights in the field of external relations, and privileges and immunities, are specifically reserved.

In addition to these general reservations, the Allied Kommandatura has legislated specifically with respect to the establishment of offices of international organisations in Berlin. In BK/O(75)3 of 9 April 1975,[75] the Allied Kommandatura raised no objection to the establishment of the European Centre for the Development of Vocational Training, subject to the reservation that –

> Allied rights and responsibilities, including those respecting privileges and immunities, shall remain unaffected.

Similarly, in BK/O(76)6 of 24 June 1976[76] the Allied Kommandatura authorised in principle the establishment of a Berlin Sub-Office of the European Patent Office, subject to "Allied reserved rights and responsibilities, notably in the field of security and status including privileges and immunities". The authorisation and reservations in BK/O(76)6 were confirmed by the Allied Kommandatura in BK/O(78)5 of 31 May 1978[77] approving the

---

[73] For the most important examples, see Schröder, *Die ausländischen Vertretungen in Berlin*, pp.52–3.

[74] *GVBl.* p.2060.

[75] *GVBl.* p.1132. The Centre was established in accordance with Regulation (EEC) No. 337/75 of the Council of the European Communities of 10 February 1975 (*Official Journal of the European Communities*, 13 February 1975, No. L 39/1).

[76] *GVBl.* p.1462. This BK/O was issued in connection with the extension to Berlin of three treaties concerning patents, including the European Patent Convention of 5 October 1973. The Centralisation Protocol attached to the latter Convention envisaged the establishment of the Berlin Sub-Office.

[77] *GVBl.* p.1168.

extension to Berlin of the Agreement of 19 October 1977 between the Government of the Federal Republic of Germany and the European Patent Organisation on the setting up of the Berlin Sub-Office of the European Patent Office.[78]

For the most part, however, the activities of international organisations in the Western Sectors of Berlin are limited and occasional. The Allied Kommandatura has also legislated specifically in relation to such activities. For example, under BK/O(73)2 of 25 May 1973[79] the Federal Ordinance on privileges and immunities of the European Organisation for the Safety of Air Navigation (EUROCONTROL) applies in Berlin only to the extent necessary to confer taxation privileges and immunities on EUROCONTROL in connection with activities of a commercial nature, such as the purchase of goods and materials, carried out in Berlin on behalf of the Organisation. In addition, the general Allied reservations in BK/O(75)10 apply,[80] which are of particular relevance to meetings of international organisations in the Western Sectors, and official visits by representatives and staff members.

---

[78] *BGBl.* II, p.337. For details of the position of the Sub-Office and its staff, see Schröder, *Die ausländischen Vertretungen in Berlin*, pp.104–5.

[79] *GVBl.* p.904. Similar limitations were imposed by BK/O(66)6 of 8 August 1966 (*GVBl.* p.1632) in relation to the European Launcher Development Organisation, and by BK/O(65)9 of 19 August 1965 (*GVBl.* p.1672) in relation to the European Space Research Organisation.

[80] This was expressly provided for in BK/O(75)12 of 9 September 1975 (*GVBl.* p.2392) in connection with the application in Berlin of the Headquarters Agreement between the Government of the Federal Republic of Germany and the European Molecular Biology Laboratory.

CHAPTER 5

THE LAW APPLICABLE IN BERLIN

HE law applicable in Berlin[1] derives from a variety of sources.
First, there is law made since the end of the Second World
War by the occupation authorities in exercise of the supreme
authority assumed with respect to Germany, including Berlin. This
may for convenience be referred to as "Allied law". Second, and
subject to this Allied law, there is law made by German (as distinct
from Allied) legislative authorities, which in part predates the
occupation. This may be referred to as "German law". These terms
are, however, to some extent misleading since all the legislative
authorities exercise their powers in the government of Germany, or
of Berlin as part of Germany. All law in force in Berlin, whether
deriving from Allied or German legislative authorities, forms part of
the law of Germany.

ALLIED LAW

Allied law in Berlin consists of a wide range of instruments, which
have over the years been given various titles, such as Laws,
Proclamations, Orders, Directives, Ordinances and Regulations.[2]
Allied decisions and directives have also been conveyed to the local
Berlin authorities in Letters. These instruments have emanated
from various Allied authorities in Germany. Although much Allied
law, particularly that issued in the early post-war years, has been
suspended or repealed[3] or has become spent, many examples of the
various types of instrument still remain in force in Berlin.

Military Government (SHAEF)[4] legislation

German territory was first occupied by Allied forces on 18
September 1944, and immediately several legislative instruments
were promulgated by the Supreme Commander of the Allied

---

[1] For the position in the Soviet Sector, see pp.304–5 below.
[2] von Schmoller/Maier/Tobler, *Handbuch des Besatzungsrechts* (1957); Heidelmeyer, *ZaöRV*,
28 (1968), pp.704–30; Schröder, *ROW*, 29 (1985), pp.181–90 .
[3] Many Allied laws were repealed in the 1950s, particularly after the Declaration on
Berlin of 5 May 1955. The practice with Control Council Laws is to suspend their effect
in Berlin rather than to repeal them outright. Further measures have been taken: see for
example BK/O(84)10 of 23 November 1984 (*GVBl.* p.1646), BK/O(85)6 of 23 August
1986 (*GVBl.* p.1932); BK/O(86)8 of 8 October 1986 (*GVBl.* p.1656).
[4] Supreme Headquarters Allied Expeditionary Force.

Expeditionary Force, General Eisenhower. In Article II of Proclamation No. 1,[5] he announced that:

> Supreme legislative, judicial and executive authority and powers within the occupied territory are vested in me as Supreme Commander of the Allied Forces and as Military Governor, and the Military Government is established to exercise these powers under my direction.

Legislation issued by the Supreme Commander during the period of belligerent occupation, that is to say, between 18 September 1944 and the assumption of supreme authority by the four Allied Powers on 5 June 1945, took various forms and dealt with a wide range of matters.[6] The subject-matter of some Military Government legislation (or SHAEF legislation, as it was sometimes called) was also covered by similar legislation enacted later by the Control Council.[7] Other pieces of Military Government legislation were applied, without the enactment of further legislation, in the Western Sectors of Berlin after Western Allied forces occupied those Sectors. An important example of such legislation which is still applied in Berlin is Military Government (SHAEF) Law No. 52 concerning the blocking and control of property.[8]

Control Council legislation

Following the assumption of supreme authority, the highest legislative authority for Germany, including Berlin, was the Allied Control Council. This functioned as the highest organ of control of Germany from its first meeting on 30 July 1945 until the withdrawal of the Soviet member on 20 March 1948. During this period the Control Council issued many legislative instruments of general application in Germany as a whole, including Berlin. These instruments were entitled Proclamations, Laws, Orders or Directives. They were published in the Official Gazette of the Control Council for Germany. Some of these instruments remain in

---

[5] *Military Government Gazette, Germany, 21 Army Group Area of Control*, No. 1, p.1.
[6] See Bathurst and Simpson, *Germany and the North Atlantic Community*, pp.3–17. The titles of Proclamation, Law and Ordinance were variously given to instruments having the force of law in the occupied territory during this period.
[7] For example, Military Government Law No. 1 and Control Council Law No. 1 each dealt with the abrogation of Nazi law.
[8] *Military Government Gazette, Germany, 21 Army Group Area of Control*, No. 1, p.24; Dölle/Zweigert, *Gesetz Nr. 52, Kommentar* (1947). This Law is of particular importance for the status of railway property and waterways in the Western Sectors: see Chapter 21 below. In certain respects Law No. 52 has been supplemented or modified by further legislation in the Western Sectors: see in particular British Sector Ordinance No. 202 of 30 December 1949 (*British Military Government Gazette*, p.255); US Military Government Law No. 19 of 20 April 1949 (*US Military Government Gazette, Issue N, 16 June 1949*, p.9); and French Sector Ordonnance of 31 August 1949 (*VOBl.* p.319).

force and are still applied. A notable example is Control Council Law No. 43 of 20 December 1946,[9] which regulates in Berlin the manufacture, import, export, transport and storage of war materials, and continues to be an important element of the demilitarised status of Berlin.

Allied Kommandatura legislation

The supreme legislative authority for Berlin is the Allied Kommandatura, which has issued numerous legislative instruments. Some are styled "Laws", a number of which remain in force and are still applied: for example, Allied Kommandatura Law No. 7 of 17 March 1950[10] concerning judicial powers in the reserved fields. These Laws, which the Allied Kommandatura began to issue only after the Soviet withdrawal,[11] were published in the Official Gazette of the Allied Kommandatura in accordance with Article I of Allied Kommandatura Law No. 1 of 9 February 1950.[12] Much more numerous, however, are Orders of the Allied Kommandatura, known as BK/Os (Berlin Kommandatura Orders). These are usually instruments of general legislative effect,[13] and with few exceptions[14] are published in the Berlin *Gesetz- und Verordnungsblatt* (regrettably only in German translation, which is not authoritative). BK/O(64)4 of 23 September 1964[15] provides that "the Berlin authorities will ensure that henceforth all BK/Os sent to them by the Allied Kommandatura shall be published forthwith in the *Gesetz- und*

---

[9] *CC Gazette*, p.234. See pp.275–6 below.

[10] *AK Gazette*, p.11. See pp.65–7 above, and pp.89–90 below.

[11] The Soviet Union appears not to have regarded the Allied Kommandatura as having legislative competence. Nevertheless, some Orders dating from the period 1945 to 1948 did have general legislative effect, e.g. Order No. 1 of 11 July 1945: Heidelmeyer, p.26; BK/O(46)61 of 24 January 1946 (p.238 below); BK/O(46)101A of 26 February 1946 on denazification: *Documentation on the question of West Berlin*, p.41.

[12] *AK Gazette*, p.1. See also Allied Kommandatura Laws Nos. 2 and 3 of 9 February 1950 (*AK Gazette*, pp.4 and 5), which contain interpretative provisions of general application to Allied legislation.

[13] Although many early BK/Os contained decisions or instructions of limited effect, the great majority of BK/Os (particularly following the Soviet withdrawal from the Allied Kommandatura) have general legislative effect. Many BK/Os modify German legislation of general application, or establish rules binding on the whole population. For many years the Allied Kommandatura has in practice used BK/Os for legislation having general effect.

[14] Limited in recent years to BK/Os dealing with occupation costs: see p.61 above.

[15] *GVBl.* p.1162. Prior to BK/O(64)4 there was no express Allied order regarding publication of BK/Os, but in practice most BK/Os were published by the *Senat* in the Berlin Law Gazette. However, some important BK/Os were not published (e.g. BK/O(52)35 on the Federal Constitutional Court) or published only in part (e.g. BK/O(51)10 on the Law on the Constitution of the Courts). The occasion for the 1964 BK/O appears to have been an oversight. The original and authentic English and French texts of BK/Os are held by the Allied authorities and the *Senat*, and copies of the English and French texts of BK/Os published in German may be obtained from them. It would clearly be desirable for the authentic texts to be published.

Verordnungsblatt für Berlin, unless the text of the BK/O itself expressly states that it is not to be published".

The Allied Kommandatura also issues Letters. These usually contain instructions or directives to the Governing Mayor or convey Allied decisions, and are binding on the local Berlin authorities. Some Letters are signed by the Chairman Commandant, and are known as BKC/Ls (Berlin Kommandatura Commandants' Letters); these are comparatively rare, the most notable example being BKC/L(55)3 of 5 May 1955 containing the Declaration on Berlin. Most, however, are known as BK/Ls (Berlin Kommandatura Letters) and are signed by the Chairman Deputy Commandant (formerly by the Chairman Secretary). In addition, Letters are addressed to particular offices of the *Senat* by the Committees of the Allied Kommandatura; these deal with routine or detailed matters falling within the Committees' respective fields of responsibility.[16] Letters from the Allied Kommandatura are not usually published officially; but, as is indeed desirable, many Letters on matters of general concern or interest are in fact made public, or at least their contents are widely known.

Allied Kommandatura Orders and Letters are dated and are cited in standard form, with the last two numbers of the year of issue placed in brackets, followed by the number of the instrument in the series for that year; for example BK/O(84)7 is the seventh Berlin Kommandatura Order of 1984.

Sector legislation

Most Allied legislative instruments in Berlin are made jointly by the occupation authorities. But a number of legislative instruments have been issued by individual Sector Commandants for application in their Sectors of Berlin. These have usually taken the form of Sector Orders or Ordinances. In some fields identical or similar Sector legislation has been enacted in each of the three Western Sectors. An example which is still regularly applied is Ordinance No. 508 of the British, French and US Sectors, dated 21 May 1951,[17] which deals with compensation for occupation damages. In other cases a piece of Sector legislation has been enacted by a Sector Commandant which has no equivalent in the other Sectors. An example is British Sector Ordinance No. 146 of 14 June 1948[18] dealing with contempt of courts-martial. In yet other cases,

[16] A Letter from the Legal Committee is known as a LEG/L, from the Civil Affairs Committee a CAC/L, from the Economic Committee an ECON/L, and from the Public Safety Committee a PUSA/L.
[17] *AK Gazette*, p.257; see p.283 below.
[18] *British Military Government Gazette*, p.107.

legislation enacted for a Western zone of occupation in Germany was expressly extended to the corresponding Sector of Berlin, and applied there as Sector legislation.[19] Sector legislation is usually published in the Official Gazette of the Allied Kommandatura. It was formerly published in the Official Gazettes of the Western Allied Military Governments.

Current practice

Allied legislative authority in Berlin is vested in the Allied Kommandatura, which is the supreme legislative authority in Berlin, and, subject to the Allied Kommandatura, in the individual Sector Commandants. The Allied Kommandatura issues a number of BK/Os and BK/Ls each year and, occasionally, other instruments. The last Allied Kommandatura Law was issued on 30 April 1955; the practice nowadays is to issue a BK/O when an instrument of general legislative effect is required. The power of each Sector Commandant to legislate for his own Sector has rarely been exercised in recent years. The field in which the Allied authorities legislate is limited, and almost all day-to-day matters are regulated by law enacted by German authorities. Only twelve BK/Os were issued in 1986.[20]

GERMAN LAW

German constitutional provisions

The German constitutional law in force in Berlin consists of the Constitution of Berlin of 1 September 1950 (p.69 above) and, to some degree, provisions of the Basic Law for the Federal Republic of Germany (pp.152–3 below). The application in Berlin of both remains limited by reservations made by the Western Allied authorities (pp.144–8 below).

Ordinary German law

The ordinary German law in force in Berlin may be subdivided in various ways. First, there is the German law, both *Reich* and Prussian, which was in force in Berlin before the occupation and which has not been repealed by Allied or German legislation.

---

[19] For example, *Ordonnance* No. 242 of 1 June 1950 issued by the French High Commissioner (*Allied High Commission Gazette*, p.421). United States High Commissioner Law No. 46 of 28 April 1955 (*AK Gazette*, p.1056) established a United States Court for Berlin and was applicable only in the American Sector of Berlin; it has subsequently been amended by Sector Ordinances (*AK Gazette*, pp.1083, 1132, 1220).
[20] The average number of BK/Os issued annually in the period 1956 to 1986 was eleven. In the period 1945 to 1949 the average was 288; from 1950 to 1955 it was 47.

Although much German legislation predating the occupation was repealed in the course of Allied denazification measures,[21] and more has been repealed or amended by local German legislation since the war, some nevertheless remains in force in Berlin. Article 48 of the Constitution of Berlin makes provision for the amendment of *Reich* and Prussian Laws still in force; it also provides that the rights accorded by such Laws to the former *Reich* Government, the former Prussian State Ministry, their members or other authorities shall devolve on the *Senat* unless the House of Representatives otherwise decides.

The second principal category of ordinary German law in force in Berlin consists of legislation made by local German legislative authorities since the end of the war. This may be further subdivided. First, there is local legislation made for Berlin alone by the Berlin House of Representatives, and subordinate legislation made by the *Senat*. Secondly, there is legislation enacted by the Berlin House of Representatives taking over provisions of legislation originally enacted by the legislature of the Federal Republic of Germany. This adoption process, which is described in Chapter 11 below, is important in maintaining a large degree of legal uniformity or harmony between the Western Sectors and the Federal Republic. Although most provisions of Federal Laws have been taken over in Berlin, there are significant exceptions. Particularly in the specific fields where the Allies retain reserved rights, the provisions of Federal Laws have either not been adopted in Berlin at all (for example, Federal military and defence legislation), or have been adopted only in part or subject to Allied reservations (for example, Federal civil aviation legislation). Mention should also be made of European Community law, virtually all of which applies in Berlin (Chapter 17 below).

THE RELATIONSHIP BETWEEN ALLIED AND GERMAN LAW

The highest legislative authority in Berlin is the Allied Kommandatura. Subject thereto, legislative power in each Sector resides with the Commandant. As was expressly confirmed by section 44 of Control Council Proclamation No. 2 of 20 September 1945,[22] Allied law overrides any provisions of German law inconsistent therewith. The Allied Kommandatura dealt further with the relationship between Allied and German law in force in Berlin in the Declaration on Berlin of 5 May 1955, which continues to govern the matter. Article I of the Declaration provides that

---

[21] See, for example, Control Council Law No.1 of 20 September 1945 (*CC Gazette*, p.6).
[22] *CC Gazette*, p.18.

Berlin shall exercise all its rights, powers and responsibilities set forth in its Constitution as adopted in 1950 subject only to the reservations made by the Allied Kommandatura in BK/O(50)75 of 29 August 1950[23] "and to the provisions hereinafter". After dealing with rights and powers reserved to the Allies, the Declaration addresses Allied legislation in Article VI. This provides that all legislation of the Allied authorities will remain in force until repealed, amended or deprived of effect. It further provides that Allied legislation may be repealed or amended by Berlin legislation, but that such repeal or amendment shall require the approval of the Allied authorities before coming into force. Article VII reads:

> Berlin legislation shall come into force in accordance with the provisions of the Berlin Constitution. In case of inconsistency with Allied legislation, or with other measures of the Allied authorities, or with the rights of the Allied authorities under this Declaration, Berlin legislation will be subject to repeal or annulment by the Allied Kommandatura.

The Allied Kommandatura has exercised, and occasionally still does exercise, its right to repeal, annul, modify, or make reservations to the application of, German legislation in Berlin. This right is generally exercised in relation to specific measures as they arise, and after consultation with the *Senat*. In addition, the Allied Kommandatura made a general reservation in BK/O(74)11 of 30 September 1974.[24] In this BK/O it reaffirmed (in relation both to laws and to treaties extended to Berlin) that "in the light of Article VI of the Declaration on Berlin of 5 May 1955 (BKC/L(55)3), even in those cases where no reservations are laid down expressly by the Allied Kommandatura, such laws and treaties do not affect the rights and responsibilities of the Allies or Allied legislation".

Allied Kommandatura Law No.7 of 17 March 1950[25] includes provisions dealing with the application of Allied law by the German courts. Article 3, paragraph 1, provides that no German court shall render a decision which impeaches the validity or legality of any legislation, regulation, directive, decision or order published by the occupation authorities. Article 3, paragraph 2, provides that whenever any question as to the existence, terms, validity or intent of any order[26] of the occupation authorities or occupying forces must be decided, the German authorities concerned shall forthwith

---

[23] *VOBl.* p.440; *Selected Documents* I, p.135; *US Documents*, p.340; Heidelmeyer, p.121.
[24] *GVBl.* p.2576.
[25] *AK Gazette*, p.11; as amended by Allied Kommandatura Law No. 17 of 27 August 1951 (*AK Gazette*, p.382) and interpreted by Allied Kommandatura Law No. 21 of 20 February 1952 (*AK Gazette*, p.458): pp.65–7 above.
[26] This means any such order, whether the subject-matter is within or outside the reserved fields: see Article 1 of Allied Kommandatura Law No. 21.

suspend further action and refer such question to the appropriate Sector Commandant; the appropriate Sector Commandant may issue a certificate determining such question, and the certificate shall be binding on the German authorities. German courts still request certificates from the Allied authorities from time to time for the purpose of ascertaining and interpreting Allied law.[27]

---

[27] For example, the certificate issued in the *Brückmann* case, a German translation of which is in *NJW*, 27 (1974), p.1970.

CHAPTER 6

THE SPECIAL BERLIN AREA

F UNDAMENTAL to an understanding of the status of Berlin is a knowledge of the area concerned. In particular, it is important to be aware of the boundaries of the special Berlin area,[1] as determined by the four Powers towards the end of the Second World War for the purpose of joint occupation and subsequently modified by agreement between them. The whole of this area remains under four-Power occupation, and the status of no part of it can be altered except by agreement of all four Powers. It is also important to be aware of the Sectors into which the special Berlin area is divided for the purpose of the joint occupation, since the division into Sectors is of continuing relevance.

ESTABLISHMENT AND DIVISION INTO SECTORS

The basic document is the London Protocol of 12 September 1944, as amended by the Agreements of 14 November 1944 and 26 July 1945.[2] The Protocol describes the special Berlin area, to be jointly occupied, as the territory of "Greater Berlin" as defined in the Law of 27 April 1920, that is to say, in the Prussian Law of that date.[3] The Law established the entity Greater Berlin and divided its territory into twenty districts (boroughs: *Bezirke*), to which a few boundary adjustments were subsequently made; this was the basis for the division of Berlin into Sectors for the purpose of the joint occupation.

The special Berlin area is dealt with in paragraph 2 of the London Protocol. As regards Berlin, the Protocol, as amended by the Agreement of 14 November 1944, provides as follows:

The Berlin area (by which expression is understood the territory of "Greater Berlin" as defined by the Law of the 27th April, 1920) will be jointly occupied by armed forces of the U.K., U.S.A. and U.S.S.R., assigned by the respective Commanders-in-Chief. For this purpose the territory of "Greater Berlin" will be divided into the following three parts:

North-Eastern part of "Greater Berlin" (districts of Pankow,

---

[1] The special Berlin area described in this Chapter is of course not the same as the Berlin Control Zone, which is the air space between ground level and 10,000 feet within a radius of 20 miles from the Allied Control Authority building: see p.113 below.

[2] Text at p.313 below. See also pp.36–7 above.

[3] *Gesetz über die Bildung einer neuen Stadtgemeinde Berlin* (*Preussische Gesetzsammlung*, p.123), with First Amendment of 30 March 1931 (*Preussische Gesetzsammlung*, p.39). See Krumholz, *Berlin ABC* (2nd ed.), pp.108–11.

Prenzlauerberg, Mitte, Weissensee, Friedrichshain, Lichtenberg, Treptow, Köpenick) will be occupied by the forces of the U.S.S.R.;

North-Western part of "Greater Berlin" (districts of Reinickendorf, Wedding, Tiergarten, Charlottenburg, Spandau, Wilmersdorf) will be occupied by the forces of the United Kingdom;

Southern part of "Greater Berlin" (districts of Zehlendorf, Steglitz, Schöneberg, Kreuzberg, Tempelhof, Neukölln) will be occupied by the forces of the United States of America.

The boundaries of districts within "Greater Berlin", referred to in the foregoing descriptions, are those which existed after the coming into effect of the decree published on 27th March, 1938 (Amtsblatt der Reichshauptstadt Berlin No. 13 of 27th March, 1938, page 215).

The London Protocol was further amended by the Agreement of 26 July 1945, which gave effect to the decision at Yalta[4] to invite France to take part in the occupation of Germany. The Agreement amended the Protocol so as to include France among the Powers participating in the joint occupation of Greater Berlin, to increase from three to four the number of Commandants in the Inter-Allied Governing Authority, and to increase from three to four the parts into which the territory of Greater Berlin was to be divided for the purpose of the joint occupation. The precise determination of the French Sector was made by Order No. 1 of the Allied Commandants of 11 July 1945[5] and by the Control Council at its first meeting on 30 July 1945. The Soviet and American Sectors remained as originally described in the London Protocol; two districts originally allotted to the British Sector, Reinickendorf and Wedding, constituted the French Sector; and the British Sector was composed of the remaining four districts of Charlottenburg, Spandau, Tiergarten and Wilmersdorf (see Map 2).

EARLY POST-WAR ALTERATIONS

British forces occupied the British Sector of Berlin at the beginning of July 1945. It was soon found that the boundary between the British Sector and the Soviet zone caused some inconvenience. The British occupation authorities required additional land for the airfield at Gatow, and the Soviet authorities had a corresponding need in order to make full use of the airfield at Staaken in the Soviet zone. Accordingly, the Co-ordinating Committee of the Control Council prepared an agreement for the exchange of territory to satisfy the requirements of both parties.

[4] *Selected Documents* I, p.34; *US Documents*, p.10; Heidelmeyer, p.8.
[5] *VOBl.* p.45; Heidelmeyer *Dokumente*, p.16.

The agreement provided for the transfer to Soviet administration of two areas at Staaken in the British Sector, in return for the transfer to British administration of two areas lying in the Soviet zone known as Weinmeisterhöhe and Gross-Glienicke-Ost. The agreement was confirmed by the Control Council on 30 August 1945,[6] and took effect on that day. This quadripartite confirmation of the alteration of the western boundary of the British Sector effectively modified the London Protocol of 12 September 1944. The areas transferred to the British Sector became part of Greater Berlin without a further formal act of incorporation.[7]

EXCHANGE OF TERRITORY UNDER THE QUADRIPARTITE AGREEMENT[8]

The fact that the special Berlin area was based on the territory of Greater Berlin as defined in the Prussian Law of 27 April 1920 led to further practical inconveniences. The territory of the area as so defined included a number of areas surrounded or almost surrounded by the Soviet zone to which access became precarious, particularly at times of tension. Notable examples were the enclave at Steinstücken in the American Sector and the area known as Eiskeller in the British Sector. These problems were addressed during the negotiation of the Quadripartite Agreement of 3 September 1971.[9] Part IIC and Annex III, paragraph 3, of the Agreement provide that "the problems of the small enclaves, including Steinstücken, and of other small areas may be solved by exchange of territory". Part IIC and Annex III, paragraph 5, further provide that detailed arrangements implementing and supplementing these provisions are to be agreed by the competent German authorities.

On 3 September 1971, the date of signature of the Quadripartite Agreement, the Allied Kommandatura issued BKC/L(71)1.[10] This recalled the provisions of the Quadripartite Agreement cited above, and authorised the *Senat* of Berlin to

---

[6] CONL/P(45)16: Heidelmeyer *Dokumente*, pp.39, 597.

[7] See Schröder, *Die Elbe-Grenze* (1986), pp.30–1. Other minor alterations agreed by the Occupying Powers involved the transfer of an area at Stolpe to French administration and its subsequent retransfer to Soviet administration with effect from 3 January 1949; and an alteration of the course of the boundary between the American Sector and the Soviet zone of occupation, in the area of Königsweg in Zehlendorf, by agreement of 25 June 1955.

[8] Zivier, pp.231–2; Schiedermair, pp.122–5.

[9] See p.335 below. For the position before the Quadripartite Agreement, see Catudal, *Steinstücken* (1971); Mahncke, *Berlin im geteilten Deutschland*, pp.231–2. For a more detailed treatment of the position following 1971, see Catudal, *Cahiers de Géographie de Québec*, 18 (1974), pp.213–26.

[10] Cmnd. 5135, p.56; *US Documents*, p.1147.

conduct appropriate negotiations on, among other matters, exchange of territory. Thus mandated by the Occupying Powers, the *Senat* and the GDR Government negotiated an Arrangement on the Resolution of the Problem of Enclaves by Exchange of Territory.[11] In BKC/L(71)2 of 16 December 1971,[12] the Allied Kommandatura stated that it considered the Arrangement to be "in conformity with the Quadripartite Agreement, which provides the standard for its interpretation and application"; that accordingly the Arrangement would enter into force on the date of signature of the Final Quadripartite Protocol by the four Powers; and that the *Senat* of Berlin was authorised to sign the Arrangement. The Arrangement was duly signed on 20 December 1971, and was listed in the Final Quadripartite Protocol and entered into force with it.[13]

The Arrangement provided that after its execution five areas (at Finkenkrug, Teufelsbruch/Eiskeller, Böttcherberg, Gross-Kuhlake, and Nuthewiesen) belonging to the Western Sectors of Berlin, amounting to about 15.6 hectares, "shall belong to the territory of the German Democratic Republic", and three areas lying within the GDR, amounting to about 17.1 hectares, "shall belong to the Western Sectors of Berlin". All except one of the areas transferred to the GDR were enclaves surrounded by GDR territory. The areas acquired by the Western Sectors were the northern part of the Frohnau cemetery together with an adjoining strip to the east, and strips of territory to provide satisfactory access to Steinstücken and Eiskeller. The Arrangement also provided for the results of the necessary surveys, together with the exact course and the demarcation of the new boundaries, to be recorded in a Protocol which, on signature, would become an integral part of the Arrangement. This Protocol was signed on 2 June 1972, and the execution of the exchange of territory pursuant to the Arrangement was recorded in a Final Statement signed on 3 June 1972, as envisaged in Article 5(2) of the Arrangement.

In consequence of the Arrangement, the Allied Kommandatura issued BK/O(72)6 on 3 June 1972.[14] Paragraph 1 of this Order provided that the areas acquired under the Arrangement would each "become part of the adjacent Sectors of Greater Berlin", as

---

[11] Cmnd. 5135, pp.122, 138; *US Documents*, pp.1182, 1184. The Arrangement (*Vereinbarung*) needs to be read with its related documents: the Protocol Notes (*Protokollvermerke*) relating to Articles 1, 2, 3 and 5; the Protocol (*Protokoll*) of 2 June 1972 concerning implementation of the Arrangement; and the Final Statement (*Schlusserklärung*) of 3 June 1972.
[12] Cmnd. 5135, p.136.
[13] For the relationship between the inner-German arrangements and the Quadripartite Agreement, see pp.51–2 above.
[14] *GVBl.* p.998; *US Documents*, p.1204.

follows: the strip of territory between Kohlhasenbrück and Steinstücken – the American Sector (*Bezirk* Zehlendorf); the strip of territory in the vicinity of Eiskeller – the British Sector (*Bezirk* Spandau); the territory north of Frohnau – the French Sector (*Bezirk* Reinickendorf). Paragraph 2 provided that all laws and decisions in force in the above-mentioned Sectors should apply in the above-mentioned areas. Paragraph 3 made provision regarding public and private property in the acquired areas.

The negotiation of the exchange of territory provided for in the Arrangement of 20 December 1971 was mandated by the four Powers, and the exchange itself was completed by their signing the Final Quadripartite Protocol. It was thus an act of the four Powers, which alone are competent to modify the boundaries of the special Berlin area laid down in the London Protocol of 12 September 1944. As a result, the occupation status of the Sectors concerned was extended to the acquired areas and ceased for those areas transferred to the GDR.

The Arrangement of 20 December 1971 did not solve all problems, but expressly left open the possibility of further negotiations and arrangements. Article 6(1) provided that "with respect to the enclaves and other small areas which have not yet been included in this Arrangement, further discussions shall take place in due course and suitable arrangements be concluded". This provision, like the rest of the Arrangement, was approved by the four Powers when they signed the Final Quadripartite Protocol. The same applies to Article 6(2) of the Arrangement, which provides that "the existing situation in respect of the remaining enclaves and other small areas shall not be changed before the entry into force of the arrangements envisaged by both sides". This preserves the *status quo ante* as regards the remaining enclaves, including existing arrangements for access thereto, pending the conclusion of further arrangements.[15]

The *Senat* of Berlin and the GDR Government took early advantage of Article 6(1), and did so in the context of an exchange of territory between Sectors. In July 1972 they concluded an Arrangement concerning the inclusion of the Area at the former Potsdamer Bahnhof in the Arrangement of 20 December 1971 on the Resolution of the Problem of Enclaves by Exchange of

---

[15] The remaining enclaves are Wüstemark (district of Zehlendorf), and Fichtenwiese, Erlengrund, Lasszinswiesen and Brieselanger (or Falkenhagener) Wiese (district of Spandau). Access to Fichtenwiese and Erlengrund is available to persons owning property there along special footpaths running across GDR territory and past a GDR control point, where identity cards are checked: Zivier, p.232. For sketches of some of the areas concerned in the exchanges of territory see Catudal, *A Balance Sheet of the Quadripartite Agreement on Berlin*, pp. 104–6.

Territory.[16] The new Arrangement provided for the transfer of the area of the former Potsdamer station, which lay in the Soviet Sector of Berlin, to the British Sector, by including it in the Arrangement of 20 December 1971. By BKC/L(72)1 of 20 July 1972,[17] the Allied Kommandatura authorised the *Senat* to sign this Arrangement. The Allied Kommandatura noted that the Arrangement had been reached on the basis of the relevant provisions of the Quadripartite Agreement and pursuant to Article 6(1) of the Arrangement of 20 December 1971; it also stated that it considered the new Arrangement, like the Arrangement of 20 December 1971 of which it formed a part, to be in conformity with the Quadripartite Agreement, which provided the standard for its interpretation and application. The Arrangement was signed on 21 July 1972, and on the same day the Allied Kommandatura issued BK/O(72)9,[18] which provided that as from that day the area in question would become part of the British Sector (*Bezirk* Tiergarten). The BK/O also provided that property of public persons in the area would become the property of *Land* Berlin, and that in all other respects the provisions of BK/O(72)6 would apply to the area. The latter provision meant in particular that all laws and decisions in force in the British Sector would apply in the acquired area. It will be noted that the Arrangement was concluded in further implementation of the Quadripartite Agreement and was thus under a clear four-Power roof.[19]

The possibility of further negotiations for the exchange of territory, envisaged in Article 6(1) of the Arrangement of 20 December 1971, was again taken up in 1983. Both the *Senat* and the GDR Government were interested in holding discussions about remaining enclaves and other small areas. In BKC/L(83)1 of 25 October 1983, the Allied Kommandatura authorised the *Senat* to conduct appropriate negotiations for a further exchange of territory, taking account of the provisions of Part IIC and of Annex III, paragraph 3, of the Quadripartite Agreement of 3 September 1971. No further arrangement had been concluded by December 1986.

ALTERATION OF BOUNDARIES BETWEEN DISTRICTS

Article 4 of the 1950 Constitution of Berlin envisages the

---

[16] *Zehn Jahre Deutschlandpolitik*, p.190.
[17] *Zehn Jahre Deutschlandpolitik*, p.191.
[18] *GVBl.* p.1450.
[19] The Arrangement of 21 July 1972 was the subject of a technical amendment negotiated in 1975 by the *Senat* and the GDR Government, with the authorisation of the Allied Kommandatura, to permit the East Berlin *U-Bahn* to continue to use the reversing facility in the area beneath the Potsdamer Platz, in return for an annual fee to be paid to the *Senat* by the GDR Government.

alteration of the boundaries of the districts into which Berlin is divided. There have been several minor alterations to these boundaries since 1945, most of which involved alterations to the boundaries between districts in the same Sector. Two cases, however, involved minor alterations to the boundaries between districts in different Sectors: the Third Ordinance on the Alteration of District Boundaries of 9 January 1967[20] altered the boundary between Tiergarten (British Sector) and Schöneberg (American Sector), and the Fifth Ordinance on the Alteration of District Boundaries of 24 June 1971[21] altered the boundary between Wilmersdorf (British Sector) and Schöneberg (American Sector). Although such legislative acts of the Berlin authorities cannot of themselves alter the Sector boundaries as determined by the four Powers in the London Protocol of 12 September 1944, the Allies have in practice raised no objection to these insignificant changes.

ESTABLISHMENT OF NEW DISTRICTS

A different sort of alteration occurred in 1979, when a new district called Marzahn was created in the Soviet Sector, made up of parts of two existing districts in that Sector, Lichtenberg and Weissensee. This was, however, an internal rearrangement within the boundaries of the Soviet Sector and did not alter the boundary between that Sector and the GDR. As the boundaries of the special Berlin area were not affected, the creation of the new district did not purport to modify the substance of the London Protocol of 12 September 1944. Accordingly, there was no change in quadripartite rights and responsibilities in the Soviet Sector of Berlin; nor indeed could any unilateral action by the GDR or East Berlin authorities have brought about such a change. This is also true of two more new districts in the Soviet Sector: Hohenschönhausen, established at the beginning of 1986, which was formed out of the existing district of Weissensee; and Hellersdorf, formed out of the eastern part of Marzahn in June 1986.

---

[20] *GVBl.* p.92.
[21] *GVBl.* p.1072.

PART THREE

ACCESS TO BERLIN

Berlin is surrounded by the GDR, and free access between the Western Sectors of Berlin and the Federal Republic of Germany across the GDR is of fundamental importance. There are four means of access: air, road, rail and waterway (see Map 3). The first three are used both by Allied traffic and by civilian traffic; the waterways are in practice used only by civilian traffic. The Soviet Union and GDR have frequently sought to exert pressure on the Western Allies, and on the Western Sectors, by challenging the right of access and by interfering with transit traffic; that these efforts have remained without success is due to the determination of Allies and Germans alike. Since the Quadripartite Agreement of 3 September 1971 the situation has been comparatively trouble-free.

Chapter 7 considers the essential basis for all use of the access routes, the Allied right of access. Chapters 8 and 9 then deal in turn with access by air and by the surface routes, including civilian access.

THE RIGHT OF ACCESS

THE LEGAL BASIS OF THE RIGHT OF ACCESS[1]

THE main agreements concluded by the four Powers in 1944 and 1945 concerning the occupation of Germany did not contain provisions on access between the Western zones of occupation and Berlin across the Soviet zone, which entirely surrounded the city. However, the right to be in Berlin necessarily carried with it the right of access; without it the Allies could not have maintained the joint occupation of Berlin which they had undertaken. The four Powers considered that this was self-evident, and that no consensual basis for the inherent right of access was required. The Allied right of access to Berlin is an original right deriving from the defeat of the German armed forces, the unconditional surrender of Germany and the assumption by the Allies of supreme authority in respect of Germany, and does not depend upon any agreement with the Soviet Union. The right of access to Berlin, as an essential corollary of the right of occupation, derives from the same source and is of the same stature as the right of occupation itself. It is in no sense a right conferred by the Soviet Union or GDR and does not depend on the consent of either, and the Western Allies have never accepted Eastern arguments to the contrary. At the same time, the inherent right of access has been confirmed by a number of express agreements reached over the years, and by long-standing practices. These also regulate certain technical aspects of the exercise of the right of access, which is however in no way diminished thereby.

At the time of the Berlin blockade, the Western Allies set out their position on access in Notes to the Soviet Union of 6 July 1948[2] in the following terms:

> The rights of the United States as a joint occupying Power in Berlin derive from the total defeat and unconditional surrender of Germany. The international agreements undertaken in connexion

---

[1] Bathurst, *BYIL*, 38(1962), pp.293–305; Franklin, *World Politics*, 16(1963), pp.1–31; Kuhn, *EA*, 14(1959), pp.447–66; Riklin, pp.262–75; Schröder, *ROW*, 21 (1967), pp.104–9; Schröder, *RuP*, 5(1969), pp.11–19; Mahnke, *DA*, 5(1972), pp.140–8, 346–87; Gusseck, *Die internationale Praxis der Transitgewährung und der Berlin–Verkehr* (1973); Mahncke, *Berlin im geteilten Deutschland*, pp.181–218; Zivier, pp.139–48, 206–20. For an Eastern view, see Görner, *DDR gewährleistet friedlichen Westberlin–Transit*, pp.34–105.

[2] *US Documents*, p.156; Heidelmeyer, p.68.

therewith by the Governments of the United States, United Kingdom, France, and the Soviet Union defined the zones in Germany and the sectors in Berlin which are occupied by these powers. They established the quadripartite control of Berlin on a basis of friendly co-operation which the Government of the United States earnestly desires to continue to pursue. These agreements implied the right of free access to Berlin. This right has long been confirmed by usage. It was directly specified in a message sent by President Truman to Premier Stalin on 14th June, 1945, which agreed to the withdrawal of United States forces to the zonal boundaries, provided satisfactory arrangements could be entered into between the military commanders, which would give access by rail, road and air to United States forces in Berlin. Premier Stalin replied on 16th June, suggesting a change in date but no other alteration in the plan proposed by the President. Premier Stalin then gave assurances that all necessary measures would be taken in accordance with the plan. Correspondence in a similar sense took place between Premier Stalin and Mr Churchill. In accordance with this understanding, the United States, whose armies had penetrated deep into Saxony and Thuringia, parts of the Soviet zone, withdrew its forces to its own area of occupation in Germany and took up its position in its own sector in Berlin. Thereupon the agreements in regard to the occupation of Germany and Berlin went into effect. The United States would not have so withdrawn its troops from a large area now occupied by the Soviet Union had there been any doubt whatsoever about the observance of its agreed right of free access to its sector of Berlin. The right of the United States to its position in Berlin thus stems from precisely the same source as the right of the Soviet Union. It is impossible to assert the latter and deny the former.

It clearly results from these undertakings that Berlin is not a part of the Soviet zone, but is an international zone of occupation. Commitments entered into in good faith by the zone commanders, and subsequently confirmed by the Allied Control Authority, as well as practices sanctioned by usage, guarantee the United States, together with other Powers, free access to Berlin for the purpose of fulfilling its responsibilities as an occupying Power. The facts are plain. Their meaning is clear. Any other interpretation would offend all the rules of comity and reason.

In order that there should be no misunderstanding whatsoever on this point, the United States Government categorically asserts that it is in occupation of its sector in Berlin with free access thereto as a matter of established right deriving from the defeat and surrender of Germany and confirmed by formal agreements among the principal Allies.

EARLY POST-WAR ARRANGEMENTS

As is well described in the Notes cited above, upon the cessation of hostilities in 1945 the areas of Germany actually occupied by the

Allied armies did not correspond to the areas of occupation provided for in the four-Power agreements. The Soviet Army was in sole occupation of Berlin; British and American forces occupied considerable areas of the Soviet zone. On 14 June 1945 Truman proposed in a letter to Stalin that the withdrawal of American troops from the Soviet zone to the American zone should be carried out –

> in accordance with arrangements between the respective Commanders, including in these arrangements the simultaneous movement of the national garrisons into Greater Berlin and provision of free access by air, road, and rail from Frankfurt and Bremen to Berlin for United States forces.[3]

Churchill made a similar proposal for British forces.[4] Stalin replied on 18 June insisting on a postponement until 1 July but making no other change in the proposed plan; his letter stated:

> On our part all necessary measures will be taken in Germany and Austria in accordance with the above-stated plan.[5]

A meeting was held in Berlin on 29 June between the British, American and Soviet Commanders. Arrangements were made for use by the Western Allies of specific roads, railway lines and air routes for the purpose of exercising their right of access to Berlin.[6] British and American troops moved into the Sectors of Berlin allocated to them at the beginning of July 1945. At the same time they withdrew from the large areas of the Soviet zone which they had hitherto occupied, and handed them over to Soviet forces. As the United States and United Kingdom Governments pointed out in the Notes of 6 July 1948 cited above:

> The United States [United Kingdom] would not have so withdrawn its troops from a large area now occupied by the Soviet Union had there been any doubt whatsoever about the observance of its agreed right of free access to its Sector of Berlin.

The Allied Control Council and its competent organs took decisions on certain aspects of access to Berlin in the months following the entry of Western Allied forces into the city: the decisions included those on rail access of 10 September 1945, on the establishment of air corridors from Berlin to the Western zones of 30 November 1945 and on Flight Rules of 22 October 1946. In June 1946 the Soviet and British zonal authorities reached agreement on

---

[3] *US Documents*, p.40; Heidelmeyer *Dokumente*, p.12.
[4] *US Documents*, p.40.
[5] *US Documents*, p.41; Heidelmeyer *Dokumente*, p.14.
[6] *US Documents*, p.42; Heidelmeyer, p.31.

the principles to cover barge traffic between the two zones. In addition, working arrangements and practices developed with respect to the exercise of the Allied right of access. All these matters were dealt with as technical questions, worked out primarily by the functional Committees and Directorates of the Control Council. They were designed to provide for the orderly exercise of the right of access, and were in no sense a substitute legal basis for the inherent right enjoyed by the Western Allies as an essential corollary of their right of occupation. These and other specific arrangements are considered in Chapters 8 and 9 below.

THE BLOCKADE; THE 1949 NEW YORK AND PARIS AGREEMENTS

On 30 March 1948, ten days after the Soviet member walked out of the Control Council, the Soviet military authorities in Germany informed the Western Allies that supplementary provisions regarding communications between the Soviet and Western zones would enter into force on 1 April 1948. These provisions were contrary to established arrangements and practices. On 31 March 1948 the Western Allies replied that the new provisions were not acceptable and that such unilateral changes of policy could not be recognised.[7] The Soviet authorities then began the restrictions on traffic to and from Berlin which culminated in the Berlin blockade.[8] The Western Allies responded with the air-lift.

The blockade was terminated by the New York agreement of 4 May 1949 (the "Jessup-Malik agreement"), in which the Governments of the four Powers agreed *inter alia* that:

All restrictions imposed since March 1, 1948, by the Government of the Union of Soviet Socialist Republics on communications, transportation, and trade between Berlin and the Western Zones of Germany and between the Eastern Zone and the Western Zones will be removed on May 12, 1949.[9]

This was implemented by Order No. 56 of the Soviet Military Government and Commander-in-Chief of the Soviet Occupation Forces in Germany, dated 9 May 1949, which provided that the arrangements in force up to 1 March 1948 concerning communications and transport between Berlin and the Western zones of Germany were to be re-established.[10]

In accordance with the New York agreement, the four-Power Council of Foreign Ministers met at Paris from 23 May to 20 June

---

[7] *Selected Documents* I, pp.339–40.
[8] See *US Documents*, p.152. The various measures are also listed in Riklin, p.79.
[9] 138 *UNTS* 123; *Selected Documents* I, p.115; *US Documents*, p.221; Heidelmeyer, p.100.
[10] *Selected Documents* I, p.340; *US Documents*, p.258; Heidelmeyer, p.101.

1949. It achieved little, other than the following agreement, set forth in the final communiqué:

> The Governments of France, the Union of Soviet Socialist Republics, the United Kingdom and the United States agree that the New York Agreement of May 4, 1949 shall be maintained. Moreover, in order to promote further the aims set forth in the preceding paragraphs and in order to improve and supplement this and other arrangements and agreements as regards the movement of persons and goods and communications between the Eastern Zone and the Western Zones and between the Zones and Berlin, and also in regard to transit, the occupation authorities, each in his own Zone, will have an obligation to take the measures necessary to ensure the normal functioning and utilisation of rail, water and road transport for such movement of persons and goods and such communications by post, telephone and telegraph.[11]

The New York and Paris agreements of 1949, which remain in force, contain a clear acknowledgement and confirmation of the Western Allied rights in Berlin, and in particular the right of access. The New York agreement guaranteed the re-establishment of the *status quo ante* as a minimum. The Paris agreement went somewhat further. In addition to confirming the New York agreement and requiring that it be maintained, it imposed an express obligation to take the measures necessary to ensure the normal functioning and utilisation of rail, water and road transport.

SUBSEQUENT DEVELOPMENTS

In the twenty years following the 1949 New York and Paris agreements, the right of access was a frequent source of controversy. On 20 September 1955, the date of signature of the Treaty of Friendship between the Soviet Union and GDR, an exchange of letters between the East German Deputy Foreign Minister, Bolz, and the Soviet Deputy Foreign Minister, Zorin, confirmed an agreement purporting to grant the East German régime control over lines of communication between the Federal Republic of Germany and West Berlin. Pending the conclusion of "an appropriate agreement", however, control over the communications of the three Western Powers between the Federal Republic and West Berlin would be exercised by the Soviet military commander.[12] The Western Allied Foreign Ministers issued a joint statement in New York on 28 September 1955 emphasising that the Soviet-East German agreements of 20 September could not affect

---

[11] *Selected Documents* I, p.122; *US Documents*, p.269; Heidelmeyer, p.104.
[12] *Selected Documents* I, p.228; *US Documents*, p.460; Heidelmeyer, p.174.

the obligations or responsibilities of the Soviet Union under existing quadripartite agreements and arrangements on Germany and Berlin, and that the Soviet Union remained responsible for carrying out these obligations.[13] This was followed by Notes from the three Powers to the Soviet Union, delivered in Moscow on 3 October 1955, which repeated that the Soviet Union had not been in any way freed from its obligations towards the three Powers concerning Germany, and that –

> in particular, the letters exchanged between Mr Zorin and Mr Bolz on the 20th September 1955 cannot have the effect of discharging the USSR from the responsibilities which it has assumed in matters concerning transportation and communications between the different parts of Germany, including Berlin.[14]

In its Note to the Western Allies of 27 November 1958[15] at the outset of the second Berlin crisis, the Soviet Union argued that the basis of "the former Allied agreements on Berlin" had been destroyed, and declared its intention to negotiate with the East German authorities concerning the handing over of functions so far carried out by Soviet organs on the basis of those agreements. The Note amounted to an ultimatum, since it specified a period of six months for negotiating a radical change in the position of Berlin, during which time the arrangements for the communications of the Western Allies between West Berlin and the Federal Republic of Germany would be left unchanged. In a communiqué issued following talks in Paris on 14 December 1958,[16] the Foreign Ministers of the Western Allies reaffirmed the determination of their Governments to maintain their position and their rights with respect to Berlin, including the right of free access. They found unacceptable the unilateral repudiation by the Soviet Government of its obligations to their Governments in relation to Allied presence in Berlin and freedom of access to the city, and the substitution of the East German authorities for the Soviet Government in so far as those rights were concerned. The Western Allied Governments replied in detail to the Soviet Note of 27 November 1958 in Notes dated 31 December 1958.[17] They stated that one Power could not repudiate four-Power agreements unilaterally. In any case, the right of the Western Allies to be in Berlin did not rest on the agreements

---

[13] *Selected Documents* I, p.229; *US Documents*, p.461; Heidelmeyer, p.175.

[14] *Selected Documents* I, p.230; *US Documents*, p.462; Heidelmeyer, p.175. The Soviet and Western Allied Governments reiterated their positions in Notes of 18 and 27 October 1955 respectively: see *Selected Documents* I, pp.230, 232; *US Documents*, pp.462, 464; Heidelmeyer, pp.176, 177.

[15] *Selected Documents* I, p.318; *US Documents*, p.552; Heidelmeyer, p.180.

[16] *Selected Documents* I, p.333; *US Documents*, p.559; Heidelmeyer, p.210.

[17] *Selected Documents* I, p.346; *US Documents*, p.573; Heidelmeyer, pp.212, 214, 220.

which the Soviet Union purported to denounce, but on the unconditional surrender of Germany and the assumption of supreme authority. The Western Powers would continue to hold the Soviet Union responsible for the discharge of its obligations in respect of Berlin under existing agreements, including specifically the Paris agreement of 20 June 1949, under which the Soviet Union assumed an obligation to assure the normal functioning of transport and communications between Berlin and the Western zones of occupation. The Governments of the three Powers –

> have the right to maintain garrisons in their Sectors of Berlin and to have free access thereto. Certain administrative procedures have been agreed with the Soviet authorities, and are in operation at the present time. Her Majesty's Government will not accept a unilateral repudiation on the part of the Soviet Government of its obligations in respect of that freedom of access. Nor will they accept the substitution of the régime which the Soviet Government refers to as the German Democratic Republic for the Soviet Government in this respect.

In 1960 the Western Allies had further occasion to deny the claim of the Soviet Union to withdraw unilaterally from the obligations undertaken in the 1949 New York and Paris agreements.[18] They also protested to the Soviet Union about renewed East German violations of existing agreements concerning freedom of access to Berlin,[19] and rejected as unfounded East German pretensions to restrict such access.[20] At the same time they reaffirmed their right to the unrestricted use of the air corridors, and rejected Soviet and East German assertions that the air corridors were allotted only for supplying the Western Powers' garrisons in Berlin. Similar exchanges between the Western Allies and the Soviet Union about the status of the air corridors took place in August and September 1961, in the course of which the Soviet Union threatened to interfere with Allied flights to Berlin.[21]

In October 1963 the Soviet authorities sought to interfere with Western Allied military traffic on the Berlin-Helmstedt *Autobahn*. In Notes of 6 November 1963 the Western Allies protested against such inadmissible attempts to prejudice their right of free access to

---

[18] Notes of 26 October 1960: *Selected Documents* I, p.440; *US Documents*, p.722; Heidelmeyer, p.270.
[19] Notes of 12 September 1960: *Selected Documents* I, p.435; *US Documents*, p.719; Heidelmeyer, p.267.
[20] Statement of 3 September 1960: *Selected Documents* I, p.433; *US Documents*, p.716; Heidelmeyer, p.266.
[21] Soviet Notes of 23 August and 2 September 1961: *Selected Documents* I, pp.473, 477; *US Documents*, pp.783, 788; Heidelmeyer, pp.296, 301. Western Allied Notes of 26 August and 8 September 1961: *Selected Documents* I, pp.474, 479; *US Documents*, pp.785, 789; Heidelmeyer, pp.298, 303. See pp.118–20 below.

Berlin.[22] In April 1965, to reinforce their objection to the holding of a session of the *Bundestag* in the city, which they regarded as contrary to the status of Berlin, the Soviet and East German authorities interfered with access to Berlin to a greater degree than at any time since the blockade. On 4 April the East German régime prohibited the transit to Berlin of members of the *Bundestag* and certain other persons.[23] At the same time, Soviet and East German forces held joint military manoeuvres to the west of Berlin, which led to serious interference with both civilian and Allied military traffic on the access routes. The Soviet authorities also attempted to limit the air space available to Allied flights in the corridors. In Notes of 7 April l965 the Western Allies objected strongly to the Soviet and East German harassment as a serious violation of freedom of access to Berlin and called on the Soviet Government to put an end to it.[24] Restrictions on the access routes ceased on 10 April. Further East German interference with access to Berlin took place in 1968, culminating in a decree of 11 June 1968 introducing passport and visa requirements for residents of the Federal Republic of Germany travelling to and from the Western Sectors.[25] The Western Allies condemned these illegal East German measures in public statements, which drew attention to the responsibility the Soviet Government shared with them for unhindered access to Berlin.[26] Further East German interference with access occurred in February 1969, in response to the decision to convene the Federal Assembly in Berlin on 5 March l969. In a joint statement of 10 February 1969 the Western Allies said that the decision to hold the Federal Assembly in Berlin was taken after due consultation with them, that there was no justification for the East German measures, and that the Soviet Union, and not the East German authorities, was responsible for assuring free and unhindered access of persons and goods to Berlin.[27]

Events such as these led the Western Allies, in consultation with the Government of the Federal Republic of Germany, to consider the possibility of holding talks with the Soviet Union aimed at reducing the risk of future crises. In the negotiations which opened on 26 March 1970, and which culminated in the signature of the Quadripartite Agreement on 3 September 1971, one of the most important Western aims was to improve the situation regarding civilian access to Berlin. Civilian transit traffic on the surface routes

[22] *Selected Documents* II, p.99; *US Documents*, p.857; *BPIL* 1963, p.213.
[23] *Selected Documents* II, p.120.
[24] *Selected Documents* II, p.121; *US Documents*, p.892.
[25] *GBl. DDR* II, p.331; *Selected Documents* II, p.189.
[26] *Selected Documents* II, p.191; *US Documents*, p.1009.
[27] *Selected Documents* II, p.200; *US Documents*, p.1028.

had been far more prone to harassment than Western Allied military traffic. After the Soviet Union handed over control of civilian access traffic to the East German authorities in 1955, the Western Allies had consistently maintained that this could not excuse the Soviet Union from its responsibilities in matters concerning transport and communications between the different parts of Germany, including Berlin.[28] In Part IIA and Annex I of the Quadripartite Agreement the Soviet Union acknowledged its responsibility for civilian access to Berlin in more specific and detailed terms than at any time since 1945. In pursuance of Part IIA and Annex I, the Governments of the Federal Republic of Germany and the GDR concluded on 17 December 1971 an Agreement on the Transit Traffic of Civilian Persons and Goods between the Federal Republic of Germany and Berlin (West) ("the Transit Traffic Agreement").[29] Part IIA and Annex I of the Quadripartite Agreement, and the Transit Traffic Agreement, deal only with civilian transit traffic by road, rail and waterways. They do not regulate Allied military traffic or access by air.[30] The Quadripartite Agreement confirms the Soviet Government's responsibility in relation to civilian as well as military transit traffic. It recognises the right of free and unhindered access to Berlin, which continues to be based on original occupation rights. The existing agreements, arrangements and practices concerning access are unaffected, including the New York and Paris agreements of 1949, and the existing situation regarding access may not be changed unilaterally. In addition, civilian transit traffic by road, rail and waterways is now regulated in detail in treaty provisions supplementing existing agreements and arrangements.

[28] *Selected Documents* I, p.230; *US Documents*, p.462; Heidelmeyer, p.175.
[29] Cmnd. 5135, p.62; *US Documents*, p.1169. See pp.129–39 below. Neither the inner-German Transport Treaty of 26 May 1972 nor the Basis of Relations Treaty deals with transit traffic between Berlin and the Federal Republic.
[30] These matters are, however, covered by the general provisions in the third and fourth paragraphs of the preamble and paragraphs 3 and 4 of Part I of the Quadripartite Agreement. Military traffic and access by air continue in accordance with the arrangements existing prior to the conclusion of the Quadripartite Agreement, and may not be changed unilaterally.

CHAPTER 8

ACCESS BY AIR

A CCESS by air to Berlin takes place along three air corridors established in 1945.[1] Flight in the corridors, and in the airspace above and immediately surrounding Berlin (the Berlin Control Zone), continues to be regulated by Flight Rules dating from 1946. Both the air corridors and the Flight Rules were agreed quadripartitely in the Allied Control Authority. Air access to Berlin remains a four-Power matter; the authorities of the GDR have no rights in relation thereto. The right of access by air is an original right deriving from the joint military defeat of Germany and the assumption of supreme authority with respect to Germany. It has been exercised openly, continuously and without interruption for more than forty years. Air access was not even interrupted during the period of the Berlin blockade; on the contrary the Allies mounted a massive air-lift to overcome the blockade, in which Allied aircraft defied considerable Soviet harassment to keep the air corridors open and Berlin supplied. The régime governing access by air was not affected by the Bolz/Zorin letters of 20 September 1955; nor is it affected by the Quadripartite Agreement of 3 September 1971, under which the situation which has developed with respect to access may not be changed unilaterally.[2] It is therefore necessary to look at the position in 1945 and 1946, and at the practices which have developed in implementation of the agreements made by the four Powers in the immediate post-war period.

ESTABLISHMENT OF THE AIR CORRIDORS

At a meeting on 29 June 1945 the British, American and Soviet Commanders-in-Chief agreed upon the use of two air corridors between Berlin and the Western zones. The question of air access was next considered in the autumn of 1945 by the competent technical bodies of the Allied Control Authority, and ultimately by the Allied Control Council. The Air Directorate drew up a Report

---

[1] Bathurst, *BYIL*, 38(1962), pp.293−305; Ruge, *Das Zugangsrecht der Westmächte auf dem Luftweg nach Berlin* (1968); Deuerlein, *DA*, 2(1969), pp.735−64; Bentzien, *Zeitschrift für Luft- und Weltraumrecht*, 19(1970), pp.11−18 and 28 (1979), pp.327−39; von Przychowski, in: *Berlin translokal*, pp.152−66. See Map 3.

[2] Preamble, third and fourth paragraphs, and Part I, paragraphs 3 and 4 of the Quadripartite Agreement.

on the Creation of a System of Air Corridors to be used for flights
in the Respective Zones of Occupation in Germany,[3] which set out
the history of the matter as follows. The Allied Control Authority
Aviation Committee had prepared and submitted a paper to the Air
Directorate proposing six air corridors: Berlin-Hamburg; Berlin-
Hanover (Bückeburg); Berlin-Frankfurt-on-Main; Berlin-Warsaw;
Berlin-Prague; Berlin-Copenhagen. Each corridor was to be twenty
English miles wide and all were to be used "by aircraft of the four
Allied Nations with full freedom of action". Following consideration
of these proposals, the Air Directorate requested the Co-ordinating
Committee:

> (1) To confirm the proposals for the establishment of air corridors
> West of Berlin as follows: Berlin-Hamburg; Berlin-Bückeburg;
> Berlin-Frankfurt-on-Main, each twenty English miles wide. Flight
> over these routes (corridors) will be conducted without previous
> notice being given, by aircraft of the nations governing Germany.
> (2) To instruct the Air Directorate to compile rules of flight and
> means of safeguarding flights along the corridors stated in paragraph
> (1) above.
> (3) To decide in principle, or transmit for consideration by
> appropriate higher authority, the question of the establishment of the
> air corridors over occupied Germany, Berlin-Warsaw, Berlin-Prague,
> Berlin-Copenhagen, and also the air corridor Bückeburg-Prague
> proposed by the British representative (as indicated in annexed Map
> A). Flights over these routes (corridors) will be conducted by aircraft
> of the nations governing Germany without previous notice being
> given.[4]

The Air Directorate's Report was considered by the Co-ordinating
Committee on 27 November 1945. General Robertson explained
that it was absolutely essential for the British to have air corridors
both for flights from Berlin to Bückeburg, Headquarters of the
British Army of the Rhine, and from Berlin to Hamburg, where the
Headquarters had a number of branches. General Clay pointed out
that the Berlin-Bückeburg air corridor was also important for the
Americans since it enabled them to maintain their connection with
Bremen. General Sokolovsky stated that he was not empowered to
settle questions concerning the other air corridors mentioned in the
paper, namely Berlin-Warsaw, Berlin-Prague, Berlin-Copenhagen
and Bückeburg-Prague, as these required decisions at governmental
level. On General Sokolovsky's proposal, the Committee approved
the Report of the Air Directorate and agreed to submit it to the

---

[3] CORC/P(45)170: *Selected Documents* I, p.60; *US Documents*, p. 69; Heidelmeyer, p.32. See
also Bathurst, *BYIL*, 38 (1962), pp.296–8.
[4] Paragraph 6 of CORC/P(45)170.

Control Council for confirmation of that portion which dealt with air corridors from Berlin to the west.[5]

At its meeting on 30 November 1945, the Allied Control Council had before it a paper on Proposed Air Routes for Inter-Zonal Flights.[6] After Marshal Zhukov had recalled that the Co-ordinating Committee had approved the establishment of three air corridors, namely Berlin-Hamburg, Berlin-Bückeburg and Berlin-Frankfurt-on-Main, the meeting approved these three corridors as defined in the paper.[7] The location of the three corridors[8] has remained unchanged since 1945. The northern and central corridors go from Berlin to Hamburg and Bückeburg (just beyond Hanover) in the former British zone, and the southern corridor goes to Frankfurt in the former American zone. As originally agreed, each corridor is twenty English miles wide. There is no upper limit to the corridors.

THE 1946 FLIGHT RULES

After the establishment of the three air corridors, further technical measures were taken by the Allied Control Authority. In December 1945, the Co-ordinating Committee agreed to the setting up of the Berlin Air Safety Center (BASC), which began to operate in February 1946. At the same time, a Berlin Control Zone was created, covering the whole of the air space up to 10,000 feet (3,000 metres) over Greater Berlin and a surrounding area of the Soviet zone. On 18 December 1945 the Air Directorate approved Rules of Flight for Aircraft Flying in the Corridors and the Berlin Control Zone.[9] These Rules were slightly revised in January 1946 and again on 22 October 1946, when they were issued as DAIR/P(45)71 Second Revise.[10] This document still provides the only quadripartitely agreed rules concerning flight in the corridors and the Berlin Control Zone, though in addition certain practices have developed.

The object of the Flight Rules, which were based on Annex

---

[5] CORC/M(45)23, agenda item 309 "Proposed Air Routes for Inter-Zonal Flights": *Selected Documents* I , p.63; Heidelmeyer, p.35.

[6] CONL/P(45)63: *US Documents*, p.72; Heidelmeyer, p.35; to which was attached the Report of the Air Directorate in CORC/P(45)170.

[7] CONL/M(45)13, agenda item 110 "Proposed Air Routes for Inter-Zonal Flights": *Selected Documents* I, p.63; *US Documents*, p.72; Heidelmeyer, p.36.

[8] Western proposals for further air corridors were turned down by the Soviet member of the Allied Control Authority Air Directorate on 30 April 1946: see DAIR/M(46)11: *US Documents*, pp.78, 82; Heidelmeyer, p.39.

[9] *US Documents*, p.75.

[10] Flight Rules by Allied Control Authority Air Directorate for Aircraft Flying in the Air Corridors in Germany and Berlin Control Zone, October 22, 1946: *US Documents*, p.99; Heidelmeyer, p.39.

2 to the Chicago Convention, is stated in paragraph 1 as follows:

> To ensure the maximum safety in flight of all aircraft flying in the
> corridors and in the Berlin Control Zone under all conditions.

Paragraph 2 notes the establishment of the three air corridors, each
of which is "20 English miles (32 kilometers) wide, ie. 10 miles (16
kilometers) each side of the center line". Paragraph 3(a) defines the
Berlin Control Zone as:

> the air space between ground level and 10,000 feet (3000 meters)
> within a radius of 20 miles (32 kilometers) from the Allied Control
> Authority Building in which is established the Berlin Air Safety
> Center (BASC).

The Berlin Control Zone covers all the air space up to 10,000 feet
over the special Berlin area, as well as over part of what is now the
GDR, including the air space over Schönefeld Airport (the main
airport serving the Eastern Sector, which lies outside Greater
Berlin). Paragraph 3(b) provides that the Berlin Control Zone is a
zone of free flight for all aircraft entering the Zone to land on the
Berlin airfields or taking off to depart therefrom. This means that
the rights of the four Powers to fly aircraft into and out of the
Berlin Control Zone are unrestricted, and subject only to observance
of the 1946 Flight Rules – including the 10,000 foot ceiling in the
Berlin Control Zone and the requirement to notify the Berlin Air
Safety Center of all flights entering or leaving the Zone.

Paragraph 3(c) of the Flight Rules states that:

> It is desirable that, whenever possible, local flights (testing, training,
> etc.) be executed above the national sectors. However, if necessary
> they may be executed above the remainder of the Control Zone,
> subject to normal clearance by the Berlin Air Safety Center.

Western Allied aircraft, both military and civil, use the whole of the
Berlin Control Zone if this is necessary for the purpose of their
flights. The Soviet Union carries out no regular military or civil
flights over the Western Sectors of Berlin.[11]

Paragraph 3(d) of the Flight Rules establishes "Airdrome Traffic
Zones" with rules for the safety of Allied aircraft while flying within
the Berlin Control Zone. These Zones cover the air space up to and
including 2,650 feet (800 metres) above the area having a radius of
2 miles from the centre of the main traffic airfields in the Berlin
Control Zone. No aircraft are to enter an Airdrome Traffic Zone
except for the purpose of landing at the airfield concerned; and no

---

[11] For an Allied protest against provocative overflight, see *US Documents*, p.893. For an
example of Allied flight within the Berlin Control Zone but over the GDR, see Catudal,
Kennedy and the Wall Crisis, p.135.

Allied aircraft are to "approach an airfield, other than their own, closer than a radius of 2 miles, or at a height of less than 2,650 feet (800 meters) without having obtained prior permission from the Berlin Air Safety Center". The rules on Airdrome Traffic Zones apply not only to the three airfields in the Western Sectors of Berlin (Tegel, Tempelhof and Gatow) but also to others within the Berlin Control Zone (including Schönefeld).[12]

Paragraph 4 of the Flight Rules notes that:

> The Berlin Air Safety Center has been established in the Allied Control Authority Building with the object of ensuring safety of flight for all aircraft in the Berlin area. The Safety Center regulates all flying in the Berlin Control Zone and also in the corridors extending from Berlin to the boundaries of adjacent control zones.

Paragraph 5 provides that control of aircraft traffic by the Berlin Air Safety Center is normally exercised through the appropriate national airfield in the Berlin Control Zone. Further provisions of the Flight Rules specify in more detail the functions of the Center, which was originally intended as the main Berlin air traffic control centre. In March 1949 it delegated the practical control of air traffic to the Berlin Air Route Traffic Control Center (BARTCC), which is located at Tempelhof Airport and operated by officers of the US Air Force with a staff of Western Allied air traffic controllers. But the Berlin Air Safety Center continues to be responsible for clearing all flights, whether Allied or non-Allied, in the corridors and the Berlin Control Zone. As aircraft of the four Powers are entitled to fly without restriction in the corridors, clearance cannot be withheld from such aircraft.

The remainder of the 1946 Flight Rules (paragraphs 6 to 70) consists of detailed general flight rules, visual flight rules and instrument flight rules, together with definitions of terms used.

Although in the early post-war years there were occasional quadripartite discussions about modifying the arrangements of 1945 and 1946, nothing came of them. There have been no changes of substance in these arrangements, nor have they been affected by any subsequent arrangements which any of the four Powers has entered into with other States.

THE BONN/PARIS CONVENTIONS AND SUBSEQUENT WESTERN ARRANGEMENTS

The Bonn/Paris Conventions of 1952/54 between the three

---

[12] However, the East German authorities long ago established separate controlled air space around Schönefeld Airport, which overlaps the Berlin Control Zone.

Powers and the Federal Republic of Germany[13] specifically reserved the rights of the Allies with regard to access to Berlin by air. In Chapter 12 of the Convention on the Settlement of Matters arising out of the War and the Occupation, the Federal Republic of Germany assumed responsibility in the field of civil aviation in the Federal territory, except for air traffic to or from the Berlin air corridors.[14] Article 5 of Chapter 12 provides:

> In the exercise of their responsibilities with respect to Berlin, the Three Powers will continue to regulate all air traffic to and from the Berlin air corridors established by the Allied Control Authority. The Federal Republic undertakes to facilitate and assist such traffic in every way on a basis no less favourable than that enjoyed on the entry into force of the present Convention; it undertakes to facilitate and assist unlimited and unimpeded passage through its air space for aircraft of the Three Powers en route to and from Berlin. The Federal Republic agrees to permit any necessary technical stops by such aircraft and further agrees that such aircraft may carry passengers, cargo and mail between places outside the Federal Republic and Berlin, and between the Federal Republic and Berlin.[15]

The functions of the Allied Embassies in Bonn, in the exercise of the rights and responsibilities retained by the three Powers in the field of civil aviation, are carried out by the Civil Air Attachés of the three Embassies. The three Civil Air Attachés act jointly. Their main task is to approve all civil flights through the air corridors, including such matters as tariffs and schedules. Air carriers of the three Powers who wish to operate flights to Berlin require prior permission, and should apply for this to their respective Embassy in Bonn.[16]

Regular consultations take place, in accordance with Article 6 of the Relations Convention, between Allied and West German authorities in the Berlin Civil Air Transport Advisory Group (BCATAG), which was established in 1972 and is composed of representatives of the three Powers and of the Federal Government, with an official of the *Senat* also present. The BCATAG is advisory only, but its terms of reference allow it to provide advice on both scheduled and non-scheduled commercial operations by Allied carriers, and on the question of scheduled operations by non-Allied carriers.

---

[13] Cmd. 9368. Article 2 of the Relations Convention contains a general reservation of Allied rights.
[14] And in respect of Soviet aircraft: see p.25 above.
[15] Cmd. 9368, p.103; *US Documents*, p.430; Heidelmeyer, p.140.
[16] Heidelmeyer, p.149.

THE BOLZ/ZORIN LETTERS

A specific reservation concerning air access to Berlin was included in the Bolz/Zorin exchange of letters of 20 September 1955, by which the Soviet Union purported to transfer to the East German authorities certain functions connected with access. The final paragraph of the letters stated that:

> The movement of military personnel and freight of the garrisons of the three Western Powers in West Berlin will be permitted on the basis of the existing four-Power agreements:
>
> ...
>
> (c) in the air corridors: Berlin-Hamburg, Berlin-Bückeburg and Berlin-Frankfurt-on-Main.[17]

In Notes to the Soviet Union dated 3 October 1955, the Western Allies stated that the Bolz/Zorin letters "cannot have the effect of discharging the USSR from the responsibilities which it has assumed in matters concerning transportation and communications between the different parts of Germany, including Berlin".[18] In practice, air access to Berlin has continued to be an exclusively quadripartite matter, and the existing four-Power arrangements were unaffected by the Bolz/Zorin exchange of letters.

SOVIET CLAIMS TO LIMIT AIR ACCESS

There have, however, been a number of differences between the Western Allies and the Soviet Union about air access. Whilst not attempting to prevent such access altogether, the Soviet Union has in various ways and at various times sought to limit use of the corridors.

First, the Soviet Union has alleged that Allied aircraft may not fly in the corridors at an altitude higher than 10,000 feet (3,050 metres). On 4 April 1959, the Soviet Government protested to the United States Government about high level flights in the Berlin-Frankfurt corridor, asserting that 3,050 metres "is the maximum for flights of the Western Powers using the air corridors".[19] In its reply of 13 April 1959,[20] the United States Government rejected "the Soviet contention that flights above 10,000 feet are precluded by regulations covering flights in the corridors", and continued:

> Flights by aircraft of the United States do not require any prior agreement from the Soviet Element [in the Berlin Air Safety Center],

---

[17] *Selected Documents* I, p.228; *US Documents*, p.460; Heidelmeyer, p.174.
[18] *Selected Documents* I, p.230; *US Documents*, p.462; Heidelmeyer, p.175.
[19] *Selected Documents* I, p.384; *US Documents*, p.617; Heidelmeyer *Dokumente*, p.431.
[20] *Selected Documents* I, p.385; *US Documents*, p.619; Heidelmeyer *Dokumente*, p.433.

and the United States never has recognised and does not recognise any limitation to the right to fly at any altitude in the corridors.

This continues to be the position of the Western Allies. The 1946 Flight Rules provide for no maximum altitude for flight in the corridors, though minimum altitudes are specified in certain circumstances.[21] However, in normal conditions Allied aircraft do generally fly below 10,000 feet.[22]

Second, the Soviet Union has sought to reserve to itself certain flight levels in the corridors during specified periods of time. In aide-mémoires to the Soviet Union dated 15 February 1962, the Western Allies protested against such attempts by the Soviet authorities in the Berlin Air Safety Center, pointing out that:

> Any effort by one of the Four Powers to arrogate to itself the exclusive use of flight levels for any period of time is entirely unacceptable. Such a practice would amount to an arbitrary limitation on the free use of air corridors by the aircraft of the Three Western Powers as guaranteed by Quadripartite Agreements.[23]

The problem of separating Soviet and Western flights in the air corridors, and of allotting appropriate flight levels in the interests of flight safety, is of continuing concern.[24] The question is essentially one of management by the four Powers in the Berlin Air Safety Center; the Western Allies have consistently maintained their legal position as set out in the aide-mémoires of 15 February 1962.

Third, the Soviet Union and GDR have from time to time claimed that the air corridors were set up only to provide, temporarily, for the Western Allied troops stationed in Berlin.[25] This claim was first made during the blockade.[26] An East German declaration of 29 August 1960 also made such an assertion, complaining that the corridors were being misused "for the carrying of militarists and revanchists from West Germany to West Berlin".[27] In a statement issued on 3 September 1960, the three Allied Ambassadors in Bonn pointed out that:

> The air corridors were established by a quadripartite decision of the

---

[21] Paragraphs 16, 24, 25 and 40 of the Rules.

[22] The practice of flying below 10,000 feet, which now tends to be observed as a matter of discretion on the part of the Allies, originated in the first years after the war, when the types of aircraft then operating flew well under 10,000 feet. As noted above, however, no legal limit of 10,000 feet was imposed for flight in the corridors (as opposed to the 10,000 foot maximum altitude for flight in the Berlin Control Zone, imposed by the 1946 Flight Rules). See Mahnke, *DA*, 5 (1972), pp.364–71.

[23] *Selected Documents* II, p.43; *BPIL* 1962, p.41; *US Documents*, p.804.

[24] See, for example, *BPIL* 1965, p.88; *BYIL*, 55 (1984), p.524. For an early incident see Cmd. 7384.

[25] Bentzien, *Zeitschrift für Luft- und Weltraumrecht*, 28 (1979), p.330; Heidelmeyer *Dokumente*, p.552.

[26] Heidelmeyer, p.85.

[27] *Selected Documents* I, p.432.

Allied Control Council on November 30, 1945, and they are no concern whatever of the East Germans. The Allied Control Council approved the creation of the three presently existing corridors for use by aircraft of the nations governing Germany. There has been no subsequent change in the status of the corridors. The three Allied Powers acknowledge no restriction on the use of the Berlin air corridors by their aircraft.[28]

When the Soviet Government took up the East German complaint in a Note of 26 September 1960,[29] the Western Allies reiterated that they had the right to use the air corridors without restriction.[30]

The Soviet Union reverted to the same point in a Note of 23 August 1961, alleging that the air corridors were being used to send "revanchists, extremists, subverters, spies, and saboteurs of all kinds" from the Federal Republic of Germany to West Berlin. The Note continued:

> Thus the United States, Britain, and France are patently abusing their position in West Berlin, profiting from the absence of control on the air communications. As a result there has been a gross violation of the Agreement reached in 1945 under which, as is well-known, air corridors were assigned to the three Western Powers, temporarily, for the supplying of the needs of their military garrisons ...[31]

In their Notes of 26 August 1961 in reply, the Western Allies protested strongly "against the suggestion that the purposes for which the Western Allies use the air corridors are within the competence of the Soviet Union". The corridors had been "established in 1945 by decision of the four-Power Allied Control Council as the manner in which the unrestricted right of air access to Berlin would be exercised by the Western Powers", and there had "never been any limitation whatsoever placed upon their use by the aircraft of the Western Powers".[32]

A further Soviet Note of 2 September 1961 amplified the assertions made in the earlier Note, and attacked commercial flights by Allied carriers:

> It is apparent from the documents of the Control Council that the air corridors between Berlin and the Western Occupation Zones of Germany which are now in use were temporarily provided solely for meeting the needs of the military garrisons of Britain, the United States, and France in West Berlin, and for ensuring the communications of these garrisons with and the transportation of

---

[28] *Selected Documents* I, p.433; *US Documents*, p.716; Heidelmeyer, p.266.
[29] *Selected Documents* I, p.437; *US Documents*, p.720.
[30] Identical Notes of 26 October 1960: *Selected Documents* I, p. 440; *US Documents*, p.722.
[31] *Selected Documents* I, p.473; *US Documents*, p.783; Heidelmeyer, p.296.
[32] *Selected Documents* I, p.474; *US Documents*, p.785; Heidelmeyer, p.298.

their personnel and freight to the headquarters of the occupation forces of the corresponding Powers in West Germany. This is referred to, in particular, in the unanimously adopted decision of November 30, 1945 of the Control Council on the Report of the Military Air Directorate. No quadripartite decisions on uncontrolled commercial air-flights along the air corridors or on the transportation along them of any German personnel or of persons not serving with the Occupation Authorities of the three Powers or, *a fortiori*, of West German revanchists and militarists were passed by the Control Council, and such decisions do not exist in actuality.[33]

In Notes of 8 September 1961[34] the Western Allies set out their legal position in some detail, dealing in particular with their right to operate civil flights along the corridors to and from Berlin. They emphasised the basis of their rights of air access to Berlin:

> Rights with respect to air access to Berlin derive from precisely the same source as do the rights of the USSR in East Germany and East Berlin, namely the joint military defeat of the German *Reich* and the joint assumption of supreme authority over Germany. These rights are confirmed by the circumstances under which the four Powers entered Germany, by their subsequent discussions and agreements, and by open and established practice over a period of fifteen years.

They pointed out that the Air Directorate Report referred to in the Soviet Note proposed air corridors "which could be used by aircraft of the four Allied nations with full freedom of action". After referring to the decision of the Control Council of 30 November 1945 approving the establishment of the three air corridors, the Notes continued:

> Contrary to what is alleged by the Soviet Government, which now finds this decision inconvenient, there is no reference in this decision or in the report of the Air Directorate to any limitation upon the use of the air corridors either as regards their duration or as regards the goods or persons to be transported by aircraft of Allied nations.
>
> Thus, from the earliest days, the Soviet Union recognised that the air corridors were to be used "by aircraft of the four Allied nations with full freedom of action". This understanding is confirmed in the records of subsequent quadripartite meetings. For example, at the meeting of the Air Directorate on April 30, 1946, the Soviet delegate, Lt.General Kutsevalov, stated:
>
> > "The Soviet Delegation thinks that the existing system of air routes through the Soviet Zone of occupation in Germany is fully sufficient, not only to meet the requirements of the Allied troops in the Sector of Greater Berlin, but also to carry out successfully all

---

[33] *Selected Documents* I, p.477; *US Documents*, p.788; Heidelmeyer, p.301.
[34] *Selected Documents* I, p.479; *US Documents*, p.789; Heidelmeyer, p.303.

the Allied transportation needs for commercial cargoes regardless of their volume."

The Notes then added:

In February 1947, in connection with preparations for the Council of Ministers Meeting, the Western Powers renewed a recommendation for establishing additional air corridors for civil flights to Berlin by aircraft of nations other than the four Powers. The Soviet Union objected, on the ground, as stated in the USSR report dated February 5, 1947,[35] that the quadripartite decisions establishing the three air corridors provided adequate facilities to meet existing requirements. The Soviet Union thus recognised that the air corridors were legitimately used by the civil aircraft of the Allied Powers. The practice of the Western Powers is equally significant in confirming the understanding as to air access. Civil aircraft of the Allied nations had been flying to and from Berlin on special charter-flights from the early days of the occupation. British European Airways inaugurated regular flights to Berlin on September 1, 1946, and in the first year of operation carried out 286 round-trip flights.[36] In 1948 there were 549 round-trip flights by all carriers; in 1949 there were 4,776; in 1950 there were 6,974. All of these flights were processed as a matter of routine through the Berlin Air Safety Center on which the Soviet Union is represented. Civil air flights to Berlin continued unrestricted throughout the Berlin blockade and thereafter.

A fourth type of restriction sought by the Soviet Union concerns non-stop flights from Berlin to points outside Germany. The Soviet authorities have claimed that such international scheduled and charter flights by Allied carriers are not permissible. Thus, the Soviet Union protested when Pan-Am commenced direct flights between Berlin and New York in 1964, and the Allies responded that the right of access included unrestricted flights by Allied aircraft, regardless of destination; the part of these flights lying west of the Berlin air corridors was of no concern to the Soviet authorities.[37] Direct international flights now take place to many destinations, including the United Kingdom, France and the United States, as well as Spain, Turkey and other holiday destinations.

Although on occasion, particularly during periods of tension (for example during the blockade and the second Berlin crisis of 1958–62), there has been some Soviet harassment of commercial

[35] US Documents, p.113.
[36] In the US Note this sentence reads: "On 20th May, 1946, the American Overseas Airlines inaugurated regular weekly flights. In 1947 there were 52 such flights by Pan-American World Airways." Air France began services on 5 January 1950.
[37] Soviet Note of 20 June 1964 and Allied replies of 22 August 1964: BPIL 1964, p.275. See also Heidelmeyer Dokumente, pp.552–3. See generally Bentzien, Zeitschrift für Luft- und Weltraumrecht, 28(1979), p.330.

flights in the corridors,[38] there have been no serious attempts to interfere with such flights for many years. The Soviet Union occasionally repeats its view that commercial flights are not permitted, and the Western Allies consistently reaffirm their unrestricted right to use the corridors for whatever purpose they see fit. In practice, all scheduled passenger services to West Berlin are, to this day, flown through the corridors by British, American and French carriers – principally by British Airways, Pan-Am and Air France. There are also several charter flights and commercial cargo flights by Western Allied air companies.

FLIGHTS TO BERLIN BY NON-ALLIED AIRCRAFT

As regards non-Allied aircraft, the three Powers, in the exercise of their responsibilities under Article 5 of Chapter 12 of the Settlement Convention, undertook that applications–

> for the authorisation of air traffic to and from the Berlin air corridors by aircraft of Powers other than the United Kingdom, the United States, the French Republic and the Union of Soviet Socialist Republics will be approved only after notification by the Federal Government to the representatives of the United Kingdom, the United States and the French Republic that the Federal Government is willing to grant the right to overfly the Federal territory.[39]

In a communication dated 5 May 1955 from the Allied High Commission Civil Aviation Board to the Federal German authorities, it was stated that air carriers registered in States other than the three Powers required prior permission to operate flights to Berlin. Permission must be sought–

> (a) for that portion of the flight over the territory of the Federal Republic of Germany, from the Federal Ministry of Transport; and
> (b) for that portion of the flight along a Berlin corridor and entry into the Berlin Control Zone, from either the British, French or United States Embassy in Bonn; and
> (c) operators must obtain authorisation for their proposed flight from "the Military Authorities, Berlin".[40]

The only regular non-four-Power flights along the corridors were conducted by the Polish airline LOT, which operated a regular service from Berlin to London before the corridors were established

---

[38] See, for example, the incidents referred to in *BPIL* 1962, p. 41; Mahnke, *DA*, 5(1972), pp.144–5; shooting of French plane on 29 April 1952, Mahnke, *DA*, 5(1972), p.365.

[39] Letters from the three High Commissioners to the Federal Chancellor dated 23 October 1954: Cmd. 9368, p.169; Heidelmeyer, p.140.

[40] Heidelmeyer, p.149. Note that the requirement in sub-paragraph (c) for "authorisation" of flight does not apply to flights by British, United States and French aircraft.

and continued to do so thereafter with the special agreement of the Allied Control Authority. There have been no LOT flights in the corridors since 1981. North-south flights to Berlin (that is, flights that neither follow nor cross the corridors, at any level) are a separate issue. The Allies have on occasion granted landing rights for such flights, but GDR permission for flight over its territory has not been forthcoming. Thus in 1972 Austrian Airlines and SAS were granted landing rights, as subsequently were KLM and THY.[41]

Flight to Berlin by German aircraft is inhibited by the demilitarised status of the city; in addition, nothing should be done which could weaken the vitally important corridor access régime.[42] The Western Allies have frequently had occasion to protest to the Soviet Union against flights by GDR helicopters in the Berlin Control Zone which had not been authorised by the four Powers and which, if over Greater Berlin, violated the demilitarised status of Berlin.[43]

[41] Bentzien, *Zeitschrift für Luft- und Weltraumrecht*, 28(1979), p. 337; Mahncke, *Berlin im geteilten Deutschland*, pp.214–18.

[42] Officials of the West German airline Lufthansa have from time to time indicated interest in flying to Berlin, for example on the Frankfurt-Moscow route. On the significance, in this regard, of the FRG-USSR Air Services Agreement of 11 November 1971 see Bentzien, *Zeitschrift für Luft- und Weltraumrecht*, 28(1979), pp.337–8.

[43] Bentzien, *Zeitschrift für Luft- und Weltraumrecht*, 28(1979), p. 337.

CHAPTER 9

ACCESS BY ROAD, RAIL AND WATERWAY

WHILE the inherent right of access applies to all access by road, rail and waterway,[1] the practical arrangements that have developed over the years differ as between military and civilian traffic. In particular, those provisions of the Quadripartite Agreement of 3 September 1971 that deal specifically with access, as well as the related Transit Traffic Agreement between the Federal Republic of Germany and GDR, do not apply to military traffic. It is therefore convenient to consider military and civilian surface access separately.

MILITARY TRAFFIC

Access to Berlin by Allied surface military traffic (including that of civilians, such as Allied dependents and civilian officials, travelling under the sponsorship of and with documentation issued by the Allied authorities) takes place by road and rail; no military traffic in practice uses the waterways. The arrangements and practices which had evolved since 1945 for military traffic by road and rail were not affected by the Quadripartite Agreement of 3 September 1971, but the situation which had developed with respect to such traffic may not be changed unilaterally.[2]

Access by road

On 29 June 1945 Western Allied and Soviet military commanders agreed upon arrangements for the entry into Berlin of Western Allied troops in conjunction with the evacuation by the latter of the areas of the Soviet zone then occupied by them. It was agreed that the *Autobahn* between Helmstedt and Berlin would be available for the movement of Allied troops to take up their stations in the Western Sectors of Berlin.[3] The practice of Allied use of this *Autobahn* between Berlin and the Western zones dates from this agreement, and has continued thereafter except during the blockade. The arrangements were restored after the lifting of the blockade in accordance with the 1949 New York and Paris

---

[1] See Chapter 7 above. For a Soviet view of surface transit traffic, see Vysotsky, *West Berlin*, pp.277–92.
[2] Preamble, third and fourth paragraphs, and Part I, paragraphs 3 and 4, of the Quadripartite Agreement.
[3] The participants took their own records of the arrangements, but there was no agreed record: *US Documents*, p.42; Heidelmeyer, p.31.

agreements, and have been maintained continuously and with minimal interference since then.[4]

The Berlin-Helmstedt *Autobahn* runs for about 106 miles through GDR territory. Western Allied checkpoints are maintained at Dreilinden in the American Sector (Checkpoint Bravo) and at Helmstedt in the Federal Republic (Checkpoint Alpha). Soviet checkpoints are maintained on GDR territory at Drewitz (between Potsdam and Berlin) and at Marienborn (just over the border from Helmstedt). Allied military traffic is processed only by these Western and Soviet checkpoints, all of which are manned by military personnel. The Berlin-Helmstedt *Autobahn* is now the only road access route in practice used by military traffic.

Access by rail

By a decision of 10 September 1945,[5] the Allied Control Council approved an arrangement recommended by its Transport Directorate concerning rail access to Berlin,[6] which provided for the movement under Russian control and supervision of thirteen trains a day for the purposes of supplying the population of the Western Sectors of Berlin, and three trains a day for the Western Allied forces in Berlin. All rail traffic was to use the Helmstedt-Berlin line. The practice of Western Allied military trains using this line arose from this arrangement, and has continued since 1945 except during the blockade. As with road traffic, the arrangements were thereafter restored pursuant to the 1949 New York and Paris agreements (with some agreed adjustments to correspond with the practices which had developed and were in effect before 1 March 1948) and they have been maintained continuously and with minimal interference since 1949.

The Western Allied authorities operate military trains for both passengers and goods along the Berlin-Helmstedt line.[7] The operation of these trains and payment for services rendered in respect of them remain a quadripartite responsibility. Trains are processed only by the Western Allied authorities in Berlin and

---

[4] For examples of interference, see *US Documents*, pp.857, 858.

[5] CONL/M(45)5.

[6] CONL/P(45)27: *US Documents*, p.65; Heidelmeyer *Dokumente*, p.40.

[7] At present, the British military passenger train runs once daily in each direction between Berlin (Charlottenburg Station) and Brunswick (Braunschweig); American military passenger trains run daily in each direction between Berlin (Lichterfelde-West Station) and both Frankfurt and Bremerhaven; and the French military passenger train runs three times a week between Berlin (Tegel Station) and Strasbourg. Western Allied military goods trains run between Berlin and the Federal Republic of Germany as required, but less frequently than the passenger trains. (The British goods train runs from Spandau Station instead of Charlottenburg Station.)

Helmstedt and the Soviet authorities at Marienborn Station. Since 1949 the trains have been pulled through GDR territory by East German (*Deutsche Reichsbahn*) locomotives manned by East German crews. By Western Allied direction, payments for this service are made by the (West German) *Deutsche Bundesbahn*. For many years increases were negotiated and agreed from time to time by the two railway administrations, acting under four-Power auspices. The matter was simplified for the future when the two railway administrations negotiated agreements containing an automatic adjustment formula, for passenger trains in 1981 and for goods trains in 1984. The negotiations leading to these agreements were authorised in advance by the four Powers; and in each case the four Powers approved the resulting arrangements.[8]

CIVILIAN TRAFFIC

Access to Berlin by surface civilian traffic takes place by road, rail and waterway (see Map 3). Arrangements and practices for such traffic were worked out by the four Powers soon after the end of the war. After the lifting of the blockade, these were restored in accordance with the 1949 New York and Paris agreements. In 1955 the Soviet Union purported to transfer responsibility for the control of civilian traffic to the East German authorities; the Western Allies have never accepted the lawfulness of this transfer. In the Quadripartite Agreement of 3 September 1971 the Soviet Union unequivocally accepted its responsibility for unimpeded access by civilian traffic, and the four Powers authorised the competent German authorities (that is, the Federal Republic of Germany and GDR) to negotiate and conclude the Transit Traffic Agreement, which contains detailed arrangements implementing and supplementing the relevant provisions of the Quadripartite Agreement. These two Agreements in no way prejudice the inherent right of access or supersede the existing quadripartite agreements, in particular the 1949 New York and Paris agreements; but they regulate such traffic in detail, and are supplemented by further detailed inner-German arrangements concluded with the concurrence of the four Powers. The more significant of these provisions will be considered later in this Chapter, as they are common to all civilian traffic. Before doing so it is necessary to mention the arrangements and practices that had developed before 1971 in respect of each of the three types of access route available to surface civilian traffic.

---

[8] Thus in 1981 the US Assistant Secretary of State referred to the "four-power agreement on railway tariffs": *US Documents*, p.1336.

Access by road

On 29 May 1946 the Allied Control Authority Co-ordinating Committee agreed that civilian self-propelled vehicles would be allowed to move between the zones of occupation provided that the driver and passengers had the necessary Inter-Zonal Travel Permits and that the movement of goods had been authorised by the appropriate authorities in each zone concerned.[9] Extensive road traffic moved between Berlin and the Western zones in the years before the blockade, and this was restored thereafter.

The four road access routes available for civilian traffic are as follows:

The Berlin-Helmstedt *Autobahn*, with crossing points at Dreilinden/Drewitz and Marienborn/Helmstedt.[10]

The Berlin-Hof *Autobahn*, with crossing points at Dreilinden/Drewitz and Hirschberg/Hof (Rudolfstein).[11]

The Berlin-Herleshausen route. This follows the Berlin-Hof *Autobahn* to the Gera turn-off, then turns westwards on an *Autobahn* to the crossing point at Wartha/Herleshausen.[11]

The Berlin-Hamburg route. The route used to follow Highway 5, with crossing points at Staaken and Horst/Lauenburg. Since November 1982 it follows a new *Autobahn*, with crossing points at Staaken (to be replaced in due course by Heiligensee/Stolpe-Süd) and Zarrentin/Gudow.[12]

In addition to checking identity cards, driving licences and vehicle documentation, from June 1968 the East German authorities required civilian road travellers to obtain transit visas. The visa was originally paid for individually, and endorsed on annexes to the

[9] CORC/P(46)189: *US Documents*, p.87. In practice the vehicle registration number was endorsed on the Inter-Zonal Travel Permit, and consignments of goods were accompanied by official documents (*Warenbegleitscheine*). On Inter-Zonal Travel Permits, see the note in Heidelmeyer *Dokumente*, p.598.

[10] The *Autobahn* was improved and modernised in accordance with an inner-German arrangement of 19 December 1975: *Zehn Jahre Deutschlandpolitik*, p.290.

[11] Sections of the route were improved and modernised in accordance with inner-German arrangements of 30 April 1980 and 15 August 1985: see *Bulletin der Bundesregierung*, 30 April 1980 and 15 August 1985.

[12] The new *Autobahn* route was established and necessary construction carried out in accordance with an inner-German arrangement of 16 November 1978: *Zehn Jahre Deutschlandpolitik*, p.343. Because of environmental difficulties in Berlin, the Staaken crossing point remains temporarily in use pending the opening of a new crossing point at Heiligensee/Stolpe-Süd.

temporary identity cards of residents of the Western Sectors of Berlin and in the passports of other travellers, including residents of the Federal Republic. In addition the East Germans imposed a toll for use of the road access routes and a tax adjustment levy (*Steuerausgleichsabgabe*) for the commercial transport of persons and goods. For consignments of goods an accompanying official document (*Warenbegleitschein*) was necessary, approved in Berlin by the Senator for Commerce or in the Federal Republic by the appropriate *Land* authority. East German customs officials checked that the goods carried conformed to the accompanying document, although after 1960 this was done by random sample checking.

Access by rail

As noted above, by its decision of 10 September 1945, the Allied Control Council approved an arrangement including thirteen goods trains a day for the purposes of supplying the population of the Western Sectors of Berlin. All these trains were to use the Berlin-Helmstedt line. In fact, the number of trains was increased during 1947-48 to a maximum of nineteen per day (including military trains), and included trains carrying non-Allied civilian passengers. After the blockade, four-Power agreement was reached to restore thirteen goods trains, plus one civilian passenger train, per day, which together with the military trains was regarded as representing the practice before 1 March 1948. The Soviet authorities insisted that henceforth all trains be pulled through GDR territory by East German (*Deutsche Reichsbahn*) locomotives manned by East German crews, and this has continued ever since.

In 1949 an agreement was reached between the *Deutsche Reichsbahn* and *Deutsche Bundesbahn* providing for additional civilian passenger trains between Berlin and the Federal Republic and new routes and crossing points. Daily passenger services were instituted on lines to Cologne (via Magdeburg and Helmstedt), Hamburg (via Wittenberge and Büchen), Munich (via Leipzig and Ludwigsstadt), and Frankfurt-on-Main (via Halle, Erfurt and Bebra). In June 1954 a further agreement between the German railway administrations added more passenger trains, and sleeping and dining car services were introduced. The two railway administrations have since held regular train scheduling negotiations.

Berlin goods traffic continued to go by way of Helmstedt/ Marienborn under quadripartite arrangements until 5 July 1965, when a new freight agreement between the *Deutsche Reichsbahn* and *Deutsche Bundesbahn* came into force. This agreement provided for daily goods trains for Berlin via Helmstedt, and added new goods trains via Schwanheide/Büchen, Gerstungen/Bebra and Gutenfürst/ Hof.

The railway access routes available for civilian traffic are as follows:

Berlin to Brunswick (Braunschweig), with crossing points at Kohlhasenbrück/Griebnitzsee[13] and Marienborn/Helmstedt.

Berlin to Hamburg, with crossing points at Staaken[14] and Schwanheide/Büchen.

Berlin to Frankfurt-on-Main, with crossing points at Kohl-hasenbrück/Griebnitzsee[13] and Gerstungen/Bebra.

Berlin to Munich, with crossing points at Kohlhasenbrück/Griebnitzsee[13] and Gutenfürst/Hof.

Berlin to Munich, with crossing points at Kohlhasenbrück/Griebnitzsee and Probstzella/Ludwigsstadt.

The last-mentioned route is used only by passenger trains, the others by passenger and goods trains. As with civilian transit traffic by road, from June 1968 the GDR authorities required rail travellers to obtain transit visas when using the access routes. The official documents required for goods traffic by rail were similar to those for civilian road traffic.

Access by waterway[15]

Berlin lies between the Elbe and Oder, and the main waterways connecting them run through the city. In addition, Berlin has long been an important inland port. It has waterway links with the Federal Republic of Germany, the GDR, Poland and Czechoslovakia. A considerable proportion of the goods coming into the Western Sectors arrives by waterway.

Waterway transport between Berlin and the Western zones was originally regulated by an Allied Control Authority Co-ordinating Committee decision of 16 May 1946,[16] which set out the principles of "maximum efficiency of movement consistent with safe and economic operation" and uniform documentation and tariffs for all

---

[13] GDR processing of passenger trains is done at Griebnitzsee Station, and of goods trains at Seddin Station.
[14] The Staaken crossing point was opened for trains to and from Hamburg in September 1976 in accordance with an inner-German arrangement of 19 December 1975: *Zehn Jahre Deutschlandpolitik*, p.290.
[15] See the note in Heidelmeyer *Dokumente*, pp.597–8.
[16] CORC/P(46)59 Final: *US Documents*, p.83; see generally Catudal, *A Balance Sheet of the Quadripartite Agreement on Berlin*, pp.61–3.

zones. An annex established rules and procedures for inland waterway vessel and crew documentation, and these were further supplemented by an agreement of 26 June 1946 between the British[17] and Soviet zonal authorities. After the blockade a further British-Soviet zonal agreement was concluded on 4 May 1951, and its provisions for vessel documentation were renewed annually until the end of 1954. On 13 October 1955 the Soviet authorities notified the British authorities that the issue of barge permits had been handed over to the East German authorities.[18] In 1956 the British took parallel action and transferred responsibility for documenting inland waterway traffic to a Federal German office in Hamburg; technical arrangements for these matters were worked out later in the year between the Federal German and GDR authorities.

The waterway access routes available to civilian traffic are as follows:

The Havel/Elbe route: from Berlin along the Havel to the junction with the Elbe near Mühlenholz, and thence to the inner-German border at Cumlosen/Schnackenburg.

The Mittelland Canal System route: from Berlin along the Havel, Elbe-Havel Canal, Elbe and (via the Rothensee shiplift) Mittelland Canal, and thence to the inner-German border at Buchhorst/Rühen.

In exceptional cases arrangements have been made for the use of other routes. The requirements for transit visas and official documents for those travelling by waterway access routes were similar to those applicable to civilian road and rail transit traffic.

THE QUADRIPARTITE AGREEMENT AND THE TRANSIT TRAFFIC AGREEMENT[19]

The general provisions of the Quadripartite Agreement of 3

---

[17] The waterway routes to the Western zones ran through the Soviet zone to points in the British zone.

[18] Lauterpacht, *ICLQ*, 8 (1959), pp.202–12.

[19] Agreement of 17 December 1971 between the Government of the Federal Republic of Germany and the Government of the German Democratic Republic on the Transit Traffic of Civilian Persons and Goods between the Federal Republic of Germany and Berlin (West): Cmnd. 5135, p.62; *US Documents*, p.1169; *Zehn Jahre Deutschlandpolitik*, p.169. See the leaflet *Reisen nach und von Berlin (West)*, published by the Federal Ministry for Inner-German Relations; Zivier, pp.209–19; Wettig, *Die Durchführung des Berlin-Transits nach dem Viermächte-Abkommen 1972–1981* (Bundesinstitut für ost-wissenschaftliche und internationale Studien 1981); Wulf, in: *Zehn Jahre Berlin-Abkommen 1971–1981*, pp.149–61.

September 1971 on transit traffic are contained in Part IIA and
Annex I, paragraph 1. Part IIA provides as follows:

> The Government of the Union of Soviet Socialist Republics declares
> that transit traffic by road, rail and waterways through the territory of
> the German Democratic Republic of civilian persons and goods
> between the Western Sectors of Berlin and the Federal Republic of
> Germany will be unimpeded; that such traffic will be facilitated so as
> to take place in the most simple and expeditious manner; and that it
> will receive preferential treatment.
> Detailed arrangements concerning this civilian traffic, as set forth in
> Annex I, will be agreed by the competent German authorities.

In paragraph 1 of Annex I, the Soviet Government, "after
consultation and agreement with the Government of the German
Democratic Republic", informed the Governments of the three
Powers that:

> Transit traffic by road, rail and waterways through the territory of the
> German Democratic Republic of civilian persons and goods between
> the Western Sectors of Berlin and the Federal Republic of Germany[20]
> will be facilitated and unimpeded. It will receive the most simple,
> expeditious and preferential treatment provided by international
> practice.

Detailed consequential provisions are set out in paragraph 2 of
Annex I; they are designed chiefly to reduce inspection procedures
to a minimum and to simplify payments in respect of civilian traffic.
Paragraph 3 provides that "arrangements implementing and
supplementing the provisions of paragraphs 1 and 2 above will be
agreed by the competent German authorities".

Although in the form of Soviet declarations to the Western Allies,
the provisions of Part IIA and Annex I constitute unequivocal legal
obligations undertaken by the Soviet Union, giving rise to
corresponding legal rights for the Western Allies.[21] The basic
provision is the unqualified Soviet undertaking that surface civilian
transit traffic will be "unimpeded", which means that no political,
administrative or other obstacles may be placed in its way. In
addition, such traffic is to be "facilitated so as to take place in the
most simple and expeditious manner", and is to receive
"preferential treatment", that is to say better treatment than other

---

[20] Article 1 of the Transit Traffic Agreement describes "transit traffic" in the same terms,
as being "the subject of this Agreement". The purpose of the transit is irrelevant, *pace*
Schiedermair, p.71. The use of the word "transit" carries no implications for the status of
Berlin: see Zivier, p.208.
[21] For an explanation of the form of the Agreement, see Zivier, pp.154–5. Schiedermair
(pp.76–83, 88, 113) has argued that Annexes I to III are not part of the Agreement. This
view is not held by any of the parties to the Agreement or by other writers: see, for
example, Frowein, *AöR*, 101 (1976), pp. 641–2; Zivier, pp.150–5.

traffic.[22] These basic obligations govern the interpretation and application of the detailed provisions in Annex I, paragraph 2, and in the Transit Traffic Agreement, the provisions of which are the "implementing and supplementing" arrangements authorised by the four Powers in Annex I, paragraph 3. The Soviet Union is responsible for the implementation of these obligations, including their implementation by the GDR. The reference to "consultation and agreement with the Government of the German Democratic Republic" in Annex I does not detract from the Soviet responsibility, but rather reflects the GDR role in implementing the supplementary provisions in Annex I. While the GDR Government clearly understood and is required to fulfil them, the primary obligation vis-à-vis the Western Allies rests with the Soviet Union. It will be noted that there is no mention of consultation and agreement with the GDR Government in Part IIA itself, which contains the basic and direct Soviet commitments on access; the provisions in Annex I are the main "detailed arrangements" envisaged in Part IIA, and flow from and are consistent with the commitments in Part IIA.

On 16 December 1971 the three Western Ambassadors in Bonn informed the Federal Chancellor that their Governments considered the provisions of the Transit Traffic Agreement to be in conformity with the Quadripartite Agreement, which "provides the standard for its interpretation and application".[23] It was signed on 17 December 1971. In BKC/L(71)3 of 18 December 1971,[24] the Allied Kommandatura noted the conclusion of the Transit Traffic Agreement, in the negotiation of which the Federal Government had been "acting also on behalf of the *Senat* of Berlin", and stated that the three Western Allied Governments considered the provisions of the Agreement "as being in conformity with the Quadripartite Agreement of 3 September 1971, which provides the standard for its interpretation and application". BKC/L(71)3 continues:

> As the Agreement of 17 December 1971 will be in force in the Western Sectors of Berlin from the date of the signature of the Final Quadripartite Protocol, the Senat of Berlin is hereby authorised and

---

[22] These general provisions are repeated in Article 2, paragraph 1, of the Transit Traffic Agreement, and are thus directly binding on the GDR also. It will be noted that the provisions of the Quadripartite Agreement and the Transit Traffic Agreement (other than the lump sum payment) are not limited to persons resident in the Federal Republic of Germany and West Berlin: see Catudal, *A Balance Sheet of the Quadripartite Agreement on Berlin*, pp.34–6; Wulf, in: *Zehn Jahre Berlin-Abkommen 1971–81*, p.158.

[23] Cmnd. 5135, p.88; *Zehn Jahre Deutschlandpolitik*, p.168. On the question of the conformity of the Transit Traffic Agreement with the Quadripartite Agreement, see Zivier, pp. 209–11.

[24] Cmnd. 5135, p.101; *Zehn Jahre Deutschlandpolitik*, p.174.

directed to participate as appropriate in the implementation in the Western Sectors of Berlin of the above-mentioned Agreement.

The Transit Traffic Agreement entered into force simultaneously with the Quadripartite Agreement on 3 June 1972 in accordance with the Final Quadripartite Protocol signed by the four Powers on that day. The preamble to the Transit Traffic Agreement states that the two Governments have agreed to conclude the Agreement in accordance with the arrangements of the Quadripartite Agreement. The Transit Traffic Agreement is thus to be interpreted and applied in the light of the provisions of the Quadripartite Agreement. Article 21 of the Transit Traffic Agreement provides that it shall enter into force simultaneously with the Quadripartite Agreement and shall remain in force together with it. This implements and supplements Part III of the Quadripartite Agreement and corresponds to paragraphs 2 and 3 of the Final Quadripartite Protocol.

The Quadripartite Agreement does not provide expressly for the number or course of the access routes, nor for the location of crossing or control points. Annex I, paragraphs 2(b) and 2(d), merely refers to "designated routes". Article 3 of the Transit Traffic Agreement provides that transit traffic "shall be conducted via the designated border crossing points and transit routes". In the Protocol Notes[25] relating to the Transit Traffic Agreement, the head of the GDR delegation, referring to Article 3 of the Agreement, stated that "use of the existing border crossing points and transit routes is envisaged for transit traffic". Provision is also made in the Protocol Notes for specified improvements in connection with these crossing points and transit routes for rail, road and waterway traffic; and for the GDR authorities to pass timely information to the authorities of the Federal Republic of Germany about "any changes that may become necessary". Thus the "designated border crossing points and transit routes" are the pre-existing ones,[26] with the stated improvements, and changes may only be made where objectively "necessary". The existence of the access routes is moreover guaranteed by the provisions of the Quadripartite Agreement concerning access (Part IIA and Annex I, paragraph 1) and the existing situation (Part I, paragraph 4).

---

[25] Cmnd. 5135, p.84; *Zehn Jahre Deutschlandpolitik*, p.173.
[26] As noted at p.126 above, a new *Autobahn* route and crossing point for traffic between Berlin and Hamburg was established in accordance with an inner-German arrangement of 16 November 1978. In a Protocol Note it was expressly stated that the Transit Traffic Agreement would extend to the new *Autobahn* and that, after its completion, transit traffic would no longer be routed over the corresponding section of GDR highway: *Zehn Jahre Deutschlandpolitik*, p.343.

It is convenient to consider the detailed provisions of the Transit Traffic Agreement under four headings: goods traffic, passenger traffic, miscellaneous provisions, and the Transit Commission.

(i) *goods traffic*

The detailed rules for civilian goods traffic distinguish between sealed and unsealed conveyances. For the former, Annex I, paragraph 2(a), of the Quadripartite Agreement provides:

> (a) Conveyances sealed before departure may be used for the transport of civilian goods by road, rail and waterways between the Western Sectors of Berlin and the Federal Republic of Germany. Inspection procedures will be limited to the inspection of seals and accompanying documents.

This is implemented and supplemented by Article 6 of the Transit Traffic Agreement, which specifies that, for the transport of civilian goods in transit traffic, conveyances (goods vehicles, railway waggons, inland waterway vessels, containers) may be used which, before departure, have been fitted with customs, railway or post office seals, or with official seals made available for the purpose. The fixing of seals is to be done by specified Federal German or Berlin authorities. The GDR authorities may affix their own seals in cases where this appears necessary as an additional safeguard against misuse, but this is not to delay the conduct of transit traffic. The GDR undertakes to provide a particularly favourable procedure for processing sealed conveyances, and to limit inspection procedures to the inspection of seals and accompanying documents.

Annex I, paragraph 2(b), of the Quadripartite Agreement concerns unsealed conveyances, and reads:

> (b) With regard to conveyances which cannot be sealed, such as open trucks, inspection procedures will be limited to the inspection of the accompanying documents. In special cases where there is sufficient reason to suspect that unsealed conveyances contain either material intended for dissemination along the designated routes or persons or material put on board along these routes, the content of unsealed conveyances may be inspected. Procedures for dealing with such cases will be agreed by the competent German authorities.

This is implemented and supplemented by Article 7 of the Transit Traffic Agreement. Article 7(1) specifies that inspection procedures with regard to conveyances which cannot be sealed will be limited to inspection of accompanying documents. Article 7(2) sets out the limited circumstances in which the contents of unsealed conveyances may be inspected, and applies the relevant provisions of Article 16 concerning misuse (pp.136–7 below).

Article 5 of the Transit Traffic Agreement contains provisions for the simplification of the official documents accompanying goods in transit, and of the procedure for completing and inspecting these documents.[27] Article 5(4) imposes an obligation on the Federal German and Berlin customs authorities to check the contents of vehicles against the entries in the accompanying documents.

(ii) *passenger traffic*

The detailed rules for civilian passenger traffic distinguish between through buses and trains on the one hand and individual vehicles on the other. Annex I, paragraph 2(c), of the Quadripartite Agreement provides:

> (c) Through trains and buses may be used for travel between the Western Sectors of Berlin and the Federal Republic of Germany. Inspection procedures will not include any formalities other than identification of persons.

Annex I, paragraph 2(c), is implemented and supplemented by detailed provisions of the Transit Traffic Agreement on through buses (Article 10) and through trains (Article 12). The only GDR inspection procedure permitted is identification of persons, which is normally to take place on board. Only if a bus halts or a train traveller leaves the train for other than certain specified reasons is GDR action under Article 16 permitted (pp.136–7 below).

Annex I, paragraph 2(d), of the Quadripartite Agreement concerns individual vehicles and reads:

> (d) Persons identified as through travellers using individual vehicles between the Western Sectors of Berlin and the Federal Republic of Germany on routes designated for through traffic will be able to proceed to their destinations without paying individual tolls and fees for the use of the transit routes. Procedures applied for such travellers shall not involve delay. The travellers, their vehicles and personal baggage will not be subject to search, detention or exclusion from use of the designated routes, except in special cases, as may be agreed by the competent German authorities, where there is sufficient reason to suspect that misuse of the transit routes is intended for purposes not related to direct travel to and from the Western Sectors of Berlin and contrary to generally applicable regulations concerning public order.

This is implemented and supplemented by several provisions of the Transit Traffic Agreement.

---

[27] See Cmnd. 5135, p.93.

The principle of freedom from individual tolls and fees is reflected in Article 18, which provides for tolls, fees and other costs relating to traffic on the transit routes, including the maintenance of adequate routes, facilities and installations used for such traffic, to be paid by the Federal Republic of Germany to the GDR in the form of an annual lump sum.[28] The lump sum covers, *inter alia*, road tolls, tax adjustment levies and visa fees. Article 4 provides for simplified visa procedures. Through travellers are to be issued visas at the GDR border crossing points, and "in order to ensure the fastest possible processing of transit traffic" this is to be done as a rule at the conveyance or inside through buses and trains. Group visas are available for travellers using through buses. Article 9 makes specific provision for individual conveyances,[29] including the requirement that procedures shall not involve delay and shall as a rule be carried out at the vehicle; it also applies the procedures for individual conveyances to the crews of goods conveyances and their personal baggage. Article 9(4) reads:

> The travellers, their vehicles and personal baggage[30] will not be subject to search, detention or exclusion from use of the designated routes, except in special cases, as specified in Article 16, where there is sufficient reason to suspect that misuse of the transit routes is intended, is being or has been committed, for purposes not related to direct travel to and from Berlin (West) and contrary to generally applicable regulations concerning public order.[31]
> This principle shall be applied on a case-by-case basis and individually.

Search, detention and exclusion are thus exceptional measures which may be carried out only in specific defined cases. There must be sufficient reason to suspect misuse, and the suspected misuse must be for purposes both not related to direct travel and contrary to public order. Moreover, the final sentence is important in

---

[28] This Article also implements and supplements Annex I, paragraph 2(e), of the Quadripartite Agreement. It was implemented in advance by the GDR authorities as from 1 January 1972.

[29] Caravans, trailers and similar conveyances not intended for the transport of goods are treated as individual conveyances: paragraph 8 of the Protocol Notes: Cmnd. 5135, p.87; *Zehn Jahre Deutschlandpolitik*, p.174.

[30] Paragraph 9 of the Protocol Notes provides: "The carrying of books, newspapers and other printed material intended only for personal use by through travellers, and not for dissemination along transit routes, shall not be interpreted as misuse": Cmnd. 5135, p.87; *Zehn Jahre Deutschlandpolitik*, p.174. See further Cmnd. 5135, p.93.

[31] The words "generally applicable regulations concerning public order" (like the same phrase in Annex I, paragraph 2(d), of the Quadripartite Agreement) imply a reference to public order regulations to be found in States generally, not just the GDR. (Other provisions specify GDR public order regulations, e.g. Articles 2 and 16.)

prohibiting search, detention or exclusion of particular groups of persons.[32]

The concept of "misuse" is defined in Article 16,[33] which applies not only in relation to individual conveyances by virtue of Article 9(4) but also in relation to unsealed conveyances (Article 7(2)), through buses (Article 10(5)) and through trains (Article 12(4)). Article 16(1) provides that misuse within the meaning of the Agreement is present –

> if after the entry into force of this Agreement a through traveller while using the transit routes culpably and unlawfully violates the generally applicable regulations of the German Democratic Republic concerning public order in that he
>
> (a) disseminates or receives material;
> (b) picks up persons;
> (c) leaves the designated transit routes, unless so caused by special circumstances such as accident or illness or with the permission of the competent authorities of the German Democratic Republic;
> (d) commits other criminal offences; or
> (e) is guilty of an infringement by contravening road traffic regulations.

Paragraph 1 also defines the circumstances in which incitement or aiding and abetting acts of misuse will itself amount to misuse. Paragraph 2 defines strictly "sufficient reason for suspecting misuse", and provides that where such reason exists the GDR authorities will search travellers, their conveyances and their personal baggage, or turn travellers back. Paragraph 3 provides that:

> If the suspicion is confirmed, the competent authorities of the German Democratic Republic will, commensurate with the gravity of the act of misuse, in accordance with the generally applicable regulations of the German Democratic Republic concerning public order
>
> (a) reprimand or impose a disciplinary penalty on, or issue a caution with fine to the person concerned, or impound articles;

---

[32] In addition, the Federal Republic of Germany and GDR reached the following understanding:
(a) Germans who had left the GDR without permission for the Federal Republic of Germany or West Berlin are to be treated in all respects as transit travellers and will suffer no disadvantages because of the fact that they left the GDR; and
(b) the GDR reserves the right to turn back from use of the transit routes persons who have previously committed in the GDR criminal offences against human life or premeditated criminal offences against human health or serious criminal offences against property.
See the Memorandum containing clarifications concerning the result of the negotiations on the Transit Traffic Agreement: Cmnd. 5135, p.97.
[33] Schiedermair, *ZaöRV*, 38(1978), pp.160–81.

(b) seize or confiscate articles;
(c) turn persons back or temporarily exclude them from the use of the transit routes; or
(d) detain persons.

The remaining paragraphs of Article 16 contain supplementary provisions; under Article 16(5) the GDR is to notify the Federal authorities "about any detentions or exclusions of persons from the use of the transit routes or their being turned back, and of the reasons therefor".[34]

Article 16, as well as the other Articles providing for its application, are of great importance in defining the limited circumstances in which civilian transit travellers may be searched, detained or excluded. The overriding obligations of both the Soviet Union and GDR to ensure unimpeded access require that these provisions be strictly interpreted. They place clear limitations upon GDR actions and upon the application of GDR law. They are not affected by the general provision in Article 2 (2) that the generally applicable regulations of the GDR concerning public order shall be applied in transit traffic, which is expressed to apply "unless otherwise provided for in this Agreement".

Article 17 sets out obligations for the Federal Government with a view to preventing misuse of the transit routes; certain difficulties have arisen because of the Federal Government's limited powers in this field.[35]

(iii) *miscellaneous provisions*

Other provisions of the Transit Traffic Agreement implement and supplement the general provisions on access in Part IIA and Annex I, paragraph 1, rather than the more detailed provisions in Annex I, paragraph 2. Article 8 requires motor vehicles using the transit routes to be covered by third-party insurance, and provides for mutual recognition of vehicle and driving licences. Article 11 contains general provisions for co-operation in relation to rail traffic. Article 13 provides that inland waterway vessels may be used for the transport of goods, and contains detailed rules relating to waterway traffic. As an exception to the general freedom from individual payments, Article 13(4) provides that tolls and fees shall be charged in accordance with GDR regulations for the use of waterways, including locks, canal-lifts, and berthing points. In Article 14, the GDR undertakes to provide the necessary assistance,

---

[34] See Wulf, in: *Zehn Jahre Berlin-Abkommen 1971–81*, pp.158–60.
[35] Ress, *ZaöRV*, 34(1974), pp.139–40; Wulf, in: *Zehn Jahre Berlin-Abkommen 1971–81*, pp.153–6.

including breakdown services and medical care, in the event of accidents, technical defects and breakdown, and to transmit reports to the authorities of the Federal Republic of Germany. In Article 15, the GDR undertakes to communicate to the Federal Republic of Germany information about road conditions, channel depths, water levels, lock times, obstacles to navigation, as well as any other information relating to traffic, including notification of diversions. The reference to diversions implies that sections of access routes may be closed temporarily, for example where repairs or reconstruction become necessary; but the general obligation to ensure unimpeded access requires adequate diversion routes to be provided.

(iv) *the Transit Commission*

Article 19 of the Transit Traffic Agreement establishes a Commission "to clarify any difficulties or differences of opinion regarding the application or interpretation" of the Agreement. The delegations in the Commission are to be headed by plenipotentiaries of the Federal Minister of Transport and the GDR Minister of Transport respectively. If the Commission is unable to settle a difficulty or difference of opinion put before it, the point at issue is to be submitted by the two sides to their respective Governments, who will resolve the matter by negotiation. There remains always the possibility of resolving a question under the four-Power consultation machinery provided for in paragraph 4 of the Final Quadripartite Protocol if any of the four Powers considers the difficulty to be serious.

Since the Transit Traffic Agreement, the Governments of the Federal Republic of Germany and GDR have, with the concurrence of the four Powers, concluded several arrangements concerning technical improvements in civilian transit traffic on the surface access routes.[36] These arrangements further implement and supplement the Quadripartite Agreement, and contain express references to the Transit Traffic Agreement.

The Quadripartite Agreement has so far largely succeeded in removing access to Berlin as a source of tension and crisis. There have, however, been occasional cases of politically-inspired interference with access, even after 1971, such as those in 1974 in connection with the establishment in Berlin of the Federal

---

[36] See, for example, the arrangements mentioned in footnotes 10, 11, 12 and 14 above. The arrangements of 19 December 1975 also improved facilities for rail transit, and the arrangements of 16 November 1978 also provided for reconstruction of parts of the waterway access routes and the opening for transit traffic of part of the Teltow Canal in GDR territory.

Environment Office.[37] The Allied reaction was firm, as the question of access is a central element of the Quadripartite Agreement and remains of fundamental importance. In their statement of 24 July 1974 they recalled that:

> The Soviet Government is responsible for ensuring that transit traffic between the Western Sectors of Berlin and the Federal Republic of Germany of civilian persons and goods remains unimpeded.[38]

---

[37] See, for example, *US Documents*, p.1272. Other incidents occurred in October 1973, August 1976, June 1978 and July 1978. See the Western statement of 14 August 1976. See Ress, *ZaöRV*, 34(1974), pp.133–47; Catudal, *A Balance Sheet of the Quadripartite Agreement on Berlin*, pp.34–48; Wulf, in: *Zehn Jahre Berlin-Abkommen 1971–1981*, pp.149–61.

[38] *US Documents*, p.1272.

PART FOUR

THE TIES BETWEEN BERLIN AND THE FEDERAL REPUBLIC

West Berlin is to a large degree included in the financial, economic, political and legal systems of the Federal Republic of Germany, and is fully integrated into its social and cultural life. These ties are essential to the survival of the city as part of the Western world. At the same time, the relationship between Berlin and the Federal Republic cannot put in question Allied occupation rights, which are the only secure legal basis for the city's survival.

The ties between Berlin and the Federal Republic have developed in a rather *ad hoc* fashion. Both remain part of Germany as a whole. It was the Western Allies themselves who first insisted on the inclusion of the Western Sectors in the economic system of the Federal Republic, and in particular in the Marshall Aid plan for the Federal Republic. Administrative and political ties followed, subject always to the Western Allied reservation that Berlin was not a *Land* of the Federal Republic and was not to be governed by it.

In the period up to 1958, such difficulties as arose in connection with the ties were, on the surface at least, principally between the Western Allies and the authorities in Bonn and Berlin. The Eastern attitude appeared essentially neutral. From 1959 onwards, however, the Soviet Union and GDR began to attack the ties with increasing vehemence, both by word and deed, for example by impeding access. Such attacks reached a peak in the late 1960s; and the question was central to the negotiation of the Quadripartite Agreement of 3 September 1971. In that Agreement the Soviet Union accepted that the ties between the Western Sectors and the Federal Republic would be "maintained and developed, taking into account that these Sectors continue not to be a constituent part of the Federal Republic of Germany and not to be governed by it". But the Agreement by no means resolved all the problems; differences of interpretation remain, and the Soviet Union and GDR continue to protest frequently against the ties, though difficulties on the access routes are now rare.

Part Four deals in turn with the principal aspects of the relationship between Berlin and the Federal Republic of Germany, considering in each case the attitudes of the Western Allies and of the Soviet Union. Chapter 10 considers the relationship in general, and in particular the constitutional and political ties. Chapter 11 concerns the taking over in Berlin of provisions of Federal Laws in accordance with procedures which have remained essentially unchanged since the early 1950s. The role of Federal agencies, including Federal courts (except the Federal Constitutional Court), in relation to Berlin is virtually indistinguishable, both in substance and in appearance, from their role in the Federal Republic of Germany, though they are in law acting as Berlin agencies and courts (Chapter 12). The temporary or permanent presence in Berlin of Federal institutions and senior officials is an impressive indication of the closeness of the ties, but (contrary to frequent Soviet assertions) does not involve the government of Berlin by the Federation (Chapter 13). The external representation of Berlin's interests, including the extension of treaties to Berlin, is also to a large degree an aspect of the relationship between Berlin and the Federal Republic of Germany, but it is sufficiently distinct to merit treatment in a separate Part (Part Five).

CHAPTER 10

THE BERLIN–FEDERAL REPUBLIC
RELATIONSHIP IN GENERAL

THE relationship between Berlin and the Federal Republic of Germany is the subject of an extensive literature.[1] But attempts to describe the relationship in terms of traditional international or constitutional legal concepts have not been particularly helpful. Berlin and the Federal Republic both remain part of Germany as a whole, which continues to exist as a State in international law (Chapter 2 above). Beyond this, the Allied position is that Berlin is not a *Land* (Federal state or province) of the Federal Republic of Germany and may not be governed by the Federation. The whole of Berlin remains under military occupation and is not part of either the Federal Republic of Germany or the GDR. At the same time, the relationship between Berlin (in practice the Western Sectors of Berlin) and the Federal Republic is very close. As was said in the tripartite statement of 26 June 1964, issued in connection with the Treaty of Friendship of 12 June 1964 between the Soviet Union and the GDR:

> While reserving their rights relating to Berlin the three Western Powers, taking account of the necessities for the development of the city, have authorised, in accordance with the Agreements of 23rd October, 1954, the establishment of close ties between Berlin and the Federal Republic of Germany, including permission to the Federal Republic to ensure representation of Berlin and of the Berlin population outside Berlin. These ties, the existence of which is essential to the viability of Berlin, are in no way inconsistent with the quadripartite status of the city and will be maintained in the future.[2]

This position was recognised in Part IIB of the Quadripartite Agreement of 3 September 1971.

---

[1] Drath, *JR*, 1951, pp.385–90; Kreutzer, *JR*, 1951, pp.641–5; Plischke, *Berlin: Development of its Government and Administration*, pp.111–34; Kreutzer, *Zeitschrift für Politik*, 1NF (1954), pp.139–58; Kreutzer, *DÖV*, 8 (1955), pp.12–16; Drath, *AöR*, 82 (1957), pp.27–75; Simpson, *ICLQ*, 6 (1957), pp.91–8, 101–2; Kröger, *Deutsche Aussenpolitik* (1958), pp.10–26; Lush, *ICLQ*, 14 (1965), pp.742–87; Wengler, in: *Fs Leibholz*, Vol. II, pp.939–62; Fijalkowski, *Berlin – Hauptstadtanspruch und Westintegration*; Czermak, *Die Stellung Berlins in der Rechts-, Gerichts- und Finanzordnung der Bundesrepublik Deutschland* (Dissertation, Bonn 1967); Finkelnburg, *JuS*, 7 (1967), pp.542–4 and *JuS*, 8 (1968), pp.10–14, 58–61; Schiedermair, pp.89–122; Zivier, pp.74–130, 182–93; Stobbe, *EA*, 32 (1977), pp.477–86; Wettig, *DA*, 11(1978), pp.1182–96 and *DA*, 12(1979), pp.278–90, 920–37; Schiedermair, *NJW*, 35 (1982), pp.2841–7; Pestalozza, *JuS*, 23 (1983), pp.241–54 and *JuS*, 24 (1984), pp.430–4; Sendler, *JuS*, 23 (1983), pp.903–10 and *JuS*, 24 (1984), pp.432–4; Kewenig, *Entwicklungslinien des völker- und staatsrechtlichen Status von Berlin* (1984).

[2] *Selected Documents* II, p.109; *US Documents*, p.877.

The special Berlin area (Greater Berlin) did not form part of any of the four zones of occupation in Germany. When the three Western Military Governors approved the establishment of the Federal Republic of Germany in the Western zones they took steps to ensure that Berlin was not included therein, having regard to both political and status considerations. On 1 July 1948 the Military Governors authorised the eleven *Länder* in the Western zones to convene a Parliamentary Council (*Parlamentarischer Rat*) to draft a democratic federal constitution. The Council, which was composed of delegates elected by the *Land* parliaments, invited five delegates from Berlin to take part in its work "as guests in an advisory capacity";[3] this decision was approved by the Military Governors. On 10 February 1949 the Main Committee of the Parliamentary Council adopted a draft Basic Law for the Federal Republic of Germany, Article 22 of which provided that the Basic Law should apply to twelve *Länder* listed by name (that is, the eleven *Länder* of the Western zones plus Greater Berlin).[4] On 2 March 1949 the Military Governors communicated their views to the Parliamentary Council as follows:

> ... in view of the existing situation, that portion of Article 22 which refers to Berlin must be suspended. Nevertheless, there would be no objection to the responsible authorities in Berlin designating a small number of representatives to attend the meetings of the Parliament.[5]

In a further message dated 22 April 1949 the Military Governors conveyed the views of the Washington meeting of the Foreign Ministers of the Three Powers as follows:

> The Foreign Ministers are not able to agree at this time that Berlin should be included as a *Land* in the initial organisation of the German Federal Republic.[6]

The Basic Law was adopted by the Parliamentary Council and transmitted to the Military Governors on 8 May 1949. The reference to Berlin in the list of *Länder* in the preamble had been deleted, but Article 23 (former Article 22) remained unchanged:

> For the time being, this Basic Law shall apply in the territory of the *Länder* of Baden, Bavaria, Bremen, Greater Berlin, Hamburg, Hesse, Lower Saxony, North Rhine-Westphalia, Rhineland-Palatinate, Schleswig-Holstein, Württemberg-Baden and Württemberg-Hohen-

---

[3] Heidelmeyer, p.107. Cf. Article 145(1) of the Basic Law.
[4] There was an immediate Soviet protest: Heidelmeyer *Dokumente*, p.112.
[5] *US Documents*, pp.204, 206; Heidelmeyer *Dokumente*, p.112. For the background to the Allied reservations, see Wetzlaugk, *Berlin und die Deutsche Frage*, pp.100–3.
[6] *Selected Documents* I, p.115; *US Documents*, p.218; Heidelmeyer *Dokumente*, p.113.

zollern. It shall be put into force for other parts of Germany on their accession.

Article 144(2) had been added:

> In so far as the application of this Basic Law is subject to restrictions in any *Land* listed in Article 23 or in any part thereof, such *Land* or part thereof shall have the right to send representatives to the *Bundestag* in accordance with Article 38 and to the *Bundesrat* in accordance with Article 50.

In their letter of 12 May 1949 approving the Basic Law the Military Governors made the following reservation:

> We interpret the effect of Articles 23 and 144(2) of the Basic Law as constituting acceptance of our previous request that while Berlin may not be accorded voting membership in the *Bundestag* or *Bundesrat* nor be governed by the Federation she may, nevertheless, designate a small number of representatives to attend the meetings of those legislative bodies.[7]

Parallel with developments in the Western zones, where the Military Governors were replaced by Allied High Commissioners and a new Occupation Statute issued, the Allied Kommandatura issued on 14 May 1949 a Statement of Principles Governing the Relationship between the Allied Kommandatura and Greater Berlin. At the same time the Allied Kommandatura referred to the Military Governors' letter of 12 May and said that –

> the Military Governors have not been able, because of the special circumstances of Berlin, to agree at this time that Berlin should be included as a *Land* in the initial organisation of the German Federal Republic.[8]

Article 144(1) of the Basic Law provided that the parliaments of the *Länder* should ratify the Basic Law. The Berlin City Assembly, however, did not do so, nor was Berlin counted for the purpose of applying Article 144. Instead, on 19 May 1949 the City Assembly passed a resolution thanking the Parliamentary Council for its desire to include Berlin in the Federal territory and regretting that it had not proved possible for this to happen.[9]

---

[7] *Selected Documents* I, p.117; *US Documents*, p.260; Heidelmeyer, p.107. See also Section 26 of the Electoral Law for the First *Bundestag* (Heidelmeyer, p.116); and the *Bundestag* resolution of 30 September 1949.

[8] *Selected Documents* I, p.117; *US Documents*, p.262; Heidelmeyer, p.108.

[9] Heidelmeyer, p.112. See also the resolution of 21 June 1949 (*US Documents*, p.271; Heidelmeyer, p.116) and BK/O(49)139 of 30 June 1949 (*US Documents*, p.272; Heidelmeyer, p.117). See also document AGSEC(52)1029 in Heidelmeyer *Dokumente*, p.126. Lush (p.753) concludes a detailed account of events in 1949 by stating that "in 1949 no one, either on the German or Allied side, had any doubt that Berlin was not included in the Federal Republic".

Article 1 of the 1950 Constitution of Berlin reads:

(1) Berlin is both a German *Land* and a city.
(2) Berlin is a *Land* of the Federal Republic of Germany.
(3) The Basic Law and the laws of the Federal Republic of Germany
are binding on Berlin.

However, Article 87 provides that paragraphs (2) and (3) shall enter into force only when "the application of the Basic Law for the Federal Republic to Berlin is no longer subject to restrictions", and makes provision for the transitional period during which the Basic Law is subject to restrictions. This was a clear reference to the reservation regarding Berlin in the Military Governors' letter of 12 May 1949 approving the Basic Law.

The Allied Kommandatura approved the Constitution of Berlin by BK/O(50)75 of 29 August 1950,[10] subject to three important reservations:

In approving this Constitution and the proposed changes thereto, the Allied Kommandatura makes the following reservations:
(a) The powers vested in the city government by the Constitution are subject to the provisions of the Statement of Principles which was promulgated on 14 May 1949, or any modifications thereof;
(b) Article 1, paragraphs (2) and (3) are suspended;
(c) Article 87 is interpreted as meaning that during the transitional period Berlin shall possess none of the attributes of a twelfth *Land*. The provisions of this Article concerning the Basic Law will only apply to the extent necessary to prevent a conflict between this law and the Berlin Constitution. Furthermore, the provisions of any Federal law shall apply to Berlin only after they have been voted upon by the House of Representatives and passed as a Berlin law.

On 5 May 1955 the Convention on Relations between the Three Powers and the Federal Republic of Germany [11] came into force, and the Federal Republic acquired the full authority of a sovereign State over its internal and external affairs. No basic changes occurred in the relationship between the Federal Republic and Berlin. The Allies maintained their reservations and at the same time full weight was given to the close relationship between the Federal Republic and Berlin. In their letter to the Federal Chancellor concerning the exercise of the reserved Allied rights relating to Berlin of 26 May 1952 in the version of letter X of 23 October 1954,[12] the three Western High Commissioners stated among other things:

As we have already advised you during our discussions on the

---

[10] *VOBl.* p.440; *Selected Documents* I, p.135; *US Documents*, p.324; Heidelmeyer, p.121.
[11] Text at p.323 below.
[12] Text at p.329 below.

Conventions between the Three Powers and the Federal Republic which have been signed today, the reservation made on 12th May, 1949, by the Military Governors concerning Articles 23 and 144(2) of the Basic Law will, owing to the international situation, be formally maintained by the Three Powers in the exercise of their right relating to Berlin after the entry into force of those Conventions.

... they have decided to exercise their right relating to Berlin in such a way as to facilitate the carrying out by the Federal Republic of its Declaration on Aid to Berlin, of which a copy is annexed, and to permit the Federal authorities to ensure representation of Berlin and of the Berlin population outside Berlin.

In its Declaration on Aid to Berlin the Federal Republic of Germany committed itself to extensive economic and financial aid, to improving communications between Berlin and the Federal territory and to ensuring the representation of Berlin outside Berlin.[13] The relationship was further emphasised by Article 6 of the Relations Convention, in which the three Powers undertook to consult with the Federal Republic of Germany in regard to the exercise of their rights relating to Berlin, and the Federal Republic, on its part, undertook to co-operate with the three Powers in order to facilitate the discharge of their responsibilities with regard to Berlin.

At the same time the Allied Kommandatura, in its Declaration on Berlin of 5 May 1955, maintained the reservations to the Constitution of Berlin. Article I of the Declaration reads:

Berlin shall exercise all its rights, powers and responsibilities set forth in its Constitution as adopted in 1950 subject only to the reservations made by the Allied Kommandatura on 29 August 1950 and to the provisions hereinafter.[14]

In its decision of 25 October 1951[15] the Federal Constitutional Court had accepted Dr Adenauer's view that the direct inclusion of Berlin in the Federation had been postponed.[16] Despite this, and despite the generally accepted view in the early years of the Federal Republic, in its decision of 21 May 1957[17] the Federal Constitutional Court held that Berlin was a *Land* of the Federal Republic. It interpreted the Military Governors' reservations as meaning that

---

[13] Text at p.330 below.

[14] BKC/L(55)3: see p.332 below. The "reservations made by the Allied Kommandatura on 29 August 1950" were those made in BK/O(50)75 of that date: see above.

[15] *BVerfGE* 1, 70 (Heidelmeyer *Dokumente*, p.125).

[16] *Bundestag* address of 21 October 1949: Heidelmeyer *Dokumente*, p.144.

[17] *BVerfGE* 7, 1 (Heidelmeyer *Dokumente*, p.128). This view has been reaffirmed on several occasions, even after the Quadripartite Agreement: *BVerfGE* 10, 229(232); 19, 377 (388) (*Niekisch* case); 20, 257 (266); 36, 1 (*Zehn Jahre Deutschlandpolitik*, p.232); 37, 57 (62) (*Brückmann* case).

Berlin was not to be governed by the Federation and that Berlin's representatives could not vote in the *Bundestag* or *Bundesrat*. The reference to Greater Berlin in Article 23 of the Basic Law had not expressly been suspended. In reaching its decision, the Court relied on the close ties that had grown up between Berlin and the Federal Republic,[18] and discounted the clear Allied statements of position. The Court's view has not been accepted by the Allies.[19]

The Western Allies had occasion to restate their position on the relationship between Berlin and the Federal Republic following the Federal Constitutional Court's decision in the *Niekisch* case (see pp.174–5 below). This they did in aide-mémoires to the Federal Government dated 18 April 1967[20] and, in similar terms, in BK/L(67)10 of 24 May 1967.[21] They reaffirmed *inter alia* that −

> It has been and remains the Allied intention and opinion that Berlin is not to be regarded as a Land of the Federal Republic of Germany and is not to be governed by the Federation.

THE TIES AND THE QUADRIPARTITE AGREEMENT

The Soviet Union has, since the late 1950s, protested with increasing force against the closeness of the ties between the Western Sectors of Berlin and the Federal Republic of Germany. Despite the clear Allied reservations, the Russians claim that the Allies have in effect allowed Berlin to become a *Land* of the Federal Republic; they also accuse the Federal Republic of seeking to turn Berlin into a Federal *Land*. One of the major objectives of the Quadripartite Agreement was to reduce tensions in this field, but this has been achieved only to a limited degree. Part IIB of the Quadripartite Agreement of 3 September 1971 reads:

> The Governments of the French Republic, the United Kingdom and the United States of America declare that the ties between the Western Sectors of Berlin and the Federal Republic of Germany will be maintained and developed, taking into account that these Sectors continue not to be a constituent part of the Federal Republic of Germany and not to be governed by it.

---

[18] The Court referred in this connection to Drath, *AöR*, 82 (1957), pp.27–75, and Kreutzer, *Zeitschrift für Politik*, 1NF (1954), pp.139–58.

[19] See, for example, the statement by the British Foreign Secretary on 10 February 1960 that Her Majesty's Government did not regard Berlin as part of the Federal Republic of Germany: H.C. Deb., Feb. 10–11 1960, Vols. 616–617, cols. 478, 490. In a written answer of 3 June 1986 a Foreign and Commonwealth Office Minister repeated that "Berlin is not part of the Federal Republic of Germany and is not governed by it": H.C.Deb., June 3 1986, Vol. 98, WA 414.

[20] *US Documents*, p.959.

[21] *Selected Documents* II, p.156.

Detailed arrangements concerning the relationship between the Western Sectors of Berlin and the Federal Republic of Germany are set forth in Annex II.

Annex II of the Quadripartite Agreement is a communication by the three Powers which is expressly stated to be made after consultation with the Government of the Federal Republic of Germany. The three Powers repeat the declaration set out in Part IIB, and do so "in exercise of their rights and responsibilities". Annex II goes on to state that:

> The provisions of the Basic Law of the Federal Republic of Germany and of the Constitution operative in the Western Sectors of Berlin which contradict the above have been suspended and continue not to be in effect.

In their letter conveying the Quadripartite Agreement to the Federal Government, the Western Allies, referring to the provisions of the Agreement relating to the relationship between Berlin and the Federal Republic, recalled *inter alia* the Military Governors' reservations, the High Commissioners' letter on reserved Allied rights and the *Niekisch* aide-mémoire, and stated that the provisions of the Agreement accorded with the position in these documents, which remained unchanged. They further stated:

> With regard to the existing ties between the Federal Republic and the Western Sectors of Berlin, it is the firm intention of our Governments that, as stated in Part II(B)(1) of the Quadripartite Agreement, these ties will be maintained and developed in accordance with the letter from the three High Commissioners to the Federal Chancellor on the exercise of the reserved rights relating to Berlin of 26 May, 1952, in the version of letter X of October 23, 1954, and with pertinent decisions of the Allied Kommandatura of Berlin.[22]

Part IIB and Annex II of the Quadripartite Agreement record agreement between the four Powers on a number of important points:

(a) The ties between the Western Sectors of Berlin and the Federal Republic of Germany will be maintained and developed.

(b) The Western Sectors of Berlin continue not to be a constituent part of the Federal Republic of Germany and not to be governed by it.

(c) The provisions of the Basic Law for the Federal Republic of Germany and of the Constitution of Berlin which contradict

---

[22] The full text of the letter is at p.346 below.

(a) and (b) have been suspended and continue not to be in effect.

(d) State bodies of the Federal Republic of Germany will not perform in the Western Sectors of Berlin acts in exercise of direct state authority over those Sectors.

(e) Limitations are placed on the presence of certain Federal organs in Berlin.

The last two points are considered in detail in Chapters 12 and 13 respectively. The first two points, which are closely related, are the basic provisions in Part IIB of the Quadripartite Agreement in this area. The Soviet Union has agreed that the existing ties[23] between West Berlin and the Federal Republic of Germany (that is, the *status quo*) will be maintained, and moreover that they do not make Berlin a constituent part of the Federal Republic nor amount to a governing of Berlin by the Federation. It has further accepted that the ties will be developed; the exclusion by Part 14 of unilateral change in the existing situation does not exclude development of the ties, subject only to the fact that Berlin continues not to be a constituent part of the Federation or governed by it. Annex II and the associated interpretative letter of 3 September 1971[24] indicate the scope of the more general provisions in Part IIB. Nevertheless, the Soviet Union continues to object strongly to particular manifestations of the ties. In so doing it frequently distorts and misquotes the Quadripartite Agreement, especially by referring in isolation to the half sentence of Part IIB that it terms the central provision: that the Western Sectors of Berlin are not part of the Federal Republic of Germany and are not to be governed by it.[25] The Western Allies consistently reject such distortions.

BERLIN, A GERMAN *LAND*[26]

The Allied position has been clear since before the establishment of the Federal Republic of Germany: Berlin is not a *Land* of the

---

[23] The Eastern side has sought to interpret the word "ties" (*liens*; *svyazi*) in a narrow sense; and the GDR insists on translating it by *Verbindungen*, which is apparently considered narrower than *Bindungen*: Blumenwitz, in: *Zehn Jahre Berlin-Abkommen*, pp.79–82; Schiedermair, footnotes 238, 438a.

[24] Letter from the Ambassadors of the three Powers to the Federal Chancellor, of which the Soviet Ambassador took note: see p.245 below.

[25] It is in the context of the ties that the formula "strict maintenance and full application" (*"strikte Einhaltung und volle Durchführung"*) has particular relevance. The Eastern side originally referred only to "strict maintenance" (and on occasion still does), with a view to a narrow interpretation of the ties; "full application" points to the dynamic aspects of the Agreement. The formula was first used in the joint communiqué of 21 May 1973 on the occasion of Brezhnev's visit to Bonn: Zündorf, p.172 and footnote 514; *Das Vierseitige Abkommen*, p.140.

[26] See Pestalozza, *JuS*, 23 (1983), pp.241–54.

Federal Republic.[27] As has been seen, the position of Federal and Berlin authorities was initially similar. But since the decisions of the Federal Constitutional Court in 1957 and 1973, Federal authorities are bound as a matter of Federal constitutional law to regard Berlin as a *Land* of the Federal Republic of Germany. The decisions are binding only on the Federal Republic and do not affect the Allied and international position. This issue has given rise to considerable debate.[28] In fact, the difference between the Allied and Federal view has little significance for the day-to-day working of the relationship between Berlin and the Federation.[29] But one unfortunate effect of the Constitutional Court's decisions has been to add weight to the Soviet argument that the Western Allies and the Federal Republic have permitted Berlin to become a *Land* of the Federal Republic.

While not a *Land* of the Federal Republic of Germany, Berlin is a German *Land* (Article 1(1) of the 1950 Constitution of Berlin) and may properly be referred to as "*Land* Berlin".[30] It is so described in Federal Laws and, whenever possible, in the Federal Republic's bilateral treaties. The Soviet Union and GDR object to this description on the ground that Berlin is not a *Land* of the Federal Republic of Germany; such objections are misconceived and, when made by the Soviet Union, are consistently refuted by the Western Allies.[31]

Part IIB of the Quadripartite Agreement states that the Western

---

[27] See the detailed analysis by Lush, *ICLQ*, 14 (1965), pp.742–87; see also Riklin, pp.256–8; Simpson, *ICLQ*, 6 (1957), pp.83, 101; Wengler, in: *Fs Leibholz*, Vol. II, pp.939–62; Pestalozza, *JuS*, 23 (1983), pp.241, 248. This position is shared by the Soviet Union, which does, however, draw different conclusions.

[28] See the writings mentioned at footnote 1 above, especially those by Drath (one of the judges who took part in the Federal Constitutional Court decision of 21 May 1957), Wengler, and Lush.

[29] As is recognised by Zivier, pp.77, 114. As Wengler puts it: "Everything necessary in order to afford West Berliners the practical advantages of full inclusion in the Federal Republic can be achieved through the "as if" (*als ob*) status, which has been authorised by the Occupying Powers. To want to go further and to this end engage in a dispute not only with the East but also with the Western Powers does not serve a *Deutschlandpolitik* aimed in the long-term at keeping open the German question": *Fünf Jahre Grundvertragsurteil des Bundesverfassungsgerichts*, p.337.

[30] Article 1(1) was not suspended by the Allied Kommandatura, unlike Article 1(2), which provided that Berlin was a "*Land* of the Federal Republic of Germany". Article II of Control Council Law No. 46 on the Abolition of the State of Prussia (*CC Gazette*, p.262) had provided that territories "which were a part of the Prussian State and which are at present under the supreme authority of the Control Council will receive the status of *Länder* or will be absorbed into *Länder*".

[31] E.g. *Multilateral Treaties*, Chapter III.3, note 2; *Das Vierseitige Abkommen*, pp.127, 135. See Vysotsky, *West Berlin*, p.75; Wengler, *AFDI*, 24 (1978), pp.234–5; Wengler, *Berlin in völkerrechtlichen Übereinkommen der Bundesrepublik Deutschland*, pp.31–2; Wengler, *ROW*, 30 (1986), p.151; Wettig, *DA*, 12 (1979), p.921. The Allies do not normally respond to observations about the status of Berlin by the GDR: see also p.46 above.

Sectors of Berlin continue not to be a constituent part[32] of the Federal Republic of Germany. This reflects the existing position whereby Berlin is not a *Land* of the Federal Republic.

THE APPLICATION OF PROVISIONS OF THE BASIC LAW

Since the reference to Greater Berlin in Article 23 of the Basic Law remains suspended, the Basic Law itself does not at present effectively provide for its application to Berlin. Provisions of the Basic Law apply in Berlin by virtue of Article 87(3) of the 1950 Constitution of Berlin, which reads:

> Insofar as the application in Berlin of the Basic Law for the Federal Republic of Germany is not subject to any restriction (paragraph 1) in the transitional period, provisions of the Basic Law are effective in Berlin also. They override the provisions of the Constitution. In specific cases the House of Representatives can, with a two-thirds majority of the members present, decide to the contrary. Article 85 of this Constitution is applicable by analogy.

Article 87(3) has to be read subject to the Allied Kommandatura's reservation in paragraph 2(c) of BK/O(50)75:

> (c) Article 87 is interpreted as meaning that during the transitional period Berlin shall possess none of the attributes of a twelfth *Land*. The provisions of this Article concerning the Basic Law will only apply to the extent necessary to prevent a conflict between this law and the Berlin Constitution.

The position following BK/O(50)75 has been analysed as follows:

> Article 87(3) of the Constitution provides that during the transitional period, while the Basic Law is still subject to Allied reservations, the Law shall be in force in Berlin to the extent that it is not subject to any restrictions, and shall override the provisions of the Constitution. Even those who do not agree that the application of the Basic Law to Berlin was wholly suspended concede that the restrictions imposed by the Military Governors' reservation cover those parts of the Basic Law which deal with the government of the Länder by the Federation. Paragraph 2(c) of BK/O(50)75 qualifies the effect of Article 87(3) of the Constitution still further, by stating that the article will only apply to the extent necessary to prevent a conflict. Very many of the articles of the Berlin Constitution are substantially the same as those of the

[32] In French *élément constitutif*; in Russian *sostavnaya chast'*. No agreement could be reached on the German translation of "constituent part": Schiedermair, pp.89–90, footnote 226a. As Rush points out, "constituent part is not a new term but had for many years been used in Allied and F.R.G. correspondence to describe the status of Berlin as established by the Allies": Catudal, *The Diplomacy of the Quadripartite Agreement on Berlin*, p.17; see also Wengler, *ROW*, 30 (1986), p.151.

Basic Law – for instance most of those dealing with basic rights – so no conflict can be said to arise. Others have no corresponding provision in the Basic Law, so again cannot be said to conflict. One is left with the conclusion that the effect of this provision is that the Basic Law only applies to Berlin in the rare cases where it contains an article which conflicts with a corresponding article in the Berlin Constitution.[33]

The position may now be somewhat different in practice.[34] It has been made clear in particular areas by the Allies: for example, the provisions of the Basic Law concerning the Federal Constitutional Court, defence and emergencies do not apply in Berlin. The Federal Constitutional Court itself held in a decision of 25 October 1951 that the basic rights provisions applied in Berlin.[35] In other areas the question of the application in Berlin of provisions of the Basic Law has not given rise to practical problems, and it has not been found necessary to clarify the position.

In the Quadripartite Agreement the four Powers recall that the provisions of the Basic Law which contradict Annex II, paragraph 1, have been suspended and continue not to be in effect. In other words, the Quadripartite Agreement reaffirmed the *status quo*.

BERLIN AND FEDERAL CONSTITUTIONAL ORGANS

The Federal Assembly (*Bundesversammlung*) meets every five years to elect the Federal President in accordance with Article 54 of the Basic Law. It consists of the members of the *Bundestag* and an equal number of members elected by the *Länder* parliaments. Since 1959 the Berlin representatives in the *Bundestag* and the members elected by the Berlin House of Representatives have participated in the Assembly with full voting rights.[36]

Article 144(2) of the Basic Law refers to the representatives of Berlin in the *Bundestag* (the Federal Diet, composed of elected members) and *Bundesrat* (the Federal Council, composed of representatives of the *Länder*). The election of the Berlin members of the *Bundestag* is now governed by paragraph 54 of the Federal Electoral Law of 7 May 1956 in the consolidated version of 1

---

[33] Lush, *ICLQ*, 14 (1965), pp.744–5.

[34] Zivier, p.77. *Land* Berlin officials swear an oath of allegiance to the Basic Law and the Constitution of Berlin; the Allied Kommandatura did not object since the form of oath took sufficiently into account Allied reservations: BK/L(56)21 of 25 July 1956: Heidelmeyer *Dokumente*, pp.127–8; *US Documents*, pp.840, 844.

[35] *BVerfGE* 1,70; Heidelmeyer *Dokumente*, p.125. These provisions do not, of course, bind the Allied authorities.

[36] In 1949 the Berlin members did not vote. In 1954 their votes were counted separately: Maunz, in: Maunz–Dürig, *Kommentar zum Grundgesetz*, Article 54, note 13.

September 1975, which has been taken over in Berlin.[37] Berlin sends twenty-two members to the *Bundestag*.[38] As a result of the Military Governors' reservations and those of the Allied Kommandatura, they are not directly elected by the people of Berlin but are elected by the Berlin House of Representatives at a special session held on the same day as the general election in the Federal Republic, on the basis of the strength of the parties in the House of Representatives. Their mandate is for the duration of the *Bundestag*, not that of the House of Representatives.

The Military Governors' reservations also stated that the Berlin members should not have the right to vote in the *Bundestag*.[39] This is not expressly regulated in the *Bundestag* rules of procedure but applies in practice as follows. Berlin members vote in committees (including the *Bundestag/Bundesrat* mediation committee provided for in Article 77 of the Basic Law) and on other occasions where the vote does not have legislative effect. Examples are votes on general resolutions, on the first and second reading of Bills (but not the final reading) and on internal *Bundestag* matters, such as the election of the President of the *Bundestag* and procedural matters. On certain occasions the Berlin representatives vote but their votes are counted separately and do not count towards the result, for example upon the election of the Federal Chancellor.[40] Apart from voting, the Berlin members are in the same position as other members of the *Bundestag*; their activities are in no way restricted by the special status of Berlin. They may, for example, be officers of the *Bundestag* or of a *Fraktion* (parliamentary party group).

The position in the *Bundesrat* is similar. The *Senat* of Berlin sends four of its members to the *Bundesrat*. The voting practice is similar to that in the *Bundestag*, though it remains somewhat more restrictive.[41] In other respects the Berlin members are in the same position as other members of the *Bundesrat*; for example they may hold office.[42]

---

[37] *BGBl.* I, p.2325, last amended by the Law of 8 March 1985: *BGBl.* I, p.521. For earlier Laws see paragraph 28 of the Federal Electoral Law of 15 June 1949: *BGBl.* I, p.21, Heidelmeyer, p.116; paragraph 55 of the Federal Electoral Law of 4 July 1953: *BGBl.* I, p.470; Berlin Law of 7 July 1953: *GVBl.* p.572; Federal Electoral Law of 7 May 1956: *BGBl.* I, p.383; *GVBl.* p.632. See also Heidelmeyer *Dokumente*, pp.133–8 and the notes at pp.607–8.

[38] Berlin originally sent eight representatives; this was increased to nineteen in 1952 and twenty-two in 1953; see Plischke, *Government and Politics of Contemporary Berlin*, p.69.

[39] This position has been confirmed on a number of occasions: see *BPIL* 1966, p.200; Wettig, *DA*, 12 (1979), p.922.

[40] Lush, *ICLQ*, 14 (1965), p.756. For suggestions in 1972 that the position be changed after the Quadripartite Agreement, see Nawrocki, *DA*, 7 (1974), p.589; Schiedermair, pp.109, 110; *Das Vierseitige Abkommen*, pp.129, 130.

[41] Zivier, p.106; Lush, *ICLQ*, 14 (1965), p.757.

[42] See the note in Heidelmeyer *Dokumente*, p.606.

Germans with a first residence in the Federal Republic and a second residence in Berlin are included in the register of voters for the *Bundestag* at their Federal residence. Germans with a first residence in Berlin and a second residence in the Federal Republic may register in the Federal Republic upon special application.[43]

Article 54 of the Basic Law provides that every German is eligible to be Federal President who is entitled to vote for *Bundestag* candidates and has attained the age of forty years. In the case of temporary incapacity or a vacancy the powers of the Federal President are exercised by the President of the *Bundesrat* or, in his incapacity, by the Vice-President of the *Bundesrat*. Under these provisions the Governing Mayor of Berlin has temporarily exercised the powers of the Federal President.[44] Germans living in Berlin may be candidates for political office in the Federal Republic of Germany; eligibility does not depend upon residence in the Federal Republic.[45]

The position of Berlin in relation to Federal constitutional organs was not affected by the Quadripartite Agreement of 3 September 1971 (except in the context of Federal presence: see Chapter 13 below).

---

[43] Zivier, p.107; paragraph 16.1 No. 1a of the Federal Election Order of 8 November 1979: *BGBl.* I, p.1805; *GVBl.* p.1950.
[44] Lush, *ICLQ*, 14 (1965), p.780; Zivier, p.106.
[45] Paragraph 18 of the Federal Election Law.

CHAPTER 11

THE APPLICATION IN BERLIN OF FEDERAL LEGISLATION

THE Allied Kommandatura and Commandants remain the supreme legislative authorities in Berlin, and Allied law overrides incompatible German law (Chapter 5 above). But Allied law covers a limited field; for most legal practitioners in Berlin, and indeed for Berliners generally, the law applicable in Berlin is to a large extent German law identical or virtually identical to that applicable in the Federal Republic. The application in Berlin of legislative provisions that are the same as Federal legislation is an important aspect of the ties between Berlin and the Federal Republic of Germany.[1] Berlin is not a *Land* of the Federal Republic of Germany and may not be governed by it, and Federal legislation cannot apply in Berlin by virtue of an act of the Federation. Instead, there is a taking over (*Übernahme*) of the provisions of most Federal Laws as Berlin Laws by the Berlin House of Representatives by means of a *Mantelgesetz* (Cover Law) procedure authorised by the Allied Kommandatura. This takes place only after the Allied Kommandatura has signified that it has no objection to the taking over of the Law or has indicated the conditions under which it may be taken over. Once a Law has been taken over, the application of its provisions in Berlin is, in nearly all cases, virtually indistinguishable from the application of the Federal Law in the Federal Republic of Germany. The resulting situation is often referred to by German authors as *Rechtseinheit* (legal uniformity or harmony); the greatest possible degree of *Rechtseinheit* is considered a desirable objective. Only in exceptional, but nevertheless significant, cases are Federal Laws not taken over, or taken over with modifications or omissions; such cases are kept to the minimum consistent with Berlin's legal status.

The Federal Republic of Germany, as a federal State, has both Federal and *Land* Laws (*Gesetze*). Federal Laws are passed by the *Bundestag*, with the participation of the *Bundesrat*; *Land* Laws by the parliaments of the different *Länder*. Laws may provide for secondary legislation, for example Ordinances (*Verordnungen*). The legislative power of the Federation is set out in detail in the Basic

---

[1] Sendler, *JR*, 1958, pp.81–6 and 127–9; Lush, *ICLQ*, 14 (1965), pp.757–71; Wengler, in: *Fs Leibholz*, Vol. II, pp.939–62; Czermak, *Die Stellung Berlins in der Rechts-, Gerichts- und Finanzordnung der Bundesrepublik Deutschland*, pp.60–101 (in this Chapter referred to as Czermak); Zivier, pp.78–83, 124–31; Sendler, *JuS*, 23 (1983), pp.905–7.

Law for the Federal Republic of Germany;[2] it may be exclusive (Article 73) or concurrent (Article 74). In other fields the *Länder* are competent. Two important characteristics of Federal law are that it overrides inconsistent *Land* law: *Bundesrecht bricht Landesrecht* (Article 31); and that only the Federal Constitutional Court may find that Federal legislation is contrary to the Basic Law and thus null and void.

THE PROCEDURE FOR TAKING OVER FEDERAL LEGISLATION

Article 1(3) of the 1950 Constitution of Berlin provides that the Basic Law and Laws of the Federal Republic of Germany are binding on Berlin, but this provision is suspended by BK/O(50)75 of 29 August 1950.[3] In anticipation thereof, Article 87(2) of the Constitution provided that:

> During the transitional period [that is, while the Basic Law is subject to restrictions in Berlin] the House of Representatives may by Law determine that a Law of the Federal Republic of Germany also applies without alteration in Berlin.

This is qualified by BK/O(50)75, paragraph 2(c) of which states *inter alia* that "the provisions of any Federal law shall apply to Berlin only after they have been voted upon by the House of Representatives and passed as a Berlin law". Until 1951 the Berlin legislature adopted "parallel Laws", that is to say, local Berlin Laws with, so far as possible, the same wording as the Federal Laws.[4] A more satisfactory procedure was then developed.[5] BK/O(51)56 of 8 October 1951 laid down the procedure as follows:

> Whereas it has become apparent that some clarification of the provisions of BK/O(50)75 is necessary, the Allied Kommandatura has decided that paragraph 2(c) of BK/O(50)75 shall be interpreted to mean that:
> (a) The Berlin House of Representatives may take over a Federal law by means of a "*Mantelgesetz*" (Cover law) which states that the provisions of the Federal law are valid in Berlin;

---

[2] *Reich* Laws are referred to in Articles 124 and 125 of the Basic Law: see Czermak, pp.90–2; Zivier, p.129.
[3] *VOBl.* p.440; *Selected Documents* I, p.135; *US Documents*, p.340; Heidelmeyer, p.121.
[4] Fijalkowski, *Berlin – Hauptstadtanspruch und Westintegration*, pp.142–4; Czermak, pp.65–9. Important parallel Laws were the Berlin *Gesetz zur Wiederherstellung der Rechtseinheit auf dem Gebiete der Gerichtsverfassung, der bürgerlichen Rechtspflege, des Strafverfahrens und Kostenrechts* of 9 January 1951 (*VOBl.* p.99) and the *Gesetz über Preisregelung* of 20 March 1950 (*VOBl.* p.95).
[5] For the development of the *Mantelgesetz* see Kreutzer, *JR*, 1951, pp.641–5.

(b) The provisions of implementing ordinances or regulations under the Federal law may be made valid in Berlin by issuance (by reference or otherwise) as Berlin ordinances or regulations;

(c) The *"Mantelgesetz"* must stipulate that references in the Federal laws, ordinances and regulations to any Federal agency or authority shall be construed as references to the appropriate Berlin agency or authority. (If doubt could exist as to what that agency or authority is, the Berlin enactment must clarify the point.) An exception may be made only in a case where the Berlin Senate or the House of Representatives decides that the practical application of the law so requires, [provided that the Allied Kommandatura is notified of such decision and raises no objection thereto within twenty-one days after the receipt of such notification].[6]

The wording of the *Mantelgesetz* was determined following BK/L(52)19 of 23 February 1952 (which permitted the provisions of several Laws to be taken over by a single *Mantelgesetz*), BK/L(52)81 of 28 August 1952 and BK/L(52)118 of 4 December 1952,[7] and is now usually as follows:

Law
on the Taking Over of Laws
of [date]

The House of Representatives has passed the following Law:

Article I

The following Laws shall apply in Berlin:
1. The Law on . . . of [date] (*BGBl.* I, p. .);
2. . . .

Article II

The text of Ordinances made pursuant to the Laws mentioned in Article I shall be published in the Berlin *Gesetz- und Verordnungsblatt*, and the text of administrative regulations in the Berlin *Amtsblatt*, by the responsible member of the *Senat*.

Article III

This Law shall enter into force on the day after its promulgation in the Berlin *Gesetz- und Verordnungsblatt*. The provisions of the Laws mentioned in Article I shall come into effect at the times specified in those Laws for their entry into force.[8]

---

[6] *US Documents*, p.355; Heidelmeyer, p.128. The words in square brackets were deleted by BK/O(55)10 of 14 May 1955: Heidelmeyer, p.153.
[7] *US Documents*, pp.360, 394; Heidelmeyer, pp.129, 135.
[8] See next page.

The *Senat* submits each proposal for taking over the provisions of Federal Laws to the Allied Kommandatura. Provided the Allied Kommandatura raises no objections, the *Mantelgesetz*, including the annexed provisions of Federal Laws, is then voted on and passed by the Berlin House of Representatives in accordance with paragraph 2(c) of BK/O(50)75 and Article 87(2) of the Constitution of Berlin. It comes into force upon promulgation by the Governing Mayor in accordance with Article 46(2) of the Constitution of Berlin and is published in full (including the annexed provisions of Federal Laws) in the Berlin *Gesetz- und Verordnungsblatt*. A special form of *Mantelgesetz* exists for Federal Laws ratifying treaties (p.203 below).

The Law of 4 January 1952 on the Position of *Land* Berlin in the Financial System of the Federal Republic[9] (known as the Third Transfer Law) is a Federal Law, taken over in Berlin, which includes provisions concerning the adoption of Federal Laws in Berlin. Paragraphs 12 and 13 provide that Federal Laws will be brought into force in Berlin in accordance with Article 87(2) of the Constitution of Berlin. Paragraph 13 deals with all Laws (other than certain tax Laws covered by paragraph 12) which expressly state that they are to apply in Berlin, and requires that they be brought

---

[8] The German reads:

Gesetz
zur Übernahme von Gesetzen
Vom
Das Abgeordnetenhaus hat das folgende Gesetz beschlossen:

Artikel I
Nachstehende Gesetze finden in Berlin Anwendung:
1. Gesetz zur . . . vom . . . (BGBl. I S. . . .);
2. . . .

Artikel II
Der Wortlaut von Rechtsverordnungen, die auf Grund der in Artikel I genannten Gesetze erlassen werden, wird im Gesetz- und Verordnungsblatt für Berlin, der Wortlaut von Verwaltungsvorschriften im Amtsblatt für Berlin von dem zuständigen Mitglied des Senats veröffentlicht.

Artikel III
Dieses Gesetz tritt am Tage nach seiner Verkündung im Gesetz- und Verordnungsblatt für Berlin in Kraft. Die Vorschriften der in Artikel I genannten Gesetze werden zu den in diesen Gesetzen bezeichneten Zeitpunkten ihres Inkrafttretens wirksam.

[9] *Gesetz über die Stellung des Landes Berlin im Finanzsystem des Bundes (Drittes Überleitungsgesetz)* (*BGBl.* I, p.1), last amended in 1971 (*BGBl.* I, p.1426): Heidelmeyer *Dokumente*, p.186. The Law also deals with Federal financial assistance to Berlin. The Allied High Commission made a number of changes to ensure that the Law did not give the impression that Berlin was included in the area of application of the Basic Law or that the provisions of Federal Laws applied in Berlin as Federal Laws: see Heidelmeyer *Dokumente*, p.192; Lush, *ICLQ*, 14 (1965), pp.760–1. On the Third Transfer Law generally see Plischke, *Berlin: Development of its Government and Administration*, pp.126–32; Sendler, *JR*, 1958, p.83; Finkelnburg, *JuS*, 8 (1968), p.11; Sendler, *JuS*, 23 (1983), pp.905–6.

into force in Berlin within one month. Each such Federal Law contains a Berlin clause, usually in the following terms:

> As provided in paragraph 13 of the Third Transfer Law of 4 January 1952 (*BGBl.* I, p.1), this Law also applies in *Land* Berlin.[10]

The Third Transfer Law was taken over in Berlin by *Mantelgesetz* of 12 June 1952.[11] Unless the Allies raise objection, the Berlin House of Representatives enacts any Federal Law which the Federal legislature decides shall apply in Berlin. Its rules of procedure provide for a simplified procedure, and it has traditionally passed *Mantelgesetze* without debate.[12]

Paragraph 14 of the Third Transfer Law provides that Federal Ordinances and regulations (that is, secondary legislation implementing provisions of Federal Laws taken over in Berlin) are directly applicable in Berlin. There is therefore no requirement for adoption by the *Senat*. Pursuant to BK/L(52)81 of 28 August 1952 they are published in the Berlin *Gesetz- und Verordnungsblatt* by the Senator for Justice (before 1966 by the Senator responsible for the subject-matter). BK/L(52)81 provides that publication "is an indispensable requirement".[13] On the other hand, Ordinances based on a *Reich* Law contain a Berlin clause providing that they apply in Berlin once put into effect there, and they are then adopted by a Berlin Ordinance made by the *Senat*.[14] Federal administrative regulations implementing provisions of Federal Laws taken over in Berlin are published in the Berlin *Amtsblatt* (BK/L(52)81).

These procedures have not changed significantly since 1952.[15] They were, for example, not altered at the time of the Bonn/Paris Conventions. Paragraph 4 of the letter from the three High

---

[10] The standard Berlin clause reads in German: *Dieses Gesetz gilt nach Massgabe des § 13 Abs 1 des Dritten Überleitungsgesetzes vom 4. Januar 1952 (Bundesgesetzbl. I.S. 1) auch im Land Berlin*. The form of the Berlin clause was the subject of a Federal Cabinet decision of 6 February 1954: Heidelmeyer *Dokumente*, p.169. In the case of a Federal Law ratifying a treaty the Berlin clause reads: This Law also applies in *Land* Berlin in so far as *Land* Berlin establishes the application of this Law: *Dieses Gesetz gilt auch im Land Berlin, sofern das Land Berlin die Anwendung dieses Gesetzes feststellt*.

[11] *GVBl.* p.393.

[12] Czermak, pp.72–3. Since the 1981 election *Alternative Liste* representatives have insisted on debating certain *Mantelgesetze*.

[13] Czermak, pp.84–8. It is, however, controversial whether publication is constitutive or declaratory. Sendler, *JuS*, 23 (1983), p.906, suggests it is declaratory because of paragraph 14 of the Third Transfer Law.

[14] Article 47 of the Constitution of Berlin; both the adopting and the adopted Ordinances are published in the Berlin *Gesetz- und Verordnungsblatt*.

[15] In 1955 a Bill, known as the *Globalgesetz*, was proposed in the House of Representatives to replace the *Mantelgesetz* procedure by one whereby Federal Laws would simply have been promulgated by the Governing Mayor at the request of the President of the House of Representatives; the Bill was not passed. Since 1966 the titles of *Mantelgesetze* no longer refer to the Federal Laws they adopt by name; they are now simply entitled Law on the Taking Over of Laws (*Gesetz zur Übernahme von Gesetzen*).

Commissioners concerning the exercise of the reserved Allied rights relating to Berlin (p.329 below) reads as follows:

> Similarly, they will have no objections if, in accordance with an appropriate procedure authorised by the Allied Kommandatura, Berlin adopts the same legislation as that of the Federal Republic, in particular regarding currency, credit and foreign exchange, nationality, passports, emigration and immigration, extradition, the unification of the customs and trade area, trade and navigation agreements, freedom of movement of goods, and foreign trade and payments arrangements.

This paragraph was repeated by the Allied Kommandatura in Article IV of its 1955 Declaration on Berlin (p.332 below), where it is expressly subject to Articles I and II thereof, that is to say, to existing Allied Kommandatura reservations and in particular to the Allies' right to take measures "to fulfil their international obligations, to ensure public order and to maintain the status and security of Berlin and its economy, trade and communications".

The Quadripartite Agreement of 3 September 1971 contains provisions relevant to the applicability of Federal legislation in Berlin. First, the application of Federal Laws is clearly among "the ties between the Western Sectors of Berlin and the Federal Republic of Germany", which are to be "maintained and developed, taking into account that these Sectors continue not to be a constituent part of the Federal Republic and not to be governed by it". Detailed arrangements concerning the relationship between Berlin and the Federal Republic of Germany are set forth in Annex II of the Quadripartite Agreement. Although Annex II does not expressly refer to Federal legislation, it clearly covers it. In point (d) of their letter of 3 September 1971 to the Federal Chancellor concerning clarifications and interpretations of the statements contained in Annex II, the three Western Ambassadors stated:

> Established procedures concerning the applicability to the Western Sectors of Berlin of legislation of the Federal Republic of Germany shall remain unchanged.

This covers not only the *Mantelgesetz* procedure itself but all the procedures relating to the application of Federal legislation in Berlin.[16] A copy of the letter was formally transmitted to, and noted by, the Soviet Ambassador in advance of its transmission. In a second letter of 3 September 1971 to the Federal Chancellor the Western Ambassadors recalled *inter alia* the 1952/54 letter cited above and the 1967 *Niekisch* aide-mémoire (p.174 below) and stated

---

[16] Zivier, p.193.

that the Quadripartite Agreement accorded with the position in these documents, which remained unchanged.

THE EXTENT TO WHICH FEDERAL LEGISLATION IS ADOPTED

The legislative powers of the German authorities in Berlin were narrowly circumscribed by the Allies in the years immediately following 1945. In 1949, when the Federal Republic of Germany came into being, Berlin's legislative powers continued to be limited in accordance with the 1949 Statement of Principles (and even under the revised Statement of 1951 and the 1955 Declaration on Berlin), but within these limitations it was possible for the House of Representatives to adopt the same provisions as those of the Laws of the Federal Republic. Under the Third Transfer Law the Berlin legislature takes over all Federal Laws which contain a Berlin clause. Where a Law has a Berlin clause this generally provides simply that the Law shall apply in Berlin in accordance with the Third Transfer Law. In certain cases, however, it contains a so-called "split" clause, which expressly qualifies its application in Berlin by reference to Allied rights and responsibilities. In yet other cases, the clause may provide that certain provisions of the Law will, or will not, apply in Berlin. The Berlin House of Representatives traditionally respects the wishes of the Federal legislature, except where the Allied Kommandatura, which checks all Federal Laws before their provisions are taken over, makes clear its opposition. The Allied Kommandatura occasionally did so in the 1950s and 1960s, but more recently advance consultation has rendered such action less necessary. The Allied Kommandatura has, nevertheless, sometimes considered it desirable to lay down specific conditions for the application of certain Federal Laws.

Some Federal legislation contains no Berlin clause and is not taken over, for example that dealing with defence matters, the Federal armed forces and NATO; with war weapons; and with civil defence and emergencies. Other Federal legislation is not taken over in Berlin despite the inclusion of a Berlin clause. An important example is the Law on the Federal Constitutional Court of 12 March 1951 (pp.173–4 below).[17]

A number of Federal Laws taken over in Berlin contain particular provisions which are not adopted. This is sometimes the result of Allied intervention, for example in connection with military matters dealt with in such Laws as the Penal Code, the Federal Passport and Nationality Law, and the Federal Atomic Law. More often, the Law itself makes express provision excluding application in Berlin either

---

[17] Lush, *ICLQ*, 14 (1965), pp.766–8. See also Chapters 21 and 22 below.

in the Berlin clause or, more commonly in recent years, in particular provisions.[18]

The Allied authorities in Berlin sometimes indicate expressly the conditions under which Federal Laws may apply. They have done so either generally in relation to all Federal Laws (for example BK/O(51)63 of 13 November 1951[19] on Federal activities); or in relation to a particular Law (for example BK/O(51)10 of 30 January 1951[20] concerning the Federal Law on the administration of justice; BK/O(59)9 of 26 May 1959[21] concerning the Air Traffic Law; BK/O(83)2 of 28 April 1983[22] concerning the Federal Law on International Assistance in Criminal Cases; BK/O(84)11 of 21 December 1984[23] concerning the General Railway Law). Quite apart from any express conditions, the provisions of Federal Laws which have been taken over in Berlin, like all German Laws there, are subject to Allied rights and responsibilities and Allied legislation. The Allied Kommandatura reiterated this in BK/O(74)11 of 30 September 1974, which reads in part:

> Considering the large number of laws and treaties being extended to Berlin, the Allied Kommandatura wishes to emphasise that, in the light of Article VI of the Declaration on Berlin of 5 May 1955 (BKC/L(55)3), even in those cases where no reservations are laid down expressly by the Allied Kommandatura, such laws and treaties do not affect the rights and responsibilities of the Allies or Allied legislation. Authorities and services responsible for the application of laws and international treaties in Berlin must continue to conform strictly with Allied legislation . . . [24]

THE NATURE AND EFFECT OF ADOPTED LEGISLATION

The provisions of a Federal Law taken over in Berlin by the *Mantelgesetz* procedure are a Berlin Law, that is to say, a Law of the Berlin legislature, and not a Law of the Federal legislature.[25] The Federal Law itself does not apply in Berlin, either by virtue of the Basic Law or otherwise; what applies is a Berlin Law incorporating provisions of the Federal Law. As has been seen, the provisions of

---

[18] Lush, *ICLQ*, 14 (1965), pp.768–70.
[19] Heidelmeyer, p.129.
[20] Published in part in *VOBl.* p.1106.
[21] *GVBl.* p.666.
[22] *GVBl.* p.772.
[23] *GVBl.* p.1845.
[24] *GVBl.* p.2576.
[25] Zivier (p.129) suggests that they are "joint legislative acts of the Federal and the Berlin legislatures". But the fact that the Allies require that the Law only be taken over after it has been published in the *Bundesgesetzblatt* does not support Zivier's view, since the reason for this requirement is entirely practical: the Allies need to see the Law before it is taken over.

the Berlin Law may be identical to those of the Federal Law, or the latter may be modified by its own terms or by Allied action. And their application may be subject to interpretations or conditions imposed by the Allied authorities.

The Federal Constitutional Court has, however, held that Federal Laws apply in Berlin as Federal law, not as Berlin law.[26] This view is followed by other courts in the Federal Republic and Berlin and by many West German authors.[27] But it is contrary to the clear position under Allied law and incompatible with the *Mantelgesetz* procedure. BK/O(50)75, which is the basic Allied legislative instrument on the matter, expressly provides that "the provisions of any Federal law shall apply to Berlin only after they have been voted upon by the House of Representatives and passed as a Berlin law". The Allied High Commissioners changed provisions of the Third Transfer Law that implied that Federal Laws taken over in Berlin applied there as Federal Laws. The Allies recalled their position following the Federal Constitutional Court's decision in the *Niekisch* case,[28] and at the time of signing the Quadripartite Agreement.[29] And in BK/O(74)2 of 23 April 1974[30] concerning the Introductory Law to the Criminal Code, the Allied Kommandatura recalled that "the provisions of Federal legislation, when they are adopted in Berlin, take effect there as provisions of Berlin legislation". The *Mantelgesetz* procedure confirms the Allied view; it makes clear that the provisions of Federal Laws do not apply in Berlin (as they apply in the Federal Republic) upon adoption by the Federal legislature acting under the Basic Law; instead they apply by virtue of the adoption of the *Mantelgesetz* by the Berlin House of Representatives acting under Article 87(2) of the Constitution of Berlin and in accordance with the procedure authorised by the Allies. The Federal legislature's inclusion of a Berlin clause indicates its view that the Law should apply in Berlin, and is regarded by the Berlin legislature as a condition precedent for application, but it is not itself effective to apply the Law.

It is not obvious that the assertion by West German courts and

---

[26] *BVerfGE* 19, 377 (388) (*Niekisch* case); 20, 257 (267); 37, 57 (62) (*Brückmann* case).

[27] BGH *NJW*, 32 (1979), p.2559 (p.2560); BGHZ 80, 87 (90). West German authors who hold that the provisions of Federal Laws apply as Federal law include Sendler, *JuS*, 23 (1983), p.903. Those taking the contrary view include Wengler, in: *Fs Leibholz* Vol. II, p.939; Czermak, pp.62–95; Pestalozza, *JuS*, 23 (1983), p.254.

[28] Allied aide-mémoires of 18 April 1967 (*US Documents*, p.959) and, in substantially the same terms, BK/L(67)10 of 24 May 1967 (*Selected Documents* II, p. 156), which stated that it "remains the Allied intention and opinion that Berlin laws, if they adopt the provisions of Federal laws, are legislative acts of the Berlin House of Representatives and are legally distinct from such Federal laws".

[29] In their letter of 3 September 1971 to the Federal Chancellor conveying the text of the Quadripartite Agreement: p.346 below.

[30] *GVBl.* p.1055.

authors that the provisions of Federal Laws apply as Federal law and not as Berlin law has major practical consequences. The debate is in most respects one of definition and appearance. Allied insistence that the provisions of Federal Laws apply in Berlin as Berlin law, like the *Mantelgesetz* procedure itself, reflects the fact that the Federal legislature has no competence in relation to Berlin: "the Federal Republic cannot be said to exercise sovereign legislative powers in relation to Berlin as it would do if Berlin were in fact an integral part of the Republic".[31] The Federal Constitutional Court's insistence on the contrary position is closely connected with its assertion that Berlin is a *Land* of the Federal Republic.

Under the Basic Law Federal law is superior to *Land* law, including *Land* constitutional law. This is an essential element of the legal system in the Federal Republic of Germany and if the position were different in Berlin this could render nugatory efforts towards *Rechtseinheit*.[32] Those who hold that adopted Federal law remains Federal law appear to have this quality of Federal law in mind. If their view were accepted there would be no doubt that the provisions of a Federal Law taken over in Berlin would be superior to ordinary *Land* Law[33] passed by the Berlin House of Representatives. But the fact that provisions of adopted Laws are Berlin Laws does not prevent them being treated as superior to other Berlin *Land* Laws. This is what happens in practice in Berlin since Berlin courts and authorities accept that the provisions of Federal Laws taken over in Berlin are superior to other Berlin *Land* law.[34] They may be regarded as doing so on the basis of legal conviction, or indeed commonsense, since any other approach would lead to confusion and run counter to *Rechtseinheit*. This position is not inconsistent with Article 87(2) of the Constitution of Berlin or indeed with Allied provisions on the matter, and may be said to have its legal basis therein.[35] In short, Allied intentions have in practice been interpreted as meaning that those Berlin Laws that consist of adopted provisions of Federal Laws should apply as if they were Federal law, and in particular override other Berlin *Land* law. They remain, of course, subject to Allied law. It is not necessary, in order to reach this result, to fly in the face of the

[31] Lush, *ICLQ*, 14 (1965), p.771.
[32] As Zivier says (p.125), "The creation of merely content-identical Berlin *Land* law would not conform to the intentions of the Federal legislature . . . nor the intentions of the Berlin legislature. Furthermore, this would not be the purpose of the Allied reservations".
[33] The term "*Land* Law" in the context of Berlin is here used to denote local legislation enacted for Berlin alone.
[34] Zivier, pp.83, 124–6.
[35] Some West German authors (Zivier, p.126; Mussgnug, in: *Fs Weber*, p.176) consider that Article 31 of the Basic Law applies in Berlin, but this view is not compatible with the fact that adopted Laws are not Federal Laws. See however Wengler, in: *Fs Leibholz* Vol. II, p.958.

express Allied provisions and hold that they actually are Federal law.

Berlin courts applying adopted Federal law can be expected to have regard to decisions of courts in the Federal Republic of Germany. This is a normal judicial approach, and is not affected by the different formal basis for the provisions. It is, moreover, consistent with the general objective of the greatest possible degree of *Rechtseinheit*, and indeed with the fact that – with the exception of the Federal Constitutional Court – Federal courts (acting as Berlin courts) also have jurisdiction in Berlin matters.

The Allies have on occasion declined to permit provisions of Federal Laws taken over in Berlin to be treated differently from other Berlin *Land* law, presumably because to do so might imply that it was indeed Federal law. Under former Article 49 of the Constitution of Berlin, which was repealed in 1974, *Land* Laws could be passed by referendum in accordance with an implementing Law. No implementing Law was passed because the Allies did not accept that it should expressly state that such *Land* Laws could not amend or annul adopted provisions of Federal Laws.[36] The Allies adopted a similar position in relation to the question of a Berlin Constitutional Court, declining to approve an implementing Law excluding adopted Federal law from its jurisdiction. The *Senat* insisted on such an exclusion, and, as a result, Article 72 of the Constitution of Berlin was suspended by a new Article 87a (p.71 above).

The provisions of the Basic Law concerning the legislative powers of the *Länder* (Articles 71 to 75) are in practice respected in Berlin. In particular, where provisions of a Federal Law in the area of concurrent powers have been taken over in Berlin the House of Representatives regards itself, in accordance with Article 87 of the Constitution of Berlin, as no longer able to pass ordinary *Land* Law in the same field. But if such Federal legislation is not taken over, Berlin's legislative power is regarded as unaffected by the adoption of the Law by the Federal legislature. The Berlin legislature regards itself as having no legislative power in the area of exclusive competence of the Federal legislature unless authorised by the Allied Kommandatura. The Berlin legislature may, of course, also be authorised by Allied action to enact Laws in areas where it would otherwise not act; likewise, legislative action even in traditional areas might be limited by the Allies.[37]

---

[36] Zivier, p.127.
[37] Zivier, pp.130-1. For the purpose of applying the provisions of Federal Laws, the Federal Republic of Germany and Berlin are treated as a single law district, though this does not of course prevent a modified application of Federal Laws in Berlin where this is specified in the Laws or by the Allied Kommandatura: Zivier, p.125.

THE SOVIET ATTITUDE TO THE ADOPTION OF FEDERAL LEGISLATION

Unlike the extension to Berlin of international treaties (Chapter 15 below), the taking over of provisions of Federal legislation has not, in general, proved a source of controversy with the Soviet Union, which appears to accept that the *Mantelgesetz* procedure adequately safeguards Berlin's status. This perhaps explains why there is no express mention of the matter in Annex II of the Quadripartite Agreement – though there is in the letter containing clarifications and interpretations which the three Ambassadors sent to the Federal Chancellor and which was communicated to and noted by the Soviet Union. Nevertheless, the Soviet Union follows developments closely. It has, of course, frequently objected in general terms to what it sees as the incorporation of Berlin into the Federal Republic of Germany, but its objections to the extension of particular pieces of legislation have been comparatively infrequent. The Soviet protest in 1973 against the proposed taking over of the Introductory Law to the Criminal Code[38] indicates its approach to this matter. The protest pointed out *inter alia* that the Law amended the Law on the Federal Constitutional Court, that it treated Berlin as a *Land* of the Federal Republic of Germany, that it dealt with activities of the Federal Government, and that it covered matters relating to the security of the Federal Republic. It further stated:

> In conformity with the Quadripartite Agreement the three Powers have also undertaken that established procedures concerning the applicability to the Western Sectors of Berlin of legislation of the FRG shall remain unchanged. In accordance with the Declaration of the authorities of the USA, Great Britain and France of 5 May 1955 that means in particular that in no case can legislation of the FRG be applied in the Western Sectors of Berlin that relates to such questions as security, disarmament and demilitarisation, civil aviation, the police etc.[39]

---

[38] *Das Vierseitige Abkommen*, p.148. The GDR protested in similar terms: *Das Vierseitige Abkommen*, p.151.

[39] In fact, the Allied Kommandatura was most careful to ensure that the taking over of the Law in no way affected the status of Berlin: BK/O(74)2 of 23 April 1974 (*GVBl.* p.1055). For further examples of Soviet protests see *Selected Documents* II, pp.123, 126; *Das Vierseitige Abkommen*, pp.203, 221, 251.

CHAPTER 12

THE ROLE OF FEDERAL AGENCIES IN RELATION TO BERLIN

FEDERAL agencies and officials derive their authority in relation to Berlin from the Berlin legislature and government. Their activities are subject to control by the Allied Kommandatura to the same extent as are the activities of local Berlin authorities. This is a consequence of Allied supreme authority, and reflects the position that Berlin is not a *Land* of the Federal Republic of Germany and may not be governed by it.

With certain important exceptions, Federal agencies and officials in practice act in relation to Berlin in the same way as in relation to the *Länder* of the Federal Republic. But the legal basis is quite different: they act not by virtue of Federal authority but by virtue of Berlin authority, and thus as Berlin organs. While this distinction is not generally apparent, it is nonetheless real, and is central to the maintenance of Allied supreme authority and the position that Berlin is not a Federal *Land* and is not to be governed by the Federation. The distinction has, moreover, certain important practical consequences: not all Federal agencies are permitted to act in Berlin matters, and those that are so permitted are just as much subject to Allied powers and jurisdiction as local Berlin authorities. BK/O(51)63 of 13 November 1951[1] set forth the position in the following terms:

> In connection with the enactment by Berlin of Federal legislation, the Allied Kommandatura directs you to take note that the powers and jurisdiction of the Occupation Authorities shall not be affected by any delegation of any authority to officials or agencies outside Berlin made by any Berlin authority. Activities in Berlin of any such officials or agencies, including activities under their instructions (the authority in Berlin of all such officials or agencies being derived from the Berlin Legislature or Government), shall be subject to the same powers and jurisdiction of the Occupation Authorities as are activities of the Berlin authorities.

This important Allied Order applies to all Federal agencies acting in Berlin matters, including Federal Ministries, officials, and courts. It makes clear a number of points: Federal agencies only exercise powers in relation to Berlin by virtue of a delegation made by a Berlin authority, that is to say, their authority is derived from the Berlin legislature or government; and they exercise such powers by

---

[1] Heidelmeyer, p.129.

virtue of provisions of Federal legislation which have been taken over in Berlin. Allied powers and jurisdiction are not affected by such delegation; in particular, the activities of Federal agencies, and activities carried out on their instructions, are subject to Allied powers and jurisdiction.

The Quadripartite Agreement of 3 September 1971 did not require changes in the activities of Federal agencies in relation to Berlin since its provisions were consistent with the existing position.[2] Part IIB provides that "the ties between the Western Sectors of Berlin and the Federal Republic of Germany will be maintained and developed, taking into account that these Sectors continue not to be a constituent part of the Federal Republic of Germany and not to be governed by it". This provision is repeated in paragraph 1 of Annex II, which goes on to state that the provisions of the Basic Law for the Federal Republic of Germany and of the Constitution of Berlin which contradict it have been suspended and continue not to be in effect. Paragraph 2 of Annex II provides that state bodies of the Federal Republic of Germany will not perform in the Western Sectors of Berlin constitutional or official acts which contradict this basic position, that is to say, they will not perform "acts in exercise of direct state authority over the Western Sectors of Berlin" (point (a) of the letter of 3 September 1971 containing clarifications and interpretations). The state bodies concerned are the Federal President, Federal Chancellor, Federal Government, Federal Cabinet, Federal Ministers and Ministries (including branch offices of Ministries), Federal Assembly, *Bundesrat* and *Bundestag* (including committees and *Fraktionen*), and all Federal courts.[3] None of these may perform in the Western Sectors of Berlin acts of direct state authority over the Western Sectors.[4] In fact, no Federal agencies are authorised to perform acts of direct state authority over Berlin. Such acts as they may be authorised to perform in relation to Berlin are at most acts of indirect state authority, since they are acts of delegated authority derived from the Berlin legislature or government and are subject to Allied powers and jurisdiction. The Quadripartite Agreement contains no general prohibition on acts of direct state authority over the Federal Republic of Germany being performed in Berlin, though some specific manifestations of Federal presence are excluded (Chapter 13 below).

[2] A related but distinct question is the presence of Federal agencies in Berlin and their activities there in relation to the Federal Republic of Germany (Chapter 13 below).
[3] See Annex II, paragraph 2, of the Agreement, together with point (e) of the letter containing clarifications and interpretations (p.345 below). "Branch offices" of Ministries means offices subordinate to the central establishment of the Ministry, and not separate agencies loosely linked to a Ministry such as the Federal Cartel Office.
[4] This term was used by the Federal Constitutional Court in its decision of 21 May 1957: *BVerfGE* 7, 1.

FEDERAL EXECUTIVE AGENCIES[5]

The relationship between the Federation and the *Länder* under the Basic Law is complex. In most cases the *Länder* execute Federal Laws, either as matters of their own concern or as agents for the Federation. In each case the Federal Government may issue general administrative regulations,[6] and it exercises a degree of supervision and may issue instructions to the *Länder* (Articles 83 to 85 of the Basic Law). The adoption of provisions of a Federal Law in Berlin normally involves acceptance of such arrangements for their execution. The Federal role does not amount to a governing of Berlin by the Federation since it results from the adoption of the provisions of the Federal Law in Berlin as a Berlin Law and is subject to the principles embodied in BK/O(51)63. In other words, even where the Federation supervises and gives instruction to Berlin its authority to do so is derived from Berlin and is subject to Allied powers and jurisdiction.

In other cases the Federation executes Federal Laws by means of Federal agencies. Thus, certain matters specified in Article 87(1) of the Basic Law are conducted as matters of direct Federal administration, for example the foreign service, the postal administration and shipping. Others are the concern of autonomous Federal higher authorities or Federal corporate bodies and institutions under public law (Article 87(2) and (3) of the Basic Law). Paragraph 1(c) of BK/O(51)56 of 8 October 1951[7] reads as follows:

> The "Mantelgesetz" must stipulate that references in the Federal laws, ordinances and regulations to any Federal agency or authority shall be construed as references to the appropriate Berlin agency or authority. (If doubt could exist as to what that agency or authority is, the Berlin enactment must clarify the point.) An exception may be made only in a case where the Berlin Senate or the House of Representatives decides that the practical application of the law so requires.

This provision envisaged that references in Federal Laws to Federal agencies should generally be read as references to the corresponding Berlin agency. Exceptions could be made on practical grounds. In fact the exception has become the norm,[8] and references to Federal agencies generally take effect in Berlin subject to the principles embodied in BK/O(51)63, that is to say, such

---

[5] Zivier, pp.93–7.
[6] These are published in the Berlin *Amtsblatt*: BK/L(52)81.
[7] Heidelmeyer, p.128.
[8] In 1955 the Allies revoked the requirement of prior notification of the "exceptional" cases: paragraph 5 of BK/O(55)10 of 14 May 1955 (Heidelmeyer, p.153).

agencies act as Berlin organs.[9] This is not, however, always so. Thus, the Federal Association Law of 5 August 1964 is modified in Berlin so that prohibitions are issued by a local Berlin organ rather than the Federal Minister of the Interior.[10]

The two principal areas where Berlin *Land* authorities execute Federal Laws which, in the Federal *Länder*, would be executed by Federal agencies are the postal service (the Berlin *Landespostdirektion*) and the financial administration (the Berlin *Oberfinanzdirektion*). Even here, special provisions largely assimilate these local Berlin organs to the corresponding Federal agencies.[11]

Certain Federal agencies have no role in relation to Berlin because the Federal Laws establishing their powers have not been taken over in Berlin. This is particularly the case in the fields of military matters (for example, the Federal Ministry of Defence and Federal armed forces), civil aviation, and civil defence and emergencies.

FEDERAL COURTS

With the important exception of the Federal Constitutional Court, Berlin is integrated into the judicial system of the Federal Republic of Germany. By BK/O(51)10 of 30 January 1951,[12] the Allied Kommandatura permitted the coming into force of the Berlin Law on the Re-establishment of Legal Unity of 9 January 1951.[13] This Law applied in Berlin, with certain amendments, provisions of the Federal Law on the Re-establishment of Legal Unity (including the Law on the Constitution of the Courts and the Codes of Civil and Criminal Procedure) of 12 September 1950.[14] Paragraph 4 of BK/O(51)10 reads:

The Allied Kommandatura reminds you, however,
(a) that the sole purpose of this law is to prevent divergencies developing between the judicial system and the jurisprudence of Berlin and those of the Federal Territory, and to bring these two systems and these two jurisprudences into as close harmony as possible;
(b) that in extending the competency of the Bundesgerichtshof to its

---

[9] As was, for example, expressly recalled in BK/O(76)8 of 10 September 1976 (*GVBl.* p.1950) and in BK/O(83)2 of 28 April 1983 (*GVBl.* p.772).
[10] *Bundesvereinsgesetz*: BGBl. I, p.593.
[11] For details, see Zivier, pp.94–6; Schröder, in: *Fs Mampel*, pp.75–6.
[12] Published in part in *VOBl.* p.106.
[13] *Gesetz zur Wiederherstellung der Rechtseinheit auf dem Gebiete der Gerichtsverfassung, der bürgerlichen Rechtspflege, des Strafverfahrens und Kostenrechts*: VOBl. p.99.
[14] *Gerichtsverfassungsgesetz*: BGBl. I, p.455. The current version of this Law is that promulgated in *BGBl.* 1975 I, p. 1077, last amended on 20 December 1984: *BGBl.* I, p.1654. See also BK/O(77)9 of 30 September 1977 (*GVBl.* p.2012).

territory, Berlin merely makes use of the possibility provided for in Article 88 of the Federal Law, under which the competency of this jurisdiction can be exercised outside the boundaries of the Federal Territory;

(c) that the law would, therefore, on no account constitute a step towards the transformation of the Western Sectors of Berlin into a Twelfth Land of the Federal Republic.

These three conditions, together with BK/O(51)63 (p.168 above), spell out the basic position of the Allies on the inclusion of Berlin in the Federal judicial system. As in the case of other Federal agencies, the authority of Federal courts in Berlin matters derives from the adoption of the provisions of Federal legislation in Berlin, that is to say, from acts of the Berlin legislature and government, not from acts of the Federation; they therefore act as Berlin courts. The law applied by these courts in Berlin matters is law which has been taken over in Berlin, and is thus Berlin law and not Federal law. When Federal courts act in Berlin matters they are subject to the same limitations as other Federal agencies, and indeed as Berlin courts.[15]

In addition to the Federal Supreme Court (*Bundesgerichtshof*), the jurisdiction of the other superior Federal courts – the Federal Administrative Court (*Bundesverwaltungsgericht*), Federal Labour Court (*Bundesarbeitsgericht*), Federal Finance Court (*Bundesfinanzhof*) and Federal Social Court (*Bundessozialgericht*) – has likewise been extended to Berlin. In each case the relevant Federal legislation, and any amendments thereto,[16] have been taken over in Berlin by the *Mantelgesetz* procedure. All Berlin courts, including Federal courts acting as Berlin courts, are subject to Allied Kommandatura Law No. 7, which places restrictions on their jurisdiction (p.65 above).

The list in the Quadripartite Agreement of 3 September 1971 of bodies which may not perform in Berlin acts in exercise of direct state authority over the Western Sectors of Berlin includes "all Federal courts". Those Federal courts which are authorised to exercise jurisdiction in Berlin matters do not exercise direct state authority over Berlin since both their authority and the law they apply derive from the Berlin legislature and government, and they therefore act as Berlin courts.[17] Thus, the exercise of jurisdiction over Berlin by the Federal Administrative Court, based in Berlin, does not contravene the Quadripartite Agreement; it is difficult to

---

[15] Zivier, p.84.

[16] See BK/O(77)9 of 30 September 1977 (*GVBl.* p.2012).

[17] See the exchange with the Soviet Union in *Das Vierseitige Abkommen*, pp.203, 221, 223. For a different view, see *BVerfGE* 7, 1 (Heidelmeyer *Dokumente*, pp.128–33).

see how the inclusion of Federal courts in the list can have practical consequences, except as regards the Federal Constitutional Court.

THE FEDERAL CONSTITUTIONAL COURT[18]

The Federal Constitutional Court (*Bundesverfassungsgericht*) is one of the supreme constitutional organs of the Federal Republic of Germany. Its establishment is provided for in the Basic Law (Articles 92 to 94), and it was established by the Law on the Federal Constitutional Court of 12 March 1951.[19] Its jurisdiction is extensive and varied.[20]

By BK/O(52)35 of 20 December 1952,[21] the Allied Kommandatura declined to permit the Law on the Federal Constitutional Court to be taken over in Berlin. The operative provisions of the BK/O read:

2. The provisions of the Federal Constitutional Court Law are so closely interwoven with the Basic Law that its adoption by Berlin would be inconsistent with the position taken by the Allied Kommandatura in BK/O(50)75.

3. One of the principal functions of the Federal Constitutional Court is to resolve differences between the constituent parts and organs of the Federation. The adoption of the Federal Constitutional Court Law by Berlin would make it appear that Berlin was a constituent part of the Federation.

4. The Allied Kommandatura regards the Federal Constitutional Court as one of the repositories of supreme governmental power in the Federal Republic. To accept the extension of its jurisdiction to Berlin as foreseen in the draft legislation submitted would conflict with the reservations of the Military Governors in their letter of approval of the Basic Law of 12 May 1949.

5. The Allied Kommandatura is therefore unable to accept the draft legislation submitted. This decision must be regarded as overriding any provisions in other Berlin legislation for reference to the Federal Constitutional Court of cases concerning Berlin.

The Western Allies thus made clear that the Court did not have

---

[18] See Zivier, pp.85–92; Apell, *Das Bundesverfassungsgericht und Berlin* (1984) (with extensive bibliography); Lerche, in: *Fs Leibholz* Vol. II, pp.465–80, and in: *Festgabe Bundesverfassungsgericht*, Vol. 1 (1976), pp.715–47; Finkelnburg, *JuS*, 7 (1967), pp.542–4; *JuS*, 8 (1968), pp.10–14, 58–61; *AöR*, 95 (1970), pp.581–95; *NJW*, 27 (1974), pp.1969–73; Delbrück, in *Ostverträge – Berlin-Status – Münchener Abkommen – Beziehungen Zwischen der BRD und der DDR* (1971), pp.214–20; Wengler, *JZ*, 29 (1974), pp.528–35; Mussgnug, in: *Fs Weber*, pp.157–86; Storost, *Der Staat*, 21 (1982), pp.113–26; Werner, *Die Zuständigkeit des BVerfG für Berlin* (Dissertation, Munich 1972); Elsas-Patrick, *Revue de droit international, de sciences diplomatiques et politiques*, 57 (1979), pp.245–77.

[19] *Gesetz über das Bundesverfassungsgericht*: BGBl. I, p.243.

[20] See Article 93 of the Basic Law, together with Articles 18, 21, 41, 89, 98 and 100.

[21] Heidelmeyer *Dokumente*, p.127.

jurisdiction in Berlin matters. To have permitted the Court to exercise its jurisdiction would have conflicted with the position that Berlin is neither part of, nor governed by, the Federation in so far as, unlike other Federal courts, the Federal Constitutional Court is one of the repositories of supreme governmental power in the Federal Republic. It is likewise clear that the provisions of the Basic Law concerning the Federal Constitutional Court are not applicable in Berlin.[22]

Paragraph 6 of BK/O(52)35 reads:

> Nevertheless, the Allied Kommandatura is willing to give consideration to suggestions which the Senate may present to obviate any practical difficulties to which this decision may give rise.

However, no such suggestions have been implemented, and nowadays any proposed change would have to be measured against the Quadripartite Agreement's exclusion of unilateral change in the existing situation.[23]

This position has not always been respected by the Federal Constitutional Court or by courts in Berlin, a fact which cannot affect the legal position. Nevertheless, the Allies have on occasion considered it desirable to reaffirm the legal position.[24] In the *Niekisch* case[25] the Court asserted that it had jurisdiction to review the constitutionality of Federal legislation taken over in Berlin since it regarded such legislation as retaining the quality of Federal law. The Western Allies thereupon restated their position to the Federal Government in aide-mémoires of 18 April 1967,[26] which read in part:

> It has been and remains the Allied intention and opinion that Berlin is not to be regarded as a Land of the Federal Republic and is not to be governed by the Federation. It also has been and remains the Allied intention and opinion that Berlin laws, if they adopt the provisions of Federal laws, are legislative acts of the Berlin House of Representatives and are legally distinct from such Federal laws. . .
> The Embassy considers that the Court does not have jurisdiction in relation to Berlin and that accordingly it is not competent to review either (1) the constitutionality of acts of Berlin authorities; or (2) the

---

[22] The Soviet Union obviously attaches importance to this position: see, for example, *Das Vierseitige Abkommen*, p.148.

[23] See Heidelmeyer *Dokumente*, p.606.

[24] The fact that they have not done so each time the Court has asserted its jurisdiction contrary to the Allied position does not signify any change in that position: see Apell, *Das Bundesverfassungsgericht und Berlin*, p.34. Cases have not always come to their attention in a timely manner, and in any event it is not necessary continually to repeat the position, which is clear and well publicised.

[25] Decision of 20 January 1966: *BVerfGE* 19, 377; Heidelmeyer *Dokumente*, p.563.

[26] *US Documents*, p.959.

constitutionality of Berlin laws including laws taking over provisions of Federal legislation. The Embassy would be grateful if the contents of the Aide-Mémoire could be brought to the attention of the Federal Constitutional Court in any case in which it may be relevant.

The Allied Kommandatura made the same points in BK/L(67)10 of 27 May 1967.[27]

The *Niekisch* aide-mémoire was recalled by the Western Ambassadors in their letter of 3 September 1971 to the Federal Chancellor conveying the text of the Quadripartite Agreement (p. 346 below). The Allied position was again made clear following the *Brückmann* case in 1974,[28] in which the Federal Constitutional Court once more asserted jurisdiction to review the constitutionality of Federal legislation taken over in Berlin. The Allies informed the Berlin *Kammergericht* (Appeal Court), upon request under Allied Kommandatura Law No. 7, that the Federal Constitutional Court could not be regarded as having jurisdiction in relation to Berlin and that the *Kammergericht* was prohibited from taking the Court's decision into consideration.[29]

The Allies have thus repeatedly made clear that the Federal Constitutional Court does not have jurisdiction in relation to Berlin. The central legal issue is the extent to which the Court has jurisdiction in cases with a Berlin connection. The Court itself has held that it does not have jurisdiction if its decision would affect acts of Berlin *Land* authority.[30] The Court has subsequently qualified this by holding that only politically important effects are excluded.[31] The Court thus accepts that it has no jurisdiction to hear a complaint under Article 100 of the Basic Law challenging the constitutionality of local Berlin *Land* Laws,[32] or to hear a complaint against a decision of a local Berlin *Land* organ[33] or court.[34] The Court has further held that it does not have jurisdiction to hear a constitutional complaint based on substantive grounds against a judgment of the Federal Supreme Court in a case on appeal from the Berlin courts, since this "must directly and indirectly have effects on acts of Berlin state

---

[27] The English text of BK/L(67)10 is in *Selected Documents* II, p.156, and Zivier, p.256; a German translation is in *NJW*, 20 (1967), p.1743 with notes by Wengler (p.1743) and Beyer (p.1991).
[28] *BverfGE* 37, 57.
[29] German translation in *NJW*, 27 (1974), p.1970.
[30] *BVerfGE* 7, 1 (Heidelmeyer *Dokumente*, p.128); 7, 190; 7, 192.
[31] *BVerfGE* 10, 229; 19, 337 (*Niekisch* case); 20, 257; 37, 57 (*Brückmann* case). See Apell, *Das Bundesverfassungsgericht und Berlin*, pp.26–9.
[32] *BVerfGE* 7, 1 (14, 15); 19, 377 (385) (*Niekisch* case). See Apell, *Das Bundesverfassungsgericht und Berlin*, pp.36–7.
[33] *BVerfGE* 7, 190 (no jurisdiction to determine the constitutionality of a decision of a Berlin constitutional organ); 37, 57 (*Brückmann* case).
[34] *BVerfGE* 7, 192 (no jurisdiction to hear constitutional complaint against a judgment of the Berlin *Kammergericht*).

authority", that is to say, it would lead automatically to the overturning of the *Kammergericht* decision and reinstatement of the decision at first instance.[35]

Other areas of jurisdiction accorded to the Federal Constitutional Court under the Basic Law are clearly excluded in Berlin cases since they would amount to a governing of Berlin by the Federation: constitutional disputes between Berlin and the Federation or within Berlin (Article 93 (1) Nos. 3 and 4 of the Basic Law); election challenges (Article 41 (2) of the Basic Law); loss of basic rights (Article 18 (2) of the Basic Law); prohibition of political parties (Article 21 (2) of the Basic Law); challenging judges (Article 98 (5) of the Basic Law).

The question of the jurisdiction of the Federal Constitutional Court in cases with a Berlin connection is one of continuing difficulty. In particular, as noted above, the Federal Constitutional Court has asserted that it may exercise jurisdiction in Berlin cases to review the constitutionality of –

(a) the provisions of Federal legislation taken over in Berlin, since it views such provisions as retaining the quality of Federal, as opposed to Berlin, law; and

(b) acts of Federal agencies, including Federal courts, in relation to Berlin, since it views such agencies as Federal, as opposed to Berlin, organs.[36]

Because this conflicts with express and fundamental Allied reservations and legislation, both as to the lack of jurisdiction of the Federal Constitutional Court in relation to Berlin and as to the legal quality of the legislation and acts concerned, it cannot be accepted by the Allies, who have on occasion felt it desirable to say so.

A second issue is the effect in Berlin of decisions of the Federal Constitutional Court. Under paragraph 31 of the Law on the Federal Constitutional Court: (1) decisions of the Court (that is, their main grounds) are binding on the constitutional organs of the Federation and of the *Länder*, as well as on all courts and authorities, and (2) decisions of the Court on the constitutionality of a Law, including any interpretations it places on the Law to ensure constitutionality, have legislative force. The Law on the Federal Constitutional Court does not apply in Berlin and therefore the Court's decisions are not binding in Berlin. But this does not mean that they are without practical effect there. If the Court finds a Federal Law to be unconstitutional and thus null and void, the provisions of the Federal Law taken over in Berlin are likewise

---

[35] *BVerfGE* 10, 229.
[36] E.g. *BVerfGE* 19, 337 (*Niekisch* case); BVerfGE 37, 57 (*Brückmann* case).

regarded as null and void. The Berlin legislature is considered to have adopted a nullity (the so-called *nullum* theory).[37] The position is less clear where the Court finds a Federal Law to be constitutional, especially where it does so on the basis of a particular interpretation which is then binding. There is nothing in the Allied reservations and legislation to prevent Berlin courts and officials adopting the same interpretation and in practice they do so, since the Berlin legislature intended to adopt the same substance as the Federal Law and not merely the same text. Action by Berlin organs may sometimes be required to reproduce in Berlin the effect of a judgment of the Federal Constitutional Court in the Federal Republic of Germany. When, for example, in April 1983 the Court issued a temporary injunction postponing the census in the Federal Republic, the *Senat* decided that, although the decision was not binding in Berlin, the census should also be postponed there.[38]

[37] The *nullum* theory first appeared in a decision of the *Bundesfinanzhof* of 22 January 1963: *Bundessteuerblatt* 1963, III p.189. While some writers oppose the theory (eg. Pestalozza, *AöR*, 96 (1971), p.27), Zivier (p.91) suggests that the practice of the German and Allied authorities support it. While the Allied authorities do not normally declare invalid provisions in Berlin Laws that have been struck down by the Federal Constitutional Court, they did so in the case of part of the Federal Restitution Law (*Bundesrückerstattungsgesetz*) by BK/O(68)13 of 21 October 1968 (*GVBl.* p.1549). Zivier points out that this was a special case given the role of the Supreme Restitution Court Berlin, which is composed of Allied, German and neutral judges. (The Supreme Restitution Court was established by Allied Kommandatura Law No. 25: *AK Gazette*, p.750).

[38] Statement by the Senator for the Interior, 13 April 1983.

CHAPTER 13

FEDERAL PRESENCE IN BERLIN

THE mere presence of Federal organs or personalities in Berlin cannot constitute a governing of Berlin by the Federation and is therefore in general not excluded by Allied reservations.[1] It is only by performing acts of direct state authority over Berlin that Federal organs could contravene these reservations. Since 1959 the Soviet Union has objected vigorously to manifestations of the Federation in Berlin, and has on occasion used such manifestations as an excuse for permitting infringements of Allied rights in regard to Berlin, particularly over access. Even before the Quadripartite Agreement of 3 September 1971 the Western Allies and the Federal Republic in practice limited certain forms of "demonstrative" Federal presence, that is, the presence of the highest organs of the Federal Republic of Germany to affirm the close ties between Berlin and the Federal Republic. They did so, however, on policy grounds. Under the Quadripartite Agreement, the Western Allies are now committed to maintaining certain of these restrictions. The Quadripartite Agreement does not, however, require any limitation on other forms of Federal presence, for example in the administrative field; indeed, an increase is not excluded. Despite the Quadripartite Agreement, this continues to be one of the areas where Soviet protests are most frequent.

BEFORE THE QUADRIPARTITE AGREEMENT

A Federal President first visited Berlin in October 1949, and later an official residence was established for the President at Schloss Bellevue in Tiergarten. He sometimes undertook official acts in Berlin, such as signing Federal Laws and nominating persons to office. The first official visit by a Federal Chancellor was in April 1950; and the first full Cabinet meeting took place on 11 October 1956.[2] Individual Federal ministers frequently visited Berlin, for example when accompanying foreign visitors.

The Federal Assembly to elect the Federal President met four times in Berlin, in 1954, 1959, 1964 and 1969. In 1954 the Allied

---

[1] Hennig, *Die Bundespräsenz in West-Berlin* (referred to in this Chapter as Hennig); Zivier, pp.107-9, 190-3. Compare the position in the Soviet Sector, where again the mere presence of GDR institutions does not contravene Berlin status (except in certain fields, such as the military: see Chapter 24 below).

[2] An "economic Cabinet" had met there in April 1955 – see Hennig, p.34. At a later stage formal Cabinet meetings no longer took place in Berlin; instead there were informal ministerial meetings.

High Commissioners made it clear in a press statement that this did not affect Berlin's status and that there was therefore no reason to object. The plenary of the *Bundestag* met several times in Berlin between October 1955 and April 1965. Meetings of *Bundestag* Committees and *Fraktionen* (parliamentary party groups) frequently took place in Berlin from the outset of the work of the *Bundestag*. Between October 1955 and June 1969 many such meetings were held simultaneously during "Berlin weeks". The plenary of the *Bundesrat* met nine times in Berlin between 1956 and 1959. *Bundesrat* Committees met there frequently even before then.

The setting up of Federal bodies in Berlin was an active issue immediately upon the establishment of the Federal Republic in 1949. The presence of Federal bodies could contribute significantly towards reducing unemployment in Berlin, which had formerly been the seat of most of the *Reich* authorities; and from a political perspective it would strengthen the relationship between Berlin and the Federation, and symbolise Berlin's position as the future capital of a reunified Germany. In 1949 the *Reich* Printer (*Reichsdruckerei*) in Berlin was turned into a branch office of the Federal Printer (*Bundesdruckerei*) and a Berlin office of the Federal Court of Accounts (*Bundesrechnungshof*) was set up. Many other bodies followed, including in 1953 the Federal Administrative Court and Federal Health Office.[3] Most Federal Ministries set up branch offices in Berlin. A proposal to transfer the seat of the Federal Government to Berlin was under active consideration in 1956 and 1957.[4] Certain manifestations of Federal presence, however, were not permitted since they would contravene specific aspects of Berlin status, primarily demilitarisation.

LEGAL BASIS OF FEDERAL PRESENCE

The Western Allies made clear from the outset that Berlin is not a *Land* of the Federal Republic and may not be governed by it; and that Allied supreme authority in Berlin cannot be affected by the development of ties between Berlin and the Federation. The mere presence in Berlin of Federal bodies, whether temporary or permanent, "in no way affects the legal status of the city".[5] It does not turn Berlin into a Federal *Land* or amount to a governing of Berlin by the Federation. The exercise by Federal bodies in Berlin

---

[3] See Hennig, pp.30–62, and the list at pp.349–54.
[4] The proposal was made by a member of the Berlin House of Representatives, Gerd Bucerius: Hennig, pp.50–62.
[5] British Note of 17 December 1962 concerning the Federal Administrative Court: *Selected Documents* II, p.67; *BPIL* 1962, p.267.

of powers over the Federation (for example, when the Federal Administrative Court decides Federal cases) does not contravene Allied reservations. Nor do acts which are not in any event acts of government, such as social events and speeches. Allied reservations could only be contravened if Federal bodies, whether in Berlin or elsewhere, were to perform acts of direct state authority over Berlin. Federal bodies located in Berlin, like those elsewhere, may perform acts in relation to Berlin, but they do so by virtue of authority derived from the Berlin legislature or government and are thus acting as Berlin organs (Chapter 12 above).

When acting as Berlin organs, Federal bodies are subject to Allied rights and responsibilities and Allied legislation. When present in Berlin Federal bodies are, like all other persons in Berlin, subject to Allied supreme authority, but this rarely has significance in practice.[6]

Neither the Soviet Union nor the East German authorities had objected to manifestations of Federal presence in Berlin before 1959. However, on 26 June 1959 the Soviet Union protested to the Western Allies about the decision to hold the Federal Assembly in Berlin on 1 July 1959; the Allies rejected this protest.[7] On 11 October 1959 the Soviet Union protested about a meeting of the *Bundesrat*, and the Western Allies once again rejected the protest.[8] Many such protests followed, in increasingly strong terms,[9] and the Eastern side sought to justify restrictions on the access routes to Berlin and on entry to East Berlin as counter-measures to "illegal" Federal presence.[10] On 23 August 1961 the Soviet Union protested in general terms about Federal presence, and this led to an extended exchange of Notes.[11] On 29 November 1962 it described the location in Berlin of the Federal Administrative Court as illegal.[12] The Soviet Union protested in strong terms against the plenary meeting of the *Bundestag* in April 1965.[13] On 6 January

---

[6] Hennig, p.51.

[7] *Selected Documents* I, p.407; *US Documents*, p.671. The Soviet Union likewise protested at the 1964 and 1969 Federal Assembly: *US Documents*, pp.865, 876, 1029.

[8] Heidelmeyer *Dokumente*, p.434.

[9] E.g. concerning *Deutschlandfunk*: *US Documents*, pp.686, 688; Heidelmeyer *Dokumente*, pp.434–6, 444, 446; Hennig, footnote 359.

[10] The East German decree of 29 August 1960 requiring "citizens from the German Federal Republic" to obtain entry permits was a "counter-measure" against a meeting of expellee organisations.

[11] Soviet Notes of 23 August 1961; Allied Notes of 26 August 1961; Soviet Notes of 2 September 1961; Allied Notes of 8 September 1961: *Selected Documents* I, pp.473–82; *US Documents*, pp.783–93; Heidelmeyer *Dokumente*, pp.520–7.

[12] *US Documents*, p.828. For the Allied response, see *US Documents*, p.831.

[13] *Selected Documents* II, p.119; *US Documents*, p.891; Heidelmeyer *Dokumente*, p.559. For the Allied response, see *Selected Documents* II, p.119; *US Documents*, p.892; Heidelmeyer *Dokumente*, p.560.

and 14 February 1968 the Soviet Union again protested in comprehensive terms against Federal presence.[14] On the occasion of the Federal Assembly in 1969 the GDR prohibited access to its territory by members of the Assembly and certain other persons.[15]

THE POSITION FOLLOWING THE QUADRIPARTITE AGREEMENT

Annex II, paragraph 2, of the Quadripartite Agreement of 3 September 1971 provides as follows:

> The Federal President, the Federal Government, the Bundesversammlung, the Bundesrat and the Bundestag, including their Committees and Fraktionen, as well as other state bodies of the Federal Republic of Germany will not perform in the Western Sectors of Berlin constitutional or official acts which contradict the provisions of paragraph 1.

This paragraph is primarily concerned with the activities of Federal bodies in relation to Berlin, and not with "Federal presence" as such. Point (a) of the letter of "clarifications and interpretations" sent by the three Western Ambassadors to the Federal Chancellor confirms that paragraph 2 concerns only acts in exercise of direct state authority over the Western Sectors of Berlin (p.345 below). Point (b) of the letter does, however, deal directly with Federal presence in the following terms:

> Meetings of the Bundesversammlung will not take place and plenary sessions of the Bundesrat and the Bundestag will continue not to take place in the Western Sectors of Berlin. Single committees of the Bundesrat and the Bundestag may meet in the Western Sectors of Berlin in connection with maintaining and developing the ties between those Sectors and the Federal Republic of Germany. In the case of Fraktionen, meetings will not be held simultaneously.

Under the Quadripartite Agreement there is thus some reduction of demonstrative Federal presence,[16] but no other limitations on Federal presence. The position may be summarised as follows:

(a) The Federal Assembly (*Bundesversammlung*) may not meet in Berlin.[17]

---

[14] *US Documents*, p.986. See also the protest of 5 March 1968 concerning a "Berlin Week": *US Documents*, p.989.

[15] *Verordnung* of 8 February 1969: *GBl.DDR* II, p.97; *US Documents*, p.1027. For the Allied protest of 10 February 1969, see *US Documents*, p.1028.

[16] As Ambassador Rush has stated: "Over the years, the Allies allowed the Federal Republic to develop this demonstrative presence as a means of counteracting Soviet claims that there were no legal ties between Berlin and the FRG. Now that these ties have been officially recognised, this demonstrative presence becomes less important" (*US Documents*, p.1163).

[17] Hennig, p.212.

(b) Plenary sessions of the *Bundesrat* and the *Bundestag* may not take place in Berlin.[18]

(c) Single committees of the *Bundesrat* and *Bundestag* may meet in Berlin in connection with maintaining and developing the ties between Berlin and the Federal Republic of Germany. This requirement is met where any matter is discussed that relates both to Berlin and to the Federal Republic of Germany, for example a Bill which is to be taken over in Berlin. The reference to "single committees" excludes the demonstrative simultaneous meeting of a large number of committees, such as used to occur during "Berlin weeks". But, unlike the provision on *Fraktionen*, it does not exclude more than one committee meeting simultaneously, or jointly, in Berlin, where there are practical reasons for this.[19]

(d) Meetings of *Fraktionen* may take place in Berlin, but only one such meeting may take place at a time. By contrast with *Bundesrat* and *Bundestag* committees, there is no requirement that such meetings be in connection with maintaining and developing the ties between Berlin and the Federal Republic.[20]

(e) In all other respects the position as regards Federal presence is unchanged by the Quadripartite Agreement. In particular, existing manifestations of Federal presence may be maintained; and further such manifestations are not excluded. The Soviet Union has sometimes suggested that what is not expressly permitted by the Quadripartite Agreement is forbidden, but this is not so.[21]

Two further provisions of the Quadripartite Agreement need to be considered: Part I4, which provides that "the situation which has developed in the area, and as it is defined in this Agreement as well as in the other agreements referred to in this Agreement, shall not be changed unilaterally"; and Part IIB, which envisages that "the ties between the Western Sectors of Berlin and the Federal Republic of Germany will be maintained and developed". Part I4 cannot be interpreted so as to preclude the development of ties (including Federal presence) as the Eastern side has argued. To do so would render this part of Part IIB meaningless, and is clearly not intended. The development of Federal presence could take various forms: the expansion of existing Federal bodies, both as to their functions and

---

[18] Hennig, p.214.
[19] Hennig, p.214; Zivier, p.191; Wettig, *DA*, 12 (1979), p.287. For a Soviet protest against a meeting of the *Bundestag* Interior Committee, see *Das Vierseitige Abkommen*, p.154. For a possible meeting of the *Bundestag Präsidium* and *Ältestenrat*, see Catudal, *A Balance Sheet of the Quadripartite Agreement on Berlin*, pp.130–2.
[20] Hennig, p.217.
[21] See examples cited in Wettig, *DA*, 12 (1979), p.929.

their staff; the transfer to Berlin of existing Federal bodies or the establishment of new Federal bodies in Berlin, such as the Federal Environment Agency. The only legal restrictions on increased Federal presence as such are those set out in point (b) of the letter of "clarifications and interpretations" and those flowing from other particular aspects of the status of Berlin, in particular its demilitarised status (Chapter 22 below).

THE FEDERAL LIAISON AGENCY

Annex II, paragraph 3, of the Quadripartite Agreement reads:

> The Government of the Federal Republic of Germany will be represented in the Western Sectors of Berlin to the authorities of the three Governments and to the Senat by a permanent liaison agency.

Point (c) of the tripartite letter of "clarifications and interpretations" reads:

> The liaison agency of the Federal Government in the Western Sectors of Berlin includes departments charged with liaison functions in their respective fields.

The liaison agency is, in fact, the Office of the Federal Plenipotentiary in Berlin (*Bevollmächtigter der Bundesregierung in Berlin*). A Federal Plenipotentiary in Berlin (*Bevollmächtigter der Bundesrepublik Deutschland in Berlin*) had first been nominated on 1 February 1950, and his office was formally established by a decree of the Federal Government of 30 November 1953.[22] He was to represent the Federal Government vis-à-vis the *Senat* and the Western Commandants, and was charged with supervising the work of Federal agencies in Berlin. Following the Quadripartite Agreement, the Federal Plenipotentiary's title has been slightly amended; but his functions vis-à-vis the Allies and *Senat* are essentially unchanged. The branch offices of Federal ministries (but not the separate agencies) have become departments of the liaison agency; this change is essentially presentational.[23]

THE SOVIET ATTITUDE SINCE THE QUADRIPARTITE AGREEMENT

The Soviet Union and other East bloc countries have continued to challenge manifestations of Federal presence in many ways. They

---

[22] *Gemeinsames Ministerialblatt* of 30 December 1953, p.565: Heidelmeyer *Dokumente*, p.195. See Görlich, *Die staatsrechtliche Stellung des Bevollmächtigten der Bundesrepublik in Berlin* (Dissertation, Würzburg 1970).
[23] Hennig, pp.94–5, 208–9. The *Länder* of the Federal Republic also have plenipotentiaries in Bonn, but only in Berlin is there a plenipotentiary of the Federal Government.

do so within international organisations and conferences, by direct protest to the Western Allies and in connection with the conclusion of bilateral treaties. The Quadripartite Agreement does not, it seems, inhibit the Soviet Union and the GDR from pressing their former point of view.

The most serious dispute in this field since the Quadripartite Agreement concerned the Federal Environment Agency (*Umwelt-bundesamt*).[24] This new Federal agency was set up in Berlin in 1974. The Soviet Union (and the GDR) protested both before and after its establishment, and even for a time imposed restrictions on the use of the transit routes by officials of the Agency. At the outset the Soviet Union claimed that the establishment of the Agency was unlawful because Federal presence was to be reduced under the Quadripartite Agreement. The Western Allies firmly rejected these protests. They rejected in particular the assertion that the Quadripartite Agreement was based on the general principle that Federal presence was to be reduced; and maintained that the establishment of the Federal Environment Agency was legally unobjectionable. In approving the taking over in Berlin of the Law on the Establishment of a Federal Environment Agency the Allied Kommandatura expressly recalled that –

> This Agency will operate in Berlin subject to the reserved rights and responsibilities of the Allies. In particular, the exercise, by the Agency, of functions in pursuance of this Law remains subject to the provisions of BK/O(51)63.[25]

The Soviet Union continues to protest regularly in international organisations and at international conferences about aspects of Federal presence in Berlin, for example when delegations of the Federal Republic include persons from Federal bodies located in Berlin, such as the Federal Health Office,[26] the Federal Cartel Office,[27] the Federal Environment Agency,[28] and the Federal Institute for Material Testing.[29] The Western Allies consistently reject such protests along the following lines:

> The establishment of the Federal Health Office in the western sectors of Berlin was approved by the French, British and American authorities acting on the basis of their supreme authority. These authorities are satisfied that the Federal Health Office does not perform, in the western sectors of Berlin, acts in exercise of direct

---

[24] Hennig, pp.97–108; Catudal, *A Balance Sheet of the Quadripartite Agreement on Berlin*, pp.123–7; *Das Vierseitige Abkommen*, pp.153, 157–8, 160–1, 183–4, 187–92, 194–6.
[25] BK/O(74)8 of 12 July 1974: *GVBl.* p.1668; *US Documents*, p.1269.
[26] *BYIL*, 54 (1983), p.472.
[27] *US Digest* 1979, pp.785–6.
[28] *BYIL*, 55 (1984), pp.525–6, 536–7, 538.
[29] *Das Vierseitige Abkommen*, pp.301–3; *BYIL*, 52 (1981), pp.458–9.

state authority over the western sectors of Berlin. Neither the location nor the activities of that office in the western sectors of Berlin, therefore, contravenes any of the provisions of the Quadripartite Agreement . . .

Furthermore, Annex IV of the Quadripartite Agreement stipulates that, provided matters of security and status are not affected, the Federal Republic of Germany may represent the interests of the western sectors of Berlin in international conferences and that western sectors of Berlin residents may participate jointly with participants from the Federal Republic of Germany in international exchanges. Finally, as a matter of principle, it is for the Federal Republic of Germany alone to decide on the composition of its delegations.

Frequent Soviet protests are also made directly to the Western Allies about visits to Berlin of leading Federal personalities, such as the Federal President and Federal Ministers,[30] even though such visits involve no acts in exercise of direct state authority over Berlin. These protests are rejected by the Western Allies, who point out that such visits do not constitute a violation of the Quadripartite Agreement and are fully compatible with the status of Berlin. The Soviet Union also sometimes protests about meetings in Berlin at the *Länder* level, since apparently they regard such meetings as suggesting that Berlin is a Federal *Land*.[31] They even on occasion protest about the presence in Berlin of non-governmental bodies; in such cases the Western Allies merely point out that the establishment and activities of such bodies cannot contravene the status of Berlin.[32]

---

[30] *Das Vierseitige Abkommen*, p.234. Similarly, the Soviet Union sometimes protests when it is announced that leading foreign personalities are visiting Berlin "in the framework of" a visit to the Federal Republic: *Das Vierseitige Abkommen*, p.242.

[31] *Das Vierseitige Abkommen*, pp.246, 264, 299.

[32] For example, the DIN-German Standardisation Institute: *BYIL*, 55 (1984), p.528.

PART FIVE

THE EXTERNAL REPRESENTATION OF BERLIN'S INTERESTS

The external representation of Berlin's interests is conducted essentially on two levels. First, the Western Allies maintain their rights and responsibilities in this field, though they do not in practice exercise them except in regard to matters of security and status. Second, under arrangements made by the Western Allies, the Federal Republic of Germany represents Berlin's interests generally in international relations, on condition that matters of security and status are not affected. In addition, the *Senat* of Berlin has entered into direct contacts with GDR authorities, or bodies in East Berlin, but only under close Allied control and on a strictly limited basis; such contacts cannot prejudice the general external representation of Berlin by the Federal Republic of Germany. On a day-to-day basis the most significant level is representation by the Federal Republic of Germany. In practice, the Federal Republic alone enters into treaties extending to Berlin, offers consular services to natural and legal persons resident in Berlin and regularly represents Berlin's interests in international organisations and conferences.

The external representation of Berlin is an area of constant friction. The Soviet Union and other East bloc countries seek to limit as far as possible the role of the Federal Republic and to treat the *Senat* as though it were the government of a separate international entity. Such pretensions are rejected by the Western Allies, Federal Government and *Senat*.

After examining external representation in general (Chapter 14),

Part Five looks in turn at the extension of international agreements and arrangements to Berlin (Chapter 15) and the position of Berlin in relation to international organisations and meetings (Chapter 16), of which a particularly important example is the European Communities (Chapter 17). Finally, because of their particular importance and special features, contacts with GDR and East Berlin authorities are dealt with separately in Chapter 18.

CHAPTER 14

EXTERNAL REPRESENTATION IN GENERAL[1]

BERLIN does not have international legal personality. It is not a State and cannot conduct international relations or enter into international agreements as though it were.[2] The Western Allies retain their rights and responsibilities relating to the external representation of the interests of Berlin and its inhabitants. At the same time, arrangements exist whereby in most fields the Federal Republic of Germany looks after these interests; the principal exceptions relate to matters of security and status. External representation by the Federal Republic is an important aspect of the relationship between Berlin and the Federal Republic. The *Senat* of Berlin may also, to a strictly limited degree, enter into contacts with authorities outside Berlin and the Federal Republic, but these are essentially of a technical or social kind.

THE PRINCIPAL ALLIED PROVISIONS

In paragraph 2(c) of the Statement of Principles governing the Relationship between the Allied Kommandatura and Greater Berlin of 14 May 1949,[3] the Allied Kommandatura specifically reserved to itself powers in the field of "relations with authorities abroad". The Revised Statement of Principles,[4] which took effect on 8 March 1951, provided in paragraph 2(c) that "this power will be exercised so as to permit the Berlin authorities to assure the representation of Berlin interests in this field by suitable arrangements".

Provision was made in 1952 for the extension to Berlin of international agreements and arrangements entered into by the Federal Republic of Germany (Chapter 15 below). In their letter to the Federal Chancellor of 26 May 1952/23 October 1954 (p.329 below), the three Powers stated that –

> they have decided to exercise their right relating to Berlin in such a way as to facilitate the carrying out by the Federal Republic of its Declaration on Aid to Berlin, of which a copy is annexed, and to

---

[1] Zivier, pp.98–101; Schiedermair, pp.130–63; van Well, *EA*, 31 (1976), pp.647–56; Knörr, *Die Kompetenz von Berlin (West) zum Abschluss völkerrechtlicher Verträge* (Dissertation, Munich 1975).
[2] "The *Senat* of Berlin has under the Quadripartite Agreement no external powers of representation; this lies with the three Powers and – in accordance with their authorisation – with the Federal Republic of Germany": van Well, *EA*, 31 (1976), p.651.
[3] *Selected Documents* I, p.117; *US Documents*, p.262; Heidelmeyer, p.108; *VOBl.* I, p.151.
[4] BK/L(51)29 of 7 March 1951: *Selected Documents* I, p.140; *US Documents*, p.348; Heidelmeyer, p.126; *VOBl.* I, p.274.

permit the Federal authorities to ensure representation of Berlin and of the Berlin population outside Berlin.

Article III(c) of the Declaration on Berlin of 5 May 1955 (p.332 below) reproduces without significant change paragraph 2(c) of the 1951 Revised Statement of Principles, and reads as follows:

> III. The Allied authorities will normally exercise powers only in the following fields:
>
> . . .
>
> (c) Relations of Berlin with authorities abroad. However, the Allied Kommandatura will permit the Berlin authorities to assure the representation abroad of the interests of Berlin and of its inhabitants by suitable arrangements.

It is in pursuance of these arrangements that, for some thirty-five years, the Federal Republic of Germany has in practice undertaken the representation abroad of Berlin's interests, except in relation to matters of security and status.

FEDERAL CONSTITUTIONAL CONSIDERATIONS

Despite some theoretical differences, the position of the Federal Republic of Germany is consistent with that described above. In addition, from the West German viewpoint, certain constitutional principles have to be considered, although these cannot of course affect the Allied position. First, according to the Federal Constitutional Court Berlin is a *Land* of the Federal Republic of Germany; while this view is not shared by the Allies, all Federal organs and officials are obliged, as a matter of Federal German constitutional law, to respect it. Moreover, the Federal Government is not merely empowered, but is obliged as a matter of constitutional law, to include Berlin in its international agreements and arrangements, except where this would be contrary to Allied rights and responsibilities.[5] Article 32 of the Basic Law also has to be considered, though its application is controversial even among West German writers.[6]

THE SOVIET ATTITUDE[7]

Consistent with their general approach of seeking to isolate West Berlin, to present it as a "separate political entity" and in particular to restrict its ties with the Federal Republic, the Soviet Union and

---

[5] *BVerfGE* 36, 1; Zivier, pp.123, 200; Pfennig/Neumann, *Verfassung von Berlin*, pp.44−5.
[6] See *BVerfGE* 36, 1; Knorr, *Die Kompetenz von Berlin (West) zum Abschluss völkerrechtlicher Verträge*, p.175; Zivier, pp. 235−6.
[7] See generally van Well, *EA*, 31 (1976), pp.647−56.

other East bloc countries seek to treat West Berlin's external relations as analogous to those of an independent State. Their efforts in this direction have hardly diminished since the Quadripartite Agreement of 3 September 1971, and take a great variety of forms. They continue to protest against the extension of certain treaties to Berlin and against the Federal Republic's representation of Berlin's interests within international organisations. They seek to isolate West Berlin by trying to deal with it directly rather than with the Federal Republic; for example, they seek to conclude agreements with it outside the framework of the Quadripartite Agreement and, as regards the GDR, the narrow range of permissible local arrangements. They try to present West Berlin as a separate entity. They would like to treat the Governing Mayor of Berlin as though he were a head of State. They interpret the external representation provisions of the Quadripartite Agreement as restrictively as possible.

EXTERNAL REPRESENTATION AND THE QUADRIPARTITE AGREEMENT

External representation proved a contentious issue with the Soviet Union, and the existing position was confirmed in Part IID and Annex IV of the Quadripartite Agreement of 3 September 1971. Part IID reads in part:

Representation abroad of the interests of the Western Sectors of Berlin . . . can be exercised as set forth in Annex IV.

Paragraphs 1 and 2 of Annex IVA read:

1. The Governments of the French Republic, the United Kingdom and the United States of America maintain their rights and responsibilities relating to the representation abroad of the interests of the Western Sectors of Berlin and their permanent residents, including those rights and responsibilities concerning matters of security and status, both in international organisations and in relations with other countries.

2. Without prejudice to the above and provided that matters of security and status are not affected, they have agreed that:
(a) The Federal Republic of Germany may perform consular services for permanent residents of the Western Sectors of Berlin.
(b) In accordance with established procedures, international agreements and arrangements entered into by the Federal Republic of Germany may be extended to the Western Sectors of Berlin provided that the extension of such agreements and arrangements is specified in each case.
(c) The Federal Republic of Germany may represent the interests of

the Western Sectors of Berlin in international organisations and international conferences.

(d) Permanent residents of the Western Sectors of Berlin may participate jointly with participants from the Federal Republic of Germany in international exchanges and exhibitions. Meetings of international organisations and international conferences as well as exhibitions with international participation may be held in the Western Sectors of Berlin. Invitations will be issued by the *Senat* or jointly by the Federal Republic of Germany and the *Senat*.

The Soviet Union accepted this in Annex IVB.

The Quadripartite Agreement confirmed the existing position on external representation, based on quadripartite rights and responsibilities and arrangements made between the Western Allies, the *Senat* and the Federal Republic. It did not establish a new legal basis for these arrangements, as is clear both from the substance and from the language used (". . . maintain their rights . . . They have agreed . . . "). The new element was the formal Soviet acceptance of these arrangements. However, the Soviet Union and other East bloc countries often assert that the Quadripartite Agreement is the legal basis for the Federal Republic of Germany's representation abroad of the interests of the Western Sectors of Berlin.

Part IID of the Quadripartite Agreement contains little more than a cross-reference to Annex IV. Annex IV consists of a communication from the three Western Allies to the Soviet Union stating the position on external representation and, in response, a Soviet communication accepting that position. The Soviet communication is virtually a mirror image of the tripartite one.[8]

Paragraph 1 of Annex IVA is a statement of fact: the Western Allies "maintain their rights and responsibilities relating to the representation abroad of the interests of the Western Sectors of Berlin and their permanent residents, including those rights and responsibilities concerning matters of security and status". The Western Allies have undertaken no commitment towards the Soviet Union to exercise those rights directly in any particular institutions or on any particular matters. The reference to representation of the interests of the Western Sectors of Berlin, rather than to the representation of the Western Sectors themselves, reflects the existing arrangements and is consistent with the Western view that the Western Sectors are not a separate political entity.

In paragraph 2 of Annex IVA the Western Allies inform the Soviet Union of three areas in which they have already agreed that the Federal Republic of Germany may represent Berlin's interests

---

[8] Part IID and Annex IV, together with Agreed Minute II, also deal with the establishment of the Soviet Consulate-General: see pp.76–7 above.

(consular services, treaties, international organisations and conferences) and of certain practical matters in the external field (participation of Berliners, meetings in Berlin). The listing in Annex IVA of these four matters, which had in the past given rise to particular difficulties with the Soviet Union, does not mean that Federal representation in other fields is contrary to the status of Berlin, but simply that the Soviet Union has not, in the Quadripartite Agreement, taken a position thereon.

The three Western Allies have agreed to the four areas listed in Annex IVA without prejudice to the maintenance of their rights and responsibilities and "provided that matters of security and status are not affected". The term "security and status" is a common one in connection with Berlin (see, for example, Article II of the ·1955 Declaration on Berlin) and includes all matters connected with the defence or protection of Berlin or with the status of Berlin derived from the assumption of supreme authority in 1945 and the agreements and decisions in force. For example, in the context of external representation military treaties or specifically military provisions of treaties are not extended to Berlin. And where questions relating to Berlin's security or status are raised in international organisations, the Western Allies take the lead, supported as appropriate by the Federal Republic of Germany.

Of the four areas listed in paragraph 2 of Annex IVA, those at (b), (c) and (d) are dealt with in the following chapters. Paragraph 2(a) provides that the Federal Republic of Germany "may perform consular services for permanent residents of the Western Sectors of Berlin". This reflects the practice before the Quadripartite Agreement, though difficulties had arisen in the Soviet Union and other East bloc countries. The expression "consular services" covers all consular functions apart from the special arrangements on passports.[9] The reference to permanent residents covers Germans with their registered domicile (*Wohnsitz*) in the Western Sectors of Berlin and legal persons based there.[10]

THE ROLE OF THE *SENAT*

Since Berlin is in no sense a State with international legal personality, the *Senat* may not itself engage in international relations as though it were. It may, and does, like other local governments, maintain contacts with other governments, including the

---

[9] On passports for residents of the Western Sectors of Berlin, see Chapter 19 below. Agreed Minute I provides that the passport or identity card therein described will serve as the basis for consular services in the Soviet Union.

[10] Schiedermair, pp.137–46; Zivier, p.197; Wettig, *DA*, 7 (1974), p.385, and *DA*, 12 (1979), p.288.

governments of States. Thus the Governing Mayor of Berlin is a frequent and welcome guest not only of the Governments of the Western Allies but also elsewhere, for example at the 1985 Big City Conference in Tokyo. Difficulties arise, however, with those countries, principally the Soviet Union and its allies, which seek to present West Berlin as a separate political entity, for example by limiting the role of the Embassy of the Federal Republic in connection with visits. As a result no Governing Mayor has yet visited Moscow.[11]

---

[11] A visit by the Governing Mayor to Moscow in 1973 was cancelled: Wettig, *DA*, 12 (1979), p.927. Hennig, *Die Bundespräsenz in West-Berlin*, pp.95–6, 185.

CHAPTER 15

THE EXTENSION OF INTERNATIONAL AGREEMENTS TO BERLIN

A N important aspect of the external representation of Berlin, for which procedures were established in the early 1950s, is the inclusion of Berlin within the terms of the international undertakings of the Federal Republic of Germany.[1] Four preliminary points should be noted. First, while the territorial application of international agreements is a complex question,[2] it is perhaps sufficient for present purposes to note that the extension of an agreement to Berlin means that it applies in respect of Berlin in the same way that it applies in respect of the territory of the Federal Republic, subject to any special exceptions that are made. We are thus concerned with territorial scope in the sense of Article 29 of the Vienna Convention on the Law of Treaties.[3] Second, the procedures that have been established for the extension of treaties to Berlin are based on the fact that, without a special act of extension, they do not so apply: Berlin is not part of the territory of the Federal Republic, and the application of a treaty in Berlin must therefore be "otherwise established" in terms of Article 29. Third, we are concerned in this Chapter only with the extension to Berlin of treaties concluded by the Federal Republic of Germany. The Allied authorities could and did enter into treaties on behalf of Germany itself, including Berlin;[4] they could continue to do so in the exercise of their rights and responsibilities relating to Berlin and Germany as a whole. But in practice they do not do so. A separate question is the extent to which they undertake obligations in respect of acts performed outside their own territory.[5] Fourth, while this Chapter is principally concerned with treaties (that is to say, legally binding international agreements between States or between States and international organisations), what is said also applies to less

---

[1] Lush, *ICLQ*, 14 (1965), pp.771–8; Wengler, *AFDI*, 24 (1978), p.227; Zivier, pp.98–101, 199–200; van Well, *EA*, 31 (1976), p.647; Hacker, in: *Zehn Jahre Berlin-Abkommen 1971–1981*, pp.241–7; Wengler, *Berlin in völkerrechtlichen Übereinkommen der Bundesrepublik Deutschland* (1984) (in this Chapter referred to as Wengler); Wengler, *ROW*, 30 (1986), pp.149–54.
[2] Sinclair, *The Vienna Convention on the Law of Treaties* (2nd ed. 1984), pp.87–92; Wengler, pp.8–14; Wengler, *ROW*, 30 (1986), pp.149–50.
[3] Article 29 reads: "Unless a different intention appears from the treaty or is otherwise established, a treaty is binding upon each party in respect of its entire territory".
[4] Bathurst and Simpson, *Germany and the North Atlantic Community*, pp.85–90. See the letter of 26 May 1952 sent in connection with the Settlement Convention: Cmd. 9368, p.121.
[5] Wengler, pp.37–8.

formal arrangements, such as memoranda of understanding, which are not necessarily legally binding.[6]

The extension of treaties to Berlin takes place in accordance with procedures established pursuant to Allied provisions. Paragraph 2(c) of the Statement of Principles governing the Relationship between the Allied Kommandatura and Greater Berlin of 14 May 1949, as amended by the Instrument of Revision of 7 March 1951, specifically reserved to the Allies "relations with authorities abroad", but went on to provide that "this power will be exercised so as to permit the Berlin authorities to assure the representation of Berlin interests in this field by suitable arrangements".[7] The arrangements for including Berlin in treaties of the Federal Republic were at first rather uncertain and unsatisfactory.[8] Following consultations with the *Senat* and the Federal Government, the Allied Kommandatura issued a Declaration on 21 May 1952 regarding the inclusion of Berlin in international treaties and undertakings of the Federal Republic of Germany.[9] Paragraph 1 reads in part:

1. The Allied Kommandatura declares that it has no objection to the inclusion of Berlin in international treaties and undertakings of the Federal Republic under the following conditions:

a) The Government of the Federal Republic of Germany and the *Senat* of Berlin will be prepared to reach an agreement to the effect that:

1) As far as possible, the Federal Republic will include Berlin within the terms of the Federal Republic's international undertakings.

2) The Berlin *Senat*, subject to the authority of the Allied Kommandatura and the Constitution of Berlin, will implement in Berlin the relevant international undertakings of the Federal Republic.

3) The name of Berlin shall be stated in the text of such treaties and agreements. If for any reason it is impossible to insert the name of Berlin into the text of a treaty, the Federal Republic, either in the instrument wherewith it adheres to the treaty or in a separate statement [issued at the time of the signing of the treaty][10] shall state that the provisions of the treaty will be

---

[6] See, for example, the question of a Berlin clause in a transfer of technology arrangement between the United States and the Federal Republic: *Der Tagesspiegel*, 28 and 30 March, 2 April 1986; *ILM*, 25 (1986), p.957.

[7] BK/L(51)29 of 7 March 1951: *Selected Documents* I, p.140; *US Documents*, p.348; Heidelmeyer, p.126; *VOBl.* I, p.274.

[8] See the Governing Mayor's letter of 9 April 1951 to the Federal Chancellor: Heidelmeyer *Dokumente*, p.174. For an example of the difficulties, see the uncertainty concerning the Treaty establishing the European Coal and Steel Community: Heidelmeyer *Dokumente*, p.177, and p.218 below.

[9] BKC/L(52)6 of 21 May 1952, amended by BKC/L(61)2 of 8 December 1961: *US Documents*, p.372; Heidelmeyer, p.130.

[10] These words were deleted in 1961.

applied in Berlin. In the matter of trade and payments agreements, it shall be construed that Berlin has been included in the treaty if it is stated that the area of purview of the treaty is the territory of DM West.

4) As long as the application of the provisions of the treaty to the territory of Berlin is not specified by the Federal Republic in any of the foregoing ways, it shall be understood that it is not intended to apply the treaty in Berlin.

. . .

b) The Berlin *Senat* undertakes to inform the Allied Kommandatura of international treaties in which Berlin is included, if possible before signature, and, at the latest, immediately after they have been signed by the Federal Republic. At the time of such notification, the Berlin *Senat* will deliver to the Allied Kommandatura 15 copies of the treaties and of the protocols or other documents regulating Berlin's inclusion.

c) Berlin can be excluded from the purview of any treaty if the Allied Kommandatura raises objections to the inclusion of Berlin in such a treaty. The right of the Allied Kommandatura to raise objections will be exercised within a period of 21 days after the notification to it by the *Senat* of the text of the treaty . . .

These procedures applied to all subsequent treaties of the Federal Republic of Germany and to treaties of the German Reich reactivated in the future.[11] Since 1973 the same procedures apply to agreements between the Federal Republic of Germany and the GDR (Chapter 18 below). Special procedures were laid down for existing treaties of the Federal Republic and *Reich* treaties that had already been reactivated. The *Senat*-Federal Republic of Germany agreement envisaged in the Allied Declaration was concluded on 19 December 1952; the *Senat* informed the Federal Government of its agreement that in concluding agreements the Federal Government should represent Berlin in accordance with the Declaration of the Allied Kommandatura, and the Federal Government undertook to do so.[12] These arrangements were expressly confirmed at the time of the Bonn/Paris Conventions. In its Declaration on Aid to Berlin the Federal Republic undertook to facilitate the inclusion of Berlin in its international agreements, provided this was not precluded by the nature of the agreements concerned (p.330 below). And BK/O(55)10 of 14 May 1955[13] provided that the procedure with respect to Berlin's participation in treaties of the Federal Republic remained as heretofore.

The inclusion of Berlin in treaties entered into by the Federal Republic of Germany was, from 1958, a source of friction with the

---

[11] Lush, *ICLQ*, 14 (1965), p.774.
[12] Heidelmeyer *Dokumente*, p.179.
[13] Heidelmeyer, p.153.

Soviet Union, and was one of the practical matters which the Quadripartite Agreement of 3 September 1971 sought to resolve. Annex IVA states that, without prejudice to Allied rights and responsibilities in the field and provided that matters of security and status are not affected:

> (b) In accordance with established procedures, international agreements and arrangements entered into by the Federal Republic of Germany may be extended to the Western Sectors of Berlin provided that the extension of such agreements and arrangements is specified in each case.

METHODS OF EXTENDING TREATIES

The Declaration of 21 May 1952 envisages two principal methods for the extension of treaties to Berlin: express mention in the text of the treaty or, where this is not possible, in the Federal Republic's instrument of adherence or in a separate statement. (The third method – reference to the territory of D-Mark West – was used in trade agreements.) Express mention in the text of the treaty is standard in the case of bilateral treaties, which normally include a provision along the following lines:

> This Treaty shall also apply to *Land* Berlin (*gilt auch für das Land Berlin*), provided that the Government of the Federal Republic of Germany does not make a contrary declaration to the Government of . . . within three months of the date of entry into force of this Treaty.[14]

Under such a provision extension to Berlin takes place provided that the Federal Government does not make a contrary declaration within three months of entry into force. This ensures that there is time to consult the Allied Kommandatura under the "twenty-one day rule" laid down in the 1952 Declaration. The Allied Kommandatura occasionally extends the twenty-one day period where more time is needed for consideration of a particular treaty. If the Allied Kommandatura does not agree, or is not deemed to have agreed, to extension within the period specified in the bilateral treaty, the Federal Republic would have to indicate to its treaty partner that the treaty does not apply to Berlin. This would not exclude later agreement between the parties to the treaty that it does apply, if the Allied objection had by then been lifted.

---

[14] Federal Cabinet decision of 6 February 1954: Heidelmeyer *Dokumente*, p.136. See, for example, *BGBl.* 1982 II, p.963. The reference to "*Land* Berlin" (p.151 above) is not acceptable to certain States. For the different forms of Berlin clause in treaties with these States, see pp.203–4 below.

In the case of multilateral treaties the Federal Republic's extension of the treaty to Berlin is generally made clear when it deposits its instrument of ratification or accession.[15] The representative of the Federal Government normally makes a statement in the following terms:

> I have the honour . . . to declare that the Agreement shall also apply to *Land* Berlin with effect from the day on which it enters [entered] into force for the Federal Republic of Germany.

There is no delay because the treaty will have already been considered by the Allied Kommandatura before ratification. Such extension is not foreseen in the multilateral treaty itself and it is open to States to object thereto. If they do not they are deemed to have accepted it.[16]

EFFECT OF EXTENDING TREATIES

The extension to Berlin of treaties entered into by the Federal Republic of Germany cannot affect Allied rights and responsibilities or Allied legislation. This was made clear in BK/O(74)11 of 30 September 1974,[17] which reads in part:

> Considering the large number of laws and treaties being extended to Berlin, the Allied Kommandatura wishes to emphasise that, in the light of Article VI of the Declaration on Berlin of 5 May 1955 (BKC/L(55)3), even in those cases where no reservations are laid down expressly by the Allied Kommandatura, such laws and treaties do not affect the rights and responsibilities of the Allies or Allied legislation. Authorities and services responsible for the application of laws and international treaties in Berlin must continue to conform strictly with Allied legislation . . .

There are many examples of treaties the extension of which is expressly qualified. This may be done either in the text of the treaty (for example, in the Berlin clause in the case of a bilateral treaty) or in the instrument whereby the Federal Republic expresses its consent to be bound or some associated instrument. Sometimes the ratification Law, or Allied legislation (BK/O or BK/L) relating to the treaty or ratification Law, may qualify its application in Berlin, but this only has direct effect as a matter of internal law and as between the Allies and the German authorities, and does not as such operate vis-à-vis other parties to the treaty. Such qualifications may be

---

[15] This is occasionally foreshadowed by a statement upon signature, e.g. in connection with the constituent instruments of the European Communities: see p.217 below.
[16] Wengler, pp.19–20, 38–41.
[17] *GVBl.* p.2576.

general or specific, or both. The following examples illustrate some of the principal types of express qualification:

i) In connection with the taking over of the Federal Law ratifying the Vienna Convention on Diplomatic Relations, the Allied Kommandatura ordered that the Law should in no way affect the legal provisions in force in Berlin with respect to privileges and immunities or the competence of the Allied Commandants to determine the extent of entitlement to privileges and immunities in Berlin: BK/O(64)3 of 11 September 1964.[18] Similar provision is made in connection with other treaties on privileges and immunities; and BK/O(75)10 of 7 August 1975[19] deals in general terms with the privileges and immunities of international organisations.

ii) The Allied Kommandatura authorised a very limited extension to Berlin of the Convention on the Prohibition of Military or any other Hostile Use of Environmental Modification Techniques: BK/O(83)1 of 21 April 1983.[20] Certain provisions of the Convention were expressly excluded from the extension, and the remainder applied only insofar as civilian, as opposed to military, implications were involved. Moreover, the BK/O expressly stated that the extension would not affect Allied rights and responsibilities and Allied legislation. On ratifying the Convention, the Federal Republic of Germany declared that its extension to Berlin was subject to the rights and responsibilities of France, the United Kingdom and the United States, including those relating to disarmament and demilitarisation. A Soviet protest at the United Nations was rejected by the Western Allies.[21]

iii) The Allied Kommandatura approved the extension of the European Agreement on Main International Traffic Arteries (AGR), but expressly stated that its application in Berlin did not derogate from Allied rights and responsibilities or affect quadripartite agreements, practices and procedures regarding roads and traffic in or serving Berlin. The Allied Kommandatura further stated that amendments to the Agreement required its prior approval: BK/O(76)10 of 29 October 1976.[22] A Soviet protest at the United Nations was rejected by the Western Allies.[23]

iv) The Federal Republic of Germany has extended to Berlin both

---

[18] *GVBl.* p.1162; see pp.77–8 above.
[19] *GVBl.* p.2060; see pp.80–1 above.
[20] *GVBl.* p.744.
[21] *BYIL*, 55 (1984), pp.526–7; *Multilateral Treaties*, Chapter XXVI. 1, note 2.
[22] *GVBl.* p.2578.
[23] *BYIL*, 55 (1984), p.532.

the International Covenant on Economic, Social and Cultural Rights and the International Covenant on Civil and Political Rights; in each case its instrument of ratification contained the following declaration:

The said Covenant shall also apply to Berlin (West) with effect from the date on which it enters into force for the Federal Republic of Germany except as far as Allied rights and responsibilities are affected.

The Soviet Union's protests over this extension were rejected by the Western Allies.[24]

The legal effect of such qualifications has to be considered (a) internally within Berlin and (b) vis-à-vis other parties to the treaty. Internally, both the general rule that Allied rights and responsibilities cannot be affected by the extension of treaties and such express qualifications as may be made are clearly fully effective. The law applicable in Berlin is not altered by the extension of treaties entered into by the Federal Republic so as to affect Allied rights and responsibilities. The extent to which the Federal Republic's obligations towards other treaty parties in respect of Berlin are modified by these qualifications is less clear. When the qualification is made known to the other parties and they do not object thereto, they may be assumed to have accepted that the treaty applies subject to the qualification. Even where this is not the case, given that the matter is a firm element of international treaty practice,[25] the other parties may be deemed to be on notice that the extension to Berlin of treaties concluded by the Federal Republic is subject to Allied rights and responsibilities.

While most treaties entered into by the Federal Republic of Germany are extended to Berlin there are important exceptions. Thus the North Atlantic Treaty and related agreements have not been extended (but see p.41 above). The same applies to certain other treaties of a military nature, for example, the Convention on the Prohibition of the Development, Production and Stockpiling of Bacteriological (Biological) and Toxin Weapons and on their Destruction.[26] Certain other treaties in this field have been extended, but the Allies have always been careful to ensure that this does not affect the status of Berlin and have made the necessary reservations: see for example BK/O(83)1 referred to above.

There are other fields in which treaties are not extended to

---

[24] *Das Vierseitige Abkommen*, pp.168, 180, 181.
[25] van Well has described the practice of extending treaties to Berlin as a *fester Bestandteil der völkerrechtlichen Vertragspraxis*: *EA*, 31 (1976), p.648.
[26] See the exchange of Notes in *BYIL*, 52 (1981), p.457.

Berlin. For example, the Chicago Convention on International Civil Aviation and bilateral air services agreements have not been extended. The Treaties of 12 August 1970 with the Soviet Union (the Moscow Treaty) and of 7 December 1970 with Poland (the Warsaw Treaty) do not extend to Berlin; nor do the Bonn/Paris Conventions of 1952/1954. A number of agreements with the GDR have likewise not been extended (p.230 below).

In other cases the text of a treaty expressly envisages the special situation of Berlin. Thus the Treaty on Franco-German Co-operation of 22 January 1963 provides for its application to Berlin except for the clauses covering defence.[27] Similarly, the bilateral treaties of the Federal Republic of Germany in the field of overseas aid routinely provide for their application to Berlin with the express exception of provisions dealing with civil air transport.[28] The Basis of Relations Treaty of 21 December 1972 and the Treaty of 11 December 1973 with Czechoslovakia (the Prague Treaty) apply only to a limited extent.

IMPLEMENTATION OF TREATIES EXTENDED TO BERLIN

In considering the question of responsibility for implementing treaties of the Federal Republic of Germany in so far as they extend to Berlin, international responsibility vis-à-vis other parties to the treaties has to be considered separately from internal responsibility for implementation. The distinction is clear in paragraph 1(a)(2) of the 1952 Declaration referred to above, which states that the Berlin *Senat* will implement in Berlin the relevant international undertakings of the Federal Republic. In his letter to the Federal Chancellor of 9 April 1951[29] the Governing Mayor had likewise stated that *Land* Berlin would fulfil all treaty requirements pursuant to its Constitution. International responsibility, on the other hand, lies with the Federal Republic of Germany; it is the Federal Republic that is a party to the treaty, not Berlin (which is not an international legal person with treaty-making capacity) or the three Western Allies, which are not in any capacity parties to treaties of the Federal Republic in respect of Berlin.[30] In concluding a treaty applying to Berlin, the Federal Republic undertakes an international obligation to ensure that the obligations under the

[27] *Selected Documents* II, p.71; for the Soviet protest see *Selected Documents* II, pp.75, 83, 89.
[28] E.g. Article 7 of the FRG-Indonesia Agreement on Financial Co-operation of 29 May 1985: *BGBl.* II, p.1101.
[29] Heidelmeyer *Dokumente*, p.174.
[30] Schröder, *Die ausländischen Vertretungen in Berlin*, p.50; Lush, *ICLQ*, 14 (1965), p.774; Wengler, *AFDI*, 24 (1978), pp.227–8; Wengler, p.35.

treaty are carried out in and in respect of Berlin to the extent that they are applicable to Berlin. The extension of treaties to Berlin carries no implication that Berlin is part of the territory of the Federal Republic of Germany.[31]

The internal implementation of treaties in so far as they extend to Berlin is carried out through the same instruments as any other legislative, executive and judicial acts in Berlin. For example, in so far as legislation is required this will normally take the form of a Berlin Law taking over a Federal ratification Law (p.159 above), although an ordinary Berlin Law or Allied legislation is also in theory possible. Similarly, executive action to implement a treaty would normally be taken by the local Berlin authorities, though Allied action is not excluded.[32] Federal ratification Laws in practice are taken over in groups by a special form of *Mantelgesetz* known as an application Law (*Anwendungsgesetz*).[33]

THE SOVIET ATTITUDE TO TREATY EXTENSION

Both before and after the Quadripartite Agreement of 3 September 1971 the Soviet Union (and States associated with it) have objected to the extension of many treaties to Berlin and refused to enter into particular bilateral treaties when the Federal Republic insisted upon extension.[34] It was hoped that the Quadripartite Agreement would have overcome these difficulties, but the Soviet attitude continues to cause problems.

The Soviet Union argues that the Quadripartite Agreement is in some way the basis for the extension. This is not accepted by the Western Allies, who consider that the Quadripartite Agreement simply confirmed existing procedures: Annex IV refers expressly to "established procedures". The wording of the Berlin clause in bilateral agreements with the Soviet Union and certain other countries is not inconsistent with the Soviet view, but equally does not prejudice the Western view. This so-called "Frank-Falin clause", first included in the Trade Agreement with the Soviet Union of 5 July 1972, reads:

In accordance with the Quadripartite Agreement of 3 September

---

[31] Wengler, footnote 41.
[32] See, for example, *Das Vierseitige Abkommen*, p.135.
[33] The text of the treaty is not published in Berlin: Zivier, p.80; Heidelmeyer, p.136. On the publication of information relating to treaties and Berlin, see Wengler, pp.21-4.
[34] For examples prior to the Quadripartite Agreement, see Zivier, pp.100–l; Abrasimov, *West Berlin—Yesterday and Today*, pp.122–3. The Soviet Union refused for eight years prior to 1972 to conclude a trade agreement because of the Federal Republic's insistence on including a Berlin clause.

1971 this Agreement is in accordance with established procedures extended to Berlin (West).[35]

In the case of some multilateral treaties the Soviet Union has expressly indicated its acceptance of extension only on the understanding that extension took place in accordance with the Quadripartite Agreement of 3 September 1971 and subject to compliance with established procedures.[36] This is apparently intended to indicate that the Quadripartite Agreement is, in the Soviet view, the basis for the extension, and usually elicits an Allied reply to the effect that the Soviet declaration contains an incomplete and misleading reference to the Quadripartite Agreement.[37]

The Soviet Union continues to object to references to "*Land* Berlin" and insists instead on "Berlin (West)" (p.151 above). In addition, it takes a narrow view of what is covered by Annex IVA, paragraph 2(b), of the Quadripartite Agreement, and frequently makes its position clear at the United Nations and elsewhere. It objects in particular to the extension of treaties which, on its own very broad interpretation, affect status or security or involve a "governing" of Berlin by the Federal Republic. It states that it considers the Federal Republic's declaration of extension to be illegal and to have no legal force. The three Powers generally[38] respond in the following manner. After describing the provisions of Annex IV concerning the established procedures for the extension of treaties, they continue along the following lines:

> The established procedures referred to above, which were endorsed in the Quadripartite Agreement, are designed *inter alia* to afford the authorities of the Three Powers the opportunity to ensure that international agreements and arrangements entered into by the Federal Republic of Germany which are to be extended to the Western Sectors of Berlin are extended in such a way that matters of security and status are not affected.

[35] Article 10 of the Long-term Agreement between the Government of the Federal Republic of Germany and the Government of the Union of Soviet Socialist Republics on Trade and Economic Co-operation (*BGBl.* 1972 II, p.483), which reads in German: *Entsprechend dem Viermächte-Abkommen vom 3. September 1971 wird dieses Abkommen in Übereinstimmung mit dem festgelegten Verfahren auf Berlin (West) ausgedehnt.* See Wettig, *DA*, 12 (1979), pp.924–6. The same provision is included in the Federal Republic's treaties with other Warsaw Pact countries and the Mongolian People's Republic, though a slightly different clause occurs in treaties with Romania: *BGBl.* 1973 II, p.1350. Further special forms of Berlin clause are used in bilateral treaties with Finland (*BGBl.* 1976 II, p.545) and with China (*BGBl.* 1985 II, p.31). The standard Berlin clause is used in bilateral treaties with international organisations, though in the case of the United Nations and its specialised agencies the clause refers to "Berlin (West)" rather than "*Land* Berlin".
[36] *Multilateral Treaties*, Chapter XII. 1, note 3; for a similar but somewhat fuller Soviet statement, see *Multilateral Treaties*, Chapter VI. 15, note 4.
[37] E.g. *BYIL*, 55 (1984), p.529.
[38] The fact that they do not do so in each individual case does not imply any change in their views: *Selected Documents* II, pp.225–6.

When authorizing the extension of the above-mentioned Convention to the Western Sectors of Berlin, the authorities of the Three Powers took such steps as were necessary to ensure that matters of security and status were not affected. Accordingly, the validity of the Berlin declaration made by the Federal Republic of Germany in accordance with established procedures is unaffected and the application of the Convention to the Western Sectors of Berlin continues in full force and effect, subject to Allied rights, responsibilities and legislation.[39]

The Federal Republic of Germany normally associates itself with the legal position of the three Powers.

The Soviet Union has objected to the extension to Berlin of multilateral treaties in the following fields among others: privileges and immunities,[40] human rights,[41] nationality and statelessness,[42] traffic in persons, and slavery,[43] inland waterways,[44] telecommunications,[45] criminal jurisdiction and extradition,[46] and disarmament.[47]

The Soviet Union sometimes objects to the extension to Berlin of international agreements that can have no practical application in Berlin.[48] The reason for their objection is not clear, but they may consider that the sole purpose of the extension is to give a misleading impression of the relationship between the Western Sectors of Berlin and the Federal Republic.

Where the Federal Republic has extended a multilateral treaty to Berlin, parties to the treaty which do not object thereto must be deemed to have accepted the extension. Where another party objects, the Federal Republic could presumably decline to regard

---

[39] *Multilateral Treaties*, Chapter XVIII. 5, note 2 (International Convention against the Taking of Hostages).

[40] *Multilateral Treaties*, Chapter III. 1, note 2 (Convention on the Privileges and Immunities of the United Nations); Chapter III. 3, note 2 (Vienna Convention on Diplomatic Relations); Chapter III. 11, note 2 (Convention on the Prevention and Punishment of Crimes against Internationally Protected Persons, including Diplomatic Agents).

[41] *Multilateral Treaties*, Chapter IV. 3, note 4 and Chapter IV. 4, note 3 (International Covenants on Economic, Social and Cultural Rights, and on Civil and Political Rights).

[42] *Multilateral Treaties*, Chapter V. 3, note 2 (Convention relating to the Status of Stateless Persons); Chapter XVI. 2, note 3 (Convention on the Nationality of Married Women).

[43] *Multilateral Treaties*, Chapter VII. 1, note 4 (Suppression of Traffic in Women and Children); Chapter XVIII. 1, note 5 (Slavery).

[44] *Multilateral Treaties*, Chapter XII. 3, note 1 (Convention relating to the Unification of Certain Rules concerning Collisions in Inland Waterways).

[45] *Selected Documents* II, p.224 (International Telecommunication Conventions).

[46] *Multilateral Treaties*, Chapter XVIII. 5, note 2 (International Convention against the Taking of Hostages).

[47] Heidelmeyer *Dokumente*, p.558 (Test Ban Treaty); *Das Vierseitige Abkommen*, pp.177, 196, (Nuclear Non-Proliferation Treaty); *US Digest* 1976, p.274 (Seabed Nuclear Weapons Treaty); *Multilateral Treaties*, Chapter XXVI. 1, note 2 and *BYIL*, 55 (1984), p.526 (Convention on the Prohibition of Military or Any Other Hostile Use of Environmental Modification Techniques).

[48] Zivier, p.199.

the treaty as in force between itself and the objecting State, but this does not appear to have happened.[49]

Even where the Soviet Union or other East bloc countries accept extension in principle (for example, by including a Frank-Falin clause) this does not necessarily overcome all obstacles to including Berlin and Berlin institutions in the practical application of treaties. Difficulties remain in connection with certain proposed treaties, for example, on Scientific and Technological Cooperation, and on Legal Assistance.[50]

[49] Wengler, pp.38–41.
[50] van Well, *EA*, 31 (1976), p.647; Hacker, in: *Zehn Jahre Berlin-Abkommen 1971–1981*, p.242; Nawrocki, *Relations between the two States in Germany* (1985), pp.68–70.

CHAPTER 16

BERLIN AND INTERNATIONAL ORGANISATIONS

THE Federal Republic of Germany, from an early date, became a party to treaties establishing international organisations; for the most part these were extended to Berlin in accordance with established procedures (Chapter 15 above). Berlin was thus, by virtue of the participation of the Federal Republic, within the area of application of the constituent instruments of the organisations concerned and hence within the competence of the organisations. Berlin's interests were in general represented by the Federal Republic though this did not exclude representation by the Allies. The Federal Republic's delegation might well include Berliners. This Chapter covers the legal aspects of Berlin's position in relation to international organisations and other international bodies.[1] Chapter 17 considers the particular case of the European Communities.

THE EXTENSION OF CONSTITUENT INSTRUMENTS TO BERLIN

The constituent instruments of most international organisations of which the Federal Republic of Germany is a member have been extended to Berlin in accordance with established procedures. These include the Convention on the Organisation for Economic Co-operation and Development, the Statute of the Council of Europe, the Statute of the International Atomic Energy Agency, the Treaties establishing the three European Communities, the Charter of the United Nations and the constitutions of most of the specialised agencies of the United Nations. In some cases express reservations have been made in connection with the extension to Berlin.

Certain constituent instruments have not been extended to Berlin, since the organisations concerned deal essentially with areas where the Federal Republic does not represent Berlin's interests. Neither the North Atlantic Treaty, establishing the Western military alliance, and related agreements,[2] nor the modified Brussels Treaty,

---

[1] van Well, *EA*, 31 (1976), pp.647–54; van Well, in: *Berlin translokal*, pp.97–113; Zündorf, pp.285–95; *Schiedermair*, pp.149–54; Mahnke, *VN*, 21 (1973), pp.112–17; Kewenig, *Zur Problematik der Vertretung West-Berlins in internationalen Organisationen und in den Vereinten Nationen* (unpublished).

[2] For example, the Agreement between the Parties to the North Atlantic Treaty regarding the Status of their Forces: UKTS 3(1955); the Agreement to Supplement this Agreement with respect to Foreign Forces stationed in the Federal Republic of Germany: UKTS 73(1963).

establishing Western European Union, extend to Berlin, though this in no way detracts from the Allied security guarantee (p.41 above). Since aviation matters are reserved to the Allies, the Federal Republic's accession to the Chicago Convention on International Civil Aviation does not extend to Berlin.

Both before and after the Quadripartite Agreement of 3 September 1971, the Soviet Union and other Eastern European countries objected to Berlin's inclusion within the area of competence of certain international organisations. In Annex IVA, paragraph 2(c), of the Quadripartite Agreement the three Western Allies informed the Soviet Union that, without prejudice to the maintenance of their rights and responsibilities and provided that matters of security and status were not affected, they had agreed that –

> (c) The Federal Republic of Germany may represent the interests of the Western Sectors of Berlin in international organisations and international conferences.

The Soviet Union indicated in Annex IVB that, provided that matters of security and status were not affected, the Soviet Union would raise no objection to such representation.

These provisions of the Quadripartite Agreement reaffirm the existing position and do not constitute the legal basis for the representation of Berlin's interests by the Federal Republic:

> The right of the Federal Republic of Germany to represent the Western Sectors of Berlin, and their permanent residents, in international organisations and international conferences derives from rights long granted by the Governments of France, the United Kingdom and the United States on the basis of their authority in the Western Sectors of Berlin.[3]

THE UNITED NATIONS

The Federal Republic of Germany and the German Democratic Republic both became members of the United Nations on 18 September 1973.[4] This was preceded by a number of important steps designed to ensure that their membership did not affect the status of Berlin or that of Germany as a whole. These steps were considered necessary since otherwise, given the terms of the Charter, membership of the United Nations might have been taken to imply acceptance of two fully sovereign States and the

---

[3] U.N. Doc. A/9598; *US Digest* 1974, p.246.
[4] Zündorf, pp.285–95; Ress, *Der Staat*, 11 (1972), pp.27–49; Korber, *VN*, 5 (1972), pp.141–2; Schaefer, *Politische Studien*, 24 (1973), pp.11–28; Mahnke, *VN*, 21 (1973), pp. 112–17; van Well, in: *Berlin translokal*, pp.97–113.

disappearance of quadripartite rights and responsibilities. The most important of these steps was the Quadripartite Declaration of 9 November 1972. As is recorded in the Declaration itself, it was negotiated in the same way as the Quadripartite Agreement. The Declaration reads:

> The Governments of the United Kingdom of Great Britain and Northern Ireland, the French Republic, the Union of Soviet Socialist Republics and the United States of America, having been represented by their Ambassadors who held a series of meetings in the building formerly occupied by the Allied Control Council, are in agreement that they will support the applications for membership in the United Nations when submitted by the Federal Republic of Germany and the German Democratic Republic and affirm in this connection that this membership shall in no way affect the rights and responsibilities of the Four Powers and the corresponding, related quadripartite agreements, decisions and practices.[5]

The Declaration was formally notified to the Federal Republic of Germany and the GDR,[6] and circulated at the United Nations[7] before the Security Council and General Assembly considered the applications.

The Federal Law of 6 June 1973[8] providing for accession to the United Nations Charter contains the following Berlin clause:

> This Law applies also in *Land* Berlin,[9] in so far as *Land* Berlin decides on the application of this Law, provided that the rights and responsibilities of the Allied authorities, including those concerning matters of security and status, are unaffected.

In BKC/L(73)1 of 13 April 1973[10] the Allied Kommandatura referred to the draft of this Law and stated:

> In accordance with the arrangements referred to in Annex IVA of the Quadripartite Agreement of September 3, 1971, and in particular with the exception of matters concerning security and status:
> (a) The Allied Kommandatura has no objection to the acceptance by the Federal Republic of Germany of the rights and obligations contained in the United Nations Charter with respect also to the Western Sectors of Berlin;
> (b) The Allied Kommandatura approves the representation of the interests of the Western Sectors of Berlin in the United Nations and its subsidiary organs by the Federal Republic.

---

[5] *Selected Documents* II, p.264; *US Documents*, p.1213–90.
[6] Zündorf, p.287.
[7] U.N. Docs. S/10952–5: *US Documents*, p.1244.
[8] *BGBl.* II, p.430; *US Documents*, p.1235.
[9] For a Soviet protest, see *Das Vierseitige Abkommen*, p.127.
[10] *US Documents*, p.1234.

The Federal Republic of Germany applied for membership of the United Nations on 15 June 1973.[11] In a letter of the same date, circulated to all members of the United Nations,[12] the Federal Minister for Foreign Affairs referred to BKC/L(73)1 in the following terms:

> In connection with the submission today of the application for membership of the Federal Republic of Germany in the United Nations (A/9070−S/10949), I have the honour, with regard to the application of the United Nations Charter to Berlin (West), to declare that, with the exception of matters concerning security and status, and in accordance with the authorisation given to the Senate in the Allied Kommandatura letter dated 13 April 1973 (BKC/L(73)1), the Federal Republic of Germany accepts, from the date on which it is admitted to membership in the United Nations, the rights and obligations contained in the United Nations Charter also with respect to Berlin (West), and will represent the interests of Berlin (West) in the United Nations and its subsidiary organs.

There followed an exchange of letters between the Soviet Union and the three Western Allies. In a letter of 26 June 1973[13] the Soviet Union accepted that the Federal Republic of Germany "may represent the interests of the Western Sectors of Berlin in certain specific spheres enumerated in Annex IV of the Quadripartite Agreement . . . The basis of such representation is the Quadripartite Agreement, which regulates its permissible nature and scope." This restrictive interpretation of the Quadripartite Agreement was rejected by the Western Allies in a letter dated 7 December 1973.[14]

THE SPECIALISED AGENCIES AND IAEA

The constituent instruments of the specialised agencies of the United Nations (except the International Civil Aviation Organisation) and of the International Atomic Energy Agency[15] have been extended to Berlin by the Federal Republic of Germany. The GDR is also a member of most of these organisations. Whenever necessary, care has been taken to ensure that matters of status and security are not affected. For example, in approving GDR membership of the Universal Postal Union the Western Allies made it clear that this did not affect the special rights and responsibilities

[11] U.N. Doc. A/9070–S/10949: *US Documents*, p.1240. The GDR applied on 12 June 1973: U.N. Doc. A/9069–S/10945: *US Documents*, p.1239. The GDR had previously applied on 28 February 1966 (U.N. Doc. S/7192): *US Documents*, p.912.
[12] U.N. Doc. A/9071–S/10950: *US Documents*, p.1241.
[13] U.N. Doc. A/9082–S/10958: *Das Vierseitige Abkommen*, p.145.
[14] U.N. Doc. A/9431–S/11150: *US Documents*, p.1255. A further Soviet response dated 20 December 1973 is in U.N. Doc. A/9471–S/11165: *Das Vierseitige Abkommen*, p.165.
[15] Heidelmeyer *Dokumente*, p.184.

which the United Kingdom, the United States and France had relating to postal traffic to and from Berlin.[16]

THE EUROPEAN HUMAN RIGHTS ORGANS

The European Convention for the Protection of Human Rights and Fundamental Freedoms of 4 November 1950, under which international organs – the European Commission and Court of Human Rights, and the Committee of Ministers of the Council of Europe – ensure the application of the rights and freedoms set forth in the Convention, has been extended to Berlin by the Federal Republic of Germany.[17] Neither the Western Allies nor the Soviet Union made any express reservations or objections. As is the case with all such extensions, however, the European Convention does not and cannot affect Allied rights and responsibilities or Allied legislation.[18] Article 1 of the Convention provides that –

> The High Contracting Parties shall secure to everyone within their jurisdiction the rights and freedoms defined in Section I of this Convention.

The extension of the treaty obligations of the Federal Republic of Germany covers all persons in Berlin in so far as they fall within the jurisdiction of Berlin authorities (including Federal authorities acting as Berlin authorities, but excluding Allied authorities).[19] It does not include persons affected by acts of the Allied authorities, since they are not within the jurisdiction of the Federal Republic of Germany. The Commission has held that the Federal Republic is not responsible under the Convention for the effects of Allied reservations to the Basic Law.[20] The Allies have not subjected themselves to German courts; to subject their acts, even indirectly through the Federal Republic, to scrutiny by the European Commission and Court of Human Rights would be incompatible

---

[16] *US Digest* 1973, p.196.

[17] Pestalozza, in: *Fs zum 125 jährigen Bestehen der Juristischen Gesellschaft zu Berlin*, p.550.

[18] See BK/O(74)11 of 30 September 1974 (*GVBl*. p.2576) and, generally, Chapter 15 above. Compare the position under the United Nations Covenants: p.201 above.

[19] The Strasbourg organs (Commission, Court, Committee of Ministers) have considered applications against the Federal Republic of Germany by Berliners in many cases: the acts complained of include decisions of Berlin courts and acts of the Berlin police and prison officers: see Pestalozza, in: *Fs zum 125 jährigen Bestehen der Juristischen Gesellschaft zu Berlin*, pp.561–7. On occasions the Commission has taken into account, as relevant facts, matters special to Berlin, such as the lack of jurisdiction of the Federal Constitutional Court and the absence of a Berlin Constitutional Court. The latter was held not contrary to the Convention: Application No. 10308/83, *Altun v FRG, Decisions and Reports* 36, p.209.

[20] Application No. 10308/83 (footnote 19 above). See also Application No. 235/56 (*Yearbook of the European Convention on Human Rights* 2, p.256), and other cases listed in Fawcett, *The Application of the European Convention on Human Rights* (1969), pp.22–3.

with the maintenance of their rights and responsibilities in regard to Berlin and to Germany as a whole.[21]

A separate question is whether the European Convention applies to acts of the British and French Military Governments in Berlin by virtue of United Kingdom and French participation in the Convention. The occupation authorities in Berlin have never accepted to be bound by the requirements of the Convention since this would be incompatible with their position as Occupying Powers exercising supreme authority. It could, moreover, impede their exercise of quadripartite rights and responsibilities and seriously diminish their ability to maintain the status of Berlin in relation to the Soviet Union. The Convention applies to the metropolitan territory of the United Kingdom and, by virtue of notifications under Article 63, to some, but not all, of the territories for whose international relations it is responsible. Likewise, it applies to France and its overseas *départements* and territories. Neither France nor the United Kingdom has extended the Convention to Berlin, let alone accepted the right of individual petition from Berlin. Indeed, they could not do so since neither Berlin, nor an individual Sector of Berlin, is a territory for whose international relations they are responsible. Responsibility for the external relations of Berlin lies with the Occupying Powers jointly. Although the jurisprudence of the Strasbourg organs shows that the Convention may apply to persons under the jurisdiction of a Contracting Party even outside the area of its territorial application as accepted by that Party,[22] persons subject to the jurisdiction of Allied authorities in Berlin, including the British and French Military Governments, are not within the jurisdiction of the United Kingdom and France for the purposes of Article 1 of the Convention. In the *Hess* case the Commission, after recalling its previous decisions to the effect that "a State is under some circumstances responsible under the Convention for the actions of its authorities outside its territory", stated that "there is in principle, from a legal point of view, no reason why acts of the British authorities in Berlin should not entail the liability of the United Kingdom under the Convention". But the Commission went on to find –

> that the joint authority cannot be divided into four separate jurisdictions and that therefore the United Kingdom's participation in

[21] Of the four Powers only the United Kingdom had ratified the Convention at the time of the Federal Republic's ratification in 1952; France ratified in 1974.
[22] *Digest of Strasbourg Case-Law relating to the European Convention on Human Rights*, Vol. I, pp.12–22: Application No. 6231/73, *Ilse Hess v UK*, *Decisions and Reports* 2, p.72; Applications Nos. 6780/74 and 6950/75, *Cyprus v Turkey*, *Decisions and Reports* 2, p.125; Application No. 8007/77, *Cyprus v Turkey*, *Decisions and Reports* 13, p.85; Frowein, in: *Fs Schlochauer* (1981), pp.289–91; Frowein/Peukert, *EMRK-Kommentar*, pp.17–18.

the exercise of the joint authority and consequently in the administration and supervision of Spandau Prison is not a matter "within the jurisdiction of the United Kingdom", within the meaning of Article 1 of the Convention.[23]

All acts of Allied authority in Berlin, whether joint (for example, of the Allied Kommandatura) or individual (for example, of a Sector Commandant), are attributable not to the United Kingdom, France, the United States and the Soviet Union, whether jointly or severally, but to Germany as a whole (p.55 above). And the reasoning in the *Hess* decision applies to all such acts since all Allied powers in Berlin derive from the joint assumption of supreme authority in respect of Germany.[24]

BERLINERS IN DELEGATIONS OF THE FEDERAL REPUBLIC

In paragraph 2(d) of Annex IVA of the Quadripartite Agreement the three Western Allies informed the Soviet Union that they had agreed that:

> Permanent residents of the Western Sectors of Berlin may participate jointly with participants from the Federal Republic of Germany in international exchanges and exhibitions.

In Annex IVB the Soviet Union stated that it would raise no objection to this.

Joint participation involves participation in a single group with participants from the Federal Republic of Germany, without special seating or name-plates. These provisions cover delegations to international organisations and conferences, but also other international exchanges and exhibitions. Insofar as the Governments concerned have a hand in the arrangements for such exchanges and exhibitions they may not object to the participation of Berliners as part of the delegation or team of the Federal Republic of Germany. The Soviet Union and others do sometimes object to such participation, claiming that it is a breach of the Quadripartite Agreement, usually on the ground that the Berliners come from some Federal body which the Soviet Union considers is illegally based in Berlin (Chapter 13 above). The Western Allies consistently reject such protests, pointing out that there is nothing in the Quadripartite Agreement which supports the contention that residents of the Western Sectors of Berlin may not be members of

---

[23] *Decisions and Reports* 2, p.72. To the same effect, the decision on Application No. 6953/75, cited in *Digest of Strasbourg Case-Law relating to the European Convention on Human Rights*, Vol I, p.17.

[24] See pp.55–6, 60 above. See also Randelzhofer, *Die Verwaltung*, 19 (1986), pp.22–6; Heidelmeyer, *ZaöRV*, 46 (1986), pp.519–20.

delegations of the Federal Republic of Germany. They refer to Annex IV thereof and state that it is, as a matter of principle, for the Federal Republic alone to decide on the composition of its delegations.[25]

INTERNATIONAL ORGANISATIONS IN BERLIN

There can be no objection to the temporary or permanent presence in Berlin of international organisations, provided that matters of security and status are not affected. Their status, privileges and immunities are ultimately governed by Allied legislation and reserved rights (p.80 above). Organisations with permanent establishments in Berlin include the European Communities (a Press and Information Sub-Office and the European Centre for the Development of Vocational Training), and the European Patent Office (Berlin Sub-Office).

MEETINGS AND EXHIBITIONS IN BERLIN[26]

In paragraph 2(d) of Annex IVA of the Quadripartite Agreement the three Western Allies informed the Soviet Union that they had agreed that:

> Meetings of international organisations and international conferences as well as exhibitions with international participation may be held in the Western Sectors of Berlin. Invitations will be issued by the Senat or jointly by the Federal Republic of Germany and the Senat.

In Annex IVB the Soviet Union informed the three Western Allies that it would raise no objection to –

> the holding in [the Western Sectors of Berlin] of meetings of international organisations and international conferences as well as exhibitions with international participation, taking into account that invitations will be issued by the Senat or jointly by the Federal Republic of Germany and the Senat.

While the Soviet communication essentially mirrors the Western one, it expressly links the holding of meetings and the invitation procedure.

These provisions cover meetings of public international organisations and international conferences having an official character. They do not cover meetings of international non-governmental organisations or private conferences. Likewise, the reference to exhibitions with international participation refers to

---

[25] *BYIL*, 52 (1981), pp.456, 459; *BYIL*, 54 (1983), pp.472, 474, 476.
[26] Möhler, *Völkerrechtliche Probleme östlicher Beteiligungen an internationalen Veranstaltungen in West-Berlin.*

those held under governmental auspices, and not to those organised privately. This is confirmed by the invitation procedure, which can only apply to official meetings. Thus, in response to a complaint by the Soviet Union the three Western Allies pointed out that "the International Waste Recycling Congress does not have an official character and can in no way contravene the status of Berlin or the provisions of the Quadripartite Agreement of 3 September 1971".[27] The invitation procedure (that is to say, invitation by the *Senat* or jointly by the Federal Government and *Senat*) is a new element introduced by the Quadripartite Agreement. In practice, since Berlin is not represented separately in international organisations, the invitation is normally a joint one and is transmitted to other participants by the Federal Government acting on its own behalf and on behalf of the *Senat*.

Despite the clear provisions of the Quadripartite Agreement difficulties continue to arise in connection with international meetings. Even after the Agreement the Soviet Union and its allies have sought to oppose the holding of meetings of international organisations in Berlin. A number of such meetings are nevertheless held. Thus, the annual meeting of the World Bank and International Monetary Fund is to take place in Berlin in September 1988, at the joint invitation of the Federal Republic and *Senat*.[28]

Meetings of a non-official kind are not governed by Allied provisions and are not within the terms of the Quadripartite Agreement of 3 September 1971. Nevertheless, considerable difficulties have been made by the Soviet Union and other East bloc countries in connection with such meetings, for example, international sporting events.[29]

REFERENCES TO BERLIN IN THE DOCUMENTS OF INTERNATIONAL ORGANISATIONS

References to Berlin in United Nations documents, and in those of the specialised agencies and other international organisations and meetings, are a constant source of friction. They are often incompatible with the legal positions held by the various interested parties, especially when they can be read as implying that the Western Sectors of Berlin are part of the Federal Republic of

---

[27] *BYIL*, 55 (1984), p.534; Notes of 28 May 1976, *Das Vierseitige Abkommen*, p.272; van Well, *EA*, 31 (1976), p.655. Similarly, meetings organised by institutions such as the German Foundation for Development (DSE), which are established under private law, and the attendance at such meetings of officials from Governments or international organisations, do not and cannot in any way affect the status of the city.

[28] *Der Tagesspiegel* of 6 October 1985.

[29] Doehring/Heilbronner, *DA*, 7 (1974), pp. 1169–87.

Germany or that the Soviet Sector is part of the German Democratic Republic or its capital. Such references cannot affect Berlin's status,[30] but one side or the other sometimes feels constrained to place its objection on record. The most protracted exchange occurred in connection with the *United Nations Demographic Yearbook 1972*.[31]

So far as the Western Sectors of Berlin are concerned current United Nations practice is as follows. The Western Sectors are referred to as "Berlin (West)". Where other towns are immediately followed by the country concerned, the document refers just to "Berlin (West)"; in lists where towns are placed under country headings "Berlin (West)" appears at the end of the list under the heading "Germany, Federal Republic of". In each case a footnote is added to the effect that the interests of Berlin (West) are represented in the United Nations by the Federal Republic of Germany. The position in the specialised agencies is similar.

United Nations documents are frequently incorrect as regards East Berlin, placing "Berlin" at the top of lists under the heading "German Democratic Republic" or implying in other ways that Berlin is the capital of the GDR, or referring to it as "Berlin, German Democratic Republic". The Western position on this matter is clearly on record at the United Nations (pp. 298–9 below) and is not repeated on every occasion. As a matter of principle the designations used in United Nations documents do not imply the expression of any opinion on the part of the Secretariat concerning the legal status of any place. An express disclaimer to this effect is frequently included in documents along the following lines:

> The designations employed and the presentation of material in this list do not imply the expression of any opinion whatsoever on the part of the Secretariat concerning the legal status of any country, city, territory or area, or its authorities, or concerning the delimitation of its frontiers. (*United Nations Demographic Yearbook 1978*)

---

[30] The Western letter of 1 May 1974 concerning the *United Nations Demographic Yearbook* affirmed that "no rights are or can be created or asserted on the basis of any data, statement or assertion in the Yearbook": U.N. Doc. A/9599.
[31] U.N. Docs. A/9599 (*US Digest* 1974, p.246); A/9633; A/9648; A/9649; A/9761; A/9855; A/10078 and Corr. 1 (*US Documents*, p. 1277); A/10084; A/10126.

CHAPTER 17

BERLIN AND THE EUROPEAN COMMUNITIES

QUESTIONS concerning the inclusion of Berlin within the area of application of the Treaties establishing the European Communities are in essence no different from those arising generally in connection with the extension to Berlin of international agreements concluded by the Federal Republic of Germany, particularly those establishing international organisations. Nevertheless, they merit treatment in some detail in view of the importance for Berlin of its position within the European Community, the particular nature of the Communities and of Community law, and the attitude of the Soviet Union.[1]

THE EXTENSION OF THE BASIC TREATIES

The 1957 Treaties of Rome were extended to Berlin in accordance with established procedures (Chapter 15 above). Upon signing the Treaties the Federal Republic of Germany reserved the right to extend them to Berlin and did so upon ratification, stating that this did not affect the rights and responsibilities of France, the United Kingdom and the United States in regard to Berlin. The Allied Kommandatura had previously approved the extension of the EEC Treaty with the following important qualifications:

> . . . the Allied Kommandatura does not object to the application
> to Berlin of the above-named treaty insofar as is compatible
> with the rights and responsibilities of the Allied authorities as defined
> in the Declaration on Berlin of May 5, 1955, which in the case
> of any conflict involving the fulfilment of the obligations set forth
> in that instrument, must be regarded as paramount. The extension
> of this treaty to Berlin, moreover, is not to be construed as

---

[1] Writing on this subject is extensive: see in particular Wengler, *AFDI*, 24 (1978), pp.217–36; Hütte, *Yearbook of European Law*, 3 (1983), pp.1–22 (in this Chapter referred to as Hütte). See also Jahn, *Die Europäische Wirtschaftsgemeinschaft (EWG) und Berlin* (Dissertation, Cologne 1968); Jahn, *EuR*, 7 (1972), pp.232–50; von Meibohm, *NJW*, 20 (1967), pp.2096–7; Heidelmeyer, *NJW*, 21 (1968), p.337–8; Zieger, in: *Fs Menzel*, p.581; Doeker-Freiberg, in: Doeker-Bruckner, *The Federal Republic of Germany and the German Democratic Republic in International Relations* 1 (1979), p.347; Schumacher, *EuR*, 15 (1980), pp.183–9; de Rosa, *La Communità Internazionale*, 36 (1981), pp.393–420; Abrasimov, *West Berlin*, pp.124-6; Pestalozza, in: *Fs zum 125 jährigen Bestehen der Juristischen Gesellschaft zu Berlin*, pp.553–9, 567–71 (in this Chapter referred to as Pestalozza); Grabitz, in: *Fs Carstens*, Vol 1, pp.125–38.

implying the repeal or amendment in any way of Allied legislation.[2]

The precise legal basis as between the Member States for the application of the Community Treaties to Berlin has been a matter of some controversy among writers; the better view is that the Treaties apply to Berlin not because of any express provision in their texts but because of the clear agreement of the Member States that they should so apply established by the Federal Republic's declaration on signature and ratification.[3]

A more practical question is the effect of extension by the Federal Republic vis-à-vis the other Member States and the Community institutions. The position has been summarised as follows:

> The Allied Kommandatura directive cited above (BK/L(57)44), with its emphasis on the pre-eminence of Allied occupation law, and the FRG's declaration on ratification set out clearly the conditions for the extension of the Treaties to Berlin. It is against these that the application of Community law in Berlin constantly has to be measured. The Allied reservations are in general terms and are not addressed to particular provisions or powers. They underlie the extension of the Treaties to Berlin, and are binding on Member States and Community organs alike.[4]

The European Communities are constantly developing. The Treaty of Rome itself contains important dynamic elements, both specific (for example, transport policy) and general (the preambular reference to "an ever closer union among the peoples of Europe", and the measures envisaged in Article 235). And it may be amended to provide for closer integration. Part 14 of the Quadripartite Agreement of 3 September 1971 clearly does not preclude such developments applying to Berlin. As has been stated:

> . . . the further dynamic development of the EC is already provided for in the Treaties of Rome. The participation of Berlin in such developments is, in principle, covered by the Allied approval, so the dynamic potential of the Community is also part of the existing situation referred to in Part 14. However, this does not alter the fact that the inclusion of Berlin would reach its ultimate limit where the

[2] BK/L(57)44 of 18 November 1957: Heidelmeyer, p.156. BK/L(57)45 of 18 November 1957 concerning EURATOM is in the same terms; the application of the EURATOM Treaty is subject to Allied provisions relating to nuclear matters (pp.276–8 below). The same procedure has been followed in connection with the accession of the United Kingdom, Denmark and Ireland; Greece; and Portugal and Spain. On the ECSC Treaty, see BK/L(65)51: Heidelmeyer *Dokumente*, p.177; Wettig, *DA*, 11 (1978), p.1186; Hütte, p.15; Pestalozza, pp.553–4. The Single European Act signed at Luxembourg on 17 and 28 February 1986 will also be extended to Berlin.

[3] Heidelmeyer *Dokumente*, p.183. See Hütte, pp.15–16. This is indeed the basis on which most multilateral treaties apply to Berlin: see p.199 above.

[4] Hütte, p.15. Pestalozza (p.550) likewise states that the occupation status of Berlin is paramount and respected by the European institutions.

development of the EC touched upon Allied reserved rights and responsibilities, including those in the field of security and status.[5]

THE APPLICATION OF COMMUNITY LAW

Many provisions of the Community Treaties and of Community secondary legislation (Regulations and certain Directives) are directly applicable in the Member States. The application in Berlin of the Community Treaties is similar to the application, under German constitutional law, of other treaties concluded by the Federal Republic. As regards secondary legislation, BK/L(57)44 states:

> As regards 'European regulations' issued under the authority of this treaty, the Allied Kommandatura will require that the same conditions apply in the case of these regulations as apply in the case of regulations issued under Federal legislation and that it be furnished with copies of all European regulations as soon after their publication as is practicable. Regulations issued under Federal legislation will continue to be provided in accordance with existing procedures.

European regulations are published (since 1964 by title only) in the Berlin *Gesetz- und Verordnungsblatt* under the signature of a Berlin Senator and thus have the force of law in Berlin (though in practice they are then regarded as having been in force as from the same date as in the rest of the Community). The *Senat* is required to inform the Allied Kommandatura about such regulations once they are published in the *Official Journal of the European Communities*; regulations may only be published in the *Gesetz- und Verordnungsblatt* if the Allied Kommandatura has not objected within twenty-one days.[6]

Conflicts between Community law and Allied rights and responsibilities are possible, but unlikely to arise in practice since "the basis for the application of Community law in Berlin does not lie just in the constituent Treaties, but rests ultimately upon the authorisation granted by the Occupying Powers and is linked to the specific reservations of the Allied Kommandatura".[7] Nevertheless it is better to avoid all doubt in the case of potential conflict, and this was done, for example, in connection with two EEC Directives in the field of civil aviation. BK/O(83)4 of 31 May 1983[8] reads:

The Allied Kommandatura has taken note of Directive 83/206/EEC of

---

[5] Hütte, p.15; see also Zündorf, pp.131–2.
[6] Pestalozza, pp.556–8; Hütte, p.17. Compare the procedure for extension of treaties: Chapter 15 above.
[7] Hütte, p.18.
[8] *GVBl.* p.916.

the Council of the European Communities and of the related communication from the Government of the Federal Republic of Germany to the Council set out in the Official Journal of the European Communities No. L 117, 4 May 1983. In view of Allied rights and responsibilities in the field of civil aviation, the Directive cannot apply in relation to Berlin.

The communication referred to in this BK/O was agreed within the Council before the Directive was adopted. In it the Federal Republic recalled its declaration on ratification of the Treaties establishing the European Communities and stated that:

> In view of the fact that civil aviation is one of the areas in which the said States have specifically reserved powers for themselves in Berlin, and following consultations with the Governments of these States, the Government of the Federal Republic of Germany states that the Council Directive amending Directive 80/51/EEC on the limitation of noise emissions from subsonic aircraft does not cover *Land* Berlin.[9]

THE EUROPEAN PARLIAMENT

The European Parliament (Assembly of the European Communities) was originally composed of persons designated by national parliaments, but the Treaties provided for eventual elections by direct universal suffrage in accordance with a uniform procedure. To this end a Decision of the Council of the European Communities was adopted on 20 September 1976, which annexed an Act concerning direct elections.[10] The Federal Republic of Germany declared that the Act applied to Berlin but that, in view of Allied rights and responsibilities, the Berlin House of Representatives would elect those members within the Federal Republic's quota that fell to Berlin. The Allied Kommandatura issued BK/O(77)8 of 19 July 1977[11] which reads:

> The Allied Kommandatura approves, subject to Allied rights and responsibilities, the extension to Berlin of the Decision and Act of the Council of the European Communities concerning the Election of the Representatives of the Assembly by Direct Universal Suffrage on the understanding that the Berlin House of Representatives will select the representatives for those seats which fall to Berlin within the quota for the Federal Republic of Germany.
>
> Extension of the Decision and Act to Berlin does not imply that Allied legislation has been repealed or modified in any way.

[9] The same procedure was followed in connection with another Air Directive in 1983: BK/O(83)6 of 12 October 1983 (*GVBl.* p.1360) and the *Official Journal of the European Communities* No. L. 237 of 26 August 1983. See Hütte, pp.1–3, 18.
[10] *UKTS* 15 (1979), p.201.
[11] *GVBl.* p.1824. See also BK/O(78)6 of 31 July 1978 (*GVBl.* p.1576) and BK/O(79)5 of 25 April 1979 (*GVBl.* p.688).

Before the introduction of direct elections the three Berlin members of the European Parliament were nominated by the *Bundestag*; they have been selected by the Berlin House of Representatives on the occasion of the direct elections of June 1979 and June 1984, pursuant to the arrangements described above.[12]

OTHER MATTERS

Unlike the Federal Constitutional Court, the jurisdiction of the European Court of Justice has not been excluded by Allied action. Berlin courts, and Federal courts acting in Berlin matters, may request preliminary rulings under Article 177 of the EEC Treaty[13] and the corresponding provisions of other Community Treaties. Berliners may challenge decisions of Community organs under Article 173. Judgments of the European Court are directly binding in Berlin as elsewhere in the Community. Like the other Community institutions the Court is bound by the limits imposed by the Allies on the application of the Treaties in Berlin.[14]

The European Communities enter into many international agreements in their own right, which in principle apply to Berlin since Berlin is within the area of application of the Treaties establishing the Communities. Agreements entered into by the Communities do not need a Berlin clause or other express mention of Berlin, unlike those entered into by the Federal Republic of Germany. Such treaties do in fact frequently include a territorial application clause along the following lines, which *inter alia* makes it clear that Berlin is covered:

> This Agreement shall apply, on the one hand, to the territories in which the Treaty establishing the European Economic Community is applied and under the conditions laid down in that Treaty and, on the other hand, to the territory of . . .[15]

As with treaties of the Federal Republic, the extension of Community treaties to Berlin cannot affect Allied rights and responsibilities, and this is so whether or not an express reservation is made.[16]

---

[12] The GDR then introduced direct elections to the *Volkskammer*: pp.303–4 below.

[13] See examples in Pestalozza, pp.568–9.

[14] Wengler, *AFDI*, 24 (1978), pp.230–1. Pestalozza, p.567. "In any case the AK would not be bound by decisions of the Court concerning Berlin and could forbid their execution in Berlin on the grounds of incompatibility with Allied rights and responsibilities": Hütte, p.21; Pestalozza, p.559. Both Hütte and Pestalozza conclude that conflicts between the European Court of Justice and Allied rights and responsibilities are unlikely.

[15] E.g. Article 9 of the Agreement for Commercial, Economic and Development Co-operation between the European Economic Community and the Islamic Republic of Pakistan of 23 July 1985: Hütte, p.19 (footnote 72).

[16] BK/O(74)11 of 30 September 1974 (*GVBl.* p.2576): p.199 above.

Two Community bodies are located in Berlin: a Press and Information Sub-Office and the European Centre for the Development of Vocational Training. In relation to the latter, the Allied Kommandatura issued BK/O(75)3 of 9 April 1975,[17] the substantive part of which reads:

> The Allied Kommandatura, having reviewed Regulation (EEC) No. 337/75 of the Council of the European Communities of 10 February 1975 which was submitted to it in accordance with the established procedures, raises no objection to the establishment of the European Centre for the Development of Vocational Training in the Western Sectors of Berlin. Allied rights and responsibilities, including those respecting privileges and immunities, shall remain unaffected.

There are frequent visits to Berlin by Community officials. Community organs likewise meet there from time to time.[18]

THE SOVIET ATTITUDE

The Soviet Union did not object to the inclusion of Berlin in the area of application of the Community Treaties until the mid-1970s, nearly twenty years after the establishment of the EEC, and the matter is not expressly referred to in the Quadripartite Agreement. Since then the Soviet authorities have protested frequently and in strong terms against Berlin's inclusion in what they term the "state-political integration of Western Europe", which they apparently see as a back-door incorporation of Berlin into the Federal Republic. These objections appear to be based upon a fear that Berlin's status will somehow be disregarded within the European Communities.

In 1974 the Soviet Union stated in Notes to the three Powers that it had always regarded as unlawful all attempts to bring West Berlin within the sphere of the European Communities; the objective of the Communities was the political integration of their Member States, and this objective was incompatible with the status of West Berlin.[19] The Soviet Union likewise objected in 1975 to the establishment in Berlin of the European Centre for the Development of Vocational Training, saying that the European Economic Community was not entitled to take any decisions concerning the Western Sectors of Berlin; that the Community had no competence in questions touching the status of the Western Sectors; that the aim of the Community was the political integration

---

[17] GVBl. p.1132.
[18] Hütte, p.22.
[19] Das Vierseitige Abkommen, p.196. The GDR press had already objected in February 1973 to a meeting in Berlin of the Presidential Council of the European Parliament.

of its Member States, and this aim was incompatible with the status of the Western Sectors, as laid down in the Quadripartite Agreement; and that the Western Sectors were not and could not be part of the Federal Republic of Germany and could not be included in the Community. They protested again following the issue of BK/O(75)3.[20] Soviet protests concerning the inclusion of Berlin in direct elections to the European Parliament were in similar terms.[21] The Western Allies rejected these protests on 15 June 1984 in the following terms:

The three Powers, in accordance with established procedures and insofar as is compatible with Allied rights and responsibilities, in 1957 approved the extension to the Western Sectors of Berlin of the Treaty establishing the European Economic Community. On the same basis they subsequently approved the extension to the Western Sectors of Berlin of other constitutive treaties of the European Community. Consequently, the Western Sectors of Berlin have since 1957 been included in the area of application of these treaties. The three Powers have throughout that period ensured that Allied rights and responsibilities, including those relating to matters of security and status, were not affected by developments in the European Community. The Quadripartite Agreement in no way affected the application in the Western Sectors of Berlin of the European Community Treaties.

Direct elections to the European Assembly, in the work of which representatives from the Western Sectors of Berlin have participated since its inception, were provided for in the EEC Treaty of 1957. As in the past, representatives from the Western Sectors of Berlin will continue to be included within the quota of the Federal Republic of Germany at the Assembly. They are not directly elected, but are selected by the Berlin House of Representatives. In these circumstances it is clear that continued participation of Berlin representatives in the European Assembly does not affect the status of Berlin. Such participation can therefore not constitute a violation of the Quadripartite Agreement.[22]

---

[20] *Das Vierseitige Abkommen*, pp.215, 219, 239; Hennig, *Die Bundespräsenz in West-Berlin*, pp.108–10; see also the Soviet protest and Allied reply concerning the holding in West Berlin of an International Waste Recycling Congress: *BYIL*, 55 (1984), pp.533–5.

[21] See, for example, the Soviet statements of 3 August 1976 and 16 November 1976 (*Das Vierseitige Abkommen*, pp.279, 297); and of 11 June 1984.

[22] *US Documents*, p.1379.

CHAPTER 18

CONTACTS WITH THE GDR AND EAST BERLIN

CONTACTS with the GDR of concern to Berlin take various forms. They may either be between the Government of the Federal Republic of Germany and the GDR Government, between the *Senat* of Berlin and the GDR Government, or between the *Senat* or other bodies in West Berlin and the municipal authorities or other bodies in East Berlin. The contacts, and any arrangements resulting from them, are of differing degrees of formality. Some take place under a quadripartite roof, express or implied; others do not. The following account necessarily deals chiefly with the more formal or significant contacts with the GDR, that is to say, those that have come to public attention.

The Quadripartite Agreement of 3 September 1971 provides for certain matters to be settled between "the competent German authorities", that is, between the Governments of the Federal Republic of Germany and the GDR (civilian transit traffic between the Federal Republic and West Berlin, posts and telecommunications) or between the *Senat* of Berlin and the GDR Government (travel and visits of West Berliners, exchange of territory, certain communications matters). In all these cases the German parties act under a quadripartite roof, and the resulting arrangements are covered by the Final Quadripartite Protocol.

The representation of Berlin's interests vis-à-vis the GDR is governed by principles analogous to those governing such representation vis-à-vis other States. But there are a number of special factors. First, the Federal Republic of Germany has, since the early 1970s, accepted the GDR as a State, but not as a foreign State. The Federal Republic has not entered into diplomatic relations with the GDR, and the rules of international law governing relations between States are only applied by analogy. Second, there is a special need for contacts, of an informal or low-level kind, on technical matters arising from the fact that West Berlin is surrounded by the GDR and East Berlin. A third, complicating factor is that East Berlin, the GDR seat of government, is regarded by the GDR as an integral part of its territory and its capital.

It is, in general, for the Federal Republic of Germany to represent Berlin's interests in relation to the GDR, as in relation to other States. Thus agreements between the Federal Republic of Germany and the GDR are, with certain exceptions, extended to Berlin and the same procedures apply as with international agreements generally (Chapter 15 above). The Permanent Representation of the Federal Republic of Germany to the GDR looks after West Berlin's interests in most fields. However, given the geographical situation, there is also a need to deal with local problems of a technical, economic, administrative or humanitarian nature. These may require contacts at appropriate levels between the *Senat* of Berlin and GDR officials or semi-official bodies. There is no general arrangement for the *Senat* to represent Berlin's interests externally comparable with that for the Federal Republic, and the *Senat* must therefore receive specific authorisation from the Western Allies on each occasion before entering into negotiations or arrangements.

Contacts between the *Senat* of Berlin and the GDR pose delicate problems, both political and legal. Given their potential for giving credence to the Eastern view that West Berlin is a separate political entity, and the fact that the Federal Republic is in general authorised to represent Berlin's interests outside Berlin, such contacts relate only to local problems of a technical nature and may not encroach upon matters where it is for the Federal Republic to represent Berlin's interests. They are normally on a technical level and are, wherever possible, informal. They cannot involve acceptance of positions contrary to the quadripartite status of Berlin, for example acceptance that the Soviet Sector is part of the GDR or its capital, that the sector boundary is the GDR state frontier, that the municipal authorities in East Berlin are lawfully constituted, or that the GDR military may be present in Berlin. There is the closest possible consultation between *Senat* and Allied authorities in advance of and, as appropriate, during such contacts to avoid any risk of harm to the status of Berlin. During the contacts over the wall pass arrangements in the 1960s (p.226 below), the *Senat* spokesman, Egon Bahr, set forth the principles upon which the *Senat* acted as follows:

1. In the interests of people, everything responsible must be tried in order to soften the hardest effects of the Wall.
2. The legal status of Berlin must not be impaired.
3. Berlin's ties with the Federation and the relationship to the Allied Protecting Powers must not be loosened.
4. No encouragement must be given to the three-State theory.[1]

These principles remain as valid today as in 1964.[2]

---

[1] Heidelmeyer *Dokumente*, p.579.
[2] Cf. the public debate about possible status and constitutional implications of the Governing Mayor's meeting with Honecker in September 1983 at Schloss Niederschönhausen in the Soviet Sector: see Kewenig, *Entwicklungslinien des völker- und staatsrechtlichen Status von Berlin*.

BEFORE THE QUADRIPARTITE AGREEMENT

Apart from the special case of inner-German trade (p.26 above), there is no example of the Federal Republic of Germany representing Berlin's interests in relation to the GDR prior to the negotiation of the Quadripartite Agreement and general Western acceptance of the GDR as a State. Contacts between authorities located in the Western Sectors and those located in the Soviet Sector were rare. There were inevitably certain contacts on a technical level between Berlin and the Soviet zone and Sector, given the previous administrative connection and the geographical position; for example, there was an open border between the city and the Soviet zone until 1952, the central administration of the Soviet zone was located in the Soviet Sector, and the operation throughout the city of the railways (including the *S-Bahn*) and certain canal locks was undertaken by administrative authorities located there.[3] Some contacts between the Western Sectors and the Soviet Sector existed prior to 1961, chiefly it seems on the municipal level. After 1961 contacts, even on a technical level, were very exceptional, one example being to save life.[4]

The negotiation of the wall pass arrangements[5] of the 1960s is of particular interest. Following the sealing-off of the Soviet Sector in August 1961 the GDR Government at first refused to agree on arrangements to enable West Berliners to visit the East except through direct negotiations and agreements between West Berlin and the GDR involving recognition of the GDR and of the separate entity *Westberlin*.[6] Eventually, on 17 December 1963, officials of the *Senat* and GDR reached agreement on a *Protokoll* (agreed record) on a temporary arrangement for West Berliners to visit relatives in East Berlin, which covered the Christmas and New Year period (18 December 1963 to 5 January 1964). The *Senat* acted "in agreement with the Federal Government and with the three Protecting Powers responsible for West Berlin". The Western Commandants stated that the arrangements in no way affected the status of Berlin.[7] The *Protokoll* was signed by State Secretary Wendt "on instructions from

---

[3] Zivier, pp.4–5; Krumholz, *Berlin ABC* (2nd ed.), p.363.

[4] *Zehn Jahre Deutschlandpolitik*, p.53.

[5] Heidelmeyer *Dokumente*, pp.568–89; *Selected Documents* II, pp.6–7 and 102–3; *US Documents*, pp.860, 879, 883. The four arrangements were signed on 17 December 1963, 24 September 1964, 25 November 1965 and 7 March 1966. Zivier, *Die Nichtanerkennung im modernen Völkerrecht* (2nd ed. 1969), pp.264, 328; Mahncke, *Berlin im geteilten Deutschland*, pp.220–3.

[6] Heidelmeyer *Dokumente*, pp.568–71. On 8 February 1963 Ulbricht proposed a "Treaty on the Normalisation of Relations between the German Democratic Republic and Westberlin". The *Senat* would, it seems, have been willing to reach agreement with the municipal authorities in East Berlin over hardship cases: Heidelmeyer, p.294.

[7] *Selected Documents* II, p.102.

the Deputy Chairman of the Council of Ministers of the GDR" and by *Senatsrat* Korber "on instructions of the Head of the *Senatskanzlei*, given with the authority of the Governing Mayor of Berlin". The *Protokoll* contained the following saving clause:

> Despite the differing political and legal standpoints both sides are guided by the principle that it should be possible to realise this humanitarian object [ie the visits]. In the talks, which took place alternately in Berlin (West) and Berlin (East)/Capital of the GDR, the attached understanding [*Übereinkunft*] was reached.
>
> Both sides declared that an agreement on common descriptions of places, authorities and offices could not be reached.

In his statement upon signature, *Senatsrat* Korber referred to the arrangements as a technical understanding (*technische Übereinkunft*), and continued:

> In this connection it is important that your side also declared that this arrangement does not have the character of an inter-state agreement.[8]

Care was also taken to ensure that East German activities under the arrangements were not of a sovereign or quasi-consular nature.[9] Similar care was taken to protect the Western legal position in connection with the three subsequent arrangements of 24 September 1964, 25 November 1965 and 7 March 1966. When, because of increased GDR demands and in particular its refusal to include the saving clause, these principles could no longer be maintained, no further wall pass arrangements were reached.[10]

FEDERAL REPUBLIC/GDR ARRANGEMENTS UNDER THE QUADRIPARTITE AGREEMENT

In Part IIA and Annex I, paragraph 3, of the Quadripartite Agreement the four Powers agreed that detailed arrangements concerning civilian transit traffic between West Berlin and the

---

[8] Heidelmeyer *Dokumente*, p.571. The Governing Mayor spoke along similar lines: "Today's understanding could only be reached because the opposing critical political and legal standpoints were excluded. The text of the understanding and the form of the signature made it clear that it is not a case of an arrangement of an international or inter-state character . . . The status of Berlin has not been changed". In a joint statement the Federal Government and *Senat* stated that "the legal status of Berlin is not altered by this arrangement": Heidelmeyer *Dokumente*, pp.577, 578.

[9] Zivier, p.30.

[10] A fifth wall pass arrangement of 6 October 1966, limited to urgent family cases, contained no saving clause, but referred back to the earlier arrangements that did: see Mahncke, *Berlin im geteilten Deutschland*, p.112. "The Federal Government and the *Senat* are ready, as before, to reach agreements on the existing basis . . . they are not however ready to join in increasing the status of the Soviet zone of occupation": joint FRG/*Senat* statement of 29 July 1966: Heidelmeyer *Dokumente*, p.589. For the Easter 1971 discussions, see *Selected Documents* II, p.19. The GDR unilaterally permitted West Berliners to visit at Easter and Whitsun 1972.

Federal Republic of Germany would be agreed by the competent German authorities; and in Part IIC they similarly agreed that detailed arrangements concerning travel, communication and the exchange of territory, as set forth in Annex III, would be agreed by the competent German authorities. In implementation of these provisions detailed arrangements on civilian transit traffic, and posts and telecommunications, were agreed by the Government of the Federal Republic and the GDR Government, while those on travel and visits of West Berliners and exchange of territory were agreed by the *Senat* and GDR Government. The Governments of the Federal Republic of Germany and the GDR negotiated an Agreement of 17 December 1971 on the Transit Traffic of Civilian Persons and Goods between the Federal Republic of Germany and Berlin (West).[11] The relationship of this Agreement to the Quadripartite Agreement has already been considered (pp.131–2 above). It is sufficient to note here that, at the explicit request of the three Allies, the Federal Government acted also on behalf of the *Senat*.[12] As the Allied Kommandatura stated in BKC/L(71)3, the Agreement is in force in the Western Sectors of Berlin and the *Senat* is therefore "authorised and directed to participate as appropriate" in its implementation there. The Governments of the Federal Republic of Germany and the GDR similarly negotiated an arrangement on Berlin post and telecommunications, contained in points 6 and 7 of the Protocol on Negotiations between a Delegation of the Federal Ministry for Post and Telecommunications of the Federal Republic of Germany and a Delegation of the Ministry for Post and Telecommunications of the German Democratic Republic, dated 30 September 1971.[13] This arrangement by its terms applies to West Berlin.

SENAT/GDR ARRANGEMENTS UNDER THE QUADRIPARTITE AGREEMENT

Two *Senat*/GDR arrangements implement and supplement Part IIC and Annex III, paragraphs 1, 2 and 3, of the Quadripartite Agreement: the Arrangement of 20 December 1971 on Facilitations and Improvements in Travel and Visitor Traffic;[14] and the Arrangement of 20 December 1971 on the Resolution of

[11] Cmnd. 5135, p.62; *US Documents*, p.1169; *Zehn Jahre Deutschlandpolitik*, p.169. See Chapter 9 above.
[12] Letter of 3 September 1971: see p.346 below. The *Senat* is not a party to the Agreement.
[13] Cmnd. 5135, p.59; *US Documents*, p.1167; *Zehn Jahre Deutschlandpolitik*, p.163. Zivier, p.220; Zündorf, p. 188.
[14] Cmnd. 5135, p.104; *US Documents*, p.1179; *Zehn Jahre Deutschlandpolitik*, p.175.

the Problem of Enclaves by the Exchange of Territory.[15] The relationship of these Arrangements to the Quadripartite Agreement has been described at p.52 above, and their substance is covered at pp.248–52 below and pp.94–5 above respectively. Each Arrangement looks forward to further arrangements, and the Travel and Visits Arrangement provides for standing commissioners (*Beauftragte*). All these activities take place under a clear quadripartite roof.

REPRESENTATION OF BERLIN'S INTERESTS BY THE FEDERAL REPUBLIC

The principles governing representation by the Federal Republic of Germany of Berlin's interests apply to representation vis-à-vis the GDR. Thus the Federal Republic is authorised by the Allied Kommandatura to represent the interests of Berlin vis-à-vis the GDR; the letter of the three High Commissioners concerning the exercise of reserved Allied rights (p.329 below) and the Declaration on Berlin of 5 May 1955 (p.332 below) are regarded as applying. The procedure laid down in BKC/L(52)6 (p.196 above) concerning the extension of international agreements is likewise applicable. Among the first inner-German agreements to extend to Berlin was the Exchange of Letters of 8 November 1972 concerning working possibilities for journalists.[16] While, given its content, the Treaty on the Basis of Relations between the Federal Republic of Germany and the GDR of 21 December 1972 (the Basis of Relations Treaty) does not in general extend to Berlin, a statement by the two parties on signature reads as follows:

> There is agreement that the extension to Berlin (West) of agreements and arrangements envisaged in the Supplementary Protocol to Article 7 may be agreed in each case in accordance with the Quadripartite Agreement of 3 September 1971.
> The Permanent Representation of the Federal Republic of Germany to the German Democratic Republic shall, in accordance with the Quadripartite Agreement of 3 September 1971, represent the interests of Berlin (West).
> Arrangements between the German Democratic Republic and the *Senat* shall remain unaffected.[17]

The Federal Republic of Germany and GDR thus expressly applied the provisions of the Quadripartite Agreement on the extension of international agreements, and on external representation, to agreements with, and representation in relation to, the GDR.

---

[15] Cmnd. 5135, p.122; *US Documents*, pp.1182, 1184; *Zehn Jahre Deutschlandpolitik*, p.178.
[16] *Zehn Jahre Deutschlandpolitik*, p.203. Extension to Berlin was agreed in oral declarations.
[17] *BGBl.* 1973 II, p.428; *US Documents*, p.1221; *Zehn Jahre Deutschlandpolitik*, p.211.

There are two points to note about the first paragraph of the statement. It refers in terms only to those agreements envisaged in the Supplementary Protocol to Article 7, that is to say, agreements on economic relations and trade, science and technology, traffic, judicial relations, post and telecommunications, health, culture, sport, environmental protection, acquisition of books, etc. and non-commercial payments and clearing procedures. But it is not exhaustive and other agreements may likewise be so extended. Second, it only states that such agreements may extend to West Berlin. As a matter of Federal constitutional law they must so extend, but the GDR is not obliged to agree to extension. Thus, for example, the following inner-German agreements extend to the Western Sectors of Berlin: the Treaty of 26 May 1972 on Questions of Transport,[18] the Agreements of 25 April 1974 on Maintenance Payments and Property Transfers,[19] the Health Agreement of 25 April 1974,[20] the Agreement on Posts and Telecommunications of 30 March 1976,[21] the Agreement of 21 December 1979 on Veterinary Matters,[22] and the Cultural Co-operation Agreement of 6 May 1986.[23] Berlin is not merely included in the area of application of these agreements in the formal sense, but also in their practical implementation. Thus, for example, Berlin is included in cultural exchanges under the recent Cultural Agreement. The Frank-Falin clause (p.203 above) is generally used for including Berlin in inner-German agreements. Agreements relating to the inner-German border, concluded under the auspices of the Border Commission (Article 3 of the Basis of Relations Treaty) are not extended to Berlin.[24]

The second and third paragraphs of the statement on signature of the Basis of Relations Treaty were repeated in *Protokollvermerk* No. 6 to the Protocol on the Establishment of Permanent Representations of 14 March 1974.[25] The cross-reference to the Quadripartite Agreement introduces the difference of view between

[18] *BGBl.* 1972 II, p.1449; *Zehn Jahre Deutschlandpolitik*, p.183; *US Documents*, p.1191. Extension to Berlin was agreed in declarations upon signature. Similarly the Agreements of 31 October 1979 on Road Taxes extend to Berlin: *Zehn Jahre Deutschlandpolitik*, pp.384, 385.
[19] *Zehn Jahre Deutschlandpolitik*, pp.261, 262. Extension to Berlin is governed by an Article of each Agreement.
[20] *Zehn Jahre Deutschlandpolitik*, p.265. Article 8 of the Agreement provides for extension to Berlin.
[21] *Zehn Jahre Deutschlandpolitik*, p.302. Extension to Berlin is expressly provided for in Article 21; Articles 9 and 13 and the related Administrative Agreements also contain special provisions.
[22] *Zehn Jahre Deutschlandpolitik*, p.387. Article 8 of the Agreement provides for extension to Berlin.
[23] See *BGBl.* II, p.710.
[24] See, for example, *Zehn Jahre Deutschlandpolitik*, pp.245, 247, 272.
[25] *Zehn Jahre Deutschlandpolitik*, p.256.

East and West on the proper scope of the representation by the Federal Republic of the interests of the Western Sectors of Berlin. In the Western view, the Federal Republic may represent those interests in general, except where this would affect Allied rights and responsibilities. The Eastern view is that the Federal Republic's role is limited to the four points listed in Annex IVA, paragraph 2, of the Quadripartite Agreement (Chapter 14 above).

OTHER *SENAT*/GDR CONTACTS

Contacts not coming under the Quadripartite Agreement are not, as a matter of law, affected by it; but the changed political climate has resulted in a greater range of West Berlin/GDR contacts than was the case prior to 1971. In so far as these contacts have resulted in agreed arrangements these have been essentially on local and technical matters, and have usually had a very informal nature. Examples include arrangements on the saving of life in the Spree,[26] sewage disposal,[27] local environment matters, waste disposal,[28] locks (Chapter 21 below), and repair work to the Glienicker Bridge. In the cultural field contacts have tended to be on a municipal level, for example, the return of the Schinkel statues to the Marx-Engels-Brücke (Schlossbrücke) and of the statue of Schiller to the Platz der Akademie (Gendarmenmarkt) in front of the Schauspielhaus.

There have been a number of contacts between *Senat* authorities and the *Deutsche Reichsbahn* on railway matters, notably the Südgelände arrangements of 21 February 1974 and 24 January 1980 (currently under revision); the 1980 arrangements concerning improvements to railway operations in the Wannsee area; and the *S-Bahn* arrangement of 30 December 1983 (under which the *Deutsche Reichsbahn* ceased to operate the *S-Bahn* in the Western Sectors on 9 January 1984). In all these contacts the Western Allies and the *Senat* were careful to ensure that nothing was done that might adversely affect status (Chapter 21 below).

[26] *Zehn Jahre Deutschlandpolitik*, p.287 (also the *Senat*/AK statement at p.289); see Catudal, *A Balance Sheet of the Quadripartite Agreement on Berlin*, pp.102–3.
[27] Arrangements of 12 December 1974 and 18 March 1980: see Catudal, *A Balance Sheet of the Quadripartite Agreement on Berlin*, pp.101–2.
[28] Mahncke, *Berlin im geteilten Deutschland*, pp.229–30; *Das Vierseitige Abkommen*, pp.320, 326, 328; *Zehn Jahre Deutschlandpolitik*, p.284.

PART SIX

BERLIN: INTERNAL

This Part covers certain matters arising from the status of Berlin which are of particular concern to individual Berliners and which are, for the most part, internal in nature. Chapter 19 deals with questions of nationality, and the travel and identity documents of Berliners. Chapter 20 examines the principle of freedom of movement throughout the special Berlin area, and the particular arrangements regarding travel and visits of West Berliners to East Berlin and the GDR. Chapter 21 deals with two of the means of transport within Berlin, the railways and waterways, which are particularly affected by the status of Berlin. Chapter 22 describes the various aspects of the special demilitarised status of Berlin; and Chapter 23 examines some important aspects of Allied responsibility in the field of security and public order.

CHAPTER 19

NATIONALITY, PASSPORTS AND IDENTITY CARDS

NATIONALITY

ALTHOUGH the special Berlin area remains under quadripartite occupation and does not form part of either the Federal Republic of Germany or the German Democratic Republic, there is no special Berlin nationality. Berlin remains, of course, part of Germany as a whole. The question of the national status of Germans resident in or connected with Berlin is inseparable from that of the national status of Germans everywhere, and the latter question is linked to the question of Germany as a whole. The question of German nationality is a matter of continuing controversy between the Federal Republic and GDR. Moreover, the four Powers retain rights and responsibilities relating to German nationality as part of their responsibilities for Germany as a whole.[1]

In Berlin as in the rest of Germany, the four Powers acted on the basis of a common German nationality from the outset of the occupation. There was no attempt to establish a special national status for persons resident in or connected with each of the four zones of occupation or the special Berlin area. With the exception of certain denazification measures,[2] the occupation authorities disturbed neither the national status of the Germans nor the pre-existing nationality legislation of the German *Reich*.[3] The *Reich*

---

[1] Grawert, *Der Staat*, 12 (1973), pp.289–312; Ipsen, *JIR*, 16 (1973), pp.266–300; Zivier, pp.132–8; Schröder, *AVR*, 21 (1983), pp.409–32; Schröder, *ROW*, 30 (1986), pp.154–60. See also Zieger, *Die Staatsangehörigkeit im geteilten Deutschland* (1971); Schröder, *AVR*, 21 (1983), pp.409–32; Scholz, in: *Staatliche und nationale Einheit Deutschlands – ihre Effektivität* (1984), p.57; von Mangoldt, in: *Deutschland als Ganzes* (1985), pp.175–89; Ruby, *L'Évolution de la Nationalité allemande* (1953).

[2] For example, Military Government Law No. 1 (*Military Government Gazette, Germany, 21 Army Group Area of Control*, No. 1, p.11) and Control Council Law No. 1 of 20 September 1945 (*CC Gazette*, p.3) repealed the *Reich* Citizenship Law (*Reichsbürgergesetz*) of 15 September 1935 (*RGBl.* I, p.1146). The latter had left nationality to be governed by existing law, but excluded Jews from the privileged status of citizenship. See Bathurst and Simpson, *Germany and the North Atlantic Community*, p.9. Allied Kommandatura Law No. 6 of 4 March 1950 (*AK Gazette*, p.10) declared null and void provisions of wartime *Reich* legislation which purported to impose German nationality on nationals of France and Luxembourg.

[3] The four Powers could have intervened more thoroughly in matters of German nationality in exercise of the supreme authority assumed on 5 June 1945. Schröder, *AVR*, 21 (1983), pp.410, 413 argues that the Hague Regulations would have inhibited them from doing so; but the Regulations no longer applied after the assumption of supreme authority: p.35 above.

Nationality Law of 22 July 1913[4] remained in force as the basic legislation regulating questions of German nationality.

The common German nationality regulated by the Law of 1913 continued after the establishment of the Federal Republic of Germany and GDR in 1949. Proceeding from the continued existence of a single German State, the Basic Law for the Federal Republic of Germany presupposes a continuing common German nationality. Article 116(1) provides as follows:

> Unless otherwise regulated by law, a German within the meaning of this Basic Law is a person who possesses German nationality or who has been accepted in the territory of the German *Reich* as at 31 December 1937 as a refugee or expellee of German stock or as the spouse or descendant of such person.

The first Constitution of the German Democratic Republic likewise emphasised the continuation of a common German nationality. Only with the GDR Citizenship Law of 20 February 1967[5] was provision made for a separate GDR citizenship as a matter of GDR law.

The Basic Law for the Federal Republic of Germany and the nationality legislation in force there continue to presuppose a common German nationality,[6] whereas the legislation of the GDR provides, since 1967, for a separate GDR citizenship for persons with defined connections with the GDR. The Treaty on the Basis of Relations between the Federal Republic of Germany and the GDR of 21 December 1972 did not resolve the matter. The Federal Republic of Germany stated upon signature that "Questions of nationality have not been regulated by the Treaty", while the GDR stated that "The German Democratic Republic proceeds from the assumption that the Treaty will facilitate a regulation of questions of nationality".[7]

The Allies have taken no steps to disturb the common German nationality. Even though GDR legislation may treat certain residents of Berlin as GDR citizens, this cannot affect the reserved rights of the four Powers. In Article IV of the Declaration on Berlin of 5 May 1955 (p.332 below), the Allied Kommandatura stated that it would not, subject to Articles I and II of the Declaration, raise any objection to the adoption by Berlin under an appropriate procedure authorised by the Allied Kommandatura of the same legislation as that of the Federal Republic regarding nationality and

---

[4] *Reichs- und Staatsangehörigkeitsgesetz*: *RGBl.* p.583; *BGBl.* III, No. 102–1.
[5] *Staatsbürgerschaftsgesetz*: *GBl.DDR* I, p.3. See Schröder, *AVR*, 21 (1983), pp.428–9.
[6] See the decision of the Federal Constitutional Court of 31 July 1973 concerning the Basis of Relations Treaty: *BVerfGE.* 36, 1; *Zehn Jahre Deutschlandpolitik*, p.232.
[7] *Zehn Jahre Deutschlandpolitik*, p.207; *US Documents*, p.1219.

passports.[8] Accordingly Federal German nationality legislation amending and supplementing the *Reich* Nationality Law of 1913 has been taken over in Berlin. There is therefore *Rechtseinheit* between the Federal Republic of Germany and the Western Sectors of Berlin in the matter of nationality legislation, based upon the continuing common German nationality. Allied legislation in force in Berlin also presupposes a common German nationality. Moreover, Article IV of the Declaration on Berlin expressly makes the authorisation to adopt nationality legislation subject to the reserved rights in Articles I and II of the Declaration.[9]

PASSPORTS

Under the same conditions, and also in accordance with Article IV of the Declaration on Berlin, Federal legislation relating to passports has been taken over in Berlin.[10] Germans resident in the Western Sectors are therefore able to obtain passports of the Federal Republic of Germany. Because of the status of Berlin, however, there is a special procedure for the issue of these passports in Berlin. In the Federal Republic, passports are issued by the passport authorities of the *Länder*. With the agreement of the Allied Kommandatura, Federal passports are issued in Berlin to residents of the Western Sectors by the Federal Minister of the Interior acting through the Police President in Berlin.[11] Outside Berlin, Federal passports are issued in the Federal Republic of Germany to Berlin residents only if they have another place of residence in the Federal Republic; or they may exceptionally be issued abroad where a resident of the Western Sectors has lost his passport in a foreign country and approaches the embassy or consulate of the Federal Republic in that country for a new passport. There is no difference in form between a Federal passport issued to a resident of the Federal Republic of Germany and one issued to a resident of Berlin; each bears the words: *Der Inhaber dieses Passes ist Deutscher* (The holder of this passport is a German).

IDENTITY CARDS

The position is different in the case of identity cards

---

[8] This reflects a similar statement made in the letter from the three High Commissioners to the Federal Chancellor of 26 May 1952 in the version of letter X of 23 October 1954 (p.329 below).

[9] AK intervention in relation to nationality legislation has been minimal: see BK/O(61)16 of 5 October 1961 (*GVBl.* p.1616), which was concerned to maintain other aspects of the status of Berlin.

[10] The principal current legislation is the Federal Passport Law (*Gesetz über das Passwesen*) of 4 March 1952 (*BGBl.* I, p.290). The new Federal Passport Law of 19 April 1986 (*BGBl.* I, p.537) enters into force on 1 January 1988.

[11] See Schröder, *AVR*, 21 (1983), pp.418–9.

(*Personalausweise*). Whereas the issue of identity cards to Germans resident in the Federal Republic is governed by Federal legislation, in Berlin the matter is governed by Allied legislation. The original (quadripartite) legislation was BK/O(46)61 of 24 January 1946. As amended,[12] paragraph 1 of this BK/O requires that a temporary identity card (*behelfsmässiger Personalausweis*) shall be issued to persons of German nationality residing in Berlin.[13] The following paragraphs state that persons aged sixteen and over must possess a temporary identity card; that the identity card of every parent shall show the names and dates of birth of all living children under the age of sixteen years; and that upon application by their legal representatives children who have completed their sixth year may be issued with a temporary identity card. The form of the temporary identity card follows the specimen attached to the BK/O (a new specimen was introduced in 1963). It differs from the identity card issued in the Federal Republic of Germany both in its special title ("*behelfsmässiger Personalausweis*") and in omitting the imprint of the Federal eagle as well as any reference to the Federal Republic. These distinctions reflect the special status of Berlin. In accordance with the BK/O it bears the trilingual inscription: *Der Inhaber dieses Ausweises ist deutscher Staatsangehöriger*: *Le titulaire de la présente carte est ressortissant allemand*: The holder of this identity card is a German national. Berlin temporary identity cards are issued by the Police President in Berlin.

THE QUADRIPARTITE AGREEMENT

The Quadripartite Agreement of 3 September 1971 does not refer to nationality. Although the confirmation in Part IIB that the Western Sectors of Berlin continue not to be a constituent part of the Federal Republic of Germany might be thought to imply a distinction in matters of nationality between those Sectors and the Federal Republic, the Agreement does not in fact support this. It is based on the existing situation, the situation which has developed in the area, which is not to be changed unilaterally. Part of the existing situation is the continuing single German nationality, which the nationality legislation in force in the Federal Republic and the Western Sectors presupposes. So indeed is the legal harmony between the Federal Republic and the Western Sectors in the matters of German nationality and nationality legislation. The establishment of this *Rechtseinheit* long predated the conclusion of

---

[12] The version currently in force can be found in the Annex to BK/O(63)9 of 31 July 1963 (*GVBl.* p.797), less paragraph 4 which was deleted by BK/O(65)8 of 23 June 1965 (*GVBl.* p.848). But see now BK/O(87)1.

[13] This wording is an example of Allied legislation based on a single German nationality.

the Quadripartite Agreement. The same considerations apply to the law and practice regarding the issue of Federal German passports to residents of Berlin.

The Quadripartite Agreement contains several provisions referring to "permanent residents of the Western Sectors of Berlin".[14] Among these are the provisions in Annex IV concerning representation abroad of the interests of the Western Sectors of Berlin and their permanent residents, including the provision that "the Federal Republic of Germany may perform consular services for permanent residents of the Western Sectors of Berlin". This confirmed the acceptability to the four Powers of a long-established practice, a practice that reflects the single German nationality shared by Germans resident in the Federal Republic and in the Western Sectors.

Agreed Minute I of 3 September 1971 contains special provisions concerning visas and passports for permanent residents of the Western Sectors visiting the Soviet Union.[15] The first paragraph reads:

> It is understood that permanent residents of the Western Sectors of Berlin shall, in order to receive at appropriate Soviet offices visas for entry into the Union of Soviet Socialist Republics, present:
> (a) a passport stamped "Issued in accordance with the Quadripartite Agreement of 3 September 1971";
> (b) an identity card or other appropriately drawn up document confirming that the person requesting the visa is a permanent resident of the Western Sectors of Berlin and containing the bearer's full address and a personal photograph.

The second paragraph provides *inter alia* that the passport or identity card will serve as the basis for consular services in accordance with the Quadripartite Agreement during the holder's stay in the Soviet Union. The third paragraph provides that the stamp will appear in all passports used by permanent residents of the Western Sectors of Berlin for journeys "to such countries as may require it".[16] Although the type of passport is not specified, Federal passports are accepted for the purposes of the Agreed Minute. The stamp is inserted in the Federal passports of West Berliners wishing to travel to the Soviet Union or such country as may require it. Those not wishing to travel to such countries do not need the stamp.

The Berlin temporary identity card (*behelfsmässiger Personal-*

---

[14] See p.193 above.
[15] See p.342 below; Zivier, pp.198–9; Zündorf, pp.161–2.
[16] The Federal Republic has made similar arrangements bilaterally with other East bloc countries.

ausweis) is an adequate identity document for the purposes of Agreed Minute I, and is accepted as such in practice. The inclusion in the temporary identity card of details of the holder's place of residence and address (*Wohnort und Wohnung*), and the fact of its issue to the holder, are sufficient confirmation that the holder is a permanent resident of the Western Sectors of Berlin.

CHAPTER 20

FREEDOM OF MOVEMENT WITHIN BERLIN

THE principle of freedom of movement throughout the special Berlin area, that is, throughout all four Sectors of the city, was fundamental to the treatment of Berlin in the London agreements of 1944 and 1945. Those agreements provided for the joint occupation of the special Berlin area by armed forces of the four Powers, and for the joint administration of that area by the Allied Kommandatura.[1] Freedom of movement throughout the special Berlin area was implicit in, and an essential concomitant of, the joint occupation and joint administration. No specific provision affirming it was required in the agreements.[2] In practice the four Powers permitted freedom of movement throughout all four Sectors of Berlin between 1945 and 1960.

With the introduction of limited controls in 1960 and the building of the Wall in 1961 the GDR, with the support of the Soviet Union, grossly violated the principle of freedom of movement throughout Berlin. They expressed the view, which they have maintained ever since, that the Soviet Sector of Berlin was part of the territory of the GDR, that the boundary between the Soviet Sector and the Western Sectors was therefore a state frontier of the GDR, and that the GDR Government was accordingly entitled to control movement across that boundary, at least as regards civilian traffic.

The position of the Western Allies is that the whole of Berlin remains under joint four-Power occupation, and that the Soviet Sector does not form part of the GDR (pp.299–302). Accordingly, the line between the Soviet Sector and the Western Sectors is in no sense a state frontier; and the Wall and the GDR restrictions on freedom of movement are illegal. The Western Allies continue to adhere to the principle of freedom of movement for all throughout Berlin[3]

---

[1] Paragraphs 2 and 5 of the London Protocol of 12 September 1944, as amended: p.313 below; and Article 7 of the Agreement on Control Machinery in Germany of 14 November 1944, as amended: p.317 below.
[2] The position is similar to that concerning the right of access to Berlin; but no four-Power arrangements were initially worked out to regulate freedom of movement in Berlin.
[3] For example, at the NATO Ministerial Meeting in Halifax in May 1986 the Foreign Ministers of the three Powers announced that they would make strong representations to the Soviet Union concerning "the recently announced measures purporting to affect freedom of movement in the city". The GDR had sought to require diplomats accredited to the GDR, consular officials and members of the Military Missions to show their passports and obtain visas at the Sector crossing points. This could have been taken to imply acknowledgement of the Sector boundary as a state frontier. The GDR referred in this connection to the measures taken by the Western Allied authorities following the bombing of a West Berlin discotheque in April 1986, but these were in no way comparable with the GDR controls and were clearly stated not to affect the principle of freedom of movement: p.289 below. See also *Der Spiegel* of 2 June 1986.

and there are no immigration controls on the western side of the boundary between the Western Sectors and the Soviet Sector.

Although the underlying legal position of the Western Allies does not distinguish between Allied and civilian movement, the practical arrangements which have developed, particularly following the Quadripartite Agreement of 3 September 1971, require Allied and civilian movement to be considered separately.

ALLIED MOVEMENT

The whole of Berlin remains a special area under joint quadripartite occupation. As participants in that joint occupation, Western Allied forces (including civilian officials and dependents) have, and have continuously exercised, the right of free movement throughout all four Sectors of the city. So also do certain persons accredited to the Allied authorities, such as the members of the Military Missions in Berlin. Any attempt by the Soviet or GDR authorities to restrict that right would violate the principle of freedom of movement inherent in the joint occupation of Berlin, and the four-Power agreements relating thereto. Moreover, any attempt by GDR authorities to restrict that right would also violate the status of Western Allied forces in Berlin, over whom the GDR has no jurisdiction or authority.[4]

The right of free movement within Berlin of Allied forces was not affected by the Quadripartite Agreement of 3 September 1971. The right forms part of Allied rights and responsibilities for Berlin, and is a necessary concomitant of the original four-Power agreements relating to the occupation of Berlin, which are not affected by the 1971 Agreement; its continuous exercise forms part of the situation which has developed in the area, which may not be changed unilaterally.[5]

Members of the Western Allied forces move daily between the Western Sectors and the Soviet Sector, both for official and off-duty purposes. They are not subject to Soviet or GDR controls either upon entering or upon leaving the Soviet Sector. Servicemen in uniform show no identification papers, their uniform being regarded as sufficient proof of status. Civilian officials and dependents may display Allied identity documents at the crossing point to establish their status, and they then proceed without further formality. In the event of difficulties they insist on dealing only with a Soviet officer. In practice the crossing points used are almost invariably those at Friedrichstrasse ("Checkpoint Charlie")

---

[4] Heidelmeyer *Dokumente*, pp.245–6.
[5] Preamble, third and fourth paragraphs, and Part I, paragraphs 3 and 4, of the Quadripartite Agreement.

for pedestrian or motor vehicle crossing, and Friedrichstrasse Station for those travelling by *S-Bahn* or *U-Bahn*.[6]

Western military patrols ("flag tours") take place daily in the Soviet Sector in exercise of the right of free movement. Soviet flag tours likewise regularly patrol the Western Sectors. Soviet servicemen also enter the Western Sectors to work at the Berlin Air Safety Center and to carry out guard duties at Spandau Allied Prison and at the Soviet War Memorial in Tiergarten.[7]

CIVILIAN MOVEMENT BEFORE THE QUADRIPARTITE AGREEMENT

Freedom of movement between all four Sectors of Berlin continued after the Soviet withdrawal from the Allied Kommandatura and the *de facto* administrative division of the city in 1948. Until August 1960, persons in the Western Sectors could go into the Soviet Sector, and *vice versa*. Eastern controls at the boundary between the Western Sectors and the Soviet Sector provided only slight impediment to the flow of traffic. About 60,000 inhabitants of the Soviet Sector travelled to work in the Western Sectors, and about 7,000 inhabitants of the Western Sectors crossed over to work in the Soviet Sector.[8]

The most serious interruption of the freedom of movement of civilians before 1960 occurred in connection with the East Berlin uprising of 17 June 1953. On that occasion the Western Commandants protested "against the arbitrary measures taken by the Soviet authorities which have resulted in the interruption of traffic between the sectors and free circulation throughout Berlin".[9] On 29 August 1960, the East German authorities issued a decree which for a limited period required "citizens of the German Federal Republic" (but not West Berliners) to obtain entry permits if they wished to visit East Berlin.[10] In spite of Western Allied protests to the Soviet authorities against this "flagrant violation of the right of free circulation in Berlin",[11] the East German restrictions were prolonged indefinitely by a further decree issued on 8 September 1960.[12] The Western Allies again protested, in Notes to the

---

[6] Use of these crossing points reflects practical arrangements, but the Western Allies have accepted no legal obligation to use these and no others: see the Western Allied Notes of 26 August 1961 protesting to the Soviet Union against East German attempts to limit Allied forces to a single crossing point: *Selected Documents* I, p.476.

[7] Rexin, in: *Berlin translokal* (1983), pp.77–96.

[8] For a description of the position before the Wall, and the changes caused by it, see the *Senat* Memorandum of July 1962: Heidelmeyer, p.291.

[9] Heidelmeyer, p.163.

[10] *GBl.DDR* I, p.489; *Selected Documents* I, p.432; *US Documents*, p.715.

[11] *Selected Documents* I, p.433; *US Documents*, p.716; Heidelmeyer, p.266.

[12] *GBl.DDR* I, p.499; *Selected Documents* I, p.434; Heidelmeyer *Dokumente*, p.451.

Soviet Government of 12 September 1960, in the following terms:

> The United Kingdom Government has never recognised any
> limitations on the freedom of movement within Greater Berlin, and
> considers this latest attempt by East German officials to control the
> movement of persons between the Eastern and Western Sectors of
> Greater Berlin as a grave violation of Berlin's four-Power status. The
> United Kingdom Government is obliged to bring the illegal actions of
> the East German authorities to the attention of the Soviet
> Government. The Soviet Government is aware that the United
> Kingdom Government have never accepted and do not accept the
> thesis that the Eastern Sector of Berlin forms part of the territory of
> the "German Democratic Republic" or that Berlin is "on the territory
> of the German Democratic Republic".[13]

After counter-measures by the Western Allies and Federal Republic,
the East German restrictions were gradually modified early in
1961.[14]

On 3 August 1961 the Western Commandants again had occasion
to protest to the Soviet Commandant about East German
restrictions imposed on residents of the Soviet Sector employed in
the Western Sectors, pointing out that "the principle of freedom of
movement is basic to the Agreements regarding Berlin which are
binding on the four Powers responsible for this city".[15] Then on 13
August 1961 the East German authorities began construction of the
Wall. They also issued a decree prohibiting East Berliners from
crossing into the Western Sectors without a special permit, and
requiring West Berliners to present their Berlin identity cards in
order to enter the Soviet Sector. The existing restrictions on
"citizens of the West German Federal Republic" remained in force.[16]

The Western Allies protested vigorously to the Soviet authorities,
holding them responsible for the illegal measures taken by the East
Germans. In a letter of 15 August 1961 to the Soviet Commandant,
the Western Commandants said that:

> Not since the imposition of the Berlin blockade has there been such a
> flagrant violation of the four Power Agreements concerning Berlin.[17]

In Notes delivered to the Soviet Government on 17 August 1961,
the Western Allies described the East German measures as a
"flagrant and particularly serious violation of the quadripartite

---

[13] *Selected Documents* I, p.435; *US Documents*, p.719; Heidelmeyer, p.267. For further
exchanges, see *Selected Documents* I, pp.436–9, 440–1; *US Documents*, pp.720–2;
Heidelmeyer, pp.269–71.
[14] *Selected Documents* I, p.22.
[15] *Selected Documents* I, p.464; *US Documents*, p.765.
[16] *Selected Documents* I, p.466; *US Documents*, p.775; Heidelmeyer, p.271.
[17] *Selected Documents* I, p.468; *US Documents*, p.776.

status of Berlin", and reiterated that they had "never accepted that limitations can be imposed on freedom of movement within Berlin" or "the pretension that the Soviet Sector of Berlin forms part of the so-called 'German Democratic Republic' and that Berlin is situated on its territory".[18]

Despite these protests, further restrictions were imposed on West Berliners only nine days later: on 22 August 1961 the East German Ministry of the Interior ordered that West Berliners would in future only be allowed to enter East Berlin if they had obtained a permit, which would be issued at branch offices of the East German State Travel Bureau in West Berlin.[19] This unilateral East German order was acceptable neither to the Western Allies nor to the *Senat*,[20] since it was wholly incompatible with the quadripartite status of Berlin and the principle of freedom of movement between all four Sectors. Accordingly, the Allied Kommandatura issued BK/O(61)11 on 25 August 1961,[21] which prohibited the establishment or operation within the Western Sectors of Berlin of offices purporting to issue permits for entry into the Soviet Sector. Two permit offices which the East Germans had opened at Zoo and Westkreuz *S-Bahn* Stations were closed down by the Berlin police the following day.

As the construction of the Wall by the East German authorities continued in the months following August 1961, attempts by East Berliners to escape to the Western Sectors were accompanied by increasing violence and shootings at the sector boundary. By June 1962 some 40 people had been killed at the Wall. The Western Allies repeatedly protested to the Soviet Union against these brutal acts of the East German régime.[22] Residents of the Federal Republic of Germany continued to be allowed into the Soviet Sector travelling on their Federal passports and obtaining entry permits at the crossing points. On the other hand, access to the Soviet Sector for residents of the Western Sectors of Berlin was barred.

Temporary improvements were brought about by the four wall pass arrangements negotiated, with Allied authority, by the *Senat* of Berlin and the GDR Government.[23] The first was concluded on 17 December 1963 and provided for East German offices in the

---

[18] *Selected Documents* I, p.469; *US Documents*, p.777; Heidelmeyer, p.279. For further exchanges, see *Selected Documents* I, pp.470–83.
[19] *Selected Documents* I, p.472; *US Documents*, p.782; Heidelmeyer, p.290.
[20] See *Senat* Memorandum of July 1962: Heidelmeyer, p.291.
[21] *GVBl.* p.1222; Heidelmeyer, p.291.
[22] See *Selected Documents* I, pp.2–3, 45–50, 58–59, 62–65, 98–99; *US Documents*, pp.825, 827. The Allies have also protested about further restrictions on freedom of movement: *US Documents*, p.853.
[23] Mahncke, *Berlin im geteilten Deutschland*, pp.220–3; Krumholz, *Berlin ABC* (2nd ed.), p.481. For the form of these arrangements and the status issues involved in their conclusion, see p.226 above.

Western Sectors to issue passes to West Berliners to visit certain classes of relatives in the Soviet Sector between 18 December 1963 and 5 January 1964. The Western Commandants, in a statement of 17 December 1963, welcomed the arrangement on humanitarian grounds, and added:

> The arrangements made in no way affect the status of Berlin, which is defined in existing International Agreements. The Commandants wish to recall that restrictions imposed on the free movement of Berliners throughout the city are quite contrary to the terms of those Agreements.[24]

Some 1,242,800 West Berliners took advantage of the arrangement. A second arrangement, concluded on 24 September 1964, was valid for a year and provided for visits in November and at Christmas, Easter and Whitsun. It also established a pass office "for urgent family business", to issue passes at short notice and at any time of the year for such occasions as funerals, weddings and serious illnesses involving close relatives. The third arrangement, signed on 25 November 1965, only covered Christmas 1965. The fourth, signed on 7 March 1966, was valid for Easter and Whitsun 1966. No further arrangements were concluded because of increased GDR demands and the GDR's refusal to include a saving clause regarding status in subsequent arrangements, thus attempting to link future arrangements to recognition of the GDR. It was agreed however on 6 October 1966 that the office for urgent family business should remain open at least until 31 January 1967, and in fact it remained open thereafter.[25]

CIVILIAN MOVEMENT AND THE QUADRIPARTITE AGREEMENT

One of the Western aims in negotiating the Quadripartite Agreement was to improve communications between the Western Sectors of Berlin and the Soviet Sector. The arrangements for travel and visits by West Berliners are one of the practical improvements of the existing situation introduced by the Agreement. The Western Allies have in no way accepted the legality of restrictions on free circulation within Berlin, as is clear from the third preambular

---

[24] *Selected Documents* II, p.102; *US Documents*, p.860. The arrangement also contained a saving clause protecting the status of Berlin and the Western legal position: see p.227 above.

[25] The establishment and operation of East German pass offices in the Western Sectors under these arrangements were authorised by the Allied Kommandatura, as exceptions to BK/O(61)11 (see above), by BK/O(64)5 of 24 September 1964 (*GVBl.* p.1042), BK/O(65)14 of 25 November 1965 (*GVBl.* p.1936), BK/O(66)4 of 7 March 1966 (*GVBl.* p.570), BK/O(66)9 of 6 October 1966 (*GVBl.* p.1576) and BK/O(67)1 of 1 February 1967 (*GVBl.* p.326).

paragraph of the Quadripartite Agreement, which states that quadripartite rights and responsibilities and the corresponding wartime and post-war agreements and decisions are not affected, and the sixth preambular paragraph, which states that the practical improvements are without prejudice to the legal positions of the four Powers. While maintaining their legal position regarding the right to freedom of movement for all within Berlin, the Western Allies, taking into account that the *de facto* situation arising from GDR restrictions was one requiring practical improvements, accepted the provisions of the Agreement notwithstanding their apparent inconsistency with a right of unrestricted movement for West Berliners.

In Part IIC of the Quadripartite Agreement the Soviet Union declared –

> that communications between the Western Sectors of Berlin and areas bordering on these Sectors and those areas of the German Democratic Republic which do not border on these Sectors will be improved. Permanent residents of the Western Sectors of Berlin will be able to travel to and visit such areas for compassionate, family, religious, cultural or commercial reasons, or as tourists, under conditions comparable to those applying to other persons entering these areas.

This clear undertaking is repeated in paragraphs 1 and 2 of Annex III. The Soviet Union had not acknowledged any responsibility in this field since the building of the Wall in 1961. The reference in Annex III to consultation and agreement with the GDR Government may reflect the Eastern position regarding competence for these matters; but it serves also to lock the GDR in to implementation of the obligations undertaken, while leaving the primary obligation upon the Soviet Union.

The expression "areas bordering on these Sectors and those areas of the German Democratic Republic which do not border on these Sectors" covers both the Soviet Sector of Berlin and the territory of the GDR, whilst avoiding any acceptance that the Soviet Sector is part of the GDR. The improvement should clearly be substantial and continuing, in contrast to the earlier temporary improvements under the wall pass arrangements. The requirement of "comparable conditions" means that permanent residents of West Berlin should receive treatment comparable to that accorded to any other persons entering the Soviet Sector or the GDR. There must be no discrimination against them, as in the ten years prior to the Quadripartite Agreement. The requirements are given specific content in the *Senat*/GDR Arrangement discussed below.

Annex III, paragraph 2, also provides that:

In order to facilitate visits and travel, as described above, by permanent residents of the Western Sectors of Berlin, additional crossing points will be opened.

The facilitation of visits and travel provides the criterion for new crossing points.

Paragraph 5 of Annex III provides that arrangements implementing and supplementing the provisions described above will be agreed by the competent German authorities. On 3 September 1971, the date of signature of the Quadripartite Agreement, the Allied Kommandatura issued BKC/L(71)1.[26] This recalled the relevant provisions of the Quadripartite Agreement and authorised the *Senat* of Berlin to conduct appropriate negotiations on, among other subjects, travel and visits.

The mandate of the four Powers in this field was carried out by the conclusion of the Arrangement of 20 December 1971 between the *Senat* and the Government of the German Democratic Republic on Facilitations and Improvements in Travel and Visitor Traffic.[27] In BKC/L(71)2 of 16 December 1971,[28] the Allied Kommandatura stated that it considered the Arrangement to be "in conformity with the Quadripartite Agreement, which provides the standard for its interpretation and application"; that, accordingly, the Arrangement would enter into force on the date of signature of the Final Quadripartite Protocol by the four Powers; and that the *Senat* of Berlin was authorised to sign the Arrangement and to exchange the letters concerning crossing points. The Arrangement was duly signed on 20 December 1971, was listed in the Final Quadripartite Protocol signed by the four Powers on 3 June 1972, and entered into force on that date.

The Arrangement is expressly stated to be in accordance with the arrangements of the Quadripartite Agreement (preamble); it provides that it shall enter into force simultaneously with the Quadripartite Agreement and shall remain in force together with it (Article 9), thus matching paragraphs 2 and 3 of the Final Quadripartite Protocol. It is therefore clearly dependent on the Quadripartite Agreement, which it implements and supplements and which governs its interpretation and application. The preamble

---

[26] Cmnd. 5135, p.56; *US Documents*, p.1147.

[27] The Arrangement (*Vereinbarung*) needs to be read with the accompanying exchange of letters concerning crossing points, the general Protocol Note (*Protokollvermerk*) relating to the Arrangement and the special Protocol Note on the activities of the Offices for Visit and Travel Affairs (Cmnd. 5135, p.104; *US Documents*, p.1179). There is, in addition, a declaration by the GDR Government: *Verträge, Abkommen und Vereinbarungen zwischen der Bundesrepublik Deutschland und der Deutschen Demokratischen Republik*, p.257. See Mahncke, *Berlin im geteilten Deutschland*, pp.233–8; Zivier, p.221; Zündorf, p.198; Schiwy, in: *Zehn Jahre Berlin-Abkommen 1971–1981*, pp.163–75.

[28] Cmnd. 5135, p.136.

reflects this by referring to the agreement of the *Senat* and the GDR Government "to facilitate and improve the travel and visitor traffic of permanent residents of the Western Sectors of Berlin/ Berlin(West)". The language of the Arrangement avoids prejudicing the Western legal position: thus, while some degree of *de facto* administrative competence is necessarily accepted, no GDR sovereign rights are recognised. Article 1 also reflects the careful and non-prejudicial language of the Quadripartite Agreement by referring to "areas bordering on Berlin (West) and those areas of the German Democratic Republic which do not border on Berlin (West)".

Article 1 of the Arrangement provides that permanent residents of West Berlin shall be granted entry one or more times into East Berlin or the GDR for visits totalling thirty days a year. This does not imply any restriction on the way visiting entitlements may be used. Paragraph 1 of the general Protocol Note states explicitly that there will be no quota restrictions within the limit of thirty days. It also provides that in case of urgent family matters entry shall be granted even in cases where the normal visiting time totalling thirty days has already been exhausted, and that "in exceptional cases" the stay shall be extended beyond the time-limits set out in the Arrangement. This reflects Article 4 (1) of the Arrangement, which restates existing procedures for hardship cases. Moreover Article 4 (2) allows for additional visiting entitlements for social, scientific, economic-commercial, or cultural purposes.

Article 2 (1) provides that, for entry, visitors require their valid identity card and an entry permit and for exit an exit permit of the GDR. The term "visa" is avoided, here as in the rest of the Arrangement. The identity card for German nationals resident in the Western Sectors is the Berlin temporary identity card (*behelfsmässiger Personalausweis*) (p.237 above). Article 2 (3) provides that permanent residents of Berlin (West) not in possession of an identity card require for entry an identity document formally issued in Berlin (West). This applies in particular to stateless or displaced persons or other foreigners not in possession of a valid passport. The special identity document, which is issued by the Police President, confirms that the holder is registered with the police in the Western Sectors. These provisions indicate that the term "permanent residents of Berlin (West)" in this Arrangement is not limited to German nationals, but also includes civilian foreigners resident in the Western Sectors.

Article 3 (1) provides that entry shall take place via the boundary crossing points (*Grenzübergangsstellen*) designated for this purpose. In an exchange of letters of 20 December 1971 between *Senat* and GDR Government representatives, crossing points are designated for entry by rail, *U-Bahn* or *S-Bahn*, for entry by pedestrians, and for entry by motor vehicles.[29] The last sentence of the *Senat* letter places on record the understanding that the number of crossing points will not be reduced in future. This means that if for some reason a crossing point has to be closed, another should be opened in its place. The use of the word *Grenze* (boundary) in these provisions is non-prejudicial; the word is consistent with the notion of district (*Bezirk*) or sector boundaries, and does not imply recognition of a state frontier within Berlin.

Article 3 (2) provides that visitors shall be issued with entry permits at the crossing points on the basis of entitlement certificates or telegrams endorsed by the competent authorities of the GDR. Paragraph 4 of the general Protocol Note makes detailed provision regarding the procedures for application. In the case of travel for compassionate, family, religious or cultural reasons, applications are made by the persons who are to be visited, at the competent local councils or GDR passport or registration offices. For travel for social, scientific, economic-commercial or cultural purposes, applications are made by the host organisations to the competent GDR passport or registration offices. For tourist travel, applications may be made to the *Generaldirektion des Reisebüros der DDR* through the *DER-Deutsches Reisebüro GmbH* in the Western Sectors (that is to say, through nominated travel agencies). Further provision regarding tourist travel is made in Article 5 of the Arrangement.

Of particular significance is Article 5 (2):

> Permanent residents of Berlin (West) who wish to enter as tourists for only one day, without staying overnight, and without using the services of a travel agency, may apply for entitlement certificates either in person or by mail directly to the Offices for Visit and Travel Affairs (*Büros für Besuchs- und Reiseangelegenheiten*) in Berlin (West). The Offices shall issue entitlement certificates and send them to the recipients by mail or hand them out directly to the applicants.

Paragraph 4 (c) of the general Protocol Note further specifies that such applications shall be processed without delay, and that on issue entitlement certificates shall be sent to the applicant by mail or handed out immediately. These provisions therefore set out the procedure for private day visits which have not been the subject of a prior invitation from a person or organisation in the Soviet Sector

---

[29] Cmnd. 5135, p.110; *Zehn Jahre Deutschlandpolitik*, p.178. The crossing points are, for entry by rail, *U-Bahn* or *S-Bahn*, at Friedrichstrasse Station; for entry by pedestrians, at Bornholmer Strasse, Chausseestrasse, Invalidenstrasse, Oberbaumbrücke, Sonnenallee, Drewitz, Staaken, Rudower Chaussee; and for entry by motor vehicle, at Bornholmer Strasse, Chausseestrasse, Invalidenstrasse, Sonnenallee, Drewitz, Staaken, Rudower Chaussee, as well as Heiligensee/Stolpe-Süd.

or the GDR. It is controversial whether a day visitor under this procedure should be able to obtain an entitlement certificate immediately on demand. In practice the GDR employees at the Offices for Visit and Travel Affairs issue a certificate immediately only if a special reason can be shown.[30]

The Offices for Visit and Travel Affairs in the Western Sectors provided for in Article 5 (2) are dealt with in greater detail in the special Protocol Note concerning their activities.[31] Although employees of the German Democratic Republic participate in the work at these Offices, they are established by the *Senat*, which exercises the legal rights of occupier (*Hausrecht*) of the premises through members of the public service nominated by it (paragraph 1 of the Protocol Note). Further provisions confirm the *Senat's* position as occupier of the Offices (paragraphs 3, 8 and 10). The limited functions which the GDR employees are authorised to perform are set out in paragraph 7. Overall control remains with the Allied Kommandatura, which authorised the establishment and operation of the Offices in BK/O(72)3 of 13 March 1972[32] and BK/O(72)7 of 3 June 1972.[33] The Offices do not constitute in any sense a GDR consular representation in the Western Sectors of Berlin.[34]

Article 6 of the Arrangement is important since it allows for future improvements under the overall quadripartite roof:

> In the light of experience gained in the implementation of this Arrangement, and in connection with a further improvement of the situation, additional facilitations may be agreed between the two sides on the basis of this Arrangement.

Examples of such improvements are the Protocol Notes on medical and health care of 12 June 1972 and 11 April 1974.[35]

Article 8 provides for the two sides to designate Commissioners (*Beauftragte*) to "clarify differences of opinion and difficulties arising in individual cases from the application and implementation of this

---

[30] Catudal, *A Balance Sheet of the Quadripartite Agreement on Berlin*, pp.78–9; Zivier, pp.225–6.

[31] Cmnd. 5135, p.118; *Zehn Jahre Deutschlandpolitik*, p.177.

[32] *GVBl.* p.510.

[33] *GVBl.* p.1014.

[34] See Schiwy, in: *Zehn Jahre Berlin-Abkommen 1971–1981*, pp. 170–2.

[35] 1972 notes, brought into force in 1974 after their content was included in FRG/GDR Health Agreement: *DA*, 7 (1974), p.652. For examples of further facilitations, see Zivier, pp.224, 226–7. For further details of visits procedures, see the leaflet *Merkheft für Besuche und Reisen von Personen mit ständigem Wohnsitz in Berlin (West) nach Ost-Berlin und in die DDR*, published annually by the *Land* Berlin Press and Information Office. For the Protocol Note concerning improvements in communications, concluded at the same time as the Travel and Visits Arrangement, see p.267 below.

Arrangement".[36] Questions which cannot be clarified by the Commissioners are to be submitted to the GDR Government and the *Senat*, "who will clarify them by negotiation". This careful language does not detract from the provision for quadripartite consultations contained in the Final Quadripartite Protocol. These so-called Visits Commissioners, who are the one standing point of contact between the *Senat* and the GDR Government, had held 162 meetings by June 1986. Despite attempts by the GDR side to raise extraneous matters, the Commissioners' functions are strictly limited to the clarification of individual differences of opinion and difficulties. They may also consider additional facilitations under Article 6.

---

[36] See also p.229 above. For discussion of the controversy surrounding the minimum exchange of currency demanded of visitors by the GDR, see Zivier, pp.228–30; Schiwy, in: *Zehn Jahre Berlin-Abkommen 1971–1981*, pp.172–5; Mampel, in: *Zehn Jahre Berlin-Abkommen 1971–1981*, pp.136–8.

CHAPTER 21

RAILWAYS AND WATERWAYS IN BERLIN

Two of the means of transport within Berlin are subject to a complex legal régime because of Berlin's special status. These are the public railways, including the city *S-Bahn* railway; and the extensive waterways, which carry considerable barge traffic and provide facilities for numerous pleasure craft. Because both the railways and the waterways were owned and controlled by the German *Reich* before and during the Second World War, they were taken under control by the Occupying Powers at the end of the War. As a result, both the railways and the waterways within the Western Sectors of Berlin remain the subject of Allied reserved rights and legislation. In short, the railways and waterways remain subject to Western Allied control, although for purely practical reasons the Western Allies have allowed aspects of their operation to be carried on by authorities situated in the Soviet Sector.

Efforts by the GDR Government to assert various forms of legal jurisdiction or authority over the railways and waterways within the Western Sectors have been consistently rejected by the Western Allies, who have repeatedly taken steps to maintain their rights and authority. The maintenance of the legal status of these railways and waterways is a particular aspect of the maintenance of the status of Berlin itself. This Chapter looks in turn at the legal status of the railways and waterways, and at examples of Western Allied action in respect of each in order to maintain that status.

RAILWAYS IN BERLIN

Legal status in general[1]

Before the end of, the Second World War the public railway system in Germany was owned and operated by the *Deutsche Reichsbahn*, which was established by *Reich* legislation in 1924.[2] The system included the Berlin *S-Bahn*, an inner-city and suburban network extending beyond the boundaries of Greater Berlin.[3] By

---

[1] Wengler, *JR*, 1950, pp.641–6, 676–82; Schröder, *ROW*, 26 (1982), pp.237–47; Seiffert, in: *Zehn Jahre Berlin-Abkommen 1971–1981*, pp.177–88; Schweisfurth, *ZaöRV*, 44 (1984), pp.482–94; Posth, *Rechtliche Grundlagen der Deutschen Reichsbahn in West-Berlin* (Dissertation, Göttingen 1973).

[2] *Verordnung über die Schaffung des Unternehmens "Deutsche Reichsbahn"* of 12 February 1924: *RGBl.* I, p.57; *Gesetz über die "Deutsche Reichsbahn Gesellschaft"* of 30 August 1924: *RGBl.* II, p.272.

[3] The *S-Bahn* should not be confused with the Berlin *U-Bahn*, the underground railway, which was not run by the *Reichsbahn* but by the city transport authority: see Krumholz, *Berlin ABC* (2nd ed.), p.667.

further *Reich* legislation of 1937 and 1939 the *Deutsche Reichsbahn* was placed directly under the authority of the *Reich* Ministry of Transport, and its property was granted the status of special state property (*Sondervermögen*).[4]

At the end of the War, the Soviet military authorities took control of all means of communication in the area of their operations. In Order No. 8 of 11 August 1945 the Soviet military administration, with effect from 1 September 1945, entrusted the operation of the railways in the Soviet zone to the German railway administration (*Reichsbahndirektion Berlin*). This Order dealt with operations, not with ownership.

Under the Potsdam Agreement of 2 August 1945[5] the four Powers agreed to establish common policies on, among other things, communications and transport. But no formal agreement was concluded concerning the operation of the railways in Berlin. While the Soviet Order No. 8 could not have effect in the Western Sectors, the Western Allies were content, for practical reasons, to allow the technical operation of the public railways in Berlin to remain in the hands of the *Reichsbahndirektion Berlin*. However, Military Government (SHAEF) Law No. 52,[6] which had been applied by the Western Allies in the areas under their occupation since its promulgation on 18 September 1944 (the date of initial occupation of German territory), placed under the control of the Western Allied authorities all property belonging to the German *Reich*, including *Reichsbahn* properties. The four Powers agreed in the Allied Kommandatura on 23 August 1945 (BK/M(45)7) that, for the control of properties within Berlin, the laws in force in the respective zones of occupation of Germany would apply in each Sector of Berlin. At least since that date, the Western Allies have exercised control over all *Reichsbahn* property and activities in the Western Sectors of Berlin. By the agreement of 23 August 1945 the Soviet authorities acknowledged that Military Government Law No. 52 was applicable within the Western Sectors of Berlin.

The Soviet Union and GDR have from time to time appeared to take the position that the GDR has certain sovereign rights, and can exercise a form of state authority, over *Reichsbahn* property within the Western Sectors of Berlin. The *Deutsche Reichsbahn* has consistently sought to evade Allied legislation and controls, as well

---

[4] *Gesetz zur Neuregelung der Verhältnisse der Reichsbank und der Deutschen Reichsbahn* of 10 February 1937, *RGBl.* II, p.47; *Reichsbahngesetz* of 4 July 1939, *RGBl.* I, p.1205. See further Schröder, *ROW*, 26 (1982), pp.237–8.

[5] Cmd. 7087; *Selected Documents* I, p.49; *US Documents*, p.54; Heidelmeyer, p.15. See p.39 above.

[6] *Military Government Gazette Germany, 21 Army Group Area of Control*, No. 1, p.24; for a commentary, see Dölle/Zweigert, *Gesetz Nr. 52, Kommentar* (1947). In areas under Soviet occupation the equivalent legislation was Order No. 124.

as the application of pre-war railway legislation still in force in the Western Sectors.

The Western legal position is as follows: the Allied authorities have allowed the *Reichsbahndirektion* to continue to operate the public railways in the Western Sectors, including until 9 January 1984 the *S-Bahn*; but this in no way alters the fact that all public railway property in each of these Sectors remains subject to the jurisdiction and control of the respective Sector Commandant by virtue of supreme Allied authority, the Allied Kommandatura decision of 23 August 1945 and Military Government Law No. 52. These reserved rights have been frequently reaffirmed by the Allied Kommandatura, for example in the many BK/Os on railway matters.

The S-Bahn

Until 9 January 1984 the *Deutsche Reichsbahn* operated the *S-Bahn* both in the Soviet Sector of Berlin and in the Western Sectors. Until 1961 the network was run as a single unified system throughout the city. But with the building of the Wall the *S-Bahn* was permanently severed between the Western Sectors, on the one hand, and the Soviet Sector and GDR, on the other, save for two lines running into Friedrichstrasse Station in the Soviet Sector. Following the severance in the network the *S-Bahn* in the Western Sectors became an increasingly heavy loss-making operation for the *Deutsche Reichsbahn*. Fewer passengers used the system, partly as a political protest, and the network fell into decay. In 1980 the *Deutsche Reichsbahn* took the opportunity presented by a strike of *Reichsbahn* employees in the Western Sectors to close down all but three *S-Bahn* tracks, leaving only 74 kilometres out of the original 145 kilometres still in operation. The *Reichsbahn* stopped maintaining unused stations and lines, which became increasingly dilapidated.

Against this background the *Deutsche Reichsbahn* made overtures to the *Senat* to relieve it of this burden (backed by threats to close down operations in the Western Sectors altogether), and the *Senat* came under political pressure to take over the operation and save the *S-Bahn* in West Berlin. By BK/O(83)7 of 27 October 1983,[7] the Allied Kommandatura authorised the commencement of negotiations in October 1983 between the *Senat* and the *Deutsche Reichsbahn*. An Arrangement (*Vereinbarung*) was signed by representatives of the *Senat* and the *Deutsche Reichsbahn* on 30 December 1983.[8] Under this Arrangement, *S-Bahn* services in the

[7] *GVBl.* p.1424.
[8] Text in *Der Tagesspiegel*, 30 December 1983. See Kewenig, *Entwicklungslinien des völker- und staatsrechtlichen Status von Berlin*; Schweisfurth, *ZaöRV*, 44 (1984), pp.482–94.

Western Sectors ceased to be operated by the *Deutsche Reichsbahn* with effect from 9 January 1984, and were taken over by the West Berlin public transport company, the *Berliner Verkehrs-Betriebe* (BVG). The same applies to the short stretch from Lehrter Station (in the British Sector) to Friedrichstrasse Station (in the Soviet Sector), although the trains are crewed by *Deutsche Reichsbahn* staff for this stretch. There was also the option for the BVG to operate the *S-Bahn* through the north-south tunnel which links the Western Sectors but runs under the Soviet Sector, an option taken up in 1984.

The Western Allied concern that their rights and responsibilities and the status of Berlin not be prejudiced by the *S-Bahn* Arrangement was satisfied. The documents making up the Arrangement use carefully non-prejudicial language, and expressly state that status questions remain unaffected. In authorising the conclusion of the Arrangement by BK/O(83)9 of 28 December 1983,[9] the Allied Kommandatura stressed that the Arrangement "cannot affect Allied rights and responsibilities in particular in the field of the control of the property and installations concerned, the status of which remains unchanged"; and that "accordingly *Reichseisenbahn* property within the Western Sectors of Berlin remains subject to control by the appropriate Sector Commandant".

Non-operating railway property: the VdeR

There is now a basic legal distinction in Berlin railway matters between operating property (rolling stock, track, service installations, and other equipment used in the actual operation of the railways) and non-operating property of the *Reichsbahn* (largely land and buildings which are not used in the operation of the railways and are for the most part leased to private and commercial tenants). All of this property in the Western Sectors is under Allied control. The *Deutsche Reichsbahn* has the use of the operating property exclusively serving goods and long-distance traffic; the BVG has the use of the operating property exclusively serving the *S-Bahn* in the Western Sectors; and the *S-Bahn* Arrangement of 1983 makes provision for the shared use of operating property serving both railway systems.

Special arrangements have been made for non-operating *Reichsbahn* property. In 1949 it was placed under compulsory sequestration pursuant to Regulation No. 14, an implementing Regulation to the (Allied) Second Monetary Reform Ordinance of 4 July 1948.[10] Regulation No. 14 provided that rental income derived

---

[9] *GVBl.* (1984), p.56.
[10] *VOBl.* I, p.165.

from real estate located in the Western Sectors of Berlin whose owner or landlord resided outside those Sectors had to be paid into a blocked account. Only with the permission of the Currency Control Agency was the owner or landlord permitted to dispose of the account proceeds. In implementation of Regulation No. 14, the *Senat* appointed the *Verwaltung des ehemaligen Reichsbahnvermögens* (*VdeR*) as the administrator of properties of the *Deutsche Reichsbahn* situate in the American, British and French Sectors of Berlin, with the exception of properties or parts of properties directly serving railway operations. It is this body, the *VdeR*, accountable to the Senator for Finance, which administers non-operating *Reichsbahn* property in the Western Sectors, subject to the control and supervision of the Allied authorities.[11]

Removal of railway property

In order to prevent systematic dismantling and removal of *Reichsbahn* property from the Western Sectors, the Allied Kommandatura issued BK/O(49)217 on 7 October 1949,[12] which provided that –

> no fixtures, or any part thereof, on or in *Reichsbahn* property in Berlin or any property or equipment which is necessary for the proper operation or administration of the railways within a Sector will be removed out of a Sector of Berlin without the permission of the Military Government of that Sector.

This BK/O remains in effect and is enforced. For example, when the BVG took over the operation of the *S-Bahn* in the Western Sectors of Berlin on 9 January 1984, a practical need arose to move *S-Bahn* property easily throughout the Western Sectors. This was impeded by BK/O(49)217. Accordingly, in July 1984 the Allied Kommandatura granted general permission to the *Senat* to move railway property serving exclusively the *S-Bahn* in the Western Sectors throughout those Sectors. They also allowed such movements of property to pass over the *S-Bahn* lines that run through the Soviet Sector, and permitted such property to be moved into the Soviet Sector temporarily for the purpose of repairs.

Police authority on railway property

The Allied Kommandatura issued BK/O(62)6 on 21 August 1962 to regulate police functions on railway properties in the Western

---

[11] See further Schröder, *ROW*, 26 (1982), pp.242, 243.
[12] *VOBl.* p.368. Compare BK/O(49)245: p.263 below. Schröder gives further examples of measures taken by the Allied Kommandatura in connection with Berlin's railways in the early post-war years: *ROW*, 26 (1982), pp.239–41.

Sectors of Berlin.[13] This Order distinguished between the authority of the West Berlin police, on the one hand, and the *Deutsche Reichsbahn* Railway Police – the *Bahnpolizei* (BAPO) – on the other. The West Berlin police have the powers and rights of access on railway premises in the Western Sectors provided for in the Ordinance on Construction and Operation of Railways of 17 July 1928,[14] in particular sections 76 and 78. However, without the permission of the Allied Sector authorities concerned, members of the West Berlin police may not enter installations containing technical equipment which are not open to the public except to arrest a person *in flagrante delicto* or when in immediate pursuit of a person suspected of having committed a penal offence. Moreover, they must take no action which would obstruct the operation of the railways in West Berlin. Members of the *Bahnpolizei* in West Berlin are required to comply with all Allied orders or instructions, which prevail in case of conflict with German railway legislation. The rights and duties of the *Bahnpolizei* are limited to those allotted to that force by the Ordinance of 17 July 1928, in particular sections 75 to 77. Members of the *Bahnpolizei* must wear distinctive uniform or insignia, must possess no weapons other than truncheons, and must be *Reichsbahn* employees – thus distinguishing them from the *Transportpolizei* (TRAPO), a branch of the GDR *Volkspolizei*. After the *S-Bahn* Arrangement of 30 December 1983, BK/O(62)6 was amended by BK/O(84)11 of 21 December 1984[15] to deprive the *Bahnpolizei* of any rights, powers or authority with respect to the *S-Bahn* and premises exclusively serving the *S-Bahn* in the Western Sectors, and to remove the restrictions imposed by BK/O(62)6 on the West Berlin police with respect to the *S-Bahn* and premises exclusively serving the *S-Bahn* in the Western Sectors.

The GDR *Transportpolizei* have no lawful authority in the Western Sectors of Berlin. From time to time members of the *Transportpolizei* have been present and attempted to conduct investigations on railway premises in the Western Sectors. Such incidents have prompted Allied protests to the Soviet Embassy complaining about these illegal activities.

Legislation

In view of the status of the railways in Berlin, and Allied rights of control over railway property in the Western Sectors, the Allied Kommandatura has had to intervene in relation to the extension to Berlin of Federal railway legislation. Most fundamentally, by

[13] *GVBl.* p.1098.
[14] *Eisenbahn-Bau- und Betriebsordnung: RGBl.* II, p.542.
[15] *GVBl.* p.1845.

BK/O(51)72 of 29 December 1951,[16] the Allied Kommandatura annulled the *Mantelgesetz* applying to Berlin the Federal Law on the Legal Position of Railway Property of 2 March 1951,[17] which transferred the property of the *Reichsbahn* in the Federal Republic of Germany to the *Deutsche Bundesbahn*. The effect of the Law was therefore limited to the territory of the Federal Republic, and the status of Berlin's railways was left unchanged.[18]

Until 1984, the General Railway Law of 29 March 1951[19] and Ordinances made thereunder – which constitute the basic Federal legislation on railway operations – did not apply to any railway operations in Berlin. The applicable law in Berlin continued to be the pre-war *Reich* railway legislation, in particular the Ordinance on Construction and Operation of Railways of 17 July 1928.[20] Following the *S-Bahn* Arrangement of 30 December 1983, the *Senat* and Allied authorities discussed the appropriate legislative basis for the operation of the *S-Bahn* in the Western Sectors by the BVG. As a result, the Allied Kommandatura issued BK/O(84)11 of 21 December 1984,[21] which authorised the application in Berlin of the General Railway Law and seven Ordinances made thereunder, subject to certain reservations. The main reservation is that the 1951 Law and the Ordinances, as well as any further Ordinance or other regulatory measure which may be made in pursuance of the Law, apply in the Western Sectors only with respect to the *S-Bahn* and to private railways (*Kleinbahnen und Privatanschlussbahnen*). The approval of the Allied Kommandatura is required before any new Ordinances made in pursuance of the Law are applied in Berlin. Moreover, in paragraph 4 of the BK/O it is recalled that:

> Allied rights and responsibilities in particular in the field of railways shall not be affected. *Reichseisenbahn* property (*Reichseisenbahn-vermögen*) within the Western Sectors of Berlin remains subject to control by the appropriate Sector Commandant.

Express reservations of Allied rights and responsibilities in the field of railways were made in connection with the adoption in Berlin of Federal legislation concerning protection against nuisances and the transport of dangerous materials.[22] Pursuant to the latter, the Allied Kommandatura has also limited the application in Berlin

---

[16] *GVBl.* (1952), p.53.

[17] *Gesetz über die vermögensrechtlichen Verhältnisse der Deutschen Reichsbahn: BGBl.* I, p.155.

[18] In the Land Register (*Grundbuch*), railway property remains registered in the name of *Deutsches Reich* (*Reichseisenbahnvermögen*): Schröder, *ROW*, 26 (1982), p.239.

[19] *Allgemeines Eisenbahngesetz: BGBl.* I, p.225.

[20] *Eisenbahn-Bau- und Betriebsordnung: RGBl.* II, p.542.

[21] *GVBl.* p.1845.

[22] BK/O(75)1 of 8 January 1975 (*GVBl.* p.192); BK/O(75)11 of 7 August 1975 (*GVBl.* p.2140).

of several Federal Ordinances on the transport of dangerous goods by rail.[23]

International agreements

The Western Allies have similarly taken action in connection with the extension to Berlin of certain international agreements on railway matters entered into by the Federal Republic of Germany. By BK/O(85)2 of 19 March 1985,[24] the Allied Kommandatura raised no objection to the extension to Berlin of the Convention relating to International Rail Transport (COTIF) and approved the action necessary to secure the inclusion of railway routes in the Western Sectors within the scope of the Convention. This was expressly subject to two reservations: first, the application of the Convention in the Western Sectors of Berlin remains subject to the rights and powers of the Allied authorities over railway operations, which are unaffected; and secondly, the German authorities, in applying the Convention, are to take full account of the special situation of railway operations in Berlin and the law in force in the Western Sectors.[25]

Construction projects

The Allied Kommandatura has had occasion in the last decade to exercise authority in relation to some major construction projects for the improvement of railway operations in the Western Sectors of Berlin. An important railway project arose out of the transit package agreed in December 1975 between the Governments of the Federal Republic of Germany and GDR. The agreement that the *Deutsche Reichsbahn* would make additional stops in its long-distance service at Wannsee, Charlottenburg and Spandau Stations required considerable work to be done to *Reichsbahn* installations in the Western Sectors. By BK/O(75)15 of 19 December 1975,[26] the Allied Kommandatura agreed in principle to the proposed modifications to the operations and installations of the *Reichsbahn* in the Western Sectors, and stipulated conditions under which they could be effected.

[23] BK/O(84)1 of 17 January 1984 (*GVBl.* p.276); BK/O(85)3 of 10 April 1985 (*GVBl.* p.1036); BK/O(85)8 of 9 October 1985 (*GVBl.* p.2240); BK/O(85)9 of 29 November 1985 (*GVBl.* p.2464).
[24] *GVBl.* p.908.
[25] Similar provision was made in BK/O(72)10 of 25 September 1972 (*GVBl.* p.1966) on the extension to Berlin of the International Conventions concerning the Carriage of Goods by Rail (CIM) and the Carriage of Passengers and Luggage by Rail (CIV). See also BK/O(86)9 of 8 October 1986 (*GVBl.* p.1656).
[26] *GVBl.* (1976), p.76.

A further major project was agreed between the *Senat* and the *Deutsche Reichsbahn* in the Südgelände Arrangement. This consists of a Basic Arrangement (*Grundsatzvereinbarung*) of 21 February 1974[27] and an implementing technical arrangement (*Festlegungen*) of 24 January 1980,[28] which the Allied Kommandatura authorised the *Senat* to sign by BK/O(80)2 of 24 January 1980.[29] Under the Arrangement, the *Deutsche Reichsbahn* agreed to forgo the use of sixty-three hectares of railway property at the former Anhalter and Potsdamer Stations, so that they could be developed by the *Senat* for other purposes. In return a large, modern goods station and shunting yard would be built at the Südgelände site south of Sachsendamm in Schöneberg; this would cost DM 490 million, of which the *Deutsche Reichsbahn* would pay DM 21 million. In authorising the conclusion of the technical arrangement by BK/O(80)2, the Western Commandants reserved their rights of control by providing that –

> the special legal position of railways and of railway traffic in the Western Sectors of Berlin cannot be affected by the provisions of the arrangement, which shall be subject to Allied rights and legislation.

The Allied Kommandatura made similar provision in BK/O(80)5 of 30 April 1980,[30] by which it authorised the *Senat* to conclude with the *Deutsche Reichsbahn* an arrangement for improvements to railway operations in the Wannsee area, in particular the construction of a second track between Wannsee and Griebnitzsee to handle long-distance traffic leaving Berlin. In this BK/O, the Kommandatura agreed in principle to the implementation in Berlin by the *Deutsche Reichsbahn* of technical measures as provided for in the arrangement; it also confirmed that –

> the said technical measures are to be executed in accordance with the usual procedures which arise from legislation and regulations in force in the Western Sectors of Berlin and which include approvals, controls, or inspections by the Allied authorities or the German authorities designated by them.

WATERWAYS IN BERLIN

Legal status in general[31]

Before the end of the Second World War, the public waterways of Berlin were owned and administered by the German *Reich* as part of

---

[27] *Dokumente zur Aussenpolitik der DDR*, 22 (1974), p.919.
[28] *Dokumente zur Aussenpolitik der DDR*, 27 (1980), p.1050.
[29] *GVBl.* p.420.
[30] *GVBl.* p.928.
[31] Wengler, *JR*, 1950, pp.641–6, 676–82.

the unified waterways system of Berlin and central Germany. The principal *Reich* waterways (*Reichswasserstrassen*) in Berlin were the Havel and Spree Rivers and the Teltow and Landwehr Canals. When Berlin was occupied by the four Powers and divided into Sectors in 1945, they assumed supreme authority over the waterways in Berlin. As *Reich* property the waterways (like the railways) in the Western Sectors were formally placed under the control of the respective Western Sector Commandants by Military Government (SHAEF) Law No. 52, which was extended to the Western Sectors of Berlin by the Allied Kommandatura decision of 23 August 1945 (BK/M(45)7) referred to at p.254 above. The waterways situated in the Western Sectors remain subject to the control of the respective Sector Commandants.

However, Berlin's waterways, like its railways, formed part of a unified transport system extending beyond Berlin. As with the railways, it would have been impractical to disturb this arrangement, for example by setting up different Sector administrations for Berlin. As the Western Allies stated in a communication to the Secretary-General of the United Nations in June 1977:

> Soon after the war it was decided, with the approval of the respective Sector Commandants, that German technical agencies situated in the Eastern Sector of Berlin would exercise limited operational functions in respect of some of the waterways in the Western Sectors of Berlin. This decision in no way conferred on those agencies any form of sovereignty or jurisdiction over any of the canals, waterways or locks located in the Western Sectors of Berlin.[32]

The main operational functions which the German technical agencies situated in the Soviet Sector were in fact permitted to carry out were the operation and maintenance of the locks at Spandau, Charlottenburg and Plötzensee and on the Landwehr Canal, as well as the receipt of fees for the use of these locks. These functions are carried out by the technical waterways authority (*Wasserstrassenhauptamt*) situated in the Soviet Sector. Otherwise, responsibility for the maintenance and administration of the waterways in the Western Sectors is largely exercised by the *Senat*. All activities of local German authorities in respect of the waterways in the Western Sectors remain subject to the supreme authority and control of the Commandant in whose Sector the waterways are located.

The legal position of the GDR, supported by the Soviet Union, on the status of the waterways appears to be that the GDR has sovereignty or sovereign or proprietorial rights over all the

---

[32] For the full exchange, see *Multilateral Treaties*, Chapter XII.3, note 1.

waterways in West Berlin. The GDR has made various attempts over the years to promote its legal position, including purporting to legislate in respect of the waterways in West Berlin. The Western position is that the waterways in the Western Sectors have a special legal status, which has remained unchanged since 1945: they are property over which the Commandant of the Sector in which they are situated has the right of control and legal disposition, by virtue of supreme Allied authority, the Allied Kommandatura decision of 23 August 1945 and Military Government Law No. 52. Any GDR claim to, or attempt to exercise, sovereignty or sovereign or proprietorial rights over the waterways in the Western Sectors is without legal foundation, and has been consistently rejected by the Western Allies and *Senat*.

Removal of property

In 1949 it became clear that the authorities in the Soviet Sector were removing property and equipment connected with the waterways from the Western Sectors of Berlin. On 9 November 1949, the Allied Kommandatura issued BK/O(49)245,[33] which provided in paragraph 1 that:

> No fixtures, or any property or equipment including all records and plans which are necessary for the proper operation, navigation and administration of the waterways, ports, and locks within a Sector of Berlin will be removed out of that Sector without the permission of the Occupation Authority of that Sector.

This Order remains in force to prevent removal of property to the detriment of efficient navigation of the waterways in the Western Sectors.

Police authority over the waterways

Subject to the supervision and control of the Allied authorities, police authority on the waterways in the Western Sectors is the exclusive responsibility of the West Berlin police. No GDR or East Berlin police authority over those waterways is permitted.

Lock and waterway fees

Although the German technical agencies in the Soviet Sector are permitted to operate certain locks in the Western Sectors and to receive fees for the use of them, the Western Allies have never accepted that the GDR or East Berlin authorities have jurisdiction to

---

[33] *VOBl.* p.436. Compare BK/O(49)217 cited at p.257 above.

impose and determine the level of fees. From time to time the GDR Government has purported to legislate levying fees for the use of locks and waterways in the Western Sectors. The Western Allied authorities have regularly protested against such measures to the Soviet Embassy in East Berlin, pointing out that they are devoid of any legal basis.[34]

The Allied Kommandatura made its position clear, as regards fees for use of those parts of the Teltow Canal in the Western Sectors, in BK/O(68)9 of 11 September 1968.[35] Having provided in paragraph 2 that the Teltowkanal A.G. was competent in the Western Sectors for the administration, operation and maintenance of the Teltow Canal, the BK/O provides:

> The levying of fees in respect of the navigation of those parts of the Teltow Canal in the Western Sectors of Berlin by or on behalf of any body other than the Teltowkanal A.G. is unauthorised. The levying of such fees in the Western Sectors by or on behalf of any such body is prohibited. Acts contrary to this prohibition shall be regarded as a breach of this Order.

Legislation

Because of the special status of the waterways in the Western Sectors of Berlin, Federal legislation which would have been incompatible with that status and with Allied rights and responsibilities in respect of the waterways has not been taken over in Berlin. For example, the Federal Law of 21 May 1951 on the Legal Position of Federal Waterways Property,[36] which provided that all former *Reich* waterways became Federal waterways with effect from 24 May 1949, was not taken over in Berlin. Its effect is limited to the territory of the Federal Republic. Likewise, the Law of 17 August 1960 on the Pollution of Waterways,[37] which dealt solely with Federal waterways and gave the Federal Ministry of Transport the responsibility for administering them, has not been taken over.

The principal legislation regulating the waterways in the Western Sectors is the Berlin Water Law of 23 February 1960.[38] As passed by the House of Representatives, this Law designated Berlin waterways as "Federal waterways". The Allied Kommandatura issued BK/O(60)4 of 19 August 1960[39] substituting the term "former *Reich*

---

[34] The lock and waterway fees in the Western Sectors are properly imposed, and their amount determined, by the *Senat*: see, for example, *Amtsblatt für Berlin* 1984, p.1485.
[35] *GVBl.* p.1332.
[36] *Gesetz über die vermögensrechtlichen Verhältnisse der Bundeswasserstrassen: BGBl.* I, p.352.
[37] *Gesetz zur Reinhaltung der Bundeswasserstrassen: BGBl.* I, p.2125.
[38] *Berliner Wassergesetz: GVBl.* p.133.
[39] *GVBl.* p.1092.

waterway" for "Federal waterway" whenever it appeared in the Law. In doing so, the Allied Kommandatura was insisting that the status of Berlin's waterways remained unchanged and saying that the Federation should not have jurisdiction and administrative competence in Berlin in the matter. The regulation of these waterways was, in the Allied view, a matter for the *Senat*. And in BK/O(62)8 of 25 September 1962,[40] the Allied Kommandatura disapplied Article 28(4) of the Berlin Water Law, thereby authorising the *Senat* to issue Ordinances under Article 28(3) applicable to former *Reich* waterways. Several such Ordinances have been issued by the *Senat*.

Some Federal waterways legislation has, however, been taken over in Berlin. As often happens in practice, in order to suggest *Rechtseinheit* between Berlin and the Federal Republic, provisions of Federal Laws have been adopted in Berlin by *Mantelgesetz* irrespective of whether they can have any practical effect there. For example, in BK/O(68)1 of 27 May 1968[41] the Allied Kommandatura noted that the provisions of the Federal Law on Waterways of 2 April 1968[42] had been taken over in Berlin by *Mantelgesetz* of 25 April 1968. The BK/O continues:

> The Allied Kommandatura notes that no Berlin waterway is listed in the annex to the Law and recalls that the former *Reich* waterways in the Western Sectors of Berlin are property over which the Sector Commandant concerned has the right of control and legal disposition. Accordingly, Berlin waterways are not affected by the provisions of this Law.

However, over the years certain provisions of adopted Federal legislation have in practice been applied to waterways in the Western Sectors, notwithstanding that these provisions apply in terms only to Federal waterways. The practice is by no means clear, but it would appear that certain provisions are followed except where they affect the status of, or Allied rights and responsibilities with respect to, the waterways, or where they apply in terms exclusively to a specific area or thing outside Berlin (for example, legislation dealing solely with Rhine shipping). Notwithstanding the somewhat opaque picture presented by this mixture of local Berlin legislation and the practice of following certain provisions of Federal waterways legislation adopted in Berlin, it would seem that shipping and other activities connected with waterways in the Western Sectors proceed in a smooth fashion.

[40] *GVBl.* p.1184.
[41] *GVBl.* p.732. For a GDR protest over the adoption of Federal waterways legislation, see *Das Vierseitige Abkommen*, p.156
[42] *Bundeswasserstrassengesetz: BGBl.* III, p.940.

Attempts by the GDR Government to legislate in respect of waterways in the Western Sectors have been consistently rejected as unlawful by the Allied authorities. Referring to the GDR Water Law of 2 July 1982,[43] they issued a press statement on 31 August 1982 in the following terms:

> On 2 July 1982 the GDR *Volkskammer* passed a new Water Law, which purports to apply to waterways in the Western Sectors of Berlin and includes an assignment of responsibility to the GDR Ministry of Transport for questions relating to these waterways.
> The Allied authorities have made an appropriate protest to the Soviet Embassy, in particular, that GDR authorities cannot legislate in respect of waterways in the Western Sectors of Berlin. Any attempt to do so or any action by the GDR authorities purporting to be taken under this new Water Law is without any legal foundation and can have no effect.

Construction projects

Questions concerning the status of Berlin's waterways have arisen in the context of arrangements concluded between the *Senat* of Berlin and German authorities in the Soviet Sector regarding construction work at Spandau Lock and on the Teltow Canal. In each case the Allied Kommandatura acted to preserve the status of the waterways and to underline the maintenance of Allied supreme authority in respect of them.

Spandau Lock links the Upper and Lower Havel in the Western Sectors of Berlin, and is one of the locks operated by the East Berlin *Wasserstrassenhauptamt*. In order to improve the facilities for inland waterway traffic, representatives of the *Senat* and of the relevant German authorities in East Berlin held discussions between 1969 and 1977 about the construction of a second, larger lock-basin for the Lock. A technical arrangement (*Vereinbarung*)[44] was eventually concluded, which dealt with the necessary arrangements for carrying out this work. In BK/O(77)11 of 30 November 1977,[45] the Allied Kommandatura authorised the *Senat* representative to sign this arrangement, and provided also that:

> The supreme authority of the appropriate Sector Commandant in respect of the waterways in his Sector, the existing responsibilities of the *Senat* and the limited operational functions of the *Wasserstrassenhauptamt* remain unaffected by this arrangement.

---

[43] *Wassergesetz*: GBl. DDR I, p.467.
[44] Arrangement of 1 December 1977: *Zehn Jahre Deutschlandpolitik*, p.332.
[45] *GVBl.* p.2292.

The Teltow Canal, originally opened in 1906, was designed essentially as a short cut for barge traffic coming from the Lower Havel near Potsdam to the Spree-Dahme near Gruenan and to the Upper Spree via the Britz Canal. Most of the Canal runs through the American Sector, but two sections lie in the GDR, and the eastern section is in the Soviet Sector. Moreover, at certain points the border between the American Sector and the GDR runs down the middle of the Canal. As a former *Reich* waterway, the parts of the Canal in the American Sector are subject to the supreme authority of the United States Commandant; they are operated by the Teltowkanal A.G. and have at no time been operated by the GDR or East Berlin authorities. Although the GDR claims ownership of and jurisdiction over the whole Canal, the Western Allies do not accept that the GDR has any rights in respect of the parts that lie in the American Sector.

By closing those sections of the Teltow Canal lying in the GDR to through traffic, the GDR Government was able to frustrate the main purpose of the Canal. After the conclusion of the Quadripartite Agreement of 3 September 1971 and the related inner-German Transit Traffic Agreement, and in implementation of the Protocol Note on communications, the GDR authorities informed the *Senat* in December 1974 that they would be willing to negotiate with the *Senat* over the opening of the Teltow Canal. With the authorisation of the Western Allies, the *Senat* began exploratory discussions with the GDR Government in 1975, and matters were carried forward between the Governments of the Federal Republic of Germany and GDR as part of a wider package of transport negotiations. In 1978, an arrangement was eventually concluded, with the approval of the Allied Kommandatura, regarding the work necessary to re-open the Canal.[46] One element of this arrangement, which was principally concluded between the Governments of the Federal Republic of Germany and GDR, consisted of an exchange of letters between the *Senat* of Berlin and the GDR Government. This stated expressly that "the status of this waterway will not be affected by these measures". By BK/O(78)9 of 16 November 1978,[47] the Allied Kommandatura authorised the Senator for Building and Housing or his representative to conclude and implement the exchange of letters with the GDR Ministry of Transport "concerning the building measures necessary for the opening of the Teltow Canal for civilian inland shipping, including the relevant declarations on maintenance measures". The BK/O further stated that:

---

[46] Arrangement of 16 November 1978: *Zehn Jahre Deutschlandpolitik*, p.346.
[47] *GVBl.* p.2204.

The supreme authority of the United States Commandant with regard to the Teltow Canal as well as the status of the Canal remain unaffected.

The building measures necessary for the re-opening of the Teltow Canal were completed, and the Canal was opened for civilian inland shipping as from 20 November 1981. Prior to this, on 30 October 1981 the GDR Government published amendments to its waterways traffic legislation, which purported to legislate with respect to the parts of the Teltow Canal which lie in the American Sector.[48] The Allied Kommandatura issued BK/O(81)8 on 20 November 1981,[49] which provided that:

> In connection with the use of and regulation of traffic on the Teltow Canal, the Allied Kommandatura recalls that complete control and administration of all property, personnel and traffic on the Teltow Canal in the US Sector of Berlin were placed under the jurisdiction of the City Government by order of the US Military Government dated 30 April 1949.

Repeating the language of BK/O(78)9, the BK/O further states that:

> The supreme authority of the United States Commandant with regard to the Teltow Canal as well as the status of the canal remain unaffected.

---

[48] *GBl. DDR I, Sonderdruck* 76/2.
[49] *GVBl.* p.1467.

CHAPTER 22

DEMILITARISATION

B ERLIN retains a special demilitarised status under quadripartite agreements and decisions of 1945 and 1946 relating to the disarmament and demilitarisation of Germany. In the Potsdam Agreement of 2 August 1945,[1] the first among "the purposes of the occupation of Germany by which the Control Council shall be guided" was stated to be:

> The complete disarmament and demilitarisation of Germany and the elimination or control of all German industry that could be used for military production.[2]

Control Council Proclamation No. 2 of 20 September 1945[3] provided in paragraphs 1 and 2 for the abolition of all German armed forces and military and quasi-military organisations, and prohibited "all forms of military training, military propaganda and military activities of whatever nature, on the part of the German people". Paragraph 13 prohibited, except as directed by the Allies, "the manufacture, production and construction, and the acquisition from outside Germany, of war material and such other products used in connection with such manufacture, production or construction as the Allied Representatives may specify, and the import, export and transit thereof". It also required the German authorities to place at the disposal of the Allies all research, experiment, development and design directly or indirectly relating to war or the production of war material. These requirements in Proclamation No. 2 were implemented in further Control Council legislation.[4]

The special demilitarised status originally imposed on Germany was superseded by the rearmament and remilitarisation permitted by the Soviet Union in its zone of occupation (later the GDR) and, in response thereto, the gradual rearmament of the Federal Republic of Germany.[5] Berlin, however, remains under four-Power

---

[1] *US Documents*, p.54; Heidelmeyer, p.15. See p.39 above.
[2] Part II, paragraph 3(i). See also related economic provisions in Part II, paragraphs 11 and 15(d).
[3] *CC Gazette*, p.8.
[4] See in particular Law No. 8 of 1 December 1945 (Elimination and Prohibition of Military Training): *CC Gazette*, p.33; Law No. 23 of 10 April 1946 (Prohibition of Military Construction in Germany): *CC Gazette*, p.136; Law No. 25 of 29 April 1946 (Control of Scientific Research): *CC Gazette*, p.138; Law No. 34 of 20 August 1946 (Dissolution of the *Wehrmacht*): *CC Gazette*, p.172; Law No. 43 of 20 December 1946 (Prohibition of the Manufacture, Import, Export, Transport and Storage of War Materials): *CC Gazette*, p.234.
[5] *Selected Documents* I, pp.8–9.

occupation and control, and retains the special demilitarised status originally agreed by the four Powers. In the Western view, just as the whole of the special Berlin area remains legally under quadripartite occupation and control, so the special demilitarised status continues to apply to the whole of Greater Berlin. Accordingly, the Western Allies have scrupulously adhered to the special demilitarised status of the city, and have regularly protested against violations of it in the Soviet Sector. The Soviet Union and GDR, on the other hand, maintain that only the Western Sectors remain under an occupation régime and retain a special demilitarised status; the Soviet Sector, in their view, is part of the GDR and neither under occupation nor subject to any special demilitarised status. The conflicting views of West and East regarding demilitarisation thus reflect those regarding the legal status of Berlin. There is a sharp contrast between the situation in the Western Sectors and that prevailing *de facto* in the Soviet Sector. The main aspects of the special demilitarised status of Berlin, as respected and applied in the Western Sectors, are considered in this Chapter. (For the position in the Soviet Sector, see pp.306–8 below.)

THE PROHIBITION OF GERMAN MILITARY ACTIVITY

Article III of the Declaration on Berlin of 5 May 1955 (p.332 below) includes the following:

> The Allied authorities will normally exercise powers only in the following fields:
> . . .
> (b) Disarmament and demilitarisation, including related fields of scientific research, civil aviation, and prohibitions and restrictions on industry in relation to the foregoing.

Demilitarisation thus remains a reserved subject, and the Allied authorities continue to exercise powers in this field as a matter of course. The Declaration also reflects four-Power agreements and decisions of 1945 and 1946 in extending the concept of demilitarisation beyond the purely military field into related spheres of research and industry.

In the military field, the special demilitarised status of Berlin means that all German military activity in Berlin is prohibited. The prohibition takes many forms. For example, Control Council Law No. 34 of 20 August 1946,[6] which dissolved the *Wehrmacht* and all German military and quasi-military organisations, also prohibits their reconstitution or any future organisations from taking over their functions. It also repealed all German military legislation. Law

---

[6] *CC Gazette*, p.172.

No. 34 remains in force in Berlin. So does Control Council Law No. 8 of 1 December 1945,[7] which prohibits all German military education and training, military parades and military formations of any kind, and any propaganda or agitation "which is aimed at keeping alive, reviving or promoting the military or Nazi spirit and institutions, or to glorify war". A further example is Allied Kommandatura Law No. 5 of 25 February 1950,[8] which prohibits German nationals from wearing, inter alia, "any uniform of regulation colour and pattern of any formation of the former German armed forces", or any uniform resembling such a uniform, as well as the manufacture, sale or purchase of any such uniform, unless authorised by the Allied Kommandatura.

In consequence of the Allied demilitarisation legislation, no Federal German military legislation has been taken over in Berlin. Thus, for example, the Soldiers Law of 19 March 1956,[9] the Conscription Law of 21 July 1956,[10] and the Military Discipline Code of 15 March 1957,[11] all of which deal with the Federal armed forces (Bundeswehr), contain no Berlin clause and have not been adopted in Berlin. The same applies to the Law on the Purchase of Land for Defence Purposes of 23 February 1957;[12] and to the Fourth Law amending the Penal Code of 11 June 1957,[13] which created new offences in connection with evasion of military service and military security.

It follows from the special demilitarised status of Berlin that members of the Federal armed forces have no function in the city. The Allied authorities have consistently maintained this prohibition both in their legislation and in practice. The Allied Kommandatura has frequently legislated to remove any suggestion that the prohibition might have lapsed. For example, BK/O(61)16 of 5 October 1961[14] ordered that those provisions of the Federal Law concerning Passports, Nationality and Registration of Citizens Abroad which referred to members of the Federal armed forces, and which prohibited the renunciation of nationality by persons subject to conscription, should not have the force of law in Berlin. A further example is BK/O(74)2 of 23 April 1974[15] concerning the

---

[7] CC Gazette, p.33. Article IV, in so far as it applied to civil decorations, honours or medals, was deprived of effect by BK/O(52)17 of 25 April 1952 (GVBl. p.308).
[8] AK Gazette, p.7. The provisions of this Law which are inconsistent with the Federal Law on Titles, Orders and Insignia were deprived of effect, to the extent only of the inconsistency, by BK/O(57)4 of 27 February 1957 (GVBl. p. 1252).
[9] Soldatengesetz: BGBl. I, p.114.
[10] Wehrpflichtgesetz: BGBl. I, p.651.
[11] Wehrdisziplinarordnung: BGBl. I, p.189.
[12] Landbeschaffungsgesetz: BGBl. I, p.134.
[13] Viertes Strafrechtsänderungsgesetz: BGBl. I, p.597.
[14] GVBl. p.1616.
[15] GVBl. p.1055.

adoption in Berlin of the Introductory Law to the Criminal Code, the second paragraph of which includes the following:

> The adoption of this Law shall not affect Allied reserved rights and responsibilities nor Allied legislation, in particular:
>
> . . .
>
> (3) The non-applicable provisions referring to the *Bundeswehr* or to members of the *Bundeswehr* cannot be interpreted as implying that these persons, as members of the *Bundeswehr*, exercise or may be permitted to exercise any function whatsoever in Berlin . . .

Similarly, for the removal of doubt, the Allied Kommandatura has legislated to disapply provisions of Federal legislation adopted in Berlin which amend or refer to provisions of Federal military legislation not in force in Berlin.[16]

A significant consequence of the demilitarised status of Berlin is the prohibition of conscription. Federal military conscription legislation[17] does not apply in Berlin. Permanent residents of Berlin may not be conscripted into the Federal armed forces. Notices of induction into the Federal armed forces are not sent to Berlin. The Western Allies have scrupulously maintained this prohibition,[18] and continue to do so. In 1969 the Western Allies clarified the extent to which judicial and administrative assistance (*Rechts- und Amtshilfe*) may be applied in Berlin to send or return persons to the Federal Republic from Berlin in connection with service in the Federal armed forces. In doing so they drew an important distinction between conscription into the Federal armed forces and desertion from those forces. The effective date of entry into the Federal armed forces for persons who are liable for military service under the Federal military conscription legislation is the date on which such persons are required to report for induction at some designated place in the Federal Republic. Because of the special status of Berlin, members of the Federal armed forces have no function in the city. Military personnel who have proceeded to Berlin without permission or for the purpose of absenting themselves from the military forces are not authorised to be in Berlin. Accordingly, taking these factors into account the Allied instructions issued to the *Senat* in 1969, which remain in force,

---

[16] For example, BK/O(61)5 of 5 May 1961 (*GVBl.* p.624); BK/O(64)1 of 20 February 1964 (*GVBl.* p.312); Lush, *ICLQ*, 14 (1965), p.769.

[17] The principal legislation is the Conscription Law (*Wehrpflichtgesetz*) of 21 July 1956 (*BGBl.* I, p.651), in the consolidated version of 6 May 1983 (*BGBl.* I, p.529).

[18] In response to a Soviet Note of 30 June 1960 (*US Documents*, p.707; Heidelmeyer *Dokumente*, p.442), the Western Allies confirmed "without hesitation that recruitment of members for the *Bundeswehr* is not taking place in Berlin. Moreover, there is no conscription, and there are no organisations which register individuals for recruitment": Note of 12 August 1960: *Selected Documents* I, p.431; *US Documents*, p.713.

provide as follows.[19] First, persons whose permanent residence is in Berlin are not liable for service under the Federal military conscription legislation. Judicial and administrative assistance with regard to military service may not be applied to such persons. Secondly, residents of the Federal Republic liable for service under the Federal military conscription legislation who leave the Federal Republic and go to Berlin prior to receipt of their notice of induction into military service may not be served with notice of induction in Berlin. Judicial and administrative assistance with regard to military service may not be applied to such persons. Thirdly, residents of the Federal Republic who received their notice of induction into the armed forces of the Federal Republic prior to their arrival in Berlin are considered to be on active military service in the Federal armed forces from the reporting date specified in that notice of induction. As members of the Federal armed forces have no function in Berlin, the presence of such persons in Berlin is unauthorised after that reporting date. Judicial and administrative assistance may therefore be applied in cases involving such persons. Thus the special demilitarised status of Berlin is respected and preserved, both by prohibiting measures to conscript, or assist in conscripting, civilians in Berlin, and by authorising measures to remove members of the Federal armed forces from Berlin.

CIVIL DEFENCE AND EMERGENCIES

In addition to Federal military legislation, Federal legislation in the field of civil defence and emergencies has not been taken over in Berlin. As the three Western Ambassadors explained in a letter of 4 September 1967 to the Soviet Ambassador:

> All aspects of planning for emergencies of every kind and the actual handling of such emergencies in the three Western Sectors have always been an important part of the responsibilities of the Commandants in Berlin and fall under their authority. The *Senat* of Berlin naturally contributes to such planning insofar as it relates to matters over which the *Senat* exercises administrative control. All such activity on the part of the *Senat* is under the direct authority and control of the Commandants.[20]

The Allied Kommandatura had already legislated with regard to civil defence in Berlin. BK/O(65)11 of 1 October 1965[21] provides that:

> Any measures that are required for protecting the civilian population

---

[19] BK/L(69)29 of 8 August 1969: cited in the decision of the *Amtsgericht* Tiergarten of 1 October 1969: *NJW*, 23 (1970), p.1281. See also the other cases cited in Zivier, p.62.
[20] *Selected Documents* II, p.158.
[21] *GVBl.* p.1432.

of Berlin, their lives and health, dwellings, places of work and the installations and properties essential for satisfying the necessities of life against the consequences of armed attack shall be prepared and taken in Berlin.

The BK/O goes on to specify a number of particular civil defence measures that are to be prepared and taken. It also enables the *Senat* to enact regulations for the implementation of the Order, but requires that these must be approved by the Allied Kommandatura before coming into effect.[22]

CONTROLS IN THE ECONOMIC FIELD: GENERAL

An important aspect of the demilitarised status of Berlin, which likewise flows from the measures agreed at Potsdam in 1945, is the system of controls in what may be described as the economic field. As can be seen from Article III(b) of the Declaration on Berlin, the Allied Kommandatura expressly included in its reserved rights relating to disarmament and demilitarisation the related fields of scientific research, civil aviation, and prohibitions and restrictions on industry in relation to disarmament and demilitarisation. Allied controls in these fields clearly affect the economic life of Berlin. The Allied authorities have therefore balanced careful adherence to the essential requirements of the demilitarised status of Berlin with certain permissible authorisations and clarifications, in relation to activities having a peaceful purpose, in the interests of the economy of the city. The scope for this is however limited by the need to maintain the status of Berlin, of which demilitarisation is an important part.[23]

The concern of the Allied authorities is illustrated by BK/O(74)11 of 30 September 1974.[24] In this BK/O the Allied Kommandatura made a general reservation regarding laws and treaties extended to Berlin, emphasising that "even in those cases where no reservations are laid down expressly by the Allied Kommandatura, such laws and treaties do not affect the rights and responsibilities of the Allies or Allied legislation". The BK/O continues by requiring authorities and services responsible for the application of laws and international treaties in Berlin to "continue to conform strictly with Allied legislation"; it then lists, in particular, Allied legislation relating to war materials, nuclear energy, scientific research and civil aviation. These four topics may conveniently be considered in turn.

[22] See *Verordnung über die Erweiterung des Katastrophenschutzes* of 25 March 1974 (*GVBl.* p.683), as amended by *Verordnung* of 29 November 1977 (*GVBl.* p.2290). See also *Ausführungsvorschriften über die Organisation des Katastrophen-Hilfsdienstes* of 19 September 1981 (*Amtsblatt für Berlin*, p.1916).
[23] For an account of post-war developments, see Schröder, *ROW*, 28 (1984), pp.210–15.
[24] *GVBl.* p.2576.

WAR MATERIALS

Two principal Control Council Laws dealing with war materials remain in force in Berlin. Law No. 23 of 10 April 1946[25] contains prohibitions in connection with the planning or construction of Germany military installations, as well as civilian construction which could be used for war purposes. The term "military installation" is defined at length in Article II, but this Article has been deprived of effect by BK/O(65)11 as regards civil defence measures taken thereunder.

Of greater significance, given its wide scope, is Control Council Law No. 43 of 20 December 1946,[26] which is still regularly applied in the Western Sectors of Berlin. Article I prohibits the manufacture, import, export, transport and storage of a broad range of "war materials" listed in Schedule A, including "components, accessories, and spare parts of such materials, which are specially designed for military use". The "war materials" listed in Schedule A range from "warships of all classes" and "aircraft of all types, heavier or lighter than air", through "tanks and armoured cars", to firearms and "military cutting or piercing weapons". Article II permits the manufacture, import, export, transport and storage of war materials listed in Schedule B, if licensed by the Allied authorities. Licences are in practice issued by the Allied Kommandatura (Economic Committee). Schedule B includes such items as sporting weapons, explosives used for industrial purposes, and certain "war chemicals which are nevertheless required for peace economy". Article V, however, provides for some flexibility: it enables materials listed in Schedule A, as an exception, to be listed in Schedule B by the Allied Control Authority or by a body acting on their behalf "in cases where it will appear that such materials are destined for peacetime requirements and not designed specifically for war purposes and are not dangerous in themselves". The Allied authorities have in fact made a number of transfers from Schedule A to Schedule B so that, subject to appropriate conditions in each case, Allied Kommandatura licences could be issued to permit specified activities in relation to the items transferred. Such transfers are authorised by the three Ambassadors in Bonn.[27]

Law No. 43 imposes restrictions on certain areas of commerce and industry in Berlin, although its effects are less drastic than is sometimes supposed. Whilst retaining control over the activities and materials covered by the Law, the Allied authorities have shown considerable readiness to use the discretionary provisions of the Law

---

[25] *CC Gazette*, p.136.
[26] *CC Gazette*, p.234.
[27] Schröder, *ROW*, 28 (1984), p.213.

to permit activities for civil or peaceful purposes, as opposed to those having a military object or purpose.

Law No. 43 has in some respects been clarified and supplemented in further Allied legislation, in particular concerning the control of weapons.[28] BK/O(74)7 of 9 July 1974, as amended,[29] clarifies certain terms used in Law No. 43, including "weapons", "projectiles", "military cutting and piercing weapons", and "sporting weapons and ammunition for sporting weapons". It authorises the Berlin police, subject to certain conditions, to issue licences for the import, export, transport and storage of sporting weapons and ammunition therefor. It also grants a general authorisation for the manufacture, import, export, transport and storage of a limited category of items, most of which are included within the definition of "sporting weapons". This legislation goes some way towards assimilating the control of weapons in Berlin with the law in the Federal Republic of Germany; because of the demilitarised status of Berlin and Allied legislation, the Federal Weapons Law (*Waffengesetz*) has not been taken over in Berlin. In addition, BK/O(77)10 of 25 October 1977[30] authorises the Berlin police to issue permits for the carriage of firearms and ammunition by employees of firms whose only business is carrying out and guarding transports of money and valuables. BK/O(65)2 of 27 January 1965,[31] as amended by BK/O(86)7 of 30 September 1986,[32] enables the Police President to issue licences to sport shooting clubs, permitting them to organise and practise target shooting and to own certain types of sporting weapons. And BK/O(85)11 of 18 December 1985[33] authorises the licensing of certain activities in relation to explosive and pyrotechnical substances. Further Allied legislation provides for the arming of the Berlin police.[34]

NUCLEAR ENERGY

Control Council Law No. 43 includes among the prohibited "war materials" in Schedule A "all weapons, including atomic means of

---

[28] Control Council Order No. 2 of 7 January 1946 (*CC Gazette*, p. 130), which is still in force in Berlin, is also relevant to the control of weapons. With exceptions for the Allied forces and German police, it prohibited the carrying, possession or ownership of arms or ammunition.
[29] BK/O(74)7 (*GVBl.* p.1646), as amended by BK/O(77)5 of 29 April 1977 (*GVBl.* p.920) and BK/O(81)5 of 24 June 1981 (*GVBl.* p.720).
[30] *GVBl.* p.2131.
[31] *GVBl.* p.281.
[32] *GVBl.* p.1628.
[33] *GVBl.* (1986), p.395.
[34] BK/O(46)35 of 12 January 1946 (unpublished); BK/O(58)3 of 14 March 1958 (*GVBl.* p.304); BK/O(71)2 of 28 May 1971 (*GVBl.* p.956).

warfare". Control Council Law No. 25 of 29 April 1946,[35] which dealt with control of scientific research, prohibited research on "applied nuclear physics". Neither of these Control Council Laws envisaged the peaceful use of nuclear energy, and indeed they predated legislative attempts to regulate this matter in various countries as the state of technology advanced. Later Allied legislation in the 1950s made initial provision with respect to the peaceful use of nuclear energy, both in the three Western zones of Germany[36] and in Berlin,[37] as exceptions to the sweeping prohibitions in the Control Council Laws. In 1957 the Hahn-Meitner Institute for Nuclear Research was established in Berlin, and in 1958 a Berlin Atomic Law came into force,[38] subject to controls and conditions imposed by the Allied Kommandatura in BK/O(58)7 of 1 July 1958.[39]

This legislation remained in force until 1961, when the Federal Law of 23 December 1959 on the Peaceful Use of Nuclear Energy and the Protection against its Dangers[40] was taken over in Berlin. The application of the 1959 Law in Berlin is subject to the important conditions and qualifications imposed by the Allied Kommandatura in BK/O(61)8 of 12 July 1961. This BK/O, as amended,[41] and subject to it the provisions of Federal legislation which have been taken over in Berlin, remain the applicable law in the field. The general scheme of the BK/O is that the Allied Kommandatura retains overall control, while the *Senat* exercises supervisory and licensing powers. There is an express prohibition of any work on the military application of nuclear energy (Article 1). The more important licensing powers of the *Senat* may only be exercised with the prior approval of the Allied Kommandatura, and licences must include regulations for the maintenance of operation records, for safeguarding information, and regarding personnel security (Articles 2 and 3). The prior approval of the Allied Kommandatura is also required for the issue of Ordinances pursuant to the 1959 Law, and for visits of inspectors (Articles 5 and

---

[35] *CC Gazette*, p.138.
[36] Allied High Commission Law No. 22 of 2 March 1950: *Official Gazette of the Allied High Commission for Germany*, p.122.
[37] Allied Kommandatura Law No. 13 of 29 January 1951 (*AK Gazette*, p.183), as amended by Allied Kommandatura Laws No. 15 (*AK Gazette*, p.266) and No. 22 (*AK Gazette*, p.502).
[38] *Atomgesetz*: *GVBl*. p.563.
[39] *GVBl*. p.605.
[40] *Gesetz über die friedliche Verwendung der Atomenergie und den Schutz gegen ihre Gefahren*: *BGBl*. I, p.814.
[41] BK/O(61)8 (*GVBl*. p.1523); BK/O(63)7 of 24 May 1963 (*GVBl*. p.586); BK/O(67)6 of 31 May 1967 (*GVBl*. p.1008); BK/O(69)5 of 17 July 1969 (*GVBl*. p.1794); BK/O(72)8 of 22 June 1972 (*GVBl*. p.1194); BK/O(73)6 of 25 September 1973 (*GVBl*. p.1740); BK/O(86)5 of 30 May 1986 (*GVBl*. p.888).

6). In Article 7 the Allied Kommandatura reserves the right to require the submission of such statistics, reports, documents, or other information, and to prescribe such controls, as it may consider necessary.

SCIENTIFIC RESEARCH

Control Council Law No. 25, as noted above, contained sweeping prohibitions and restrictions on scientific research. It extended beyond nuclear research into such fields as aerodynamics, rocket propulsion, hydrodynamics, ship construction, electronics, explosives and chemicals, ball and roller bearings, and synthetic oil and rubber. It also dissolved and prohibited all technical military organisations, and prohibited fundamental scientific research of a wholly or primarily military nature. In the years following the suspension of the Control Council's activities in 1948, a series of BK/Os introduced some relaxations; and whilst these did not formally repeal Law No. 25, it was provided that they should prevail over any inconsistent legislation.[42] The BK/Os were repealed by the Allied Kommandatura in BK/O(57)1 of 8 January 1957,[43] which in turn provided that its provisions should supersede any inconsistent provisions in existing legislation. This BK/O re-enacted in similar language some basic provisions of Law No. 25, but otherwise introduced significant and far-reaching relaxations in the field of scientific research. BK/O(57)1 in effect replaced Law No. 25 and is the applicable Allied legislation on the subject.

Articles 1 and 2 of BK/O(57)1 prohibit "all military organisations, technical or scientific", and "scientific research which is solely or predominantly of a military nature". Thus, reflecting similar provisions in Law No. 25, the basic purpose of demilitarisation in the field of scientific research is preserved. Article 3 provides:

> Scientific research on matters listed in the Schedule to the present Order is prohibited, except in so far as research establishments are authorised by the Allied Kommandatura to carry on such research. The prohibition contained in this article does not extend to academical teaching and demonstrating. An authorisation shall be deemed to be granted, if no objection has been registered by the Allied Kommandatura within 30 days after the date of the acknowledgement of receipt by the Allied Kommandatura of a written application.

Applications are made by the *Senat*.[44] "Research establishments" are

---

[42] BK/O(49)237 and BK/O(49)238 of 7 November 1949 (*VOBl.* pp.442, 444); BK/O(51)31 of 31 May 1951 (*GVBl.* p.402): see Schröder, *ROW*, 28 (1984), p.212.
[43] *GVBl.* p.130.
[44] BK/L(58)7 of 6 March 1958: Schröder, *ROW*, 28 (1984), p.212.

defined in Article 7 as "any natural or juristic person or group of persons engaged even incidentally in scientific research". The "matters listed in the Schedule" are confined to high-speed aerodynamics (>0.7 Mach); high-speed hydrodynamics (>35 knots) or underwater hydrodynamics; and rocket, ram-jet or gas turbine propulsion, including fuels therefor, and methods of guiding projectiles.[45] To ensure compliance with Articles 1, 2 and 3 of the Order, Article 4 subjects all scientific research and scientific research establishments to such prohibitions, restrictions, safeguards, inspections and supervision (including the submission of reports) as may be ordered by the Allied Kommandatura. Articles 4 and 5 also make provision regarding the confidentiality of information regarding scientific research.

A further step for the benefit of the Berlin economy, but without prejudice to Allied reserved rights in the field of demilitarisation, was the issue of BK/O(77)4 of 27 April 1977,[46] by which the Allied Kommandatura authorised the extension to Berlin of the Convention for the Establishment of a European Space Agency. This authorisation was expressly given in order that Berlin scientific research institutions and commercial enterprises concerned with space research and technology might benefit from and participate in the co-operation for peaceful purposes envisaged in the Convention. The BK/O provides that the extension of the Convention does not affect Allied rights and responsibilities and Allied legislation.

CIVIL AVIATION

The reservation by the Allied authorities of their rights in respect of civil aviation was placed, in the Declaration on Berlin of 5 May 1955, in the context of disarmament and demilitarisation. Article I and Schedule A, Group V(a), of Law No. 43 prohibit the manufacture, import, export, transport and storage of:

> Aircraft of all types, heavier or lighter than air, with or without means of propulsion, including kites, captive balloons, gliders, and model aircraft, and all auxiliary equipment, including aircraft engines and component parts, accessories, and spare parts specifically designed for aircraft use.

Although some very limited exceptions have been permitted, pursuant to Article V of the Law, for non-military components,

---

[45] The Schedule originally included experiments in the nuclear field, but on the introduction of Berlin atomic legislation this was repealed by BK/O(58)7 of 1 July 1958 (*GVBl.* p.605).
[46] *GVBl.* p.888.

ultra-light aircraft and such items as model aircraft, kites and balloons,[47] the basic prohibition of aircraft in Law No. 43 inhibits the presence of full-size German aircraft, whether military or civil, in Berlin. In addition, the four Powers retain exclusive rights and responsibilities with respect to the Berlin air corridors and the Berlin Control Zone, and all non-Allied flights require four-Power authorisation in the Berlin Air Safety Center (pp.121–2 above). The three airfields in the Western Sectors of Berlin are under the authority of the Western Commandants, and serve as military airfields. Moreover, the three Powers retain, vis-à-vis the Federal Republic of Germany, reserved rights to regulate all air traffic to and from the Berlin air corridors,[48] and all air carriers require the prior permission of the Western Allied authorities to operate flights to Berlin.[49]

The Allied Kommandatura has had frequent occasion to legislate in the field of civil aviation. It has permitted only partial application of Federal air traffic legislation in Berlin, subject always to Allied control.[50] The same applies to the adoption in Berlin of Federal legislation relating to aircraft noise.[51] Express reservations of Allied rights and responsibilities in the field of civil aviation were made in connection with the adoption in Berlin of Federal legislation concerning protection against nuisances and the transport of dangerous materials.[52] The Allied Kommandatura has also enacted substantive rules in the interests of flight safety, dealing with such matters as building restrictions in the vicinity of airport navigational aids,[53] removal of hazards to flight safety,[54] and the flying of model aircraft, kites, balloons and hang-gliders.[55] It has recently legislated too with respect to the investigation of civil aircraft accidents in the Western Sectors of Berlin.[56] And European Community legislation in the field of civil aviation does not apply in Berlin.[57]

---

[47] For example, BK/O(84)9 of 9 October 1984 (*GVBl.* p.1561), which regulates the flying of model aircraft, kites, balloons and non-motorised hang-gliders.
[48] See p.115 above.
[49] See p.115 above.
[50] BK/O(82)6 of 30 June 1982 (*GVBl.* p.1203).
[51] BK/O(71)6 of 7 October 1971 (*GVBl.* p.1912), and paragraph 4 of BK/O(82)6 of 30 June 1982 (*GVBl.* p.1203).
[52] BK/O(75)1 of 8 January 1975 (*GVBl.* p.192) and BK/O(75)11 of 7 August 1975 (*GVBl.* p.2140).
[53] BK/O(80)8 of 30 May 1980 (*GVBl.* p.1202), and BK/O(82)1 of 29 January 1982 (*GVBl.* p.471).
[54] BK/O(79)8 of 17 July 1979 (*GVBl.* p.1200) and BK/O(86)12 of 28 November 1986 (*GVBl.* p.2040).
[55] BK/O(84)9 of 9 October 1984 (*GVBl.* p.1561).
[56] BK/O(86) 6 of 29 August 1986 (*GVBl.* p.1455).
[57] BK/O(83)4 of 31 May 1983 (*GVBl.* p.916); BK/O(83)6 of 12 October 1983 (*GVBl.* p.1360): see p.219 above.

CHAPTER 23

SECURITY AND PUBLIC ORDER

FOR Berlin, status and security are inseparable. The maintenance of the status of Berlin, and through it the continued freedom and democratic way of life enjoyed in the Western Sectors, depend ultimately on security. Responsibility for the preservation of security in and in respect of the Western Sectors rests with the Western Allied authorities. It is indispensable that the Allied authorities retain the rights and powers to enable them to fulfil that responsibility. Status and security are together at the heart of Allied rights and responsibilities in respect of Berlin.

This is most clearly demonstrated in the arrangements made in connection with the conclusion of the Bonn/Paris Conventions of 1952/54. In a joint declaration of 3 October 1954, the Governments of the United States, the United Kingdom and France stated that:

> The security and welfare of Berlin and the maintenance of the position of the Three Powers there are regarded by the Three Powers as essential elements of the peace of the free world in the present international situation. Accordingly, they will maintain armed forces within the territory of Berlin as long as their responsibilities require it. They therefore reaffirm that they will treat any attack against Berlin from any quarter as an attack upon their forces and themselves.[1]

In the Declaration on Berlin of 5 May 1955 (p.332 below) which came into effect on the same day as the Bonn/Paris Conventions, the Allied Kommandatura made appropriate reservations of rights. Article II provides as follows:

> The Allied authorities retain the right to take, if they deem it necessary, such measures as may be required to fulfil their international obligations, to ensure public order and to maintain the status and security of Berlin and its economy, trade and communications.

In addition to this general reservation, the Declaration contains specific reservations touching matters of security. Article III includes the following:

> The Allied authorities will normally exercise powers only in the following fields:
>
> (a) Security, interests and immunities of the Allied Forces, including their representatives, dependents and non-German employees . . .

---

[1] *Selected Documents* I, p.189; *US Documents*, p.424; Heidelmeyer, p.137; on the Allied security guarantee for Berlin see pp.41–2 above.

(e) Authority over the Berlin police to the extent necessary to ensure the security of Berlin.[2]

Article VIII contains the following provision of general application, but which is particularly relevant to security:

> In order to enable them to fulfil their obligations under this Declaration, the Allied authorities shall have the right to request and obtain such information and statistics as they deem necessary.

The Western Allied security guarantee for Berlin remains undiminished. The Declaration on Berlin of 5 May 1955 remains in effect. It is against this background, and in the light of these fundamental statements of policy, that the exercise of Allied rights and responsibilities in the fields of security and public order have to be considered.

EXECUTIVE MEASURES

In practice, most of the measures taken by the Allied authorities in the field of security and public order are executive acts. There is also some important Allied legislation, which will be considered later in this chapter, and Allied executive action is sometimes taken in implementation of such legislation. But measures in the security field are more often taken simply in exercise of the joint supreme authority assumed in 1945 and of the rights reserved in the Declaration on Berlin of 5 May 1955. If they are to be able to protect Berlin's security, the Allied forces stationed there must train regularly and remain at a high state of readiness, as is the case with all armed forces. To this end frequent decisions are taken regarding such matters as military exercises, border patrols, guarding of installations, and the construction and use of training facilities. Decisions must also be taken in the interests of the welfare, fitness and morale of the forces and their dependents, including such matters as their housing, medical care and education. The difficulty of reconciling such security interests with the private interests and environmental concerns of members of the public is illustrated by the fact that it is in this field in particular that attempts have been made to challenge Allied measures in the national courts of the Allied Powers. The decision to build new housing for American troops in the area of Düppel forest led in 1979 to legal action in the United States courts.[3] The decision to construct a new shooting

---

[2] Article III (d) of the Declaration states that occupation costs will be fixed at the lowest level consistent with maintaining the security of Berlin and of the Allied forces located there: see p.61 above.
[3] *Dostal v Haig*: 652 F.2d.173 (1981); *US Digest* 1979, pp.787–90.

range at Gatow airfield led in 1983 to local inhabitants seeking an injunction in the British courts to stop its construction and use.[4] In each case the national courts declined jurisdiction.[5]

COMPENSATION

Allied legislation makes detailed provision with respect to compensation in the case of loss or damage, suffered in Berlin by natural or juridical persons, caused by the occupation authorities and forces. These provisions are contained in the three parallel Sector Ordinances No. 508 of 21 May 1951, as amended, and in various provisions issued in implementation thereof.[6] Subject to certain specific exceptions, Article 3 sets out the general principle that:

> The act or omission must be such as would have given the person who suffered the loss or damage a right according to the provisions of German Law to recover compensation from the person who committed the act or omission or who was responsible for it.

Detailed provision is made as regards valuation and assessment of compensation, time limits and questions of procedure. The machinery for determining whether compensation is to be awarded and for assessing the amount of compensation is established in the implementing Regulations, which vary somewhat as between the three Western Powers. The basic provisions are, however, similar in granting competence to Berlin administrative authorities and courts. The decision-making authority is the Berlin Occupation Costs Office (*Landesamt für Besatzungslasten, Berlin*), against whose decisions there is a right of appeal to the Senator for Finance. Decisions on compensation may be challenged in the German courts in the same manner as other administrative acts of German authorities. The German courts and authorities are expressly authorised to exercise jurisdiction in such cases notwithstanding

---

[4] *Trawnik v Lennox* [1985] 1 W.L.R. 532; see also *R v Secretary of State for Foreign and Commonwealth Affairs, ex p. Trawnik* (*The Times* of 21 February 1986), discussed in Mann, *Foreign Affairs in English Courts* (1986), pp.19, 50.

[5] The French *Conseil d'État* has likewise declined jurisdiction in a series of cases involving the French occupation authorities in Germany, holding that those authorities exercised powers attributable to the government of Germany and not authority of the French State: p.55 above and Heidelmeyer, *ZaöRV*, 46 (1986), pp.519–38. See also, Geulen, *NJW*, 38 (1985), pp.1055–7; Schröder, *RuP*, 21 (1985), pp.24–31; Randelzhofer, *Die Verwaltung*, 19 (1986), pp.9–38.

[6] Ordinance No. 508 (*AK Gazette*, p.257), as amended by Ordinances No. 518 (*AK Gazette*, p.534) and No. 520 (*AK Gazette*, p.578) of the British, French and United States Sectors. These are implemented by Regulation No. 1-A of 1 April 1952 (*AK Gazette*, p.485) of the British, French and United States Sectors; British Sector Regulation No. 4 of 14 February 1955 (*AK Gazette*, p.1022); French Sector *Ordonnance* of 21 July 1955 (*AK Gazette*, p.1071); United States Sector Regulation No. 1 of 19 November 1954 (*AK Gazette*, p.1002).

Article 2(b) of Allied Kommandatura Law No. 7.[7] Successful claims are paid out of the occupation costs budget. Whilst claims are determined in accordance with the Ordinances and implementing Regulations (applying rules of German law where they so provide), Article 1 of Ordinance No. 508 allows for "such modifications with respect to particular applications or classes of applications as may be necessary for equity or the accomplishment of the basic purposes of the Occupation".

In addition to these general provisions, compensation is specifically provided for in other Allied legislation dealing with particular measures affecting individuals. For example, BK/O(80)8 of 30 May 1980,[8] as amended by BK/O(82)1 of 29 January 1982,[9] imposes in the interests of flight safety certain building restrictions around airport navigational aids in the Western Sectors. Building projects in certain defined areas require the prior approval of the Allied Kommandatura, which may also order the removal of buildings or other structures in those areas. Paragraph 4 of the BK/O provides that the provisions of Article 19 of the Federal Air Traffic Law[10] shall apply in matters of compensation *mutatis mutandis*. Similarly, BK/O(79)8 of 17 July 1979[11] required trees or bushes which constituted hazards to flight safety in the area of the approach flight paths to Gatow airfield to be removed or lopped. Paragraph 2(v) of the BK/O provided that compensation was payable in respect of private properties in accordance with the provisions of Article 19 of the Federal Air Traffic Law.

Allied legislation in the field of employment also provides for compensation awards to individuals consistent with German law. The Allied authorities and forces employ a considerable number of locally-engaged civilian personnel. BK/O(80)13 of 30 December 1980[12] regulates such employment in detail. By virtue of this BK/O the provisions of German labour and social law are made applicable in principle to the employment of civilian personnel, subject to certain reservations. These reservations, which are maintained chiefly in the interests of security, include the right of the Allied authorities to refuse to employ any particular individual, and to refuse to re-employ a person after having dismissed him. A Commandant may also prevent reasons for dismissal being

[7] *AK Gazette*, p.11. Article 2(b) of Allied Kommandatura Law No. 7 prohibits German courts from exercising jurisdiction in any civil case in which the issues to be decided include any matter arising out of or in the course of performance of duties or services with the Allied Forces: p.65 above.
[8] *GVBl.* p.1202.
[9] *GVBl.* p.471.
[10] *Luftverkehrsgesetz*: *BGBl.* I, p.61.
[11] *GVBl.* p.1200; see now BK/O(86)12 of 28 November 1986: *GVBl.* p.2040.
[12] *GVBl.* (1981), p.230.

discussed in court if he certifies that the circumstances relating to the dismissal touch on security matters which, in the interest of the Allies, should not be disclosed. The BK/O does however authorise the German courts to exercise jurisdiction in disputes arising from employment or from social insurance. Accordingly, subject to the special reservations and rules set out in the BK/O, employment disputes are dealt with in the German courts according to German law. *Land* Berlin acts as the party to the proceedings in place of the Allied employing authority concerned. Compensation is paid out of the occupation costs budget.

LEGISLATION CONTROLLING CERTAIN ACTIVITIES

Allied legislation in force in Berlin controls or regulates various types of activity in the interests of maintaining public order or security. Of particular importance to the security of the Allied authorities and forces is Ordinance No. 511 of 15 October 1951,[13] which creates a number of offences against the interests of the Occupation. These include offences specifically directed against the security or interests of the Allied forces, such as espionage, sabotage, armed attack and assault on members of the forces. There are also more general public order offences, such as incitement to or participation in rioting or public disorder. The Ordinance also contains provisions of general significance for other legislation and measures of the Western Allied authorities. For example, Article 3(13) creates the offences of "violation of any legislation of the Occupation Authorities or of any regulation issued under such legislation where no penalty is provided for such violations", and "disobedience of any directive or order issued by the Occupation Authorities or Occupation Forces". Article 5 contains provisions of general application to offences under Allied legislation. Article 6 specifies which provisions of the Ordinance are applicable to the Allied forces themselves as well as to other persons.

Another important area concerns Nazi and neo-Nazi activities. In the immediate post-war period the four Powers took sweeping measures to eliminate all vestiges of Nazism in Germany.[14] In accordance with Control Council Proclamation No. 2 of 20 September 1945[15] and Control Council Law No. 2 of 10 October

---

[13] Ordinance No. 511 (*AK Gazette*, p.408), as amended by Ordinance No. 534 (*AK Gazette*, p.1192) of the British, French and US Sectors and by BK/O(85)6 of 23 August 1985 (*GVBl.* p.1932): Schröder, *ROW*, 29 (1985), pp.187, 189.

[14] Krumholz, *Berlin ABC* (2nd ed.), pp.200–3; Schröder, *ROW*, 29 (1985), pp.183–4; and for the measures already taken in the period of belligerent occupation before the unconditional surrender, see Bathurst and Simpson, *Germany and the North Atlantic Community*, pp.3–17.

[15] *CC Gazette*, p.8.

1945,[16] the Nazi Party (NSDAP) and all Nazi organisations were dissolved and they remain prohibited organisations. Article 2(3) of Ordinance No. 511 discussed above creates the offence of "acts or conduct in aid or support of any person, group or government hostile to the interests of the Allied Forces, or intended to accomplish the reconstitution in any form whatsoever of any prohibited organisation". Allied Kommandatura Law No. 5 of 25 February 1950[17] prohibits *inter alia* the wearing, manufacture, sale, or purchase of any uniform or decoration of the NSDAP or of any affiliated or subordinate organisation, or any uniform resembling such a uniform. Further outward manifestations of Nazism also remain prohibited, such as propaganda. In addition to the provisions of German criminal law in this field, Article VII of Control Council Law No. 8 of 30 November 1945[18] prohibits "any propaganda or agitation, whether conducted in writing or orally or by any other method, which is aimed at keeping alive, reviving or promoting the military or Nazi spirit and institutions, or to glorify war".

Allied legislation has limited, but not altogether prohibited, the activities in Berlin of the *Nationaldemokratische Partei Deutschlands* (NPD) and its affiliated organisations. The Allied Kommandatura has for many years imposed temporary restrictions on various NPD activities. NPD participation in local Berlin elections, and NPD public activities in the period prior to elections, have frequently been prohibited.[19] The Allied Kommandatura, expressly in exercise of its responsibilities for the maintenance of public order, has also issued several BK/Os prohibiting the holding in Berlin of NPD party congresses or public meetings, as well as the public display or dissemination of NPD propaganda and similar material. These are limited in time, the practice in recent years being that the BK/O provides for its own expiry after seven months.[20]

For wider reasons of maintaining public order and security, each Sector Commandant occasionally legislates to restrict or require prior authorisation for certain activities, such as public assemblies or processions, in a precisely defined area within his Sector. These are known as *Bannmeile* Orders, and are usually issued in connection with a specific event at a particular place and provide for their own expiry after twenty-four hours or a few days. The only standing

[16] *CC Gazette*, p.19.
[17] *AK Gazette*, p.7.
[18] *CC Gazette*, p.33. See also Article 2(3) of Ordinance No. 511, cited above. The principal Federal German legislation is Articles 86 and 86A of the Criminal Code (*Strafgesetzbuch*), of which there are special versions in force in Berlin.
[19] For example, BK/O(84)8 of 23 August 1984 (*GVBl.* p.1278).
[20] For example, BK/O(86)2 of 29 April 1986 (*GVBl.* p.616).

Bannmeile Order is that in respect of the areas immediately surrounding the headquarters of the United States Mission and certain American military installations.[21]

Certain other activities are also controlled by Allied legislation in the general interests of security. BK/O(62)5 of 23 July 1962[22] subjects to the supervision and control of the *Senat* "any enterprise of an economical, publicity (*werbender*) or cultural nature directly or indirectly promoting the interests of a non-German state or of a German territory other than the territory of DM-West, and whose activities are capable of impairing the economical, cultural or political life of West Berlin". The *Senat* is empowered to investigate such enterprises, to decide whether they may continue their activities and under what conditions, and to decide at any time that their activities should be discontinued. In the case of a breach of a prohibition or condition imposed by the *Senat*, the activity or enterprise is to be prevented or closed by the police.

In the particular context of Berlin airports, BK/O(70)3 of 29 June 1970[23] requires the Police President in Berlin to carry out a control of the travel documents of persons who arrive by air direct from outside Germany or who depart by air from Berlin. This control is to be carried out in accordance with the legislation in force concerning passports, identification documents and aliens, without prejudice to Allied provisions and instructions. The BK/O adds that:

> Although an examination of the travel documents of persons arriving by air from other points in Germany will not ordinarily be required, the Allied Kommandatura or the Sector Commandants, each for his own Sector, may from time to time instruct that such an examination be performed in certain cases.

This BK/O is of particular relevance to Tegel Airport in the French Sector, which is the main airport for civilian use. Security and public order at Tegel Airport are a particular responsibility of the French Sector authorities, and are provided for in two French Sector Ordinances of 6 February 1979.[24]

---

[21] United States Sector Ordinance of 27 July 1972 (*AK Gazette*, p.1208), as amended by Ordinance of 2 July 1975 (*AK Gazette*, p.1212). For examples of temporary *Bannmeile* Orders, see BCO(86)1 of 29 May 1986 (*AK Gazette*, p.1263) and USCOB(86)3 of 27 June 1986 (*AK Gazette*, p.1267).

[22] *GVBl.* p.872. This BK/O has been used, for example, to close down a GDR broadcasting studio (Schröder, *ROW*, 29 (1985), p.188) and a Soviet-promoted firm called Helios-Handelszentrale: Schröder, *Die ausländischen Vertretungen in Berlin*, pp.37–8, 55, 153–4.

[23] *GVBl.* p.1138.

[24] *Ordonnance sur l'institution d'un Comité de sûreté d'aéroport à Berlin-Tegel* (*AK Gazette*, p.1228), *and Ordonnance sur la sécurité et l'ordre public sur l'aéroport de Berlin-Tegel* (*AK Gazette*, p.1230).

SUPERVISION OF THE POLICE

The relationship between the Allied authorities and the Berlin police is of fundamental importance to the maintenance of security and public order. Article III(e) of the Declaration on Berlin expressly includes among the powers the Allied authorities will normally exercise:

> Authority over the Berlin police to the extent necessary to ensure the security of Berlin.

BK/O(58)3 of 14 March 1958[25] sets out the manner in which this provision is to be interpreted . Paragraph 1 states that:

> Except as otherwise provided in this Order the police shall be subordinate to the *Senat* of Berlin in accordance with the stipulations of Article 44, Section I of the Berlin Constitution.

Other provisions of the BK/O deal with the organisation of the police, and liaison between the different branches of the police force and with the Allied authorities; prohibit members of the police force from striking; and prohibit the existence of secret police. Paragraph 3 enables the Allied Kommandatura to suspend action on the appointment of the most senior police officers. Paragraph 5 requires the approval of the Allied Kommandatura regarding the total strength of the police force and their weapons. Under paragraph 6 the Police President must report to the Allied Kommandatura "any matter which may seriously affect public order or security to a degree which would prejudice the security of the Occupation Forces". Under paragraph 8 the Allied authorities reserve the right to make all necessary inspections and to require the supply of information, reports, publications and copies of police orders. From the point of view of security, especially in a period of tension or crisis, the most important provision is paragraph 9:

> The Allied Kommandatura and Sector Commandants reserve the right to issue direct instructions to the police. The Allied Kommandatura reserves the right to assume full and direct control of the police if it considers it necessary to do so in the interests of the security of Berlin.

Most of the provisions of BK/O(58)3, and in particular paragraphs 8 and 9, are repeated in BK/O(62)9 of 24 October 1962 concerning supervision of the *Grenzaufsichtdienst* (Customs Frontier Service).[26] Members of this Service "who exercise police functions on the borders of the three Western Sectors of Berlin" are required to

---

[25] *GVBl.* p.304.
[26] *GVBl.* p.1259.

observe the directives and instructions given to the Berlin police by the Allied authorities. In the exercise of their border service Berlin customs agents are to operate under the command of the *Berliner Schutzpolizei* as the Western Allied authorities may direct. For the purpose of Western Allied supervision they are largely assimilated to the Berlin police. So too, by virtue of BK/O(61)6 of 19 May 1961,[27] are the part-time *Freiwillige Polizeireserve* (Voluntary Police Reserve) when called up for duty; and the Western Allied authorities reserve the right to order that this reserve force be called up for duty. A further force under the supervision and administration of the Police President, and thus ultimately of the Allied authorities, is the *Wachpolizei* (Auxiliary Watch Police). This force was first established in 1947, its purpose being "to guard public property and property of the Occupation authorities".[28]

In the civil field, the Berlin police are clearly vital to the preservation of public order and security. In practice, the Allied authorities enjoy the close co-operation and support of the Berlin police in the exercise of their responsibilities. At the working level, regular liaison, consultation and co-operation is maintained between the Berlin police and the Public Safety Branches of the Allied administrations. The Berlin police also work closely with the Allied military police forces, particularly in the handling and investigation of incidents or suspected offences where both members of the Allied forces and local inhabitants may be involved.

Despite the retention of wide powers, the Allied authorities do not normally intervene in the day-to-day work of the Berlin police, which is carried out under the responsibility of the *Senat* (paragraph 1 of BK/O(58)3). The Allies are involved only in so far as their responsibilities for public order and security require. For example, the fight against terrorism is of concern both to the Allies and to the local Berlin organs, who work closely together.[29] A terrorist incident on an Allied installation would, in the first place at least, be handled by the Allied authorities; and one directed specifically against Allied targets is clearly of direct concern to them.[30]

---

[27] *GVBl.* p.694.

[28] BK/O(47)277 of 30 September 1947, as amended by BK/O(48)89 of 14 June 1948 and BK/O(71)2 of 28 May 1971 (*GVBl.* p.956).

[29] The Berlin Office for the Protection of the Constitution (*Landesamt für Verfassungsschutz*) remains under Allied supervision and control.

[30] The Allied Kommandatura took special security measures in April 1986 after the bomb outrage at the La Belle Discothèque in the American Sector, in which several American soldiers were injured and two killed. In a press statement on 12 April the Kommandatura announced: "With immediate effect the Berlin authorities have been asked to remove from the Western Sectors persons identified as posing a threat to the population of Berlin. These measures are exceptional and provisional and do not affect the principle of freedom of movement throughout Berlin": *Der Tagesspiegel* of 12 and 13 April 1986.

CONTROLS ON STAY AND RESIDENCE

As the Western Allies adhere to the principle of freedom of movement within Greater Berlin, there are no controls on entry into the Western Sectors from the Soviet Sector.[31] There are, however, controls on stay and residence of non-Germans who have entered the Western Sectors. Paragraph 1 of BK/O(67)7 of 17 July 1967[32] reads:

> No alien may reside in the British, American or French Sectors of Berlin unless his residence is permitted under Allied legislation (including the present Order) or under German legislation in force in those Sectors or unless an authorisation for residence has been given by or on behalf of the Allied Control Authority, the Allied Kommandatura or the Commandants of the British, American or French Sectors of Berlin.

The latter part of this provision covers members of the Allied Forces and accredited members of Military Missions and consular posts, whose residence is authorised by the Allied authorities. The residence of other aliens is for the most part governed by German legislation in force in the Western Sectors.[33] The Western Allies have however imposed certain controls themselves, of which the following are the most significant.

Paragraph 2 of BK/O(67)7 permits nationals of certain East Bloc countries listed in the Annex to stay in the Western Sectors for up to thirty-one days provided that the stay is for scientific, technical, cultural, sports or tourist purposes or is in connection with a specific event for the promotion of international trade, and provided also that the stay is notified to the Police President in advance or immediately upon arrival in the Western Sectors.[34] The required notification must include details of name, nationality, purpose and expected duration of stay, and local address. Under paragraph 4(a) any person who disobeys these provisions, for example by staying longer than thirty-one days without further authorisation, is liable to removal from the Western Sectors. Paragraph 3 takes account of the status of the Soviet occupation authorities in Berlin. It exempts from the provisions of paragraph 2 Soviet nationals who are officials of or who are officially connected with the Soviet authorities in

---

[31] West Berlin customs controls near the crossing points are not immigration controls.

[32] *GVBl.* p.1028.

[33] The principal German legislation is the Aliens Law (*Ausländergesetz*) of 28 April 1965 (*BGBl.* I, p.353), the Law on Entry and Stay of Nationals of European Community Member States (*Gesetz über Einreise und Aufenthalt von Staatsangehörigen der Mitgliedstaaten der Europäischen Gemeinschaft*) of 31 January 1980 (*BGBl.* I, p.113), and the Asylum Law (*Gesetz über das Asylverfahren*) of 16 July 1982 (*BGBl.* I, p.946).

[34] The countries listed in the Annex are Albania, Bulgaria, Czechoslovakia, Hungary, Poland, Romania, Soviet Union and Yugoslavia. For the background to this BK/O, see Schröder, *Die ausländischen Vertretungen in Berlin*, pp.38–9.

Berlin, or dependents of such persons. It provides too that if such persons intend to stay in the Western Sectors, they shall notify the Commandant of the Sector in which they intend to stay. Failure to comply with this requirement would also, under paragraph 4(a), render the person concerned liable to removal from the Western Sectors. Paragraph 4 (b) contains a saving clause in the following terms:

> The powers of the Allied Kommandatura and the Commandants of the Western Sectors under Allied Kommandatura Law No. 8 and other legislation in force to terminate the stay in the Western Sectors of any person at any time are not affected by the present Order.

Under Article 3 of Allied Kommandatura Law No. 8 of 28 April 1950,[35] the Allied Kommandatura or any authority designated by it for this purpose may order any German national not ordinarily resident in Greater Berlin or any person not a German national to be expelled from Greater Berlin if, *inter alia*, his presence is "liable to endanger the maintenance of public order or the prestige or security of the Allied Forces". Pursuant to this Article, implementing Regulation No. 1 of 28 April 1950[36] established an Expulsion Board, appointed by the Allied Kommandatura, to examine and adjudicate on requests for expulsion and, where it so decides, to issue orders of expulsion. The Board is composed of the Allied Legal Advisers. Article 4 of Law No. 8 empowers each Sector Commandant to order unilaterally the expulsion from his area of control of any non-German national whose expulsion is, in his opinion, required in the interest of public order, prestige or security. Article 7 of Regulation No. 1 further empowers each Sector Commandant to order the expulsion from Greater Berlin of any of his fellow nationals (but not one who is also a German national) present in his Sector. Law No. 8 and Regulation No. 1 make further provision for powers of arrest and detention, the manner of expulsion, the procedures of the Expulsion Board, and appeals.[37] The Allies have also reserved to themselves limited rights in relation to extradition. In connection with the adoption in Berlin of the Federal Law of 23 December 1982 on International Assistance in Criminal Cases,[38] the Allied Kommandatura issued BK/O(83)2 of 28 April 1983,[39] which provides that:

---

[35] *AK Gazette*, p.18.

[36] *AK Gazette*, p.21; Article 4 of Regulation No. 1 was deleted by Regulation No. 2 of 29 August 1955: *AK Gazette*, p.1078.

[37] In practice, expulsion under Law No. 8 is infrequent, although the power has been exercised recently in the fight against terrorism: for examples of the use of this power, see Schröder, *Die ausländischen Vertretungen in Berlin*, pp.107–8, and *Der Tagesspiegel* of 26 February and 28 November 1986.

[38] *Gesetz über die internationale Rechtshilfe in Strafsachen*: BGBl. I, p.2071.

[39] *GVBl.* p.772.

Extradition or other transfer from Berlin under the Law or in pursuance of an international agreement of any national of the Occupying Powers or of any person exempted from the jurisdiction of the German courts pursuant to the provisions of Allied Kommandatura Law No. 7 shall not take place without the express consent of the appropriate Sector Commandant or of the Allied Kommandatura.

Further Allied controls are founded on four-Power agreements and decisions. As noted at pp.76–7 above, under Agreed Minute II of 3 September 1971 the assignment of personnel to the Soviet Consulate-General in the Western Sectors of Berlin is subject to agreement with the Western Allied authorities. The number of such personnel is not to exceed twenty Soviet nationals, and such personnel and their dependents may reside in the Western Sectors of Berlin upon individual authorisation.

Agreed Minute II also deals with certain Soviet commercial organisations represented in the Western Sectors of Berlin, although this matter is not referred to in the Quadripartite Agreement itself. The second paragraph of Agreed Minute II provides as follows:

> The three [Western Allied] Governments are willing to authorise an increase in Soviet commercial activities in the Western Sectors of Berlin as described below. It is understood that pertinent Allied and German legislation and regulations will apply to these activities. This authorisation will be extended indefinitely, subject to compliance with the provisions outlined herein. Adequate provision for consultation will be made. This increase will include establishment of an "Office of Soviet Foreign Trade Associations in the Western Sectors of Berlin", with commercial status, authorised to buy and sell on behalf of foreign trade associations of the Union of Soviet Socialist Republics. Soyuzpushnina, Prodintorg and Novoexport may each establish a bonded warehouse in the Western Sectors of Berlin to provide storage and display for their goods. The activities of the Intourist office in the British Sector of Berlin may be expanded to include the sale of tickets and vouchers for travel and tours in the Union of Soviet Socialist Republics and other countries. An office of Aeroflot may be established for the sale of passenger tickets and air freight services.

Agreed Minute II also provides that the assignment of personnel to permitted Soviet commercial organisations will be subject to agreement with the Western Allied authorities. The number of such personnel will not exceed twenty Soviet nationals in the Office of Soviet Foreign Trade Associations; one each in the bonded warehouses; six in the Intourist office; and five in the Aeroflot office. The personnel of permitted Soviet commercial organisations and their dependents may reside in the Western Sectors of Berlin upon individual authorisation.

The presence of representatives of Soviet commercial organisations in the Western Sectors is founded upon the authorisation of the Western Allies. As Agreed Minute II makes clear, the continuation of this authorisation is dependent on compliance with the provisions outlined in the Agreed Minute. The permitted Soviet commercial organisations are neither diplomatic missions nor consular posts; nor do they form part of the Soviet Embassy to the GDR or the Soviet Consulate-General in the Western Sectors. The Consulate-General is dealt with specifically and separately from the Soviet commercial organisations in Agreed Minute II. The Soviet commercial organisations represented in the Western Sectors have no special status, and neither they nor their personnel enjoy special privileges and immunities.

Western Allied offices in the Western Sectors of Berlin are the issuing authorities for residence permits and travel documents for certain non-German nationals. The Allied Travel Office[40] is the competent authority for issuing residence permits to employees of the permitted Soviet commercial organisations, to officially sponsored Soviet visitors such as lecturers, scientists and artists, and to private Soviet citizens, as well as to non-accredited staff of the Czechoslovak, Polish, and Yugoslav Military Missions,[41] and to dependents of such persons. The Allied Travel Office also issues passport extensions to the very few stateless persons residing in Berlin who still use passports originally issued by the Allied Travel Office. The Inter-Zonal Facilities Bureau, an Allied office co-located with the Allied Travel Office, is the issuing authority for passes for travel to or through the Federal Republic of Germany by members of the Soviet forces and by accredited members of the Czechoslovak, Polish and Yugoslav Military Missions, and dependents of such persons. The Bureau may also issue such passes to members of the Soviet Embassy in East Berlin, though applications have been rare in recent years.

---

[40] Krumholz, *Berlin ABC* (2nd ed.), p.28; *BPIL* 1964, p.27.

[41] Accredited members of Military Missions and their dependents require no residence permit, as the Allied Control Authority identity card issued to them is sufficient evidence of their right to stay in Berlin. This card also refers to the holder's right of free movement within Berlin, expressly accorded by four–Power decision (CORC/P(45)86, para 5): see Schröder, *Die ausländischen Vertretungen in Berlin*, pp.76, 126–8; and p.73 above.

PART SEVEN

THE SOVIET SECTOR OF BERLIN

The Soviet or Eastern Sector of Berlin remains part of the special Berlin area established by the London Protocol of 12 September 1944. The quadripartite status of Berlin applies to the whole of this area, that is, to the Soviet Sector as well as to the three Western Sectors. The Soviet Sector is not part of the territory of the GDR, nor is it the capital city of the GDR. It is, however, the place where most of the organs of government of the GDR are located, and may therefore be described as the seat of government of the GDR. The *Senat* and House of Representatives of Berlin are the lawful municipal authorities for the whole of Berlin; the municipal authorities in the Soviet Sector are unlawfully constituted. The Soviet Union has by unilateral act purported to withdraw the Soviet Sector from the area under quadripartite control, and permits widespread violation there of quadripartite agreements and decisions, for example as regards demilitarisation.

After noting certain historical developments in the Soviet Sector, in particular the formal reduction of Soviet authority there, Chapter 24 deals in turn with the following matters: the claim that the Sector is part of the territory of the GDR and its capital city, the position of the local German authorities set up in the Sector, participation of the Sector in the GDR *Volkskammer*, the law applied there, external representation, and demilitarisation.

Other aspects have already been considered in previous Chapters: the Soviet Embassy (Chapter 4), the status of Allied authorities and forces (Chapter 4), boundaries (Chapter 6), the air régime (Chapter 8), and freedom of movement and flag tours (Chapter 20).

CHAPTER 24

THE SOVIET SECTOR OF BERLIN

D EVELOPMENTS in the Soviet Sector have, on the surface, been similar to those in the Western Sectors, though the reduction of Soviet authority and the "incorporation" into the GDR were both more far-reaching, at least in appearance, and less clear than corresponding developments in the Western Sectors. But any tendency to view developments as parallel in legal terms overlooks an important and fundamental distinction. In the Western Sectors, the Western Allies have respected the quadripartite status of Berlin, applying so far as possible (given limited Soviet participation) all relevant quadripartite agreements, decisions and practices. They have maintained their supreme authority and hence their ability to exercise quadripartite rights and responsibilities and they have not allowed the Western Sectors to become part of the Federal Republic of Germany or to be governed by it. The local German authorities in the Western Sectors are those established under the Constitution of Berlin of 1950, which was adopted pursuant to the quadripartite Temporary Constitution of 1946 and approved by the Allied Kommandatura. In the Soviet Sector, by contrast, the Soviet Union has purported to surrender supreme authority to the GDR and has unilaterally permitted the establishment of unconstitutional local authorities.[1]

The Soviet zonal authorities had their headquarters at Karlshorst (Lichtenberg) in the Soviet Sector of Berlin whereas the British, French and United States headquarters were in the zones themselves. The Soviet Commandant Berlin also had his headquarters at Karlshorst. In addition, the German authorities for the Soviet zone tended to be based in the Soviet Sector. The geographical position of Berlin, entirely surrounded by the Soviet zone, was itself conducive to a close integration of the Soviet Sector into the Soviet zone; the unclear position that arose no doubt suited Soviet policy objectives.

Following the establishment of the GDR in 1949 the Soviet authorities transferred to the GDR Government the administrative functions that had previously been exercised by the Soviet Military Administration in Germany. The Military Administration was

---

[1] Brunn, *Die rechtliche, politische und wirtschaftliche Lage des Berliner Sowjetsektors* (1955); Mampel, *Der Sowjetsektor von Berlin* (1963); Legien, in: *Berlin Sowjetsektor* (1965), pp.41–53; Mahncke, *Berlin im geteilten Deutschland*, pp.49–54; Jung, *ROW*, 19 (1975), pp.217–23; Zivier, *ROW*, 19 (1975), pp.223–5; Zivier, pp.63–73; Mahnke, *ROW*, 23 (1979), pp.185–93; Wettig, *Die Statusprobleme Ost-Berlins 1949–1980*; Mampel, in: *Zehn Jahre Berlin-Abkommen 1971–1981*, pp.121–46.

dissolved, and a Soviet Control Commission established to control the implementation of the Potsdam Agreement and other joint decisions of the four Powers with respect to Germany. Thus, administrative functions were transferred to the "German democratic authorities in Berlin"; and the representative of the Soviet Control Commission in Berlin, on behalf of the Commission, was to conduct the necessary relations with the Western occupation authorities.[2] At the same time, there continued to be a Soviet Commandant Berlin, with whom the Western Commandants continued to deal. Soviet intervention during the uprising in East Berlin in June 1953 showed that the Soviet occupation authorities in reality retained very extensive powers.[3] In August 1962 the post of Soviet Commandant was abolished (p.62 above); in a statement of 23 August 1962 the three Western Allies responded as follows:

> They will continue to consider the Soviet officials responsible for carrying out their obligations regarding the Soviet sector of Berlin. Moreover, the Soviet announcement can in no way affect the unity of Berlin as a whole ... Berlin remains a single city. No unilateral action by the Soviet Government can change this.[4]

The Soviet Union thus permitted the gradual incorporation of the Soviet Sector into the GDR. A number of reminders of its special status were removed from the mid-1970s. The *Verordnungsblatt für Gross-Berlin* ceased publication in 1976 (p.305 below); a visa requirement for foreign visitors on day visits was introduced with effect from 1 January 1977; and the fixed control posts on the boundary between the Sector and the GDR were replaced at the same time by mobile police controls. The most serious development was the direct election of the Soviet Sector's representation to the GDR *Volkskammer* in June 1981.

Such unilateral acts could not affect the rights of the United Kingdom, France and the United States of America throughout Greater Berlin. The Western Allies protested to the Soviet Union on many occasions, and set out their position in the United Nations and elsewhere. For example, in a letter of 14 April 1975 to the Secretary-General of the United Nations they reaffirmed that:

> 1. The quadripartite status of greater Berlin stems from the original rights and responsibilities of the Four Powers. Quadripartite wartime and post-war agreements and decisions based on these rights and

---

[2] Statement by General Chuikov on the establishment of the Soviet Control Commission, 11 November 1949: Heidelmeyer, p.161.
[3] Order of the Soviet Commandant of 17 June 1953 declaring a state of emergency in East Berlin: *Neues Deutschland*, 18 June 1953. A considerable number of people were summarily executed on the order of the Soviet Commandant.
[4] For the full text of this statement, see *Selected Documents* II, p.60.

responsibilities stipulated that greater Berlin was to be a special area under the joint authority of the Four Powers entirely distinct from the Soviet zone of occupation in Germany.

2. Any change in the status of greater Berlin as reflected in these agreements and decisions would require the agreement of all Four Powers. No such agreement altering the status of Berlin or providing for a special status for any of its sectors has ever been concluded. No unilateral steps taken by the Soviet Union in violation of the quadripartite agreements and decisions relating to greater Berlin, nor the fact that the seat of government of the German Democratic Republic is currently located in the Eastern sector of the city, can imply that the quadripartite rights and responsibilities relating to the Eastern sector are in any way affected. In fact, the Four Powers continue to exercise their quadripartite rights and responsibilities in all four sectors of the city.[5]

The London Declaration on Berlin of 9 May 1977[6] likewise reaffirmed that the status of the special Berlin area could not be modified unilaterally.

THE CLAIM THAT THE SOVIET SECTOR IS PART OF THE GDR

The GDR considers that the Soviet Sector of Berlin is part of its territory and indeed its capital. It frequently refers to East Berlin as *Berlin, Hauptstadt der DDR* (Berlin, capital of the GDR). It has even been asserted that the whole of Berlin lies on its territory. These claims are rejected by the Western Allies.[7] The Soviet Union supports the GDR position,[8] as do other East bloc countries, and now takes the position that only the Western Sectors continue to have an occupation status. But the Soviet Union accepts that the three Powers have a special position in the Eastern Sector, such as the right to conduct flag tours and otherwise visit the Sector.

Despite the clear language of the London Protocol, the Soviet Union claimed as early as 1947 that Greater Berlin was part of the Soviet zone of occupation, a claim repeated on various occasions and always firmly rebutted by the Western Allies (see p.35 above). Since the late 1950s, however, Soviet claims have been chiefly confined to stating that East Berlin is no longer subject to an occupation status. For example, the Soviet representative refused to discuss East Berlin at the Geneva Conference of 1959.[9] The

---

[5] UN Doc A/10078 and Corr. 1 (*US Documents*, p.1277). This statement has been recalled on many occasions: *BYIL*, 53 (1982), p.441; *BYIL*, 55 (1984), p.535. See also BK/O(75)2 of 28 January 1975 (*GVBl.* p.708); BK/O(75)6 of 25 April 1975 (*GVBl.* p.1152); and the Allied statements of 11 January 1977, *Das Vierseitige Abkommen*, p.309.
[6] *US Documents*, p.1309.
[7] See the Allied letter cited above. "We do not accept ... the claim that ... the Eastern Sector ... is the capital or part of the territory of the GDR": *US Digest* 1974, p.246.
[8] Soviet note of 6 January 1958: Heidelmeyer *Dokumente*, p.184.
[9] Heidelmeyer, p.260.

fundamental difference of view over the Eastern Sector between the Soviet Union and the Western Allies was a major obstacle during the negotiation of the Quadripartite Agreement of 3 September 1971. The Western position is that, while the particular provisions set out in Part II of the Agreement relate expressly to the Western Sectors of Berlin, the remaining provisions, and in particular the general provisions in Part I, concern the whole of the special Berlin area, that is, all four Sectors of the city. The text of the Quadripartite Agreement is fully consistent with the Western position, though the Soviet Union claims that it supports its own position.

The GDR Constitution of 7 October 1949 provided that Germany was an indivisible democratic republic and that the capital of the Republic was Berlin.[10] GDR Laws often referred to Berlin as "the capital of Germany". The Constitution of 8 April 1968 provided that the capital of the German Democratic Republic was Berlin,[11] and this provision remains unchanged in the 1974 revision.[12] It appears that neither Constitution was formally brought into force in the Soviet Sector. Nevertheless, East Berlin has in practice acted as the seat of government of the GDR, and the GDR Government, supported by the Soviet Union, makes strenuous efforts to assert and project the claim that it is the capital. This claim may carry an implication that (East) Berlin is part of the territory of the GDR.[13] Neither the three Powers, the Federal Republic nor the *Senat* accept that the Soviet Sector is the capital of the GDR. They acknowledge that many of the organs of government of the GDR are situated in the Soviet Sector, and that this Sector may therefore be regarded as the GDR "seat of government". This is not inconsistent with their legal position as to the status of the Soviet Sector. Even before the establishment of the GDR the Soviet Sector contained the central administration and was thus the "seat of government" of the Soviet zone of occupation in Germany, although not forming part of that zone.

As the Soviet Sector is the seat of government of the GDR, and as in particular the GDR Foreign Ministry is located there, embassies to the GDR are also situated in the Sector. On this basis, and not on

---

[10] *US Documents*, p.278; Heidelmeyer, p.158; von Münch, *Dokumente des geteilten Deutschland*, Vol. I, p.301.
[11] *Selected Documents* II, p.178; von Münch, *Dokumente des geteilten Deutschland*, Vol. I, p.525.
[12] von Münch, *Dokumente des geteilten Deutschland*, Vol. II, p.463. For parallel texts of the 1968 and 1974 versions of the GDR Constitution, see *DA*, 7 (1974), p.1188.
[13] Riklin (p.159) points out that the Allies did not originally object specifically to the description of Berlin as "capital". In response, Zivier (p.73) suggests that international law gives no particular relevance to the word "capital"; see also Silagi, in: *Zehn Jahre Berlin-Abkommen 1971–1981*, pp.115–17.

the basis of East Berlin purporting to be the "capital" of the GDR, the three Western Allies opened embassies in East Berlin on establishing diplomatic relations with the GDR, following the conclusion of the Quadripartite Agreement of 3 September 1971 and the Basis of Relations Treaty of 21 December 1972 between the Federal Republic of Germany and the GDR. These embassies are carefully described as embassies "to the GDR" (*bei der DDR*), rather than "in the GDR" (*in der DDR*). The position was made clear by the British Government at the time of the negotiations concerning the establishment of diplomatic relations with the GDR. In answer to a Parliamentary Question on 29 January 1973, the Minister of State for Foreign and Commonwealth Affairs said:

> Our Embassy when it is opened will be in East Berlin, which is the seat of Government of the GDR, but this will in no way affect the special legal status of the Berlin area.[14]

In practice the GDR applies the provisions of the Vienna Convention on Diplomatic Relations to embassies situated in East Berlin, and to members of those embassies whilst in East Berlin. In a press statement of 9 February 1973, the British and GDR Governments announced that they had decided to establish diplomatic relations and exchange ambassadors, and that:

> The Governments of the two States are agreed that the provisions of the Vienna Convention on Diplomatic Relations of 18 April 1961 shall apply to the diplomatic relations between the United Kingdom of Great Britain and Northern Ireland and the GDR.[15]

Since the Federal Republic of Germany does not recognise the GDR as a foreign State they do not have diplomatic relations with each other. Instead, they exchange Permanent Representations at each other's seat of government, and indeed the Permanent Representation of the Federal Republic of Germany to the GDR (*Ständige Vertretung der Bundesrepublik Deutschland bei der DDR*) is one of the largest missions in the Soviet Sector. It is not a diplomatic mission, and its head is not an ambassador; this reflects the special nature of relations between the Federal Republic of Germany and the GDR (two States within Germany, which itself continues to exist as a State), as distinct from that of normal inter-State relations. The Permanent Representation was established in accordance with Article 8 of the Basis of Relations Treaty, which provides that the Federal Republic of Germany and the GDR will exchange Permanent Representations, which "will be established at the

---

[14] *Selected Documents* II, p.266. For a similar US statement, see *US Documents*, p.1274. See also Catudal, *A Balance Sheet of the Quadripartite Agreement on Berlin*, pp.39–40.
[15] *Selected Documents* II, p.268. See also *US Documents*, pp.1273–6.

respective seat of government". This careful language avoids prejudicing the Western legal position on the status of Berlin, and in particular of the Soviet Sector.[16]

LOCAL GERMAN AUTHORITIES

Under the 1946 Temporary Constitution of Berlin (p.69 above) the local German authorities of Greater Berlin consisted of a *Magistrat* and City Assembly (*Stadtverordnetenversammlung*). They were based at the Berlin town hall in the Soviet Sector (a redbrick building known as the *Rote Rathaus*). However, following the Soviet withdrawal from the Allied Kommandatura and attempts to disrupt the work of the constitutional organs, they moved to the Western Sectors, as they were fully entitled to do. Thereupon, an "extraordinary City Assembly", for which there was no legal basis, met in the Soviet Sector on 30 November 1948 and purported to declare the constitutional *Magistrat* of Berlin to be removed from office and to elect a "provisional *Magistrat*". The new *Magistrat* was recognised by the Soviet Commandant on 2 December 1948 as the only legitimate administrative body for the city;[17] in practice its activities were limited to the Soviet Sector. It acted as though the 1946 Constitution did not exist, and – since there was no City Assembly for the Soviet Sector – itself functioned as a legislative and executive body.

In 1950 the illegal *Magistrat* sought to place itself on a more regular footing by adopting rules of procedure[18] and a statute.[19] In January 1953, it brought the local administration of the Soviet Sector into line with the highly centralised system of government in the GDR.[20] People's Representations (*Volksvertretungen*) were established for Greater Berlin (in practice for the Soviet Sector) and for the districts (*Bezirke*). In January 1957, in a further major move to incorporate the Soviet Sector into the GDR, the People's Representations were subordinated to the GDR People's Chamber

[16] The Federal Republic's Permanent Representation is formally responsible to the Federal Chancellery in Bonn, rather than the Federal Foreign Office or Inner-German Ministry (which in practice draw up many of the instructions). In East Berlin it deals with the GDR Ministry for Foreign Affairs. The GDR Representation in Bonn deals with the Federal Chancellery. For the privileges and immunities of the Permanent Representations, see pp.78–9 above. See also Zündorf, pp.260–6; Blumenwitz, *Die Errichtung Ständiger Vertretungen im Lichte des Staats- und Völkerrechts* (1975); Ress, *Die Rechtslage Deutschlands nach dem Grundlagenvertrag vom 21. Dezember 1972*, pp.272–97.

[17] *VOBl.* p.435; Heidelmeyer, pp.76, 77; Mampel, *Der Sowjetsektor von Berlin*, pp.67–70.

[18] *Geschäftsordnung* of 29 March 1950 (*VOBl.* I, p.69); Heidelmeyer *Dokumente*, p.196; Mampel, *Der Sowjetsektor von Berlin*, pp.74–5.

[19] *Hauptsatzung* of 8 June 1950 (*VOBl.* I, p.145); Heidelmeyer *Dokumente*, p.197; Mampel, *Der Sowjetsektor von Berlin*, pp.76–8.

[20] Mampel, *Der Sowjetsektor von Berlin*, p.78; Heidelmeyer *Dokumente*, pp.199, 201.

(*Volkskammer*) and the *Magistrat* to the GDR Council of Ministers (*Ministerrat*).[21] The Berlin People's Representations were once again known as the City Assembly (*Stadtverordnetenversammlung*) and District Assemblies (*Stadtbezirksversammlungen*). The *Magistrat*, headed by an *Oberbürgermeister*, the City Assembly and the District Assemblies remain the local German authorities in the Soviet Sector.

The local German authorities in the Soviet Sector are not regarded by the Western side as having any lawful basis or authority, since their establishment was incompatible with the legal status of Berlin. The only Berlin constitutional provisions in force approved by the Allied Kommandatura, the highest authority for Greater Berlin, are those in the 1950 Constitution of Berlin. The only lawful local Berlin authorities are those established in accordance with that Constitution, even though their authority is limited *de facto* to the Western Sectors.

PARTICIPATION IN THE *VOLKSKAMMER*

Until 1976, the GDR Election Law distinguished between *Volkskammer* delegates (*Abgeordnete*) and the sixty-six representatives (*Vertreter*) representing East Berlin, who were not directly elected but nominated by the City Assembly.[23] In the Election Law of 24 June 1976[24] the term "representative" was dropped, but the sixty-six Berlin delegates continued not to be directly elected. It is difficult to say whether Berlin members had full voting rights, since decisions were almost invariably unanimous.[25] The Law of 28 June 1979 amending the Election Law[26] introduced a major change, the direct election of the Berlin members of the *Volkskammer*. The first direct elections were held on 14 June 1981. The 1979 Law may be seen as

[21] *Gesetz der Volksvertretung von Gross-Berlin zur Übernahme des Gesetzes über die örtlichen Organe der Staatsmacht* of 28 January 1957: Heidelmeyer *Dokumente*, p.253; Mampel, *Der Sowjetsektor von Berlin*, pp.329–44; decision of the *Volksvertretung* of 28 January 1957 on the application of the GDR *Volkskammer* Law on the Rights and Duties of the *Volkskammer* in relation to local *Volksvertretungen*: Heidelmeyer *Dokumente*, p.270. See also the *Gesetz über die Vervolkommnung und Vereinfachung der Arbeit des Staatsapparats* of 14 February 1958: Heidelmeyer *Dokumente*, p.277.
[22] See Wettig, *Die Statusprobleme Ost-Berlins*, pp.6–7; Riklin, p.161; Zivier, p.69; Mampel, *Der Sowjetsektor von Berlin*, pp.95–6. Berlin representatives in the *Länderkammer*, which was abolished in December 1958, only had advisory capacity.
[23] *GBl. DDR* I, p.743 and subsequent Election Laws.
[24] *GBl. DDR* I, pp.301, 396. From 1 November 1976 the East Berlin members of the *Volkskammer* had the same identity cards as other members: Wettig, *Die Statusprobleme Ost-Berlins*, p.33.
[25] Even in the exceptional case of the Abortion Law in the mid-seventies, where voting was not unanimous, the actual voting figures were not published.
[26] *GBl. DDR* I, p.139; *Zehn Jahre Deutschlandpolitik*, p.378. See the Tokyo statement of the Foreign Ministers of the United Kingdom, United States, France and Federal Republic of Germany: *US Documents*, p.1325. The three Allied Embassies delivered protests in Moscow on 9 and 10 July 1979: *BYIL*, 52 (1981), p.456.

a response to the introduction of direct elections to the European Parliament, though the Allied Kommandatura had not in fact permitted the Berlin members of the European Parliament to be directly elected (see pp.220–1 above). The three Powers protested through their Embassies in Moscow. In a press release dated 15 June 1981, the British Foreign and Commonwealth Office stated *inter alia* that the practice of nominating the East Berlin *Volkskammer* representatives –

> was part of the existing situation to which the Quadripartite Agreement of 3 September 1971 refers. The new procedures which the GDR has introduced in the eastern sector of Berlin treat this sector as though it were part of the territory of the GDR. This is in contradiction with the wartime and post-war agreements defining the status of the special Berlin area and accordingly also in contradiction with the Quadripartite Agreement of 3 September 1971 which applies to the whole of Berlin.[27]

The three Powers likewise protested on the occasion of the second direct elections held on 8 June 1986.[28]

THE LAW APPLIED IN THE SOVIET SECTOR[29]

Occupation law made for Germany as a whole by the Allied Control Council or for Greater Berlin by the Allied Kommandatura before the Soviet representatives walked out of those organs in 1948 applied to all four Sectors of Berlin. Since the Soviet withdrawal, Allied Control Council legislation already in force in Berlin, and Allied Kommandatura legislation, have continued to be enforced in the Western Sectors. The extent to which such occupation legislation, made for the whole of Berlin and *de jure* in force in all four Sectors, has in practice been applied and enforced in the Soviet Sector since the division of the city in 1948 has of course depended upon the will of the Soviet and German authorities exercising power *de facto* in that Sector.

Following the breakdown of effective four-Power government of Berlin in 1948, the Soviet Commandant continued for some months to issue Orders applicable in the Soviet Sector.[30] The declaration of a state of emergency in the Soviet Sector following the popular uprising of 17 June 1953 represented a major exercise

---

[27] *BYIL*, 52 (1981), p.456; *US Documents*, p.1336.
[28] Press release issued by the Foreign and Commonwealth Office on 8 June 1986, which will be published in United Kingdom Materials on International Law 1986 in *BYIL*, 56 (1986).
[29] For a detailed treatment see Mampel, *Der Sowjetsektor von Berlin*, pp.189–306.
[30] The last such Order was on 1 April 1949 (*VOBl.* p.82); see Mampel, p.73.

of Soviet occupation power. Otherwise, however, the Soviet authorities appear to have made no use of their occupation rights in the field of legislation and have transferred additional powers to local German organs in the GDR and in the Soviet Sector.

Following the division of the city in 1948, the German legislation in force in the Soviet Sector naturally diverged from that in force in the Western Sectors. The illegal *Magistrat* claimed jurisdiction over the entire city, but in practice its activity was limited to the Soviet Sector. It functioned as a legislative body, disregarding the 1946 Temporary Constitution, and continued to do so under the 1950 statute and under the reforms of January 1953 and 1957. Legislation by the *Volksvertretung* was very rare. Until September 1976, the Laws of the GDR were in general not directly valid in the Soviet Sector. They were usually made applicable in Berlin by *Magistrat* Ordinance (*Verordnung*) and published in a separate Gazette, the *Verordnungsblatt für Gross-Berlin* (after 1968 by title only). There was however no standard adoption procedure, and there were a number of exceptions to the general rule.[31]

A GDR Law of 12 September 1960 dissolved the office of President of the Republic and replaced it with a collective organ, the State Council (*Staatsrat*). While the President had had no jurisdiction in the Soviet Sector, the jurisdiction of the State Council was extended to the Sector. Thus, as an exception to the adoption procedure initially used for the application of GDR Laws in the Soviet Sector, decrees of the State Council in general applied to the Sector without any additional act by a Berlin authority.

In September 1976 the separate *Verordnungsblatt für Gross-Berlin* ceased publication. With it disappeared any remaining outward indication of a special adoption procedure for the application of GDR Laws in the Soviet Sector. The GDR newspapers *Die Wahrheit* and *Neues Deutschland* drew attention to this in January 1977, asserting that all Laws and Ordinances issued by the *Volkskammer* and the GDR Council of Ministers were valid for Berlin, and denying that Berlin had any special status. The Western Allies protested to the Soviet Union about this development on 19 and 28 January 1977, holding the Soviet authorities responsible for ensuring the maintenance of the status of Greater Berlin and for any action taken by the GDR authorities in the Soviet Sector which purported to change this status unilaterally in violation of the Quadripartite Agreement of 3 September 1971.

---

[31] Mahnke, *ROW*, 23 (1979), pp.188–9; Wettig, *Die Statusprobleme Ost-Berlins*, pp.7, 14, 32–3.

EXTERNAL REPRESENTATION

Since under international law the Soviet Sector is not part of the territory of the GDR, the question arises whether, and if so how, international agreements and arrangements concluded by the GDR extend to the Soviet Sector.[32] Treaties concluded by the Federal Republic of Germany are expressly extended to the Western Sectors in accordance with established procedures authorised by the Allied Kommandatura (Chapter 15 above). No such procedures exist for the extension to the Soviet Sector of agreements concluded by the GDR. Presumably the GDR itself, and those States which share its legal position on Berlin, consider that such agreements apply automatically in the Soviet Sector; in their eyes, the Sector is part of the territory of the GDR. For the Western Allies, and those who share their view that the Soviet Sector is not part of the territory of the GDR, treaties concluded by the GDR can only apply there if they have been extended. It is not always clear whether the other parties to treaties concluded by the GDR have accepted extension to the Soviet Sector. In the case of bilateral treaties, the other party may make a statement upon signature to the effect that it assumes that the GDR intends the treaty to apply also to the Eastern Sector of Berlin and that it agrees that the treaty should so apply.[33] Where the other party does not agree to extension (for example, because it deals with military matters), this may also be stated. The position as regards multilateral treaties is often less clear; evidence that the other parties accept extension may take various forms. For example, the United Kingdom and GDR Governments expressly agreed that the provisions of the Vienna Convention on Diplomatic Relations should apply to the diplomatic relations between the United Kingdom and the GDR.[34] It may also be clear from implementing legislation that the extension is accepted. But silence does not necessarily indicate acceptance of the extension to East Berlin.

These and other cases of *de facto* GDR representation of the Soviet Sector of Berlin internationally (for example, at the United Nations) cannot affect the quadripartite status of the whole of Berlin, and this is so even where no express statement is made.

DEMILITARISATION

Berlin's demilitarised status has for many years been grossly violated in the Soviet Sector. The GDR National People's Army

---

[32] Wengler, *Berlin in völkerrechtlichen Übereinkommen der Bundesrepublik Deutschland*, pp. 40–1; Wengler, *ROW*, 30 (1986), pp.149–54.
[33] For example, the United Kingdom made such a statement in connection with the UK-GDR Consular Convention of 4 May 1976.
[34] *Selected Documents* II, p.268; see also *US Documents*, pp.1273–4.

(*Nationale Volksarmee*) has taken part in large military parades there since 1 May 1956. The Western Allies regularly protest against such activities.[35] They had particular occasion to protest against the deployment of East German troops in 1961 to assist with building the Wall and to enforce travel restrictions illegally imposed by the East German authorities. The Western Commandants stated in a letter to the Soviet Commandant of 15 August 1961:

> In carrying out these illegal actions, military and para-military units, which were formed in violation of four-Power Agreements and whose very presence in East Berlin is illegal, turned the Soviet Sector of Berlin into an armed camp.[36]

The Western Allied authorities also protest on the occasion of particularly blatant acts by members of the *Nationale Volksarmee*.[37]

GDR military legislation has been extended to the Soviet Sector. As the Western Allies pointed out in a Note of 12 August 1960 to the Soviet Union, Control Council Law No. 43 is no longer respected in the Soviet Sector; an Ordinance on General Conditions for Delivery to and Provisioning of Armed Forces of the GDR was published in the Soviet Sector in 1959.[38] Further GDR defence and military legislation, including that relating to conscription, was adopted in the Soviet Sector on 26 January 1962.[39] These measures provoked a vigorous protest from the Western Commandants to the Soviet Commandant in a letter dated 10 February 1962, which reads in part:

> Having already flagrantly violated the provisions of agreements forbidding militarism by bringing East German military and para-military forces into the Soviet Sector, the German authorities in the Soviet Sector have now been permitted further to violate these agreements by introducing conscription. It cannot fail to be noted that there is a strong contrast between the condonation by the Soviet authorities of such further flagrant steps towards re-militarisation and its pretensions that it desires a decrease of international tensions. These actions also contrast sharply with the careful observance of

---

[35] See, for example, Western Allied protests against a para-military demonstration in January 1956 (*US Documents*, p.472) and September 1983 (*Berliner Morgenpost* of 9 September 1983); and against the 1960 May Day Parade in the Soviet Sector: *Selected Documents* I, pp.428 and 431; *US Documents*, p.705. The Western Commandants regularly protest against GDR military participation in parades in the Soviet Sector: see, for example, the British statement of 7 October 1984: *BYIL*, 55 (1984), p.537.
[36] *Selected Documents* I, p.469; *US Documents*, p.776.
[37] See, for example, the protest of 14 July 1976: Zivier, p.62.
[38] *Anordnung über die allgemeinen Bedingungen für Lieferungen und Leistungen an die bewaffneten Organe der Deutschen Demokratischen Republik* of 1 July 1959 (*GBl. DDR* II, p.221), applied by Soviet Sector *Anordnung* of 27 November 1959 (*VOBl.* I, p.877); *Selected Documents* I, p.431.
[39] Ordinance of 26 January 1962: *VOBl.* I, p.45; Heidelmeyer *Dokumente*, p.463.

quadripartite agreements in this field by the Western Allies in Berlin.[40]

The three Powers have maintained the position that the special demilitarised status applies to the whole of Berlin not only by statements[41] but also in their acts and practices in the Soviet Sector. They do not recognise the East German City Commandant.[42] Official Western visitors to East Berlin decline to take part in ceremonies attended by members of the GDR armed forces, such as are traditionally held at the Memorial (*Mahnmal*) to the Victims of Fascism and Militarism (Schinkel's *Neue Wache*) on Unter den Linden, which is permanently guarded by armed GDR soldiers. The Ambassadors of the three Powers to the GDR insist that no troops are present when they present their credentials; the traditional military salute is performed not by the *Nationale Volksarmee* but by a police detachment, the *Wachregiment Feliks Dzierzynski* of the State Security Service (*Staatssicherheitsdienst*).[43] And there are no military attachés at Western Allied Embassies in East Berlin. Although the GDR Defence Ministry no longer has its headquarters in the Soviet Sector, the presence of military attachés could nevertheless imply that the conduct in East Berlin of military business with the GDR authorities and armed forces would be permissible, which would be incompatible with the demilitarised status of Berlin. In all these matters the practice of the Western Allies is shared by the Federal Republic of Germany and other members of the North Atlantic alliance.[44]

---

[40] *Selected Documents* II, p.43. See also Letters of 4 September 1967 from the Ambassadors of the three Powers in Bonn to the Soviet Ambassador in East Berlin, drawing attention to the extension to the Soviet Sector of these and other East German "texts of an outright military nature": *Selected Documents* II, p.158.

[41] For example, *BYIL*, 55 (1984), p.527.

[42] Whose post was established in 1962 following the abolition of the post of Soviet Commandant: Heidelmeyer, p.334.

[43] Mampel, *Der Sowjetsektor von Berlin*, p.321. Felix Edmundovich Dzherzhinsky (1877 – 1926) organised the Soviet Secret Police (*Cheka*).

[44] The practice of neutral States varies, particularly in the appointment of military attachés: see Schröder, *Die ausländischen Vertretungen in Berlin*, p.89.

POSTSCRIPT

DEVELOPMENTS in Berlin since 1945 fall into three broad periods, reflecting changes in international politics on the wider stage. From 1945 to 1948 there was a period of quadripartite administration, a period of continuing co-operation among the four wartime Allies, at least on the surface. Beneath the surface there were increasing differences, especially between the Soviet Union and the three Western Allies. Following the Soviet walkout from most of the organs of quadripartite administration, the second period – from 1948 to 1971 – was essentially one of confrontation between the Soviet Union and the three Powers, and ever greater unity among the three Powers and the West Germans, including the West Berliners. In the first half of this period, until approximately 1960, Soviet pressure was directed chiefly at the Allied presence in Berlin; thereafter, having completed the division of the city but having failed to drive the Allies out, the Soviet Union sought to isolate West Berlin from the Federal Republic by attacking the ties between the two. The third period, from 1971 to the present, has been more relaxed. As has frequently been noted in NATO communiqués, the situation in and around Berlin has remained calm following the Quadripartite Agreement of 3 September 1971, and it was scarcely affected by the breakdown of *détente* in the late 1970s and early 1980s.

But the more relaxed climate in and around Berlin since 1971 does not mean that the dangers to Berlin, so evident in earlier periods, have disappeared. Soviet and GDR objectives are unlikely to have changed, though the manner of pursuing them may have. The Soviet Union did not abandon its legal position with the Quadripartite Agreement in 1971, any more than did the three Powers. On the contrary, it has continued to permit the integration of East Berlin into the GDR and to propagate the view that only West Berlin remains subject to quadripartite status. This cannot be accepted by the Western side since it would undermine the legal basis of the Allied position in Berlin. The same is true of the Soviet and GDR policy of treating West Berlin as a separate political entity. At the same time the Soviet Union continues to protest against many aspects of Federal presence in West Berlin and other examples of the ties with the Federal Republic. It attacks Berlin's position within the European Communities. And with the GDR and its other friends, the Soviet Union frequently advances its views in international fora. In these and other ways, they seek to isolate West Berlin. The Soviet Union can be in no doubt as to the West's resolve to maintain the status of Berlin until the divisions in Europe are overcome. This status remains the essential basis of West Berlin's position within the Western world. The Soviet authorities should recognise that the Western Allies have been and will continue to be scrupulous in their adherence to Berlin's status.

The calmer climate since 1971 has brought many practical benefits. But it carries with it the danger of a false sense of security, which could contribute to an erosion of Berlin's status. There are some risks, for example, in the development of direct contacts between West Berlin and the GDR, which if not handled carefully could weaken the traditional Federal role in representing Berlin's interests outside Berlin and give currency to the East's "three State theory". And there are likewise risks in assuming that the ties between West Berlin and the Federal Republic can be developed without restriction and without jeopardising the delicate *modus vivendi* established by the Quadripartite Agreement. Further development of the ties must always, as a matter of law, be judged against the need to avoid fundamental change in the existing situation, and must take into account that West Berlin continues not to be a part of the Federal Republic and not to be governed by it. Even as a matter of law, the scope for further major development of the ties is limited.

A further aspect of the changing attitude in the West is the greater readiness to question the exercise of Allied rights and responsibilities in Berlin. But in practical terms it is, unfortunately, not possible for the Allies to be in a position to defend and protect the city without impinging upon the lives of its inhabitants. Soldiers need to train if they are to do their duty effectively. West Berlin has a limited area, and the people of Berlin are bound to be affected from time to time. It is thus precisely in the field of security that the Allies most need to exercise their rights, in ways that may affect Berliners directly, in order to be in a position to carry out their responsibilities, ultimately in the interests of the Berliners themselves. And in defending their legal position, the Allied authorities still occasionally need to act in the legislative sphere, although nowadays they normally exercise their rights in very limited fields. It would be regrettable if Soviet and GDR efforts to undermine the status of Berlin were assisted by a process of erosion from within. It is at best optimistic, and at worst irresponsible, to believe that since the Quadripartite Agreement of 1971 there is no longer any real threat. The Soviet Union may no longer use the rhetoric of the Kruschev era, but it would be dangerous to assume that its underlying goals have changed.

What then of the future? As was stated in a joint declaration of the *Bundestag* of 9 February 1984:

Berlin remains the touchstone of relations between East and West . . .
The city, divided and under four-Power responsibility, makes clear
that the consequences of the division are not yet overcome and that
the German question is open.

It seems clear that the situation in and around Berlin will not
change significantly except in conjunction with developments in
Germany as a whole and in Europe. Only when the divisions in
Europe and in Germany are overcome will Berlin once again be
united and assume its full role. The re-unification of Germany
remains a distant goal, and for the foreseeable future the three
Powers and the Federal Republic have no option but to maintain
Berlin's status essentially unchanged. This does not exclude
practical measures to improve life for Berliners. But it does require
constant vigilance on the part of all concerned, and this includes not
only the officials of the various authorities involved, but also all
those who can influence or instruct – politicians, journalists,
teachers and others – to ensure that the status of Berlin is not
fundamentally changed or eroded.

DOCUMENTS

PROTOCOL OF 12 SEPTEMBER 1944 ON THE ZONES OF OCCUPATION IN GERMANY AND THE ADMINISTRATION OF "GREATER BERLIN" (AS AMENDED)

The Governments of the United Kingdom of Great Britain and Northern Ireland, the United States of America, and the Union of Soviet Socialist Republics and the Provisional Government of the French Republic have reached the following agreement with regard to the execution of Article 11 of the Instrument of Unconditional Surrender of Germany: —

1. Germany, within her frontiers as they were on the 31st December, 1937, will, for the purposes of occupation, be divided into four zones, one of which will be allotted to each of the four Powers, and a special Berlin area, which will be under joint occupation by the four Powers.

2. The boundaries of the four zones and of the Berlin area, and the allocation of the four zones as between the U.K., the U.S.A. and the U.S.S.R. and the French Republic will be as follows: —

Eastern Zone (as shown on the annexed map "A")

The territory of Germany (including the province of East Prussia) situated to the East of a line drawn from the point on Lübeck Bay where the frontiers of Schleswig-Holstein and Mecklenburg meet, along the western frontier of Mecklenburg to the frontier of the province of Hanover, thence, along the eastern frontier of Hanover, to the frontier of Brunswick; thence along the western frontier of the Prussian province of Saxony to the western frontier of Anhalt; thence along the western frontier of Anhalt; thence along the western frontier of the Prussian province of Saxony and the western frontier of Thuringia to where the latter meets the Bavarian frontier; then eastwards along the northern frontier of Bavaria to the 1937 Czechoslovakian frontier, will be occupied by armed forces of the U.S.S.R., with the exception of the Berlin area, for which a special system of occupation is provided below.

North-Western (United Kingdom) Zone (as shown on the annexed map "D")

The territory of Germany situated to west of the line defined in the description of the Eastern (Soviet) Zone, and bounded on the south by a line drawn from the point where the frontier between the Prussian provinces of Hanover and Hessen-Nassau meets the western frontier of the Prussian province of Saxony; thence along the southern frontier of Hanover; thence along the south-eastern and south-western frontiers of the Prussian province of Westphalia and along the southern frontiers of the Prussian Regierungsbezirke of Köln and Aachen to the point where this frontier meets the Belgian-German frontier will be occupied by armed forces of the United Kingdom.

South-Western (United States) Zone (as shown on the annexed map "D")

The territory of Germany situated to the south and east of a line commencing at the junction of the frontiers of Saxony, Bavaria and Czechoslovakia and extending westwards along the northern frontier of Bavaria to the junction of the frontiers of Hessen-Nassau, Thuringia and Bavaria; thence north and west along the eastern and northern frontiers of Hessen-Nassau to the point where the frontier of the district of Dill meets the frontier of the district of Oberwesterwald; thence along the western frontier of the district of Dill, the north-western frontier of the district of Oberlahn, the northern and western frontiers of the district of Limburg-an-der-Lahn, the north-western frontier of the district of Untertaunus and the northern frontier of the district of Rheingau; thence south and east along the western and southern frontiers of Hessen-Nassau to the point where the River Rhine leaves the southern frontier of Hessen-Nassau; thence southwards along the centre of the navigable channel of the River Rhine to the point where the latter leaves Hessen-Darmstadt; thence along the western frontier of Baden to the point where the frontier of the district of Karlsruhe meets the frontier of the district of Rastatt; thence south-east along the southern frontier of the district of Karlsruhe; thence north-east and south-east along the eastern frontier of Baden to the point where the frontier of Baden meets the frontier between the districts of Calw and Leonberg; hence south and east along the western frontier of the district of Leonberg, the western and southern frontiers of the district of Böblingen, the southern frontier of the district of Nürtingen and the southern frontier of the district of Göppingen to the point where the latter meets the Reichsautobahn between Stuttgart and Ulm; thence along the southern boundary of the Reichsautobahn to the point where the latter meets the western frontier of the district of Ulm; thence south along the western frontier of the district of Ulm to the point where the latter meets the western frontier of the State of Bavaria; thence south along the western frontier of Bavaria to the point where the frontier of the district of Kempten meets the frontier of the district of Lindau; thence south-west along the western frontier of the district of Kempten and the western frontier of the district of Sonthofen to the point where the latter meets the Austro-German frontier will be occupied by armed forces of the United States of America.

For the purpose of facilitating communications between the South-Western Zone and the sea, the Commander-in-Chief of the United States forces in the South-Western Zone will

(a) exercise such control of the ports of Bremen and Bremerhaven and the necessary staging areas in the vicinity thereof as may be agreed hereafter by the United Kingdom and United States military authorities to be necessary to meet his requirements;

(b) enjoy such transit facilities through the North-Western Zone as may be agreed hereafter by the United Kingdom and United States military authorities to be necessary to meet his requirements.

Western (French) Zone (as shown on the annexed map "D")

The territory of Germany, situated to the south and west of a line commencing at the junction of the frontiers of Belgium and of the Prussian Regierungsbezirke of Trier and Aachen and extending eastward along the northern frontier of the Prussian Regierungsbezirk of Trier; thence north, east, and south along the western, northern, and eastern frontier of the Prussian Regierungsbezirk of Koblenz to the point where the frontier of Koblenz meets the frontier of the district of Oberwesterwald; thence east, south, and west along the northern, eastern, and southern frontiers of the district of Oberwesterwald and along the eastern frontiers of the districts of Unterwesterwald, Unterlahn, and Sankt Goarshausen to the point where the frontier of the district of Sankt Goarshausen meets the frontier of the Regierungsbezirk of Koblenz; thence south and east along the eastern frontier of Koblenz; and the northern frontier of Hessen-Darmstadt to the point where the River Rhine leaves the southern frontier of Hessen-Nassau; thence southwards along the centre of the navigable channel of the River Rhine to the point where the latter leaves Hessen-Darmstadt; thence along the western frontier of Baden to the point where the frontier of the district of Karlsruhe meets the frontier of the district of Rastatt; thence south-east along the northern frontier of the district of Rastatt; thence north, east, and south along the western, northern, and eastern frontiers of the district of Calw; thence eastwards along the northern frontiers of the districts of Horb, Tübingen, Reutlingen, and Münsingen to the point where the northern frontier of the district of Münsingen meets the Reichsautobahn between Stuttgart and Ulm; thence south-east along the southern boundary of the Reichsautobahn to the point where the latter meets the eastern frontier of the district of Münsingen; thence south-east along the north-eastern frontiers of the districts of Münsingen, Ehingen, and Biberach; thence southwards along the eastern frontiers of the districts of Biberach, Wangen, and Lindau to the point where the eastern frontier of the district of Lindau meets the Austro-German frontier will be occupied by armed forces of the French Republic.

The frontiers of States (Länder) and Provinces within Germany, referred to in the foregoing descriptions of the zones, are those which existed after the coming into effect of the decree of 25th June, 1941 (published in the Reichsgesetzblatt, Part I, No. 72, 3rd July, 1941).

Berlin Area (as shown on the annexed 4 sheets of map "B")

The Berlin area (by which expression is understood the territory of "Greater Berlin" as defined by the Law of the 27th April, 1920) will be jointly occupied by armed forces of the U.K., U.S.A., and U.S.S.R., and the French Republic, assigned by the respective Commanders-in-Chief. For this purpose the territory of "Greater Berlin" will be divided into four parts:—

North-Eastern part of "Greater Berlin" (districts of Pankow, Prenzlauerberg, Mitte, Weissensee, Friedrichshain, Lichtenberg, Treptow, Köpenick) will be occupied by the forces of the U.S.S.R:

North-Western part of "Greater Berlin" (districts of Reinickendorf,* Wedding,* Tiergarten, Charlottenburg, Spandau, Wilmersdorf) will be occupied by the forces of the United Kingdom:

Southern part of "Greater Berlin" (districts of Zehlendorf, Steglitz, Schöneberg, Kreuzberg, Tempelhof, Neukölln) will be occupied by the forces of the United States of America.

The boundaries of districts within "Greater Berlin", referred to in the foregoing descriptions, are those which existed after the coming into effect of the decree published on 27th March, 1938 (Amtsblatt der Reichshauptstadt Berlin No. 13 of 27th March, 1938, page 215).

3. The occupying forces in each of the four zones into which Germany is divided will be under a Commander-in-Chief designated by the Government of the country whose forces occupy that zone.

4. Each of the four Powers may, at its discretion, include among the forces assigned to occupation duties under the command of its Commander-in-Chief, auxiliary contingents from the forces of any other Allied Power which has participated in military operations against Germany.

5. An Inter-Allied Governing Authority (Komendatura) consisting of four Commandants, appointed by their respective Commanders-in-Chief, will be established to direct jointly the administration of the "Greater Berlin" Area.

6. This Protocol has been drawn up in quadruplicate in the English, Russian and French languages. The three texts are authentic. The Protocol will come into force on the signature by Germany of the Instrument of Unconditional Surrender.

---

* These districts became the French Sector by virtue of Order No. 1 of 11 July 1945 (see p.92 above).

AGREEMENT OF 14 NOVEMBER 1944 ON CONTROL MACHINERY IN GERMANY (AS AMENDED)

The Governments of the United Kingdom of Great Britain and Northern Ireland, the United States of America, and the Union of Soviet Socialist Republics, and the Provisional Government of the French Republic, have reached the following Agreement with regard to the organisation of the Allied control machinery in Germany in the period during which Germany will be carrying out the basic requirements of unconditional surrender: –

Article 1

Supreme authority in Germany will be exercised, on instructions from their respective Governments, by the Commanders-in-Chief of the armed forces of the United Kingdom, the United States of America, the French Republic and the Union of Soviet Socialist Republics, each in his own zone of occupation, and also jointly, in matters affecting Germany as a whole, in their capacity as members of the supreme organ of control constituted under the present Agreement.

Article 2

Each Commander-in-Chief in his zone of occupation will have attached to him military, naval and air representatives of the other three Commanders-in-Chief for liaison duties.

Article 3

(a) The four Commanders-in-Chief, acting together as a body, will constitute a supreme organ of control called the Control Council.

(b) The functions of the Control Council will be:–

(i) to ensure appropriate uniformity of action by the Commanders-in-Chief in their respective zones of occupation;

(ii) to initiate plans and reach agreed decisions on the chief military, political, economic and other questions affecting Germany as a whole, on the basis of instructions received by each Commander-in-Chief from his Government;

(iii) to control the German central administration, which will operate under the direction of the Control Council and will be responsible to it for ensuring compliance with its demands;

(iv) to direct the administration of "Greater Berlin" through appropriate organs.

(c) The Control Council will meet at least once in ten days; and it will meet at any time upon request of any one of its members. Decisions of the Control Council shall be unanimous. The chairmanship of the Control Council will be held in rotation by each of its four members.

(d) Each member of the Control Council will be assisted by a political adviser, who will, when necessary, attend meetings of the Control Council. Each member of the Control Council may also, when necessary, be assisted at meetings of the Council by naval or air advisers.

Article 4

A permanent Co-ordinating Committee will be established under the Control Council, composed of one representative of each of the four Commanders-in-Chief, not below the rank of General Officer or the equivalent rank in the naval or air forces. Members of the Co-ordinating Committee will, when necessary, attend meetings of the Control Council.

Article 5

The duties of the Co-ordinating Committee, acting on behalf of the Control Council and through the Control Staff, will include:–

(a) the carrying out of the decisions of the Control Council;

(b) the day-to-day supervision and control of the activities of the German central administration and institutions;

(c) the co-ordination of current problems which call for uniform measures in all four zones;

(d) the preliminary examination and preparation for the Control Council of all questions submitted by individual Commanders-in-Chief.

Article 6

(a) The members of the Control Staff, appointed by their respective national authorities, will be organised in the following Divisions:–

Military; Naval; Air; Transport; Political; Economic; Finance; Reparation, Deliveries, and Restitution; Internal Affairs and Communications; Legal; Prisoners of War and Displaced Persons; Man-power.

Adjustments in the number and functions of the Divisions may be made in the light of experience.

(b) At the head of each Division there will be four high ranking officials, one from each Power. The duties of the four heads of each Division, acting jointly, will include:–

(i) exercising control over the corresponding German Ministries and German central institutions;

(ii) acting as advisers to the Control Council and, when necessary, attending meetings thereof;

(iii) transmitting to the German central administration the decisions of the Control Council, communicated through the Co-ordinating Committee.

(c) The four heads of a Division will take part in meetings of the Co-ordinating Committee at which matters affecting the work of their Division are on the agenda.

(d) The staffs of the Divisions may include civilian as well as military personnel. They may also, in special cases, include nationals of other United Nations, appointed in their personal capacity.

Article 7

(a) An Inter-Allied Governing Authority (Komendatura) consisting of four Commandants, one from each Power, appointed by their respective Commanders-in-Chief, will be established to direct jointly the administration of the "Greater Berlin" area. Each of the Commandants will serve in rotation, in the position of Chief Commandant, as head of the Inter-Allied Governing Authority.

(b) A Technical Staff, consisting of personnel of each of the four Powers, will be established under the Inter-Allied Governing Authority, and will be organised to serve the purpose of supervising and controlling the activities of the local organs of "Greater Berlin" which are responsible for its municipal services.

(c) The Inter-Allied Governing Authority will operate under the general direction of the Control Council and will receive orders through the Co-ordinating Committee.

Article 8

The necessary liaison with the Governments of other United Nations chiefly interested will be ensured by the appointment by such Governments of military missions (which may include civilian members) to the Control Council, having access, through the appropriate channels, to the organs of control.

Article 9

United Nations' organisations which may be admitted by the Control Council to operate in Germany will, in respect of their activities in Germany, be subordinate to the Allied control machinery and answerable to it.

Article 10

The Allied organs for the control and administration of Germany outlined above will operate during the initial period of the occupation of Germany immediately following surrender, that is, the period when Germany is carrying out the basic requirements of unconditional surrender.

Article 11

The question of the Allied organs required for carrying out the functions of control and administration in Germany in a later period will be the subject of a separate Agreement between the Governments of the United Kingdom, the United States of America, and the Union of Soviet Socialist Republics, and the Provisional Government of the French Republic.

DECLARATION OF 5 JUNE 1945 REGARDING THE DEFEAT OF GERMANY AND THE ASSUMPTION OF SUPREME AUTHORITY WITH RESPECT TO GERMANY BY THE GOVERNMENTS OF THE UNITED KINGDOM, THE UNITED STATES OF AMERICA AND THE UNION OF SOVIET SOCIALIST REPUBLICS AND THE PROVISIONAL GOVERNMENT OF THE FRENCH REPUBLIC

[Preamble]

The German armed forces on land, at sea and in the air have been completely defeated and have surrendered unconditionally and Germany, which bears responsibility for the war, is no longer capable of resisting the will of the victorious Powers. The unconditional surrender of Germany has thereby been effected, and Germany has become subject to such requirements as may now or hereafter be imposed upon her.

There is no central Government or authority in Germany capable of accepting responsibility for the maintenance of order, the administration of the country and compliance with the requirements of the victorious Powers.

It is in these circumstances necessary, without prejudice to any subsequent decisions that may be taken respecting Germany, to make provision for the cessation of any further hostilities on the part of the German armed forces, for the maintenance of order in Germany and for the administration of the country, and to announce the immediate requirements with which Germany must comply.

The Representatives of the Supreme Commands of the United Kingdom, the United States of America, the Union of Soviet Socialist Republics and the French Republic, hereinafter called the "Allied Representatives", acting by authority of their respective Governments and in the interests of the United Nations, accordingly make the following Declaration:

The Governments of the United Kingdom, the United States of America and the Union of Soviet Socialist Republics, and the Provisional Government of the French Republic, hereby assume supreme authority with respect to Germany, including all the powers possessed by the German Government, the High Command and any state, municipal, or local government or authority. The assumption, for the purposes stated above, of the said authority and powers does not effect the annexation of Germany.

The Governments of the United Kingdom, the United States of America and the Union of Soviet Socialist Republics, and the Provisional Government of the French Republic, will hereafter determine the boundaries of Germany or any part thereof and the status of Germany or of any area at present being part of German territory.

In virtue of the supreme authority and powers thus assumed by the four Governments, the Allied Representatives announce the following requirements arising from the complete defeat and unconditional surrender of Germany with which Germany must comply:

[remainder of text not reproduced]

Berlin, 5 June, 1945
18.00 Hours, Central European Time

Signed by the Allied Representatives:

DWIGHT EISENHOWER
General of the Army, USA

ZHUKOV

B. L. MONTGOMERY

J. DE LATTRE-TASSIGNY
Général d'Armée

CONVENTION ON RELATIONS BETWEEN THE THREE POWERS AND THE FEDERAL REPUBLIC OF GERMANY, DONE AT BONN ON 26 MAY 1952, AS AMENDED AT PARIS ON 23 OCTOBER 1954

The United States of America, the United Kingdom of Great Britain and Northern Ireland, the French Republic, and the Federal Republic of Germany

Have entered into the following Convention setting forth the basis for their new relationship:

ARTICLE 1

1. On the entry into force of the present Convention the United States of America, the United Kingdom of Great Britain and Northern Ireland and the French Republic (hereinafter and in the related Conventions sometimes referred to as "the Three Powers") will terminate the Occupation régime in the Federal Republic, revoke the Occupation Statute and abolish the Allied High Commission and the Offices of the Land Commissioners in the Federal Republic.

2. The Federal Republic shall have accordingly the full authority of a sovereign State over its internal and external affairs.

ARTICLE 2

In view of the international situation, which has so far prevented the re-unification of Germany and the conclusion of a peace settlement, the Three Powers retain the rights and the responsibilities, heretofore exercised or held by them, relating to Berlin and to Germany as a whole, including the re-unification of Germany and a peace settlement. The rights and responsibilities retained by the Three Powers relating to the stationing of armed forces in Germany and the protection of their security are dealt with in Articles 4 and 5 of the present Convention.

ARTICLE 3

1. The Federal Republic agrees to conduct its policy in accordance with the principles set forth in the Charter of the United Nations and with the aims defined in the Statute of the Council of Europe.

2. The Federal Republic affirms its intention to associate itself fully with the community of free nations through membership in international organisations contributing to the common aims of the free world. The Three Powers will support applications for such membership by the Federal Republic at appropriate times.

3. In their negotiations with States with which the Federal Republic maintains no relations, the Three Powers will consult with the Federal

Republic in respect of matters directly involving its political interests.

4. At the request of the Federal Government, the Three Powers will arrange to represent the interests of the Federal Republic in relations with other States and in certain international organisations or conferences, whenever the Federal Republic is not in a position to do so itself.

ARTICLE 4

1. Pending the entry into force of the arrangements for the German Defence Contribution, the Three Powers retain the rights, heretofore exercised or held by them, relating to the stationing of armed forces in the Federal Republic. The mission of these forces will be the defence of the free world, of which Berlin and the Federal Republic form part. Subject to the provisions of paragraph 2 of Article 5 of the present Convention, the rights and obligations of these forces shall be governed by the Convention on the Rights and Obligations of Foreign Forces and their Members in the Federal Republic of Germany (hereinafter referred to as "the Forces Convention") referred to in paragraph 1 of Article 8 of the present Convention.

2. The rights of the Three Powers, heretofore exercised or held by them, which relate to the stationing of armed forces in Germany and which are retained, are not affected by the provisions of this Article insofar as they are required for the exercise of the rights referred to in the first sentence of Article 2 of the present Convention. The Federal Republic agrees that, from the entry into force of the arrangements for the German Defence Contribution, forces of the same nationality and effective strength as at that time may be stationed in the Federal Republic. In view of the status of the Federal Republic as defined in Article 1, paragraph 2 of the present Convention, and in view of the fact that the Three Powers do not desire to exercise their rights regarding the stationing of armed forces in the Federal Republic, insofar as it is concerned, except in full accord with the Federal Republic, a separate Convention deals with this matter.

ARTICLE 5

1. Pending the entry into force of the arrangements for the German Defence Contribution, the following provisions shall be applicable to the forces stationed in the Federal Republic:

(a) the Three Powers will consult with the Federal Republic, insofar as the military situation permits, with regard to all questions concerning the stationing of these forces. The Federal Republic will, according to the present Convention and the related Conventions, co-operate, within the framework of its Basic Law, to facilitate the mission of these forces;

(b) the Three Powers will obtain the consent of the Federal Republic before bringing into the Federal territory, as part of their forces, contingents of the armed forces of any nation not now providing such contingents. Such contingents may nevertheless be brought into the Federal territory without the consent of the Federal Republic in the event of external attack or imminent threat of such attack, but, after the elimination of the danger, may only remain with its consent.

2. The rights of the Three Powers, heretofore held or exercised by them, which relate to the protection of the security of armed forces stationed in the Federal Republic and which are temporarily retained, shall lapse when the appropriate German authorities have obtained similar powers under German legislation enabling them to take effective action to protect the security of those forces, including the ability to deal with a serious disturbance of public security and order. To the extent that such rights continue to be exercisable they shall be exercised only after consultation, insofar as the military situation does not preclude such consultation, with the Federal Government and with its agreement that the circumstances require such exercise. In all other respects the protection of the security of those forces shall be governed by the Forces Convention or by the provisions of the Agreement which replaces it and, except as otherwise provided in any applicable agreement, by German law.

ARTICLE 6

1. The Three Powers will consult with the Federal Republic in regard to the exercise of their rights relating to Berlin.

2. The Federal Republic, on its part, will co-operate with the Three Powers in order to facilitate the discharge of their responsibilities with regard to Berlin.

ARTICLE 7

1. The Signatory States are agreed that an essential aim of their common policy is a peace settlement for the whole of Germany, freely negotiated between Germany and her former enemies, which should lay the foundation for a lasting peace. They further agree that the final determination of the boundaries of Germany must await such a settlement.

2. Pending the peace settlement, the Signatory States will co-operate to achieve, by peaceful means, their common aim of a re-unified Germany enjoying a liberal-democratic constitution, like that of the Federal Republic, and integrated within the European community.

3. Deleted.

4. The Three Powers will consult with the Federal Republic on all matters involving the exercise of their rights relating to Germany as a whole.

ARTICLE 8

1. (a) The Signatory States have concluded the following related Conventions:

Convention on the Rights and Obligations of Foreign Forces and their Members in the Federal Republic of Germany;
Finance Convention;
Convention on the Settlement of Matters Arising out of the War and the Occupation.

(b) The Convention on the Rights and Obligations of Foreign Forces and their Members in the Federal Republic of Germany and the Agreement on Tax Treatment of the Forces and their Members signed at Bonn on 26 May, 1952, as amended by the Protocol signed at Bonn on 26 July 1952, shall remain in force until the entry into force of new arrangements setting forth the rights and obligations of the forces of the Three Powers and other States having forces in the territory of the Federal Republic. The new arrangements will be based on the Agreement Between the Parties to the North Atlantic Treaty Regarding the Status of Their Forces, signed at London on 19 June, 1951, supplemented by such provisions as are necessary in view of the special conditions existing in regard to the forces stationed in the Federal Republic.

(c) The Finance Convention shall remain in force until the entry into force of the new arrangements negotiated in pursuance of paragraph 4 of Article 4 of that Convention with other member Governments of the North Atlantic Treaty Organisation who have forces stationed in the Federal territory.

2. During the transitional period provided for in paragraph 4 of Article 6 of Chapter One of the Convention on the Settlement of Matters Arising out of the War and the Occupation, the rights of the three Signatory States referred to in that paragraph shall be retained.

ARTICLE 9

1. There shall be established an Arbitration Tribunal which shall function in accordance with the provisions of the annexed Charter.

2. The Arbitration Tribunal shall have exclusive jurisdiction over all disputes arising between the Three Powers and the Federal Republic under the provisions of the present Convention or the annexed Charter or any of the related Conventions which the parties are not able to settle by negotiation or by other means agreed between all the Signatory States, except as otherwise provided by paragraph 3 of this Article or in the annexed Charter or in the related Conventions.

3. Any dispute involving the rights of the Three Powers referred to in Article 2, the first two sentences of paragraph 1 of Article 4, the first sentence of paragraph 2 of Article 4 and the first two sentences of paragraph 2 of Article 5 or action taken thereunder, shall not be subject to the jurisdiction of the Arbitration Tribunal or of any other tribunal or court.

ARTICLE 10

The Signatory States will review the terms of the present Convention and the related Conventions

(a) upon request of any one of them, in the event of the re-unification of Germany or an international understanding being reached with the participation or consent of the States parties to the present Convention on steps towards bringing about the re-unification of Germany, or the creation of a European Federation; or

(b) in any situation which all of the Signatory States recognise has resulted from a change of a fundamental character in the conditions prevailing at the time of the entry into force of the present Convention.

In either case they will, by mutual agreement, modify the present Convention and the related Conventions to the extent made necessary or advisable by the fundamental change in the situation.

ARTICLE 11

1. Deleted.

2. Deleted.

3. The present Convention and the related Conventions shall be deposited in the Archives of the Government of the Federal Republic of Germany, which will furnish each Signatory State with certified copies thereof and notify each such State of the date of the entry into force of the present Convention and the related Conventions.

IN FAITH WHEREOF the undersigned representatives duly authorised thereto by their respective Governments have signed the present Convention.

Done at Bonn this twenty-sixth day of May, 1952, in three texts, in the English, French and German languages, all being equally authentic.

For the United States of America:
DEAN ACHESON

For the United Kingdom of Great Britain and Northern Ireland:
ANTHONY EDEN

For the French Republic:
ROBERT SCHUMAN

For the Federal Republic of Germany:
ADENAUER

CONVENTION ON RELATIONS BETWEEN THE THREE POWERS
AND THE FEDERAL REPUBLIC OF GERMANY, DONE AT BONN ON
26 MAY 1952, AS AMENDED AT PARIS ON 23 OCTOBER 1954
(*continued*)

ANNEX A
Deleted.

ANNEX B

CHARTER OF THE ARBITRATION TRIBUNAL
[not reproduced]

LETTER OF THE THREE HIGH COMMISSIONERS TO THE FEDERAL CHANCELLOR CONCERNING THE EXERCISE OF THE RESERVED ALLIED RIGHTS RELATING TO BERLIN OF 26 MAY 1952 IN THE VERSION OF THE LETTER X OF 23 OCTOBER 1954; AND THE DECLARATION OF THE FEDERAL REPUBLIC ON AID TO BERLIN

Mr. Chancellor,

As we have already advised you during our discussions on the Conventions between the Three Powers and the Federal Republic which have been signed today, the reservation made on 12 May 1949 by the Military Governors concerning Articles 23 and 144(2) of the Basic Law will, owing to the international situation, be formally maintained by the Three Powers in the exercise of their right relating to Berlin after the entry into force of these Conventions.

The Three Powers wish to state in this connection that they are nonetheless conscious of the necessity for the Federal Republic to furnish aid to Berlin and of the advantages involved in the adoption by Berlin of policies similar to those of the Federation.

For this reason they have decided to exercise their right relating to Berlin in such a way as to facilitate the carrying out by the Federal Republic of its Declaration on Aid to Berlin, of which a copy is annexed, and to permit the Federal authorities to ensure representation of Berlin and of the Berlin population outside Berlin.

Similarly, they will have no objections if, in accordance with an appropriate procedure authorised by the Allied *Kommandatura*, Berlin adopts the same legislation as that of the Federal Republic, in particular regarding currency, credit and foreign exchange, nationality, passports, emigration and immigration, extradition, the unification of the customs and trade area, trade and navigation agreements, freedom of movement of goods, and foreign trade and payments arrangements.

In view of the declaration of the Federal Republic concerning material aid to Berlin and the charge on the Federal budget of the occupation costs of the Three Powers in Berlin in accordance with the provisions of existing legislation, the Three Powers will be prepared to consult with the Federal Government prior to their establishment of their Berlin occupation cost budgets. It is their intention to fix such costs at the lowest level consistent with maintaining the security of Berlin and of the Allied Forces located there.

For the Government of the United States of America:
JOHN J. McCLOY.

For the Government of the Republic of France:
ANDRÉ FRANÇOIS-PONCET.

For the Government of the United Kingdom of Great Britain and Northern Ireland:
IVONE KIRKPATRICK.

ANNEX

DECLARATION OF THE FEDERAL REPUBLIC ON AID TO BERLIN

In view of the special role which Berlin has played and is destined to play in the future for the self-preservation of the free world,

aware of the ties connecting the Federal Republic with Berlin as the prospective capital of a free, reunified, Germany,

resolved to consolidate these ties within the framework of the status of Berlin,

resolved to continue its aid to the political, cultural, economic and financial reconstruction of Berlin, and

motivated by the desire to strengthen and to reinforce the position of Berlin in all fields,

and in particular to bring about in so far as possible an improvement in the economic and financial situation in Berlin including its productive capacity and level of employment,

the Federal Republic undertakes

(a) to take all necessary measures on its part in order to ensure the maintenance of a balanced budget in Berlin through appropriate assistance;

(b) to take adequate measures for the equitable treatment of Berlin in the control and allocation of materials in short supply;

(c) to take adequate measures to ensure that Berlin also benefits from resources at the disposal of the Federal Republic received from outside sources, for the necessary further economic reconstruction of Berlin;

(d) to take all appropriate measures designed to promote the placing of public and private orders in the Berlin economy;

(e) to promote the development of Berlin's external trade, to accord Berlin such favoured treatment in all matters of trade policy as circumstances warrant and to provide Berlin within the limit of possibility and in consideration of the participation of Berlin in the foreign currency control by the Federal Republic, with the necessary foreign currency;

(f) to take all necessary measures on its part to ensure that the city remains in the currency area of the Deutsche Mark West, and that an adequate money supply is maintained in the city;

(g) to assist in the maintaining in Berlin of adequate stock-piles of supplies for emergencies;

(h) to use its best efforts for the maintenance and improvement of trade and of communications and transportation facilities between Berlin and the Federal territory, and to co-operate in accordance with the means at its disposal in their protection or their re-establishment;

(i) to continue its efforts to compensate, as heretofore, the disproportionate burden placed on Berlin as a result of the admission of refugees;

(j) to ensure the representation of Berlin and of the Berlin population outside Berlin, and to facilitate the inclusion of Berlin in the international agreements concluded by the Federal Republic, provided that this is not precluded by the nature of the agreements concerned.

ADENAUER.

DECLARATION ON BERLIN OF 5 MAY 1955

ALLIED KOMMANDATURA BERLIN

BKC/L(55)3
5 May 1955

SUBJECT: Declaration on Berlin
TO: The Governing Mayor, Berlin
The President of the House of Representatives
The President of the Kammergericht

1. Enclosed herewith is a copy of a Declaration on Berlin, which replaces the present Statement of Principles Governing the Relationship between the Allied Kommandatura and Greater Berlin, and which comes into effect today.
2. The Statement of Principles Governing the Relationship between the Allied Kommandatura and Greater Berlin, as amended on 7 March, 1951, is hereby repealed.

UNITED STATES
Major General
G. HONNEN

FRANCE
Général de Brigade
GEZE

UNITED KINGDOM
Major General
R. C. COTTRELL-HILL

ALLIED KOMMANDATURA BERLIN

Declaration on Berlin

Taking into consideration the new relations established between France, the United Kingdom of Great Britain and Northern Ireland, the United States of America, and the Federal Republic of Germany and
wishing to grant the Berlin authorities the maximum liberty compatible with the special situation of Berlin,
the Allied Kommandatura makes this declaration:

I.

Berlin shall exercise all its rights, powers and responsibilities set forth in its Constitution as adopted in 1950 subject only to the reservations made by the Allied Kommandatura on 29 August 1950 and to the provisions hereinafter.

II.

The Allied authorities retain the right to take, if they deem it necessary, such measures as may be required to fulfil their international obligations, to ensure public order and to maintain the status and security of Berlin and its economy, trade and communications.

III.

The Allied authorities will normally exercise powers only in the following fields:

(a) Security, interests and immunities of the Allied Forces, including their representatives, dependents and non-German employees. German employees of the Allied Forces enjoy immunity from German jurisdiction only in matters arising out of or in the course of performance of duties or services with the Allied Forces.

(b) Disarmament and demilitarisation, including related fields of scientific research, civil aviation, and prohibitions and restrictions on industry in relation to the foregoing.

(c) Relations of Berlin with authorities abroad. However, the Allied Kommandatura will permit the Berlin authorities to assure the representation abroad of the interests of Berlin and of its inhabitants by suitable arrangements.

(d) Satisfaction of occupation costs. These costs will be fixed after consultation with the appropriate German authorities and at the lowest level consistent with maintaining the security of Berlin and of the Allied Forces located there.

(e) Authority over the Berlin police to the extent necessary to ensure the security of Berlin.

IV.

The Allied Kommandatura will not, subject to Articles I and II of this Declaration, raise any objection to the adoption by Berlin under an appropriate procedure authorised by the Allied Kommandatura of the same legislation as that of the Federal Republic, in particular regarding currency, credit and foreign exchange, nationality, passports, emigration and immigration, extradition, the unification of the customs and trade area, trade and navigation agreements, freedom of movement of goods, and foreign trade and payments arrangements.

V.

In the following fields:

(a) restitution, reparations, decartelisation, deconcentration, foreign interests in Berlin, claims against Berlin or its inhabitants,

(b) displaced persons and the admission of refugees,

(c) control of the care and treatment in German prisons of persons charged before or sentenced by Allied courts or tribunals; over the carrying out of sentences imposed on them and over questions of amnesty, pardon or release in relation to them,

the Allied authorities will in the future only intervene to an extent consistent with, or if the Berlin authorities act inconsistently with, the principles which form the basis of the new relations between France, the United Kingdom and the United States on the one part and the Federal Republic of Germany on the other, or with Allied legislation in force in Berlin.

VI.

All legislation of the Allied authorities will remain in force until repealed, amended or deprived of effect.
The Allied authorities will repeal, amend or deprive of effect any legislation which they deem no longer appropriate in the light of this Declaration.
Legislation of the Allied authorities may also be repealed or amended by Berlin legislation; but such repeal or amendment shall require the approval of the Allied authorities before coming into force.

VII.

Berlin legislation shall come into force in accordance with the provisions of the Berlin Constitution. In case of inconsistency with Allied legislation, or with other measures of the Allied authorities, or with the rights of the Allied authorities under this Declaration, Berlin legislation will be subject to repeal or annulment by the Allied Kommandatura.

VIII.

In order to enable them to fulfil their obligations under this Declaration, the Allied authorities shall have the right to request and obtain such information and statistics as they deem necessary.

IX.

The Allied Kommandatura will modify the provisions of this Declaration as the situation in Berlin permits.

X.

Upon the effective date of this Declaration the Statement of Principles Governing the Relationship between the Allied Kommandatura and Greater Berlin of May 14, 1949, as modified by the First Instrument of Revision, dated March 7, 1951, will be repealed.

5 May 1955.

THE QUADRIPARTITE AGREEMENT OF 3 SEPTEMBER 1971

The Governments of the United Kingdom of Great Britain and Northern Ireland, the French Republic, the Union of Soviet Socialist Republics and the United States of America,

Represented by their Ambassadors, who held a series of meetings in the building formerly occupied by the Allied Control Council in the American Sector of Berlin,

Acting on the basis of their quadripartite rights and responsibilities, and of the corresponding wartime and post-war agreements and decisions of the Four Powers, which are not affected,

Taking into account the existing situation in the relevant area,

Guided by the desire to contribute to practical improvements of the situation,

Without prejudice to their legal positions,

Have agreed on the following:

PART I

General provisions

1. The four Governments will strive to promote the elimination of tension and the prevention of complications in the relevant area.

2. The four Governments, taking into account their obligations under the Charter of the United Nations, agree that there shall be no use or threat of force in the area and that disputes shall be settled solely by peaceful means.

3. The four Governments will mutually respect their individual and joint rights and responsibilities, which remain unchanged.

4. The four Governments agree that, irrespective of the differences in legal views, the situation which has developed in the area, and as it is defined in this Agreement as well as in the other agreements referred to in this Agreement, shall not be changed unilaterally.

PART II

Provisions relating to the Western Sectors of Berlin

A. The Government of the Union of Soviet Socialist Republics declares that transit traffic by road, rail and waterways through the territory of the

German Democratic Republic of civilian persons and goods between the Western Sectors of Berlin and the Federal Republic of Germany will be unimpeded; that such traffic will be facilitated so as to take place in the most simple and expeditious manner; and that it will receive preferential treatment.

Detailed arrangements concerning this civilian traffic, as set forth in Annex I, will be agreed by the competent German authorities.

B. The Governments of the French Republic, the United Kingdom and the United States of America declare that the ties between the Western Sectors of Berlin and the Federal Republic of Germany will be maintained and developed, taking into account that these Sectors continue not to be a constituent part of the Federal Republic of Germany and not to be governed by it.

Detailed arrangements concerning the relationship between the Western Sectors of Berlin and the Federal Republic of Germany are set forth in Annex II.

C. The Government of the Union of Soviet Socialist Republics declares that communications between the Western Sectors of Berlin and areas bordering on these Sectors and those areas of the German Democratic Republic which do not border on these Sectors will be improved. Permanent residents of the Western Sectors of Berlin will be able to travel to and visit such areas for compassionate, family, religious, cultural or commercial reasons, or as tourists, under conditions comparable to those applying to other persons entering these areas.

The problems of the small enclaves, including Steinstuecken, and of other small areas may be solved by exchange of territory.

Detailed arrangements concerning travel, communications and the exchange of territory, as set forth in Annex III, will be agreed by the competent German authorities.

D. Representation abroad of the interests of the Western Sectors of Berlin and consular activities of the Union of Soviet Socialist Republics in the Western Sectors of Berlin can be exercised as set forth in Annex IV.

PART III

Final provisions

This Quadripartite Agreement will enter into force on the date specified in a Final Quadripartite Protocol to be concluded when the measures envisaged in Part II of this Quadripartite Agreement and in its Annexes have been agreed.

DONE at the building formerly occupied by the Allied Control Council in the American Sector of Berlin, this 3rd day of September 1971, in four originals, each in the English, French and Russian languages, all texts being equally authentic.

For the Government of the United Kingdom of Great Britain and Northern Ireland:
R. W. JACKLING

For the Government of the French Republic:
J. SAUVAGNARGUES

For the Government of the Union of Soviet Socialist Republics:
P. ABRASIMOV

For the Government of the United States of America:
KENNETH RUSH

ANNEX I

Communication from the Government of the Union of Soviet Socialist Republics to the Governments of the French Republic, the United Kingdom and the United States of America

The Government of the Union of Soviet Socialist Republics, with reference to Part IIA of the Quadripartite Agreement of this date and after consultation and agreement with the Government of the German Democratic Republic, has the honour to inform the Governments of the French Republic, the United Kingdom and the United States of America that:

1. Transit traffic by road, rail and waterways through the territory of the German Democratic Republic of civilian persons and goods between the Western Sectors of Berlin and the Federal Republic of Germany will be facilitated and unimpeded. It will receive the most simple, expeditious and preferential treatment provided by international practice.

2. Accordingly,

(a) Conveyances sealed before departure may be used for the transport of civilian goods by road, rail and waterways between the Western Sectors of Berlin and the Federal Republic of Germany. Inspection procedures will be limited to the inspection of seals and accompanying documents.

(b) With regard to conveyances which cannot be sealed, such as open trucks, inspection procedures will be limited to the inspection of accompanying documents. In special cases where there is sufficient reason to suspect that unsealed conveyances contain either material intended for dissemination along the designated routes or persons or material put on board along these routes, the content of unsealed conveyances may be inspected. Procedures for dealing with such cases will be agreed by the competent German authorities.

(c) Through trains and buses may be used for travel between the Western Sectors of Berlin and the Federal Republic of Germany. Inspection procedures will not include any formalities other than identification of persons.

(d) Persons identified as through travellers using individual vehicles between the Western Sectors of Berlin and the Federal Republic of Germany on routes designated for through traffic will be able to proceed to their destinations without paying individual tolls and fees for the use of the transit routes. Procedures applied for such travellers shall not involve delay. The travellers, their vehicles and personal baggage will not be subject to search, detention or exclusion from use of the designated routes, except in special cases, as may be agreed by the competent German authorities, where there is sufficient reason to suspect that misuse of the transit routes is intended for purposes not related to direct travel to and from the Western Sectors of Berlin and contrary to generally applicable regulations concerning public order.

(e) Appropriate compensation for fees and tolls and for other costs related to traffic on the communication routes between the Western Sectors of Berlin and the Federal Republic of Germany, including the maintenance of adequate routes, facilities and installations used for such traffic, may be made in the form of an annual lump sum paid to the German Democratic Republic by the Federal Republic of Germany.

3. Arrangements implementing and supplementing the provisions of paragraphs 1 and 2 above will be agreed by the competent German authorities.

ANNEX II

Communication from the Governments of the French Republic, the United Kingdom and the United States of America to the Government of the Union of Soviet Socialist Republics

The Governments of the French Republic, the United Kingdom and the United States of America, with reference to Part IIB of the Quadripartite Agreement of this date and after consultation with the Government of the Federal Republic of Germany, have the honour to inform the Government of the Union of Soviet Socialist Republics that:

1. They declare, in the exercise of their rights and responsibilities, that the ties between the Western Sectors of Berlin and the Federal Republic of Germany will be maintained and developed, taking into account that these Sectors continue not to be a constituent part of the Federal Republic of Germany and not to be governed by it. The provisions of the Basic Law of the Federal Republic of Germany and of the Constitution operative in the Western Sectors of Berlin which contradict the above have been suspended and continue not to be in effect.

2. The Federal President, the Federal Government, the Bundes-versammlung, the Bundesrat and the Bundestag, including their Committees and Fraktionen, as well as other state bodies of the Federal Republic of Germany will not perform in the Western Sectors of Berlin constitutional or official acts which contradict the provisions of paragraph 1.

3. The Government of the Federal Republic of Germany will be represented in the Western Sectors of Berlin to the authorities of the three Governments and to the Senat by a permanent liaison agency.

ANNEX III

Communication from the Government of the Union of Soviet Socialist Republics to the Governments of the French Republic, the United Kingdom and the United States of America

The Government of the Union of Soviet Socialist Republics, with reference to Part IIC of the Quadripartite Agreement of this date and after consultation and agreement with the Government of the German Democratic Republic, has the honour to inform the Governments of the French Republic, the United Kingdom and the United States of America that:

1. Communications between the Western Sectors of Berlin and areas bordering on these Sectors and those areas of the German Democratic Republic which do not border on these Sectors will be improved.

2. Permanent residents of the Western Sectors of Berlin will be able to travel to and visit such areas for compassionate, family, religious, cultural or commercial reasons, or as tourists, under conditions comparable to those applying to other persons entering these areas. In order to facilitate visits and travel, as described above, by permanent residents of the Western Sectors of Berlin, additional crossing points will be opened.

3. The problems of the small enclaves, including Steinstuecken, and of other small areas may be solved by exchange of territory.

4. Telephonic, telegraphic, transport and other external communications of the Western Sectors of Berlin will be expanded.

5. Arrangements implementing and supplementing the provisions of paragraphs 1 to 4 above will be agreed by the competent German authorities.

ANNEX IV

A

Communication from the Governments of the French Republic, the United Kingdom and the United States of America to the Government of the Union of Soviet Socialist Republics

The Governments of the French Republic, the United Kingdom and the United States of America, with reference to Part IID of the Quadripartite Agreement of this date and after consultation with the Government of the Federal Republic of Germany, have the honour to inform the Government of the Union of Soviet Socialist Republics that:

1. The Governments of the French Republic, the United Kingdom and the United States of America maintain their rights and responsibilities relating to the representation abroad of the interests of the Western Sectors of Berlin and their permanent residents, including those rights and responsibilities concerning matters of security and status, both in international organisations and in relations with other countries.

2. Without prejudice to the above and provided that matters of security and status are not affected, they have agreed that:

(a) The Federal Republic of Germany may perform consular services for permanent residents of the Western Sectors of Berlin.

(b) In accordance with established procedures, international agreements and arrangements entered into by the Federal Republic of Germany may be extended to the Western Sectors of Berlin provided that the extension of such agreements and arrangements is specified in each case.

(c) The Federal Republic of Germany may represent the interests of the Western Sectors of Berlin in international organisations and international conferences.

(d) Permanent residents of the Western Sectors of Berlin may participate jointly with participants from the Federal Republic of Germany in international exchanges and exhibitions. Meetings of international organisations and international conferences as well as exhibitions with international participation may be held in the Western Sectors of Berlin. Invitations will be issued by the Senat or jointly by the Federal Republic of Germany and the Senat.

3. The three Governments authorise the establishment of a Consulate-General of the USSR in the Western Sectors of Berlin accredited to the appropriate authorities of the three Governments in accordance with the usual procedures applied in those Sectors, for the purpose of performing consular services, subject to provisions set forth in a separate document of this date.

B

Communication from the Government of the Union of Soviet Socialist Republics to the Governments of the French Republic, the United Kingdom and the United States of America

The Government of the Union of Soviet Socialist Republics, with reference to Part IID of the Quadripartite Agreement of this date and to the communication of the Governments of the French Republic, the United Kingdom and the United States of America with regard to the representation abroad of the interests of the Western Sectors of Berlin and their permanent residents, has the honour to inform the Governments of the French Republic, the United Kingdom and the United States of America that:

1. The Government of the Union of Soviet Socialist Republics takes note of the fact that the three Governments maintain their rights and responsibilities relating to the representation abroad of the interests of the Western Sectors of Berlin and their permanent residents, including those rights and responsibilities concerning matters of security and status, both in international organisations and in relations with other countries.

2. Provided that matters of security and status are not affected, for its part it will raise no objection to:

(a) the performance by the Federal Republic of Germany of consular services for permanent residents of the Western Sectors of Berlin;

(b) in accordance with established procedures, the extension to the Western Sectors of Berlin of international agreements and arrangements entered into by the Federal Republic of Germany provided that the extension of such agreements and arrangements is specified in each case;

(c) the representation of the interests of the Western Sectors of Berlin by the Federal Republic of Germany in international organisations and international conferences;

(d) the participation jointly with participants from the Federal Republic of Germany of permanent residents of the Western Sectors of Berlin in international exchanges and exhibitions, or the holding in those Sectors of meetings of international organisations and international conferences as well as exhibitions with international participation, taking into account that invitations will be issued by the Senat or jointly by the Federal Republic of Germany and the Senat.

3. The Government of the Union of Soviet Socialist Republics takes note of the fact that the three Governments have given their consent to the establishment of a Consulate-General of the USSR in the Western Sectors of Berlin. It will be accredited to the appropriate authorities of the three Governments, for purposes and subject to provisions described in their communication and as set forth in a separate document of this date.

AGREED MINUTE I

It is understood that permanent residents of the Western Sectors of Berlin shall, in order to receive at appropriate Soviet offices visas for entry into the Union of Soviet Socialist Republics, present:

(a) a passport stamped "Issued in accordance with the Quadripartite Agreement of 3 September 1971";

(b) an identity card or other appropriately drawn up document confirming that the person requesting the visa is a permanent resident of the Western Sectors of Berlin and containing the bearer's full address and a personal photograph.

During his stay in the Union of Soviet Socialist Republics, a permanent resident of the Western Sectors of Berlin who has received a visa in this way may carry both documents or either of them, as he chooses. The visa issued by a Soviet office will serve as the basis for entry into the Union of Soviet Socialist Republics, and the passport or identity card will serve as the basis for consular services in accordance with the Quadripartite Agreement during the stay of that person in the territory of the Union of Soviet Socialist Republics.

The above-mentioned stamp will appear in all passports used by permanent residents of the Western Sectors of Berlin for journeys to such countries as may require it.

R. W. J.
J. S.
P. A.
K. R.   3 September 1971.

AGREED MINUTE II

Provision is hereby made for the establishment of a Consulate-General of the USSR in the Western Sectors of Berlin. It is understood that the details concerning this Consulate-General will include the following. The Consulate-General will be accredited to the appropriate authorities of the three Governments in accordance with the usual procedures applying in those Sectors. Applicable Allied and German legislation and regulations will apply to the Consulate-General. The activities of the Consulate-General will be of a consular character and will not include political functions or any matters related to quadripartite rights or responsibilities.

The three Governments are willing to authorise an increase in Soviet commercial activities in the Western Sectors of Berlin as described below. It is understood that pertinent Allied and German legislation and regulations will apply to these activities. This authorisation will be extended indefinitely, subject to compliance with the provisions outlined herein. Adequate provision for consultation will be made. This increase will include establishment of an "Office of Soviet Foreign Trade Associations in the Western Sectors of Berlin", with commercial status, authorised to buy and sell on behalf of foreign trade associations of the Union of Soviet Socialist Republics. Soyuzpushnina, Prodintorg and Novoexport may each establish a bonded warehouse in the Western Sectors of Berlin to provide storage and display for their goods. The activities of the Intourist office in the British Sector of Berlin may be expanded to include the sale of tickets and vouchers for travel and tours in the Union of Soviet Socialist Republics and other countries. An office of Aeroflot may be established for the sale of passenger tickets and air freight services.

The assignment of personnel to the Consulate-General and to permitted Soviet commercial organisations will be subject to agreement with the appropriate authorities of the three Governments. The number of such personnel will not exceed twenty Soviet nationals in the Consulate-General; twenty in the office of the Soviet Foreign Trade Associations; one each in the bonded warehouses; six in the Intourist office; and five in the Aeroflot office. The personnel of the Consulate-General and of permitted Soviet commercial organisations and their dependents may reside in the Western Sectors of Berlin upon individual authorisation.

The property of the Union of Soviet Socialist Republics at Lietzenburgerstrasse 11 and at Am Sandwerder 1 may be used for purposes to be agreed between appropriate representatives of the three Governments and of the Government of the Union of Soviet Socialist Republics.

Details of implementation of the measures above and a time schedule for carrying them out will be agreed between the four Ambassadors in the period between the signature of the Quadripartite Agreement and the signature of the Final Quadripartite Protocol envisaged in that Agreement.

R. W. J.
J. S.
P. A.
K. R.   3 September 1971.

The Ambassadors of the French Republic, the United Kingdom and the United States to the Ambassador of the Soviet Union

The Ambassadors of the French Republic, the United Kingdom of Great Britain and Northern Ireland and the United States of America have the honor, with reference to the statements contained in Annex II of the Quadripartite Agreement to be signed on this date concerning the relationship between the Federal Republic of Germany and the Western Sectors of Berlin, to inform the Ambassador of the Union of Soviet Socialist Republics of their intention to send to the Chancellor of the Federal Republic of Germany immediately following signature of the Quadripartite Agreement a letter containing clarifications and interpretations which represent the understanding of their Governments of the statements contained in Annex II of the Quadripartite Agreement. A copy of the letter to be sent to the Chancellor of the Federal Republic of Germany is attached to this Note.

The Ambassadors avail themselves of this opportunity to renew to the Ambassador of the Union of Soviet Socialist Republics the assurances of their highest consideration.

September 3, 1971

J. SAUVAGNARGUES
R. W. JACKLING
KENNETH RUSH

The Ambassadors of the French Republic, the United Kingdom and the United States to the Chancellor of the Federal Republic of Germany

September 3, 1971

Your Excellency:

With reference to the Quadripartite Agreement signed on September 3, 1971, our Governments wish by this letter to inform the Government of the Federal Republic of Germany of the following clarifications and interpretations of the statements contained in Annex II, which was the subject of consultation with the Government of the Federal Republic of Germany during the quadripartite negotiations.

These clarifications and interpretations represent the understanding of our Governments of this part of the Quadripartite Agreement, as follows:

(a) The phrase in paragraph 2 of Annex II of the Quadripartite Agreement which reads: ". . . will not perform in the Western Sectors of Berlin constitutional or official acts which contradict the provisions of paragraph 1" shall be interpreted to mean acts in exercise of direct state authority over the Western Sectors of Berlin.

(b) Meetings of the Bundesversammlung will not take place and plenary sessions of the Bundesrat and the Bundestag will continue not to take place in the Western Sectors of Berlin. Single committees of the Bundesrat and the Bundestag may meet in the Western Sectors of Berlin in connection with maintaining and developing the ties between those Sectors and the Federal Republic of Germany. In the case of Fraktionen, meetings will not be held simultaneously.

(c) The liaison agency of the Federal Government in the Western Sectors of Berlin includes departments charged with liaison functions in their respective fields.

(d) Established procedures concerning the applicability to the Western Sectors of Berlin of legislation of the Federal Republic of Germany shall remain unchanged.

(e) The term "state bodies" in paragraph 2 of Annex II shall be interpreted to mean: the Federal President, the Federal Chancellor, the Federal Cabinet, the Federal Ministers and Ministries, and the branch offices of those Ministries, the Bundesrat and the Bundestag, and all Federal courts.

Accept, Excellency, the renewed assurance of our highest esteem.

For the Government of the French Republic:
J. SAUVAGNARGUES

For the Government of the United Kingdom of Great Britain and
Northern Ireland:

R. W. JACKLING

For the Government of the United States of America:
KENNETH RUSH

*The Ambassador of the Soviet Union to the Ambassadors of the French Republic, the
United Kingdom and the United States*

The Ambassador of the Union of Soviet Socialist Republics has the
honour to acknowledge receipt of the Note of the Ambassadors of the
French Republic, the United Kingdom of Great Britain and Northern
Ireland and the United States of America of 3 September 1971 and takes
note of the communication of the three Ambassadors.

The Ambassador avails himself of this opportunity to renew to the
Ambassadors of the French Republic, the United Kingdom and the United
States of America the assurances of his highest esteem.

P. ABRASIMOV
3 September 1971

*The Ambassadors of the French Republic, the United Kingdom and the United States
to the Chancellor of the Federal Republic of Germany*

September 3, 1971.

Your Excellency:

We have the honor by means of this letter to convey to the Government
of the Federal Republic of Germany the text of the Quadripartite
Agreement signed this day in Berlin. The Quadripartite Agreement was
concluded by the Four Powers in the exercise of their rights and
responsibilities with respect to Berlin.

We note that, pursuant to the terms of the Agreement and of the Final
Quadripartite Protocol which ultimately will bring it into force, the text of
which has been agreed, these rights and responsibilities are not affected
and remain unchanged. Our Governments will continue, as heretofore, to
exercise supreme authority in the Western Sectors of Berlin, within the
framework of the Four Power responsibility which we share for Berlin as a
whole.

In accordance with Part II(A) of the Quadripartite Agreement,
arrangements implementing and supplementing the provisions relating to
civilian traffic will be agreed by the competent German authorities. Part III
of the Quadripartite Agreement provides that the Agreement will enter
into force on a date to be specified in a Final Quadripartite Protocol which
will be concluded when the arrangements envisaged between the

competent German authorities have been agreed. It is the request of our Governments that the envisaged negotiations now take place between authorities of the Federal Republic of Germany, also acting on behalf of the Senat, and authorities of the German Democratic Republic.

Part II(B) and (D) and Annexes II and IV of the Quadripartite Agreement relate to the relationship between the Western Sectors of Berlin and the Federal Republic. In this connection, the following are recalled *inter alia*:

the communications of the three Western Military Governors to the Parliamentary Council of 2 March, 22 April and 12 May, 1949,

the letter of the three High Commissioners to the Federal Chancellor concerning the exercise of the reserved Allied rights relating to Berlin of 26 May, 1952 in the version of the letter X of 23 October, 1954,

the *Aide Mémoire* of the three Governments of 18 April, 1967 concerning the decision of the Federal Constitutional Court of 20 January, 1966 in the Niekisch case.

Our Governments take this occasion to state, in exercise of the rights and responsibilities relating to Berlin, which they retained in Article 2 of the Convention on Relations between the Three Powers and the Federal Republic of Germany of 26 May, 1952 as amended October 23, 1954, that Part II(B) and (D) and Annexes II and IV of the Quadripartite Agreement concerning the relationship between the Federal Republic of Germany and the Western Sectors of Berlin accord with the position in the above-mentioned documents, which remains unchanged.

With regard to the existing ties between the Federal Republic and the Western Sectors of Berlin, it is the firm intention of our Governments that, as stated in Part II(B)(1) of the Quadripartite Agreement, these ties will be maintained and developed in accordance with the letter from the three High Commissioners to the Federal Chancellor on the exercise of the reserved rights relating to Berlin of 26 May, 1952, in the version of letter X of October 23, 1954, and with pertinent decisions of the Allied Kommandatura of Berlin.

Accept, Excellency, the renewed assurance of our highest esteem.

For the Government of the French Republic:
J. SAUVAGNARGUES

For the Government of the United Kingdom of Great Britain and Northern Ireland:
R. W. JACKLING

For the Government of the United States of America:
KENNETH RUSH

The Chancellor of the Federal Republic of Germany to Her Majesty's Ambassador at
Bonn

[Translation]

Bonn,
September 3, 1971.

Your Excellency,

I have the honour to confirm receipt of the letter of the Ambassadors of France, the United Kingdom and the United States of America of September 3 together with which the text of the Quadripartite Agreement signed on September 3, 1971, in Berlin was communicated to the Government of the Federal Republic of Germany.

I also have the honour to confirm receipt of the letter of the three Ambassadors of the same date containing clarifications and interpretations which reflect what their Governments understand by the declarations contained in Annex II to the Quadripartite Agreement with regard to the relationship between the Federal Republic of Germany and the Western Sectors of Berlin.

The Government of the Federal Republic of Germany intends taking steps immediately in order to arrive at agreements on concrete arrangements relating to civilian traffic as envisaged in Part IIA of the Quadripartite Agreement.

The Government of the Federal Republic of Germany has taken note of the contents of Your Excellency's letter which were communicated to it in exercising the rights and responsibilities which were retained in pursuance of Article 2 of the Convention on Relations between the Federal Republic of Germany and the Three Powers of May 26, 1952, as amended on October 23, 1954, and which will continue to be respected by the Government of the Federal Republic of Germany.

The Government of the Federal Republic of Germany shares the view and the determination that the ties between the Federal Republic of Germany and Berlin shall be maintained and developed.

I beg to express my highest consideration.

WILLY BRANDT

FINAL QUADRIPARTITE PROTOCOL

The Governments of the United Kingdom of Great Britain and Northern Ireland, the French Republic, the Union of Soviet Socialist Republics and the United States of America,

Having in mind Part III of the Quadripartite Agreement of 3 September 1971 and taking note with satisfaction of the fact that the agreements and arrangements mentioned below have been concluded,

Have agreed on the following:

1. The four Governments, by virtue of this Protocol, bring into force the Quadripartite Agreement, which, like this Protocol, does not affect quadripartite agreements or decisions previously concluded or reached.

2. The four Governments proceed on the basis that the agreements and arrangements concluded between the competent German authorities:

"Agreement between the Government of the Federal Republic of Germany and the Government of the German Democratic Republic on the Transit Traffic of Civilian Persons and Goods between the Federal Republic of Germany and Berlin (West)" ("Abkommen zwischen der Regierung der Bundesrepublik Deutschland und der Regierung der Deutschen Demokratischen Republik über den Transitverkehr von zivilen Personen und Gütern zwischen der Bundesrepublik Deutschland und Berlin (West)") dated 17 December 1971;

"Arrangement between the Senat and the Government of the German Democratic Republic on Facilitations and Improvements in Travel and Visitor Traffic" ("Vereinbarung zwischen dem Senat und der Regierung der Deutschen Demokratischen Republik über Erleichterungen und Verbesserungen des Reise- und Besucherverkehrs") dated 20 December 1971;

"Arrangement between the Senat and the Government of the German Democratic Republic on the Resolution of the Problem of Enclaves by Exchange of Territory" ("Vereinbarung zwischen dem Senat und der Regierung der Deutschen Demokratischen Republik über die Regelung der Frage von Enklaven durch Gebietsaustausch") dated 20 December 1971;

Points 6 and 7 of the "Protocol on Negotiations between a Delegation of the Federal Ministry for Post and Telecommunications of the Federal Republic of Germany and a Delegation of the Ministry for Post and Telecommunications of the German Democratic Republic" ("Protokoll über Verhandlungen zwischen einer Delegation des Bundesministeriums für das Post- und Fernmeldewesen der Bundesrepublik Deutschland und einer Delegation des Ministeriums für Post- und

Fernmeldewesen der Deutschen Demokratischen Republik") dated 30 September 1971;

shall enter into force simultaneously with the Quadripartite Agreement.

3. The Quadripartite Agreement and the consequent agreements and arrangements of the competent German authorities referred to in this Protocol settle important issues examined in the course of the negotiations and shall remain in force together.

4. In the event of a difficulty in the application of the Quadripartite Agreement or any of the above-mentioned agreements or arrangements which any of the four Governments considers serious, or in the event of non-implementation of any part thereof, that Government will have the right to draw the attention of the other three Governments to the provisions of the Quadripartite Agreement and this Protocol and to conduct the requisite quadripartite consultations in order to ensure the observance of the commitments undertaken and to bring the situation into conformity with the Quadripartite Agreement and this Protocol.

5. This Protocol enters into force on the date of signature.

DONE at the building formerly occupied by the Allied Control Council in the American Sector of Berlin, this third day of June 1972, in four originals, each in the English, French and Russian languages, all texts being equally authentic.

For the Government of the United Kingdom of Great Britain and Northern Ireland:
ALEC DOUGLAS-HOME

For the Government of the French Republic:
MAURICE SCHUMANN

For the Government of the Union of Soviet Socialist Republics:
A. GROMYKO

For the Government of the United States of America:
WILLIAM P. ROGERS

MAP SECTION

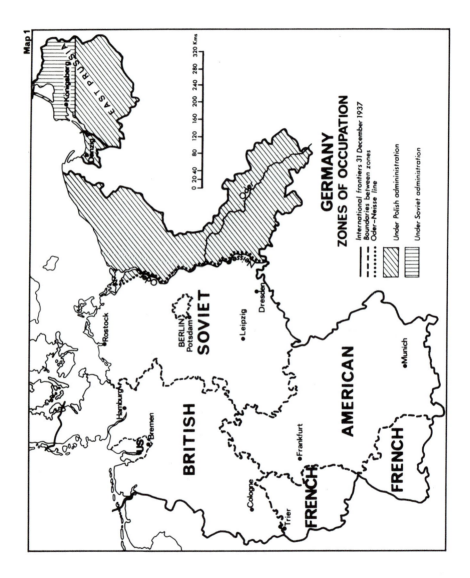

Map 1

GERMANY
ZONES OF OCCUPATION

International frontiers 31 December 1937
Boundaries between zones
Oder–Neisse line
Under Polish administration
Under Soviet administration

0 20 40   80   120   160   200   240   280   320 Kms

EAST PRUSS.

Königsberg

Danzig

Rostock

Hamburg

Bremen

BRITISH

BERLIN
Potsdam

SOVIET

Leipzig

Dresden

Cologne

Trier

FRENCH

Frankfurt

AMERICAN

Munich

FRENCH

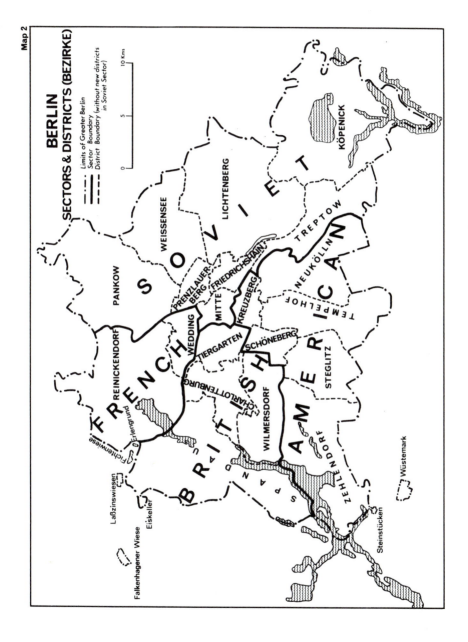

Map 2

BERLIN
SECTORS & DISTRICTS (BEZIRKE)

Limits of Greater Berlin
Sector Boundary
District Boundary (without new districts
  in Soviet Sector)

0   5   10 Kms

Map 3

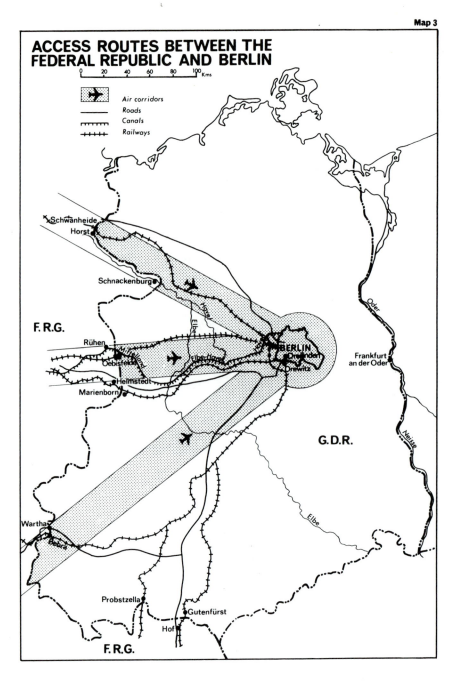

ACCESS ROUTES BETWEEN THE FEDERAL REPUBLIC AND BERLIN

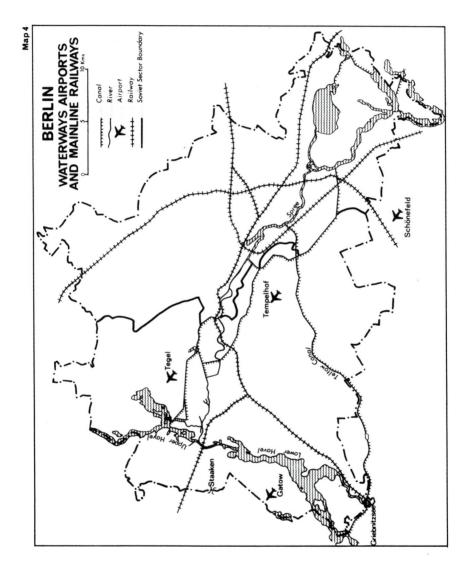

Map 4

BERLIN
WATERWAYS AIRPORTS
AND MAINLINE RAILWAYS

Canal
River
Airport
Railway
Soviet Sector Boundary

0   5   10 Kms

Tegel

Tempelhof

Schönefeld

Staaken

Gatow

Griebnitzsee

Upper Havel

Lower Havel

Spree

Teltow Canal

PRINCIPAL TREATIES AND OTHER INTERNATIONAL INSTRUMENTS, AS WELL AS PRINCIPAL INNER-GERMAN ARRANGEMENTS

1949

4 April — North Atlantic Treaty, 9, 41–2, 162, 201, 207

4 May — New York agreement terminating the Berlin blockade, 6, 40, 48, 104–5, 107, 109

20 June — Communiqué on the sixth session of the Council of Foreign Ministers, 6, 40, 48, 104–5, 107, 109

20 June — Charter of the Allied High Commission, 57

1950

19 September — New York Foreign Ministers' Communiqué, 7–8, 19, 20, 41

4 November — European Convention for the Protection of Human Rights and Fundamental Freedoms, 211–13

1951

18 April — Treaty establishing the European Coal and Steel Community, 196, 207, 218

19 June — Agreement between the Parties to the North Atlantic Treaty regarding the Status of their Forces, 25, 43, 207

20 September — Berlin Agreement on Trade between the currency areas of the German Mark (DM-*West*) and the currency areas of the German Mark of the *Deutsche Notenbank* (DM-*Ost*) (as amended in 1960), 26–7

1952

26 May — Bonn Convention on Relations between the Three Powers and the Federal Republic of Germany, as amended by the Paris Convention of 23 October 1954, 8–9, 20, 23, 25, 26, 32, 42, 43–4, 57, 72, 115, 146–7, 202, 323

26 May — Bonn Convention on the Settlement of Matters arising out of the War and the Occupation, as amended by the Paris Convention of 23 October 1954, 25, 43–4, 115, 121, 202

26 May — Declaration of the Federal Republic of Germany concerning Aid to Berlin, 9, 44, 147, 197, 330

26 May — Letter from the Three High Commissioners to the Federal Chancellor concerning the exercise of the reserved Allied rights relating to Berlin, in the version of letter X of 23 October 1954, 9, 44, 61, 72, 146–7, 161, 189, 229, 237, 329

TABLE OF LEGISLATIVE MEASURES

A. ALLIED MEASURES

(i) *SHAEF*

(ii) *Allied Control Council*

1946

20 August   Law No. 34, 269, 270

22 October   DAIR/P(45)71 Second Revise: Flight Rules by ACA Air
                 Directorate for Aircraft flying in Air Corridors in
                 Germany and Berlin Control Zone, 39, 103, 110,
                 112–14, 117

20 December Law No. 43, 40, 85, 269, 275–6, 279, 307

1947

25 February   Law No. 46, 151

(iii) *Western Zones of Occupation in Germany*

1949

20 April   US Military Government Law No. 19, 84

1950

2 March   Allied High Commission Law No. 22, 277

1 June   French High Commissioner *Ordonnance* No. 242, 60, 87

1955

28 April   US High Commissioner Law No. 46, 60, 87

(iv) *Soviet Zone of Occupation in Germany*

1945

11 August   Order No. 8, 254

1949

9 May   Order No. 56, 104

(v) *Allied Kommandatura Berlin*

1945

11 July   Order No. 1, 4, 85, 92

23 August   BK/M(45)7: Decision on control of property, 254, 262

1946

12 January   BK/O(46)35, 276

24 January   BK/O(46)61, 85, 238

26 February BK/O(46)101A, 85

1946
13 August   BK/O(46)326: Temporary Constitution of Greater Berlin,
                5, 7, 58, 69, 295

1947
30 September   BK/O(47)277, 289

1948
14 June   BK/O(48)89, 289

21 December   Declaration by Western Commandants, 6–7, 42, 58–9

1949
14 May   Statement of Principles governing the relationship
                between the Allied Kommandatura and Greater Berlin,
                8, 42, 145, 189, 196

30 June   BK/O(49)139, 145

7 October   BK/O(49)217, 257

7 November   BK/O(49)237 and 238, 278

9 November   BK/O(49)245, 263

1950
9 February   Law No. 1, 85

9 February   Law No. 2, 65, 76, 85

9 February   Law No. 3, 85

25 February   Law No. 5, 271, 286

4 March   Law No. 6, 235

17 March   Law No. 7, 65–7, 74, 76, 77, 78, 85, 89–90, 172, 284

28 April   Law No. 8, 291

29 August   BK/O(50)75, 43, 71, 89, 145, 152, 164

1951
29 January   Law No. 13, 277

30 January   BK/O(51)10, 85, 163, 171

7 March   BK/L(51)29: First Instrument of Revision of the Statement
                of Principles, 8, 42, 189, 196

1951

31 May   BK/O(51)31, 278

27 August   Law No. 17, 65, 89

8 October   BK/O(51)56, 43, 157–8, 170

13 November   BK/O(51)63, 43, 163, 168, 170

29 December   BK/O(51)72, 259

1952

20 February   Law No. 21, 65, 89

23 February   BK/L(52)19, 158

25 April   BK/O(52)17, 271

21 May   BKC/L(52)6, 43, 196–7, 229

28 August   BK/L(52)81, 158, 160, 170

4 December   BK/L(52)118, 158

20 December   BK/O(52)35, 71, 85, 152, 173–4

1955

5 May   BKC/L(55)3: Declaration on Berlin, 9, 42, 43, 61, 65, 80, 81, 86, 88–9, 147, 161, 190, 229, 236, 270, 281–2, 288, 332

14 May   BK/O(55)10, 158, 170, 197

1956

25 July   BK/L(56)21, 153

1957

8 January   BK/O(57)1, 278–9

27 February   BK/O(57)4, 271

18 November   BK/L(57)44, 217–19

18 November   BK/L(57)45, 218

1958

6 March   BK/L(58)7, 278

14 March   BK/O(58)3, 276, 288

1958

1 July   BK/O(58)7, 277, 279

1959

26 May   BK/O(59)9, 163

1960

19 August   BK/O(60)4, 264

1961

5 May   BK/O(61)5, 272

19 May   BK/O(61)6, 289

12 July   BK/O(61)8, 277

1961

25 August   BK/O(61)11, 245, 246

5 October   BK/O(61)16, 237, 271

1962

23 July   BK/O(62)5, 287

21 August   BK/O(62)6, 257–8

25 September   BK/O(62)8, 265

24 October   BK/O(62)9, 288

1963

24 May   BK/O(63)7, 277

31 July   BK/O(63)9, 238

1964

20 February   BK/O(64)1, 272

11 September   BK/O(64)3, 77–8, 80, 81, 200

23 September   BK/O(64)4, 85

24 September   BK/O(64)5, 246

1965

27 January   BK/O(65)2, 276

23 June   BK/O(65)8, 238

19 August   BK/O(65)9, 82

23 August   BK/L(65)51, 218

1 October   BK/O(65)11, 273, 275

25 November   BK/O(65)14, 246

1966

7 March   BK/O(66)4, 246

8 August   BK/O(66)6, 82

1966

6 October   BK/O(66)9, 246

1967

1 February   BK/O(67)1, 246

24 May   BK/L(67)10, 148, 164, 175

31 May   BK/O(67)6, 277

17 July   BK/O(67)7, 290

1968

27 May   BK/O(68)1, 265

11 September   BK/O(68)9, 264

21 October   BK/O(68)13, 177

1969

17 July   BK/O(69)5, 277

8 August   BK/L(69)29, 272–3

1970

29 June   BK/O(70)3, 287

26 October   BK/O(70)8, 66, 75–6

1971

28 May   BK/O(71)2, 276, 289

3 September   BKC/L(71)1, 93, 248

7 October   BK/O(71)6, 280

16 December   BKC/L(71)2, 94, 248

18 December   BKC/L(71)3, 131–2, 228

1972

13 March   BK/O(72)3, 251

1972

3 June	BK/O(72)6, 94, 96
3 June	BK/O(72)7, 251
22 June	BK/O(72)8, 277
20 July	BKC/L(72)1, 96
21 July	BK/O(72)9, 96
25 September	BK/O(72)10, 260

1973

13 April	BKC/L(73)1, 209
25 May	BK/O(73)2, 82
25 September	BK/O(73)6, 277
28 September	BK/O(73)7, 79

1974

23 April	BK/O(74)2, 164, 167, 271
19 June	BK/O(74)6, 79
9 July	BK/O(74)7, 276
12 July	BK/O(74)8, 184
30 September	BK/O(74)11, 43, 67, 89, 163, 199, 211, 221, 274

1975

8 January	BK/O(75)1, 259, 280
9 April	BK/O(75)3, 81, 222
7 August	BK/O(75)10, 81, 82, 200
7 August	BK/O(75)11, 259, 280
9 September	BK/O(75)12, 82

1975

19 December	BK/O(75)15, 260

1976

24 June	BK/O(76)6, 81
10 September	BK/O(76)8, 171
29 October	BK/O(76)10, 200

1977

27 April	BK/O(77)4, 279
29 April	BK/O(77)5, 276
19 July	BK/O(77)8, 220
30 September	BK/O(77)9, 171, 172
25 October	BK/O(77)10, 276
30 November	BK/O(77)11, 266

1978

31 May	BK/O(78)5, 81–2
31 July	BK/O(78)6, 220
16 November	BK/O(78)9, 267

1979

25 April	BK/O(79)5, 220
17 July	BK/O(79)8, 280, 284

1980

24 January	BK/O(80)2, 261
30 April	BK/O(80)5, 261
30 May	BK/O(80)8, 280, 284
30 December	BK/O(80)13, 66, 284

1981

24 June	BK/O(81)5, 276
20 November	BK/O(81)8, 268

1982

29 January	BK/O(82)1, 280, 284
30 June	BK/O(82)6, 280

1983

21 April	BK/O(83)1, 200
28 April	BK/O(83)2, 163, 171, 291
31 May	BK/O(83)4, 219, 280
12 October	BK/O(83)6, 220, 280
25 October	BKC/L(83)1, 96
27 October	BK/O(83)7, 255
28 December	BK/O(83)9, 256

1984

17 January	BK/O(84)1, 260
26 July	BK/O(84)7, 80
23 August	BK/O(84)8, 286
9 October	BK/O(84)9, 280

1984

23 November	BK/O(84)10, 83
21 December	BK/O(84)11, 163, 258, 259

1985

19 March	BK/O(85)2, 260
10 April	BK/O(85)3, 260
23 August	BK/O(85)6, 83, 285
9 October	BK/O(85)8, 260
29 November	BK/O(85)9, 260
18 December	BK/O(85)11, 276

1986

29 April	BK/O(86)2, 286
30 May	BK/O(86)5, 277
29 August	BK/O(86)6, 280
30 September	BK/O(86)7, 276
8 October	BK/O(86)8, 83
8 October	BK/O(86)9, 260
28 November	BK/O(86)12, 280, 284

1987

10 March	BK/O(87)1, 238

(vi) *British Sector of Berlin*

1948

14 June	Ordinance No. 146, 86
4 July	Second Monetary Reform Ordinance, 256

1949

30 December	Ordinance No. 202, 84

1951

21 May   Ordinance No. 508, 66, 68, 86, 283

2 July   Ordinance No. 68 (Amended 2), 60

15 October   Ordinance No. 511, 285, 286

1971

1 March   Ordinance No. 535, 68

1986

29 May   BCO(86)1, 287

(vii) *French Sector of Berlin*

1948

4 July   Second Monetary Reform *Ordonnance*, 256

1949

31 August   *Ordonnance* on property control, 84

1950

1 June   French High Commissioner *Ordonnance* No. 242, 60, 87

1951

21 May   *Ordonnance* No. 508, 66, 68, 86, 283

15 October   *Ordonnance* No. 511, 285, 286

1971

1 March   *Ordonnance* No. 535, 68

1979

6 February   Two *Ordonnances* on security at Tegel Airport, 287

(viii) *American Sector of Berlin*

1948

4 July   Second Monetary Reform Ordinance, 256

1949

20 April   US Military Government Law No. 19, 84

1951

21 May   Ordinance No. 508, 66, 68, 86, 283

15 October   Ordinance No. 511, 285, 286

1955
28 April   US High Commissioner Law No. 46, 60, 87

1971
1 March   Ordinance No. 535, 68

1972
27 July   Ordinance establishing certain restricted areas, 287

1975
2 July   Ordinance establishing certain restricted areas, 287

1986
27 June   USCOB(86)3, 287

(ix) *Soviet Sector of Berlin*

1953
17 June   Order of Soviet Commandant declaring a State of Emergency in the Soviet Sector of Berlin, 298

B. GERMAN MEASURES

(i) *German Reich*

1913
22 July   Nationality Law, 27, 236

1924
12 February   Ordinance creating the *"Deutsche Reichsbahn"*, 253

30 August   Law on the *"Deutsche Reichsbahn Gesellschaft"*, 253

1928
17 July   Ordinance on Construction and Operation of Railways, 258, 259

1935
15 September   Citizenship Law, 235

1937
10 February   Law regulating the *Reichsbank* and the *Deutsche Reichsbahn*, 254

1939
4 July   Railway Law, 254

(ii) *Prussia*

1920

27 April   Law constituting a new City Community of Berlin, 91, 93

(iii) *Federal Republic of Germany*

1949

23 May   Basic Law for the Federal Republic of Germany, 26, 144–5, 152–3, 156–7, 165–6, 170, 173, 175–6, 236

15 June   Election Law, 145

1950

12 September   Law on the Re-establishment of Legal Unity (including the Law on the Constitution of the Courts and the Codes of Civil and Criminal Procedure), 163, 171

1951

2 March   Law on the Legal Position of Railway Property, 259

12 March   Law on the Federal Constitutional Court, 162, 173, 174

29 March   General Railway Law, 163, 259

21 May   Law on the Legal Position of Federal Waterways Property, 264

1952

4 January   Law on the position of *Land* Berlin in the Financial System of the Federal Republic ("Third Transfer Law"), 159–60, 162

4 March   Passport Law, 237

1956

19 March   Soldiers Law, 271

7 May   Election Law, 153

21 July   Conscription Law, 271–2

1957

23 February   Law on the Purchase of Land for Defence Purposes, 271

15 March   Military Discipline Code, 271

11 June   Fourth Law amending the Penal Code, 271

1957

19 July   Restitution Law, 177

26 July   Law on Titles, Orders and Insignia, 271

1959

23 December   Law on the Peaceful Use of Nuclear Energy and Protection against its Dangers, 277

1960

17 August   Law on the Pollution of Waterways, 264

1964

5 August   Association Law, 171

6 August   Law to ratify the Vienna Convention on Diplomatic Relations, 77–8

1965

28 April   Aliens Law, 290

1968

27 May   Law on Waterways, 265

1969

26 August   Law to ratify the Vienna Convention on Consular Relations, 75

1973

6 June   Law on Accession of the Federal Republic of Germany to the United Nations Charter, 209

16 November   Law to provide Privileges and Immunities to the Permanent Representation of the German Democratic Republic, 78–9

1974

2 March   Introductory Law to the Penal Code, 164, 167

30 April   Ordinance to provide Privileges and Immunities to the Permanent Representation of the German Democratic Republic, 79

1980

31 January   Law on Entry and Stay of Nationals of European Community Member States, 290

1982

16 July   Asylum Law, 290

1982

23 December   Law on International Assistance in Criminal Cases, 163, 291

1984

17 July   Second Law to amend the Federal Central Register Law, 80

1986

19 April   Passport Law, 237

(iv) *Berlin*

1950

1 September   Constitution of Berlin, 69, 88, 96–7, 157, 165–6

1951

9 January   Law on the Re-establishment of Legal Unity, 171

1958

26 June   Atomic Law, 277

1960

23 February   Berlin Water Law, 264–5

1967

9 January   Third Ordinance on Alteration of District Boundaries, 97

1971

24 June   Fifth Ordinance on Alteration of District Boundaries, 97

1976

25 March   Ordinance on Protection against Catastrophes, 274

(v) *German Democratic Republic and East Berlin*

1949

7 October   Constitution of the GDR, 236, 300

1957

28 January   (East) Berlin Law on adoption of Law on Local Organs of State Power, 303

1959

1 July   Ordinance on General Conditions for Delivery to and Provisioning of Armed Forces of the GDR, 307

1960

29 August   Decree restricting entry to (East) Berlin, 243

8 September   Decree prolonging Decree of 29 August, 243

12 September   Law dissolving the Office of President and establishing the State Council, 305

1961

13 August   Decree restricting free movement within Berlin, 244

22 August   Order restricting free movement within Berlin, 245

1962

26 January   Conscription Ordinance, 307

1967

20 February   Citizenship Law, 27, 236

1968

8 April   Constitution of the GDR, 300

11 June   Decree on visas, 108

1974

7 October   Revision of GDR Constitution, 300

1976

24 June   Election Law, 303

1979

28 June   Election Law, 303

1981

30 October   Law amending Waterways Traffic Law, 268

1982

2 July   Water Law, 266

BIBLIOGRAPHY

The bibliography lists official and non-official collections of documents, and certain books and articles referred to in the text. It is not intended to be exhaustive. For more detailed bibliographies reference may be made to:

Wetzlaugk, *Berlin und die Deutsche Frage*, pp.257–72.
Heidelmeyer and Hindrichs, *Documents on Berlin 1943–1963*, pp.364–73.
Riklin, *Das Berlinproblem*, pp.405–34.
von Münch, *Dokumente des geteilten Deutschland*, Vol. I, pp.571–81; Vol. II, pp.628–37.
Berlin-Bibliographie (up to 1960) (1965).
Berlin-Bibliographie 1961–1966 (1973).
Berlin-Bibliographie 1967–1977 (1985).
The annual bibliographies in the *Jahrbuch des Landesarchiv Berlin* (since 1982).

OFFICIAL DOCUMENTATION

United Kingdom

Selected Documents on Germany and the Question of Berlin 1944–1961, Germany No. 2 (1961) (Cmnd 1552).
Selected Documents on Germany and the Question of Berlin 1961–1973, Miscellaneous No. 16 (1975) (Cmnd 6201).
Documents on British Policy Overseas, Series I, Vol. I, The Conference at Potsdam July–August 1945 (1984).

United States of America

Documents on Germany, 1944–1985 (United States Department of State Publication 9446).
Foreign Relations of the United States (volumes dealing with the wartime and post-war conferences relating to Germany).

West German

The Berlin Settlement. The Quadripartite Agreement on Berlin and the Supplementary Arrangements, published by the Press and Information Office of the Government of the Federal Republic of Germany (1972).
Berlin – Materialien zur Rechtslage und zur politischen Entwicklung seit 1945 (Informationszentrum Berlin, 6th ed., 1985).
Zehn Jahre Deutschlandpolitik – Die Entwicklung der Beziehungen zwischen der Bundesrepublik Deutschland und der Deutschen Demokratischen Republik 1969-1979 – Bericht und Dokumentation (1980), published by the Federal Ministry for Inner-German Relations.
Berichte über Durchführung des Viermächte–Abkommens und der ergänzenden Vereinbarungen (Annual Reports of the *Senat* to the House of Representatives, since 1973).

Soviet Union/GDR

Documentation on the question of West Berlin (1964), issued by the GDR Ministry of Foreign Affairs.

Das Vierseitige Abkommen über Westberlin und seine Realisierung: Dokumente 1971–1977 (1977), issued by the USSR and GDR Ministries of Foreign Affairs.

Dokumente zur Aussenpolitik der DDR (1954–).

The Soviet Union at the international conferences of the period of the Great Patriotic War 1941–1945 (in Russian), Vols. I, II, IV, VI (1978, 1980).

OTHER COLLECTIONS OF DOCUMENTS

Heidelmeyer and Hindrichs, *Documents on Berlin 1943–1963* (1963).
Heidelmeyer and Hindrichs, *Dokumente zur Berlin-Frage 1944–1966* (1967).
von Münch, *Dokumente des geteilten Deutschland*, Vols. I and II (1968, 1974).

BOOKS

Abrasimov, *West Berlin – Yesterday and Today* (1981).
Apell, *Das Bundesverfassungsgericht und Berlin* (1984).
Bark, *Agreement on Berlin – a Study of the 1970–1972 Quadripartite Negotiations* (1974).
Bathurst and Simpson, *Germany and the North Atlantic Community* (1956).
Catudal, *The Diplomacy of the Quadripartite Agreement on Berlin* (1978).
Catudal, *A Balance Sheet of the Quadripartite Agreement on Berlin* (1978).
Czermak, *Die Stellung Berlins in der Rechts-, Gerichts- und Finanzordnung der Bundesrepublik Deutschland* (Dissertation, Bonn 1967).
Doehring/Ress, *Staats- und Völkerrechtliche Aspekte der Berlin-Regelung* (1972).
Fijalkowski *et al.*, *Berlin – Hauptstadtanspruch und Westintegration* (1967).
Görner, *DDR gewährleistet friedlichen Westberlin-Transit* (1969).
Hennig, *Die Bundespräsenz in West-Berlin* (1976).
Knörr, *Die Kompetenz von Berlin (West) zum Abschluss völkerrechtlicher Verträge* (Dissertation, Munich 1975).
Krumholz, *Berlin – ABC* (2nd ed., 1968).
Landy, *Berlin et son statut* (1983).
Mahncke, *Berlin im geteilten Deutschland* (1973).
Mampel, *Der Sowjetsektor von Berlin* (1963).
Möhler, *Völkerrechtliche Probleme östlicher Beteiligungen an internationalen Veranstaltungen in West-Berlin* (1985).
Pfennig/Neumann, *Verfassung von Berlin* (1978).
Plischke, *Berlin. Development of its Government and Administration* (1952).
Plischke, *Government and Politics of Contemporary Berlin* (1963).
Ress, *Die Rechtslage Deutschlands nach dem Grundlagenvertrag vom 21. Dezember 1972* (1978).
Riklin, *Das Berlinproblem* (1964).
Rottmann, *Das Viermächte Status Berlins* (2nd ed., 1959).

Ruge, *Das Zugangsrecht der Westmächte auf dem Luftweg nach Berlin* (1968).
Schiedermair, *Der völkerrechtliche Status Berlins nach dem Viermächte-Abkommen vom 3. September 1971* (1975).
Schröder, *Die ausländischen Vertretungen in Berlin* (1983).
Schröder, *Die Elbe-Grenze* (1986).
Vysotsky, *West Berlin* (1974).
Wetzlaugk, *Berlin und die Deutsche Frage* (1985).
Zieger ed., *Zehn Jahre Berlin-Abkommen 1971–1981* (1983).
Zivier, *The Legal Status of the Land Berlin* (1980); this is a translation, with some changes, of Zivier, *Der Rechtsstatus des Landes Berlin* (3rd ed., 1977), to which reference should also be made.
Zündorf, *Die Ostverträge* (1979).

ARTICLES AND SHORTER WORKS

Arndt, "Legal Problems of the German Eastern Treaties", *AJIL*, 74 (1980), pp.122–33.

Bandorf, "Formelle Kontakte zwischen Bundestag und Volkskammer", *Zeitschrift für Rechtspolitik* 1985, pp.99–103.
Bathurst, "Legal aspects of the Berlin problem", *BYIL*, 38 (1962), pp.255–306.
Bentzien, "Die sowjetische Auslegung der mitteldeutschen Lufthoheitsrechte, insbesondere im Hinblick auf die bestehenden Vier-Mächte-Vereinbarungen", *Zeitschrift für Luft- und Weltraumrecht*, 19 (1970), pp.11-18.
Bentzien, "Probleme des Luftverkehrs von und nach Berlin, gestern – heute – morgen", *Zeitschrift für Luft- und Weltraumrecht*, 28 (1979), pp.327–39.
Boldyrew, *Westberlin und die europäische Sicherheit* (1973).

Carstens, "Zur Interpretation der Berlin-Regelung von 1971", *Fs Scheuner* (1973), pp.67–83.
Catudal, "The Berlin Agreement of 1971: Has it worked?", *ICLQ*, 25 (1976), pp.766–800.
Colard, "L'accord quadripartite sur Berlin du 3 Septembre 1971", *RGDIP*, 76 (1972), pp.401–44.

Dehnhard, "Verfassungsrecht im Vier-Mächte-Status", *DVBl*, 101 (1986), pp.176–81.
Delbrück, "Die staatsrechtliche Stellung Berlins in der Rechtsprechung des Bundesverfassungsgerichts und der Bundesgerichte", in: *Ostverträge – Berlin Status – Münchner Abkommen – Beziehungen zwischen der BRD und der DDR* (1971), pp. 214–20.
Deuerlein, "Die Entstehung der Luftkorridore nach Berlin", *DA*, 2 (1969), pp.735–64.
Doehring/Hailbronner, "Rechtsfragen der Einbeziehung West-Berlins in den internationalen Sportverkehr der Bundesrepublik Deutschland und ihrer Sportorganisationen," *DA*, 7 (1974), pp.1169–87.

Doeker/Melsheimer/Schröder, "Berlin and the Quadripartite Agreement of 1971", *AJIL*, 67 (1973), pp.44–62.

Drath, "Berlin und Bonn. Die Rechtsstellung Berlins in der Bundesrepublik", *JR*, 1951, pp.385–90.

Drath, "Die staatsrechtliche Stellung Berlins", *AöR*, 82 (1957), pp. 27–75.

Elsas-Patrick, "German Federal Constitutional Jurisdiction in Berlin: Bless'd be the ties that bind?", *Revue de droit international, de sciences diplomatiques et politiques*, 57 (1979), pp.245–77.

Ermacora, "Berlin – Relikt der Einheit Deutschlands?", in: *Gedächtnisschrift H. Peters* (1967), pp.480–92.

Finkelnburg, "Die Rechtsstellung Berlins im Bund", *JuS*, 7 (1967), pp.542–4; *JuS*, 8 (1968), pp.10–14, 58–61.

Finkelnburg, "Die Rechtsprechung des Bundesverfassungsgerichts in Berliner Sachen", *AöR*, 95 (1970), pp.581–95.

Finkelnburg, "Die Bundeszugehörigkeit Berlins und die Rechtsprechung des Bundesverfassungsgerichts in Berliner Sachen", *NJW*, 27 (1974), pp.1969–73.

Forch, "Mitwirkung deutscher Geschworener an der Ausübung amerikanischer Besatzungsgerichtsbarkeit in Berlin", *ZaöRV*, 40 (1980), pp.760–81.

Franklin, "Zonal Boundaries and Access to Berlin", *World Politics*, 16 (1963), pp.1–31.

Frowein, "Legal Problems of the German Ostpolitik", *ICLQ*, 23 (1974), pp.105–26.

Frowein, review of Schiedermair, *AöR*, 101 (1976), pp.638–45.

Frowein, "Die Rechtslage Deutschlands und der Status Berlins", in: *Handbuch des Verfassungsrechts der Bundesrepublik Deutschlands* (1983), pp.29–58.

Geulen, "Rechte Betroffener und gerichtlicher Rechtsschutz gegenüber hoheitlichen Massnahmen der Alliierten in West-Berlin", *NJW*, 38 (1985), pp.1055–7.

Grabitz, "Gemeinschaftsgewalt, Besatzungsgewalt und deutsche Staatsgewalt in Berlin", in: *Fs Carstens* (1984), pp.125–38.

Grawert, "Die Staatsangehörigkeit der Berliner", *Der Staat*, 12 (1973), pp.289–312.

Green, "The Legal Status of Berlin", *Nederlands Tijdschrift voor Internationaal Recht*, 10 (1963), pp.113–38.

Hacker, "Der Viermächte-Status von Berlin", in: *Berlin Fibel* (1975), pp.321–48.

Hacker, "Die aussenpolitische Resonanz des Berlin-Abkommens", in: *Zehn Jahre Berlin-Abkommen 1971–1981*, pp.217–52.

Heidelmeyer, "Besatzungsrecht und deutsches Recht im Land Berlin", *ZaöRV*, 28 (1968), pp.704–30.

Heidelmeyer, "Immunität und Rechtschutz gegen Akte der Besatzungshoheit in Berlin", *ZaöRV*, 46 (1986), pp.519–38.

Hütte, "Berlin and the European Communities", *Yearbook of European Law*, 3 (1983), pp.1–22.

Ipsen, "Die Staatsangehörigkeit der Bürger West-Berlins", *JIR*, 16 (1973), pp.266–300.

Jennings, "Government in Commission", *BYIL*, 23 (1946), pp. 112–41.

Jung, "Vierseitiges Abkommen und sowjetischer Sektor Berlins", *ROW*, 19 (1975), pp. 217–23.

Kewenig, "Entwicklungslinien des völker- und staatsrechtlichen Status von Berlin", *Schriftenreihe der Juristischen Gesellschaft zu Berlin*, No. 88 (1984).

Kreutzer, "Die Geltung von Bundesrecht in Berlin", *JR*, 1951, pp.641–5.

Kreutzer, "Berlin im Bund: Die Einbeziehung Berlins in die politische und rechtliche Ordnung der Bundesrepublik", *Zeitschrift für Politik*, 1 NF (1954), pp.139–58.

Kreutzer, "West-Berlin Stadt und Land", in: *Berlin, Brennpunkt deutschen Schicksals* (1960).

Kröger, "Zu einigen Fragen des staatsrechtlichen Status von Berlin", *Deutsche Aussenpolitik*, 3 (1958), pp.10–26.

Kröger, "Strikte Einhaltung des Westberlin-Abkommens – ein Gebot der Vernunft und des Rechts," *Deutsche Aussenpolitik*, 12 (1977) pp.57–65.

Legien, *Die Viermächte-Vereinbarungen über Berlin* (2nd ed., 1961).

Legien, "Der rechtliche Status des Sowjetsektors", in: *Berlin Sowjetsektor* (1965), pp.41–53.

Lerche, "Berliner Sachen als verfassungsprozessualer Begriff", in: *Fs Leibholz* Vol. II (1966), pp.465–80.

Lush, "The Relationship between Berlin and the Federal Republic of Germany", *ICLQ*, 14 (1965), pp.742–87.

Mahnke, "Das Recht des zivilen Zugangs nach Berlin", *DA*, 2 (1969), pp.148–54.

Mahnke, "Berlin – fünfte Besatzungszone oder Teil des sowjetischen Besatzungsgebiets", *DA*, 2 (1969), pp.473–82.

Mahnke, "Zur Rechtslage Berlins – Einige korrigierende Bemerkungen", *DA*, 4 (1971), pp.901–9.

Mahnke, "Der Zugang nach Berlin: Die historische Entwicklung", *DA*, 5 (1972), pp.140–8, 346–87.

Mahnke, "Zum Status von Berlin", *DA*, 8 (1975), pp.835–42.

Mahnke, "Rechtliche Aspekte des Status von Berlin (Ost)", *ROW*, 23 (1979), pp.185–93.

Mampel, "Der Status von Berlin (Ost)", in: *Zehn Jahre Berlin-Abkommen 1971–1981*, pp.121–46.

von Mangoldt, "Zur Einheit der deutschen Staatsangehörigkeit im Spiegel jüngerer Konsularverträge", *AVR*, 22 (1984), pp.138–71.

Mann, "The present legal status of Germany", *ILQ*, 1 (1947), pp. 314–35; *Studies in International Law* (1973), pp.634–59.

Mann, "Germany's present legal status revisited", *ICLQ*, 16 (1967), pp.760–99; *Studies in International Law* (1973), pp.660–705.

Mosely, "Dismemberment of Germany. The Allied negotiations from Yalta to Potsdam", *Foreign Affairs*, 28 (1949/50), pp.487–98.

Mosely, "The Occupation of Germany. New light on how the zones were drawn", *Foreign Affairs*, 28 (1949/50), pp.580–604.

Mussgnug, "Die Bindungen Berlins an die Entscheidungen des Bundesverfassungsgerichts", in: *Fs Weber* (1974), pp.157–86.

Mussgnug, "Wem gehört Nofretete?", *Schriftenreihe der Juristischen Gesellschaft zu Berlin*, No. 52 (1977).

Nawrocki, "Schwierigkeiten mit den "drei Z": Die DDR und das Viermächte-Abkommen über Berlin", *DA*, 7 (1974), pp.582–95.

Pestalozza, "Berlin – ein deutsches Land", *JuS*, 23 (1983), pp. 241–54.

Pestalozza, "Noch einmal: Der Status von Berlin", *JuS*, 24 (1984), pp.430–2.

Pestalozza, "Berlin unter Europäischem Rechtsschutz", in: *Fs zum 125 jährigen Bestehen der Juristischen Gesellschaft zu Berlin* (1984), pp.549–71.

von Przychowski, "Luftkreuz Berlin?", in: *Berlin translokal* (1983), pp.152–66.

Randelzhofer, "Untersuchung über die Möglichkeiten des Rechtsschutzes der Einwohner Berlins gegen Akte der Alliierten", *Die Verwaltung*, 19 (1986), pp.9–38.

Ress, "La disciplina giuridica del traffico in transito fra la Repubblica Federale di Germania e Berlino-Ovest", *La Comunità Internazionale*, 28 (1973), pp.41–71.

Ress, "Das privilegierte rechtliche Regime des Transitverkehrs von und nach West-Berlin", *ZaöRV*, 34 (1974), pp.133–47.

Rexin, "Die Sowjets in West-Berlin", in *Berlin translokal* (1983), pp.77–96.

von Richthofen, "Das Viermächte-Abkommen über Berlin", *Evangelische Kommentare*, 4 (1971), pp.586, 591.

Rush, "The Berlin Agreement: An Assessment", *The Atlantic Community Quarterly* (1972), pp.52–65.

Schaefer, "Die völkerrechtliche Vertretung von Berlin bei einer Aufnahme beider deutscher Staaten in die UNO", *Politische Studien*, 24 (1973), pp.11–28.

Schiedermair, "Das Verbot des Rechtsmissbrauchs und die Regelung des Transitverkehrs nach Berlin", *ZaöRV*, 38 (1978), pp.160–81.

Schiedermair, "Die Bindungen West-Berlins an die Bundesrepublik", *NJW*, 35 (1982), pp.2841–7.

Schiwy, "Probleme der Besuchsregelung", in: *Zehn Jahre Berlin-Abkommen 1971–1981*, pp.163–75.

Schröder, "Die Bedeutung der Drei-Staaten-These für die Rechtslage des Verkehrs von und nach Berlin", *ROW*, 21 (1967), pp.104–9.

Schröder, "Die Bedeutung der Berliner Rechte der Alliierten für den Zugang von Deutschen nach Berlin", *RuP*, 5 (1969), pp.11–19.

Schröder, *The Legal Status of the Lines of Communication to and from Berlin* (1970).

Schröder, "Monstro simile – zum heutigen Status von Berlin", in: *Finis Germaniae* (1977), pp.27–33.

Schröder, "Der Status der Deutschen Reichsbahn in Berlin", *ROW*, 26 (1982), pp.237–47.

Schröder, "Besatzungsgewalt und Personalhoheit", *AVR*, 21 (1983), pp.409–32.

Schröder, "Der Status Deutschlands in Berlin", in: *Fs Mampel* (1983), pp.71–91.

Schröder, "Der Status von Berlin – ein Problem der Wirtschaftspolitik", *ROW*, 28 (1984), pp.210–15.

Schröder, "Die gegenwärtigen Kontrolleinrichtungen der Vier Mächte in Deutschland", *AVR*, 23 (1985), pp.42–73.

Schröder, "Besatzungsgewalt und Rechtsschutz in Berlin", *RuP*, 21 (1985), pp.24–31.

Schröder, "Zweck und Grenzen des Besatzungsrechts in Berlin", *ROW*, 29 (1985), pp.181–90.

Schröder, "Vier-Mächte-Verantwortlichkeit und Personalhoheit der beiden deutschen Staaten", *ROW*, 30 (1986), pp.154–60.

Schweisfurth, "Der Status der Deutschen Reichsbahn in Berlin (West) im Lichte der Berliner S-Bahn-Vereinbarung vom 30. Dezember 1983", *ZaöRV*, 44 (1984), pp.482–94.

Seiffert, "Gesamtberliner Probleme der S-Bahn", in: *Zehn Jahre Berlin-Abkommen 1971–1981*, pp.177–88.

Sendler, "Bundesrecht in Berlin", *JR*, 1958, pp.81–6 and 127–9.

Sendler, "Berlin – nur ein "deutsches Land"?", *JuS*, 23 (1983), pp. 903–10.

Sendler, "Berlin – juristisch betrachtet aus der Sicht eines richterlichen Praktikers", *JuS*, 24 (1984), pp.432–4.

Simpson, "Berlin: Allied Rights and Responsibilities in the Divided City", *ICLQ*, 6 (1957), pp.83–102.

Stobbe, "Bindungen: Das Verhältnis Berlins zum Bund und das Viermächte-Abkommen", *EA*, 32 (1977), pp.477–86.

Storost, "Alliierte Kommandantur und Bundesverfassungsgericht", *Der Staat*, 21 (1982), pp.113–26.

Wagner, "Das Berlin-Problem als Angelpunkt eines Ausgleiches zwischen West und Ost in Europa", *EA*, 26 (1971), pp.375–82.

Walter, Kleinwächter, "Zur Entstehung des Vierseitigen Abkommens über Westberlin und zum Kampf um seine Verwirklichung", *Forschungshefte des Instituts für Internationale Politik und Wirtschaft der DDR*, No. 4/1978.

van Well, "Die Teilnahme Berlins am internationalen Geschehen: ein dringender Punkt auf der Ost-West-Tagesordnung", *EA*, 31 (1976), pp.647–56.

van Well, "Berlin und die Vereinten Nationen", in: *Berlin translokal* (1983), pp.97–113.

Wengler, "Die Rechtslage der Eisenbahnen und Wasserstrassen in Berlin", *JR*, 1950, pp.641–6, 676–82.

Wengler, "Die Übernahme von Bundesgesetzen für Berlin", in: *Fs Leibholz* Vol. II (1966), pp.939–62.

Wengler, "Das Schreiben der Alliierten Kommandantur vom 24. Mai 1967 über den Status von Berlin," *NJW*, 20 (1967), pp.1742–4.

Wengler, "Juristische Luftbrücken von Karlsruhe nach West-Berlin", *JZ*, 29 (1974), pp.528–35.

Wengler, "Berlin-Ouest et les Communautés européennes", *AFDI*, 24 (1978), pp.217–36.

Wengler, "Die Geltung völkerrechtlicher Verträge der beiden 'deutschen Staaten' für West-Berlin und Ost-Berlin", *ROW*, 30 (1986), pp.149–54.

Wettig, "Die Entwicklung der Bindungen West-Berlins vor dem Viermächteabkommen von 1971", *DA*, 11 (1978), pp.1182–96.

Wettig, "Die Bindungen West-Berlins als Verhandlungs- und Vertragsgegenstand der vier Mächte 1970/71", *DA*, 12 (1979), pp.278–90.

Wettig, "Das Problem der Bindungen West-Berlins bei der Anwendung des Viermächteabkommens", *DA*, 12 (1979), pp.920–37.

Wettig, "Die Statusprobleme Ost-Berlins 1949–1980", *Berichte des Bundesinstituts für ostwissenschaftliche und internationale Studien* 44–1980.

Wetzlaugk, *Die alliierten Schutzmächte in Berlin* (1982).

Wilke, "Das Viermächte-Abkommen über Berlin 1971–1976, Bilanz der politischen Praxis", *German Yearbook of International Law*, 21 (1978), pp.252–71.

Wulf, "Probleme des Transitverkehrs von und nach Berlin (West)", in: *Zehn Jahre Berlin-Abkommen 1971–1981*, pp.149–61.

Zieger, "Berlin 1945 bis zum Viermächte-Abkommen 1971", in: *Berlin Fibel* (1975), pp.11–66.

Ziekow, "Bundesverwaltungsgericht und Berlin–Vorbehalt", *NJW*, 39 (1986), pp.1595–7.

Zivier, "Zur Interpretation von Kompromissformeln im Viermächteabkommen", *ROW*, 19 (1975), pp.223–5.

Zivier, "Anwendung und Beachtung des Berlin-Abkommens aus östlicher und westlicher Sicht", in: *Zehn Jahre Berlin-Abkommen 1971–1981*, pp.191–215.

Zorgbibe, "L'accord quadripartite sur Berlin du 3 septembre 1971", *Revue belge de droit international*, 8 (1972), pp.419–30.

INDEX